YORKTOWN, VIRGINIA

THROUGH TIME

YORKTOWN, VIRGINIA
THROUGH TIME

AMY WATERS YARSINSKE

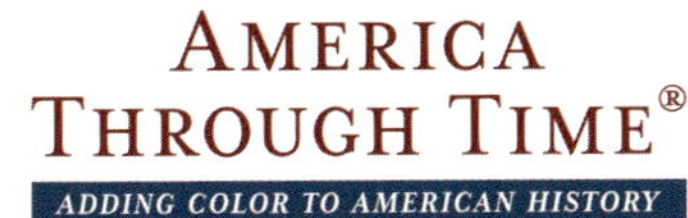

America Through Time is an imprint of Fonthill Media LLC
www.through-time.com
office@through-time.com

Published by Arcadia Publishing by arrangement with Fonthill Media LLC
For all general information, please contact Arcadia Publishing:
Telephone: 843-853-2070
Fax: 843-853-0044
E-mail: sales@arcadiapublishing.com
For customer service and orders:
Toll-Free 1-888-313-2665
Visit us on the internet at www.arcadiapublishing.com

First published 2023

ISBN 978-1-63499-438-5

Typeset in Mrs Eaves XL Serif Narrow
Printed and bound in England

Contents

ABOUT THE AUTHOR

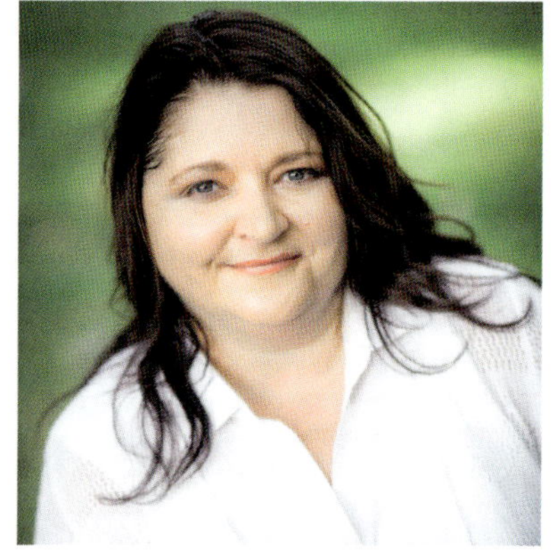

Amy Waters Yarsinske is the author of several best-selling, award-winning nonfiction books, notably *An American in the Basement: The Betrayal of Captain Scott Speicher and the Cover-up of His Death*, which won the Next Generation Indie Book Award for General Non-fiction in 2014. To those who know this prolific author and Renaissance woman, it's no surprise that she became a writer. Amy's drive to document and investigate history-shaping stories and people has already led to publication of over 85 nonfiction books, most of them spotlighting current affairs, the military, history and the environment. Amy graduated from Randolph-Macon Woman's College in Lynchburg, Virginia, where she earned her Bachelor of Arts in English and Economics, and the University of Virginia School of Architecture, where she earned her Master of Planning and was a DuPont Fellow and Lawn/Range resident. She also holds numerous graduate certificates, including those earned from the CIVIC Leadership Institute and the Joint Forces Staff College, both headquartered in Norfolk, Virginia. Amy serves on the national board of directors of Honor-Release-Return, Inc. and the National Vietnam and Gulf War Veterans Coalition, where she is also the chairman of the Gulf War Illness Committee. She is a member of the American Society of Journalists and Authors (ASJA), Investigative Reporters and Editors (IRE), Authors Guild, the North Carolina Literary and Historical Association (NCLHA), and the Western North Carolina Historical Association (WNCHA), among her many professional and civic memberships and activities.

If you want to know more about Amy and her books, go to
www.amywatersyarsinske.com

Introduction

Yorktown, the county seat of York County [one of the eight original shires formed in colonial Virginia in 1682], was established by the Act for Ports of 1691, passed by the Virginia House of Burgesses[1] at Jamestown, the seat of government in the new colony for nearly a century, largely for the purpose of exporting tobacco to Europe. The lawyer Thomas Ballard Jr.[2] (1655–1710) was the principal founder of the colonial town along with Joseph Ring (1646–1703), and it was called York until after the Revolutionary War, when the name Yorktown came to be the commonly used name. The legislation that established the town was but another in a succession of disputed and unsuccessful efforts by the colonial government to encourage growth of towns in rural lower Tidewater Virginia.[3] Yorktown, however, succeeded despite initial delays and the setbacks induced by man and nature that were shared by many of Great Britain's first colonial settlements. According to the National Park Service's narrative, although Yorktown, variously called Port of York, Borough of York, York, Town of York, and Yorktown, was not established until 1691, the area around Yorktown had been well known to the English for generations. The river itself had been explored, and frequently visited, by English explorer captain John Smith[4] (1580–1631) and his fellow settlers at Jamestown. They came most frequently by water, but it was not until the 1630 to 1632 period that early Virginians began to push overland from the James River and to establish homes on the banks of the York, which they named thusly for the ancient city of York in Yorkshire, Northern England. Among the men who braved the Indians, the forests, and natural enemies to establish homes on the creeks and tidewaters above and below Yorktown were Captain John West (1590–1659), who became acting crown governor[5] from 1635 to 1636; Captains John Utie[6] (1570–1638), of Utimara, York County, Virginia, and Robert Felgate (1578–1644), and, a little later, Dr. Henry Lee[7] (1597–1657), a justice of the peace and burgess in 1652 and the ancestor of the Lees on the Virginia Peninsula. The Indians before them had seen, and recognized, the strategic value and beauty of this location. Chief Powhatan (1545–1618), whose proper name was Wahunsenacawh and the paramount chief of Tsenacommacah, an alliance of Algonquian-speaking Tidewater Indians, resided on the north side of the river, above Gloucester Point, when Smith first saw him in 1607, and the Kiskiack[8] Indians, part of the Powhatan Confederacy, lived on the south side near present-day Yorktown until pressure from English and other European settlers caused them to move.[9]

The particulars of Yorktown's establishment bear repeating. Nicolas Martiau[10] (1591–1657), a French Huguenot military engineer who emigrated to the Virginia colony via Jamestown in June 1620 and considered the earliest emigrant ancestor of future president George Washington, settled eventually on a large tract of land overlooking the York River, and it was part of his tract, which originally lay between the holdings of crown governor Sir John Harvey[11] (1581–1646) and the estate of Captain Richard Townsend[12] (1593–1652), that in 1691 was acquired and laid out into the original eighty-five lots of Yorktown. Through the marriages of his descendants, Martiau became the earliest-known American ancestor of George Washington. A granite marker in his honor now stands on Yorktown's Ballard Street. Fifty acres of land along the York River were also purchased from Benjamin Read (1647–1712), originally of Gloucester County [located across the York River from Yorktown], for ten thousand pounds of "merchantable sweet-scented tobacco and cask" for the site of the new town. This land had first been patented sixty years earlier by Nicolas Martiau, Read's grandfather. Martiau had carved his home and plantation from what was just then forested frontier wilderness. Surveyor major Lawrence Smith[13] (1629– 1700) was tasked to subdivide the town into the eighty-five lots, which York County court-appointed town trustees, akin to European feoffees, offered for sale. Smith left the area between the bluff line and the York River—the waterfront—outside the town limits, labeling it a "common shore." Smith believed that this York River frontage had "no value" but he was quite wrong in that determination—it proved to have great value. Along it developed wharves, loading places, ships, stores, lodging accommodations and all manner of development. But the waterfront would not be made part of the town until 1738—still designated a commons—until surveyed into lots fifty years later.[14]

Yorktown's first lots each measured one hundred and thirty-two by one hundred and sixty-five feet, which left some seven-and-a-half acres that [with the exception of the steeply sloping sides of the so-called Great Valley, not surveyed into lots at that time] was set aside for streets and ways. Lot prices were one hundred and eighty pounds of tobacco and sales contracts carried forfeit provisions if the lot was not developed. On the first day of sale, November 24, 1691, thirty-six lots were recorded. Within a year, sixty-one had been sold. The axis of the town was a main street that generally bisected the fifty acres from its southeast to its northwest boundaries. Main Street, which extended some two thousand five hundred feet, ran roughly parallel with the river bank and had a width of thirty-three feet. This street ran in a straight line except for one bend at the spot where Read Street crossed it.[15] Several vales, or ravines, cut up from the waterfront and there was, unlike today, some rise and fall of the street level at various points. This was particularly true at the head of the Great Valley and also where the rising grade of the Read Street vale cut across the street. Both dips are largely obscured now by road grading though the old grades could be established.[16] The better homes, inns, and public buildings on the bluffs were in the town proper. Among the lots developed below the bluffs was one belonging to Royal African Company agent colonel Charles Chiswell (1677–1737), of Scotchtown Plantation, Saint Martin's Parish, Hanover County, Virginia, who was given a patent for land on the York River waterfront on which to build accommodations "for his greater Conveniency in Victualing His Majesties Ships of War according to his Contract."[17] On the survey plan, cross streets led off the Main Street giving access to each of the half-acre town lots except numbers two and three. There were six of these ways on the riverside and seven on the inland side. All were shown as straight lines and evidently—except for the Great Valley—had a width of some twenty-eight feet. This resulted in five direct crossings of Main Street with an additional three entries not producing direct crossings.[18]

As early as October 10, 1691, Thomas Mountfort[19] (1650–1708/9) was named surveyor of the town's roads and directed to take "Immediate care to see that there be soe mainy good and Convenient Landings made for Rolling or Carrying upp to the said Towne any sort of goods whatsoever that any person or persons shall or may hereafter have occasions to send them by water, and to be Landed and laid in the Towne, as he shall thinks Fitt and necessary."[20] Repair of roads and ways was a continuing problem and at one point, in 1757, it was necessary to declare an emergency and get special legislation and funding to "widen and support" Yorktown streets even to the extent of using brick walls where necessary to keep them from "being washed away by the hasty showers of rain."[21] But soon more repairs were in order and the court specified that the surveyor get the work done. This was in January 1760, and late in the year surveyor and property owner Patrick Matthews[22] was "for the hire of carts &c to repair the Streets in York Town." There was nothing indicated in the park service research that any structures such as bridges and causeways, which had been funded for Williamsburg's main street, were ever built or needed in Yorktown where the Main Street topography was less severe. Neither did research produce any reference to pavement, or to any special kind of street surface, or even to the existence of sidewalks, or any form of curbs and gutters in Yorktown in the colonial and later periods.[23] In due course Main Street's southeastern terminus curved southwestward along the southeastern edge of the town and then southward for connection with the road down the peninsula to Hampton. At the other end of town, it soon extended beyond the town limits, curving around what became known as Windmill Point, to Yorktown Creek where it formed a connection with the road to Williamsburg. Virginia militia major William Buckner[24] (1661–1716) was directed, as early as June 24, 1710, to construct a "Good and substantial Bridge" over this creek. Later his son, John Buckner Jr. [the "Jr." added to set him apart from his grandfather] (1693–1748), who inherited his Yorktown property interests after his older brother, William (1691–1722), died at the age of thirty-one, continued to keep this bridge in repair as in 1726 when the court awarded him one thousand pounds of tobacco "for the bridge." Again in 1746 there is the entry "To Majr John Buckner for keeping the Bridge over the Creek," and payment of eight hundred pounds of tobacco.[25]

Yorktown's first cross streets did not all open through to the water even when the town was at its busiest. This is still true of Church Street today. In colonial times there was no street where Comte de Grasse now runs. The opening of Ballard Street, for example, evidently was a mid-nineteenth century development. Park service documentation indicates that the first cross streets in use were those that ran down the Read Street vale and the other along the

Great Valley, with another along the line of Buckner Street coming shortly thereafter. It is of record under date of July 15, 1745, that a court order specified "that the public Landings from York Town down to the River side be for the future that by Thos Nelson [Great Valley], by Richard Amblers [Read Street] down to the Ware house [Buckner Street] and no others." This latter followed down Tobacco Warehouse Hill to Buckner's Landing and was noted in 1783.[26] Per the same source, in 1781, these same streets were shown to have been the primary—and only—connections between Main and Water streets. French army officer [later marshal] Louis-Alexandre Berthier[27] (1753–1815) sketched their routes prominently in his drawings of early Yorktown, showing that the Great Valley had a turnaround at its river end and Read Street was not laid out along a straight line but rather with a slight s-curve that it still retains today. When the Gwyn Read[28] [also transposed as Reade] (1694–1762) subdivision on its inland side [the addition to the town] was laid out after 1738 it evidently was separated from the original lots, at least southeastward from Read Street, by a street behind the town parallel to Main that came to be known as "back-street." The regular cross streets perpendicular to Main crossed this back street and led into the Gwyn Read development.[29] Of interest, in at least one circumstance in the first half of the nineteenth century, present Ballard Street was denoted as Court House Street. At the same time, historical record indicates that Church Street was specifically given that name and presumably the reference of "Hill Road to River" was the Great Valley, with "Street by Rows" being Buckner Street.[30] Over a century later, on a survey document dating to 1848, a full set of cross street names was given—Buckner, Ballard, Church, Read, Pearl (now Nelson), Smith and Bacon—and at this time Read Street extended directly south to a crossing of Yorktown Creek.

As Yorktown blossomed, it became an important tobacco port, exporting crops from area plantations. At peak prosperity (1740–1770), Yorktown reached the height of its development in or about 1750, when it had between two hundred and fifty to three hundred buildings and a population of nearly two thousand people, making it a substantial eighteenth-century community, and rivaling the size of the nearby colonial capital of Williamsburg. There were men of all types and classes along the streets and on the wharves—merchants, planters, prosperous yeomen, shopkeepers, indentured servants and slaves, travelers and seamen. Apprentices rose to become partners, as in the case of Augustine Moore (1730–1788) [in 1781, owner of the house in which the surrender terms for the British army were negotiated] in the Nelson firm. Prominent families were united by birth and marriage with the wealthy gentry of the region. The most noted citizen of Yorktown was Thomas Nelson Jr. (1738–1789), a signer of the Declaration of Independence, governor of Virginia and commander of the Virginia Militia at the siege of 1781. An English visitor to the town in 1736 wrote:

> You perceive a great Air of Opulence amongst the Inhabitants, who have some of them built themselves Houses, equal in Magnificence to many of our superb ones at St. Jame's ... almost every considerable Man keeps an Equipage ... The Taverns are many here and much frequented ... The Courthouse is the only considerable public Building, and is no unhandsome structure ... The most considerable Houses are of Brick; some handsome ones of Wood, all built in the modern Taste; and the lesser Sort, of Plaister. There are some very pretty Garden spots in the Town.[31]

Between 1691 and 1781, fortunes were made at Yorktown in the tobacco trade. No tobacco was better known, perhaps, that that produced under the famous "E.D." brand Edward Digges' Bellfield Plantation, four miles west of Yorktown. The plantation site and family graveyard, located off the Colonial Parkway some three hundred yards to the east, was the home of two early Virginia colonial governors—Captain John West in 1632 and Edward Digges[32] (1620–1674/5), who bought the property from West in 1650. Here, Digges produced superior tobacco and led early attempts to develop silk culture in the colony. Ships from Great Britain came to Yorktown's piers to get hogsheads of tobacco, which had been examined by government inspectors. Tobacco, and later in the eighteenth century more diversified cargoes, went out from the town's warehouses. Incoming freight included clothing, wines and liquor, furniture, jewelry and silver plate, riding gear and coaches, swords, firearms, books and slaves. This trade made Yorktown a thriving business center in the eighteenth century—a port that led in Chesapeake Bay commerce for a number of important decades.

While Yorktown's growth and prosperity peaked about 1750, the town's shops and wharves were busy for perhaps another quarter of a century. Yorktown became the headquarters of British major general Charles Edward Cornwallis V, Lord Cornwallis[33] (1738–1805) during the siege of 1781, which was the last major battle of the Revolutionary War. When the waterways were critical to transportation, Yorktown was thought to occupy a strategic location controlling upstream portions of the York River and its tributaries and their access to the Chesapeake Bay. In his *Notes on the State of Virginia*, published in 1781/2, Thomas Jefferson (1743–1826) observed that the "York River, at York town, affords the best harbour in the state for vessels of the largest size. The river there narrows to the width of a mile, and is contained within very high banks, close under which the vessels may ride. It holds 4 fathom water at high tide for 25 miles above York to the mouth of Poropotank, where the river is a mile and a half wide, and the channel only 75 fathom, and passing under a high bank."[34] Arguably, the town's future potential was wiped out by the destruction and waste that came with the British siege of 1781 and the Great Fire of 1814. But there were three factors that assuredly changed Yorktown as a prosperous port: soil quality in and around Yorktown became poor as tobacco exhausted the soil and planters shifted to mixed crops, which required less slave labor [especially after the Civil War and the end of slave practices]; the center of tobacco culture shifted southwest, and other points of trade developed. Commensurate with these changes and the relocation of the state capital from Williamsburg to Richmond, Yorktown and other areas of the largely rural Virginia Peninsula saw a sharp decline in population.

The tides of history that swept over Yorktown would also continue to shape and reshape everything from political and commercial importance to the naming of town streets. When Benson John Lossing (1813–1891), a prolific and popular nineteenth-century historian, visited Yorktown in 1866, he commented in his *Pictorial Field Book of the Civil War in the United States of America* (New York, 1868): "We observe that the names of the few streets in Yorktown have changed, and have those of 'McClellan,' 'Keyes,' 'Ellsworth,' and others."[35] As explanation, the names of these streets continued to change and in a handbook published at the time of the Yorktown centennial celebration in 1881 only three street names were given in Yorktown— Main, Church and Keyes—the latter named for Union major general Erasmus Darwin Keyes[36]

(1810–1895), who commanded the IV Corps that moved up the Peninsula during the 1862 campaign. Keyes Street is now Nelson Street. Ellsworth Street was named for Union colonel Ephraim Elmer Ellsworth (1837–1861), of Malta, New York, a law clerk and the first Union officer killed in the Civil War when he was died at Alexandria, Virginia, on May 24, 1861. Ellsworth had studied the Zouave soldiers, French colonial troops in Algeria, and was impressed enough by their fighting capabilities that he ran a drill company called the Zouave Cadets and once the war broke out, he commanded the Eleventh New York Volunteer Infantry Regiment, also called the New York Fire Zouaves. Ellsworth's troops wore short open-fronted jackets, baggy trousers, sashes and oriental head dress. After his death, the regiment was stationed near Hampton Roads during the Peninsula Campaign and it is highly likely that the men of this command had the street in Yorktown named in his honor. McClellan Street bore the name of Major General George Brinton McClellan (1826–1885), who commanded the Union army in the Peninsula Campaign from March through July 1862. By the time of the sesquicentennial in 1931, most of these cross-street names had been assigned—and in some cases reassigned—names.

Notably, one of the more prominent features of Yorktown's nineteenth century landscape, seen clearly from the York River or from the west side of Yorktown Creek, was the windmill [seen in early pictorial works of the town]. This structure, built about 1711, was a landmark in the area for nearly one hundred and fifty years. This structure gave the name Windmill Point to that steep marl bluff that projects toward Yorktown Creek a little distance from the initial western boundary of Yorktown. It was adjacent, but up the hill, from the road that extended Main Street westward to its crossing [by bridge] of Yorktown Creek.[37] The tract of land on which it was built in 1711 had been owned by John Lewis (1669–1725) and his wife, the former Elizabeth Warner (1672–1720/21), of Warner Hall, Abingdon Parish, Gloucester County. On July 16 of that year they agreed with William Buckner, already well known as a prominent surveyor and enterprising merchant of Yorktown and a town trustee, to allow him the use of one acre of ground "for to build a Windmill upon."[38] Buckner's intent was to build a merchant or custom (toll) mill that he would operate as another of his business enterprises. Mills for grinding corn into meal and/or wheat into flour (whether powered by wind or water) constituted an important part of the Virginia economy both on the plantations, or at points well suited to trade, as Yorktown. Buckner was following a profitable course. Park service reporting tells the backstory, informing that in the case of the merchant, mill grinding for export or ship supply was perhaps of more concern than for local consumption. Profit came from grinding one's own grain as well as grinding that brought in by others in the vicinity. In the latter case a toll, as fixed by law and custom, was exacted by the mill operator.[39] As the story goes, Buckner came to an agreement with John Lewis that he would build a mill and keep it in good repair for a period of at least seven years or forfeit any right in the acre of land. A further consideration, the principal one in fact, was that he obligated himself to grind twelve barrels of Indian corn each year for Lewis free of toll or other charge. Presumably William Buckner performed all of the requirements of the agreement in good order and eventually came into full possession of the mill development. At his death it passed to his son, John Buckner Jr., and when John died in 1748, he bequeathed this "wind Mill with the Lot of Ground it stands on" to his nephew, Griffin Stith[40] (1720–1784).[41]

There is no account of the actual construction of Buckner's windmill that has survived and it is not possible to be specific about its initial type. When British navy midshipman John Gauntlett (1737–1783) sketched Yorktown from his perch on board the HMS *Norwich* anchored in the York River in 1755, he clearly showed a windmill on the proper site. Though he labeled his perspective on each end of his *View of the Town of York* (and the windmill was shown off the northeast end of town) he seems to have detailed a smock[42] mill, a variant of the earlier post mill design, and a 1781 siege maps also suggests this type. It may be significant, however, that when James Peale (1749–1831), the younger brother of noted painter Charles Willson Peale (1741–1827), painted *Washington and his Generals at Yorktown* [dating to 1782–1791] he sketched in some detail what seems clearly to have been a full tower windmill of some size.[43] Roughly fifty years after Peale painted the mill and in poor condition, the full tower is clearly shown with its wood construction and octagonal shape. In 1801 it was specifically referred to as the "old Tower Windmill." This language may suggest that the mill was even then inoperative.[44] When the park service later analyzed a body of 1781 siege maps and map variants, it was noted that six of them have a sketch of a windmill as standing on the point at the time of the battle. Some twenty others give the simpler building symbol, some using a circular shaped symbol rather than the more conventional square or rectangular block. At the time of the siege, the mill came to have company on the point.[45] From those maps, it is known that the British erected an earthwork collocated with the windmill, presumably a battery, on the very tip of the bluff. On some of the maps, the work was delineated alone, yet in others in association with the windmill. This point, juxtaposed on the bluff, was a strategic one overlooking Yorktown Creek and it was also close enough to offer some artillery cover to the otherwise exposed and detached Royal Welch Fusiliers redoubt[46] just across the creek.

History informs that there are at least two engraved views of the old Yorktown windmill tower as it stood as a decaying landmark into the nineteenth century but both seem to have a common ancestry and may in truth stem from a single plate or sketch. One appeared as part of a scene titled "Yorktown Virginia," in an undated *Family Magazine*. The other was a plate in the Robert Sears (1810–1892) work titled *A Pictorial History of the American Revolution*, published by Sears in New York in 1853. But the illustration in Sears' book is actually a bit late for the old tower to have still been standing in good repair. When a survey of the "Lands of Washington Rowe Esq called Wind Mill point" was made in 1850, it delineated, among other things, the "site of the Old Wind Mill" showing it on the high ground overlooking the York River a little distance downriver from the tip of the point. Evidently the life of the Yorktown windmill [or windmills (if it was rebuilt at any given time)] on this site had run its course, but the name remained.[47]

Certainly, the events of September and October 1781 gave Yorktown its position of first rank in the story of the American Revolution, yet its earlier and less publicized history in that war is both interesting and significant. The leaders of opinion in Yorktown were merchants who stood to suffer much as supporters of the patriotic cause. Their losses were heavy in many cases, but they stood behind the Revolution practically to a man. But history informs that when the siege of 1781 was over, Yorktown quickly entered upon its decline. The damages of the siege had been devastating, trade fell off, and citizens—even whole families—moved away. It quickly became a village with no major commercial or business activity. In this category it has continued. Its history in the nineteenth century was punctuated by only an occasional significant event or development.[48] Point of fact, near midsummer of 1782, less than one year after the Yorktown victory, with the prospect of military activity diminishing in and around the town, some concern was expressed regarding the considerable—and expansive—standing earthworks still present. The French army was just about to depart the area that July 1. Past park service guidebooks inform that if the situation had not become confused later in the month, the British works, or most of them, may have been leveled at that time. Had it not been for the intervention of fifth governor of Virginia, Benjamin Harrison V[49] (1726–1791) pointing out that "The forts and platforms to the Water were all built by the State, and are necessary for the defence of the river and Its Trade," the British works would not have survived the war. Harrison wrote to French lieutenant colonel [later brigadier general] Charles François Chaudron, Chevalier de la Valette[50], then in command of the Yorktown garrison, on July 29 that:

> It appears extremely hasty in [Major] General [Benjamin] Lincoln to order all the fortifications at York Town to be destroy'd, those that have been thrown up round the Town either by the Enemy or your Army will be useless to us, but the Fort and the platforms were built by the State and ought to be preserved for it and you have my thanks for offering to deliver them up when you mean to evacuate them—you'l [sic] please to send Notice to Colo Dabney who has orders to take possession and they will be enclosed by such Works or pallisades [sic] as will be sufficient to defend them against a small force.[51]

Benjamin Lincoln (1733–1810), overall commander of the American wing of the Allied army and second in command of American forces, accepted the surrender sword from British major general Charles O'Hara (1740–1802). He was appointed secretary of war on October 30, 1781, a position he held until 1783. Harrison was certain Lincoln had bypassed him in regard to British fortifications—and he turned it into a personal mission to make his position on what remained of them known to Lincoln. La Valette, however, was quite agreeable to leaving the works. The American garrison left behind after the French departed, under the command of Colonel Charles Dabney[52] (1745–1829), was either too small to accomplish the task of leveling the works, not inclined to do it, or had to direct attention to far more pressing duties. Nothing further came of subsequent state recommendations to destroy the British fortifications, despite the protestations of Yorktown residents who considered them an impediment to commerce and travel, not to mention a visual nuisance. These complaints fell on deaf ears—a turn of luck that preserved the history on display in Yorktown today. Travelers documented the existence of the wartime fortifications around the town until they were obliterated from view by Civil War entrenchments in 1861 and 1862.[53] But also of note, even though the local residents complained regularly of the inconveniences caused by the entrenchments, they were already becoming points of interest for the travelers who documented their existence before the Civil War. Such was the case of Robert Hunter Jr., a young merchant from London who visited Yorktown on February 26, 1786. On his arrival, crossing the York River by ferry, he and his companion, another London merchant, immediately sought out Dr. Corbin Griffin[54] (1740–1814), a prominent physician active on side of Virginia forces in the Revolutionary War, to whom they had a letter of reference. They ate breakfast that morning, before walking around the town, "which consists of a few scattered houses; some of them have been elegant, but a good deal battered during the siege."

> The Doctor introduced us to General Nelson [Thomas Nelson Jr.], with whom we had some conversation about the war. He afterwards showed us the different works that were raised by the British and Americans and where the Continental Army, the French, and the militia were drawn up under General Washington.[55]

Hunter and his friend also visited and made special reference to Cornwallis Cave and, of course, to the Thomas Nelson House. Remarkably, however, most travelers who toured and then wrote about their experiences seeing the earthworks around Yorktown were absent significant detail. The exception to this, documented in a decades' old study by the park service, was Irish topographical writer, explorer and artist Isaac Weld Jr. (1774–1856) who arrived in Yorktown in 1796 and wrote of seeing the aging and otherwise collapsed fortifications:

> A few of the redoubts which were erected by each army, are still remaining, but the principal fortifications are almost quite obliterated; the plough has passed over some of them, and groves of pine trees sprang up about others, though during the siege every tree near the town was destroyed. The first and second parallels can just be traced, when pointed out by a person acquainted with them in a more perfect state.[56]

Weld also related that the shell-pocked ruins of the Secretary Nelson House "in the skirt of the town" were still standing solidly. "There are trenches thrown up round it, and on every side are deep hollows made by the bombs that fell near it."[57]

British neoclassical architect Benjamin Henry Boneval Latrobe[58] (1764–1820) was in Yorktown about the same time as Weld and he sketched the Thomas Nelson House and set it among the entrenchments that he drew boldly. Commenting on the scene, he wrote: "The history of the siege of York is well known to everybody. The works were badly constructed and well attacked. Those represented in the drawing," he continued, "were thrown up by the French after the town was taken, by way of keeping their army in exercise. They are now gone much to decay but still betray the design of a skillful engineer."[59] Latrobe first immigrated to the United States in 1796, initially settling in Virginia where he worked on the Virginia State Penitentiary project in Richmond.

During French aristocrat and military officer Marie Joseph Paul Yves Roch Gilbert du Motier, Marquis de Lafayette's visit to Yorktown on October 18–20, 1824, to mark the forty-third anniversary of Lord Cornwallis' surrender, there were incidental references to the old British works but little that was particularly specific. The October 23, 1824 *Norfolk and Portsmouth Herald*, in relating the unfolding celebratory events that involved Norfolk, Virginia native major general Robert Barraud Taylor (1775–1834), a second-generation American patriot and War of 1812 defender of that city, that he and his men, consisting of regular troops and volunteers, were quartered "about a mile out of town, contiguous to the Hampton road." There were others to the east, some encamped "near the bank of the river" but beyond the area of the sites of British Redoubts Nos. 9 and 10 around which the festivities centered.

> The field, including the town, we should judge to be about 3 miles in circuit, broken into alternate hills and vallies [*sic*]. The embankment thrown around the town by Cornwallis, is in some parts nearly perfect — of the second line there remain no traces, [this was a reference to the Allied Second Siege Line] the plough-share having effectually removed them.[60]

In the previous day's newspaper, the October 22 *Herald* informed that three days earlier, after exercises and a lengthy banquet that "the General again paid a visit to the encampment, as on the evening before, and was entertained with a brilliant exhibition of fireworks, which concluded the ceremonies of the day." In another account of this spectacle, published in Robert D. Ward's[61] *An Account of General Lafayette's Visit to Virginia in the Years 1824–1825* [Richmond, Virginia, 1881]:

> The whole company rose from the table at 9 o'clock, and many of them, with hundreds of spectators, *attended in the open fields east of the town,* to witness the uncommonly fine fire-works, which had been prepared at public expense, for general gratification. La Fayette was present, sitting on one of the old British embankments.[62]

Per the park service report, in both of these instances the general import could be, though not necessarily, that the earthworks alluded to were those forming the southeast sector of the old British line beyond the deep ravine used by the so-called Tobacco Road. In one instance, which the document makes clear, there is specific reference to what must have been the inner line developed and strengthened by the French on the town side of the ravine just after the siege. A few yards beyond the edge of town to the east, locals and visitors could see the nearest British lines, the mounds of the entrenchment, and the ditch; the mound considerably sunk from the trend of cattle and the washing of the rains, and the ditch rapidly filling up.[63]

When journalist, artist, soldier, politician and diplomat David Hunter Strother[64] (1816–1888), better known as Port Crayon, his *nom de plume*, visited Yorktown for a day in November 1849 with his uncle, having come from Williamsburg, they described seeing a "most desolate village." Even though "it was morn when we arrived, we saw no living soul on its streets." Strother opined that "[T]he village is supposed to contain about 250 inhabitants, mostly asleep at the date of our visit." In a footnote to the park service documentation, Strother also wrote on the Swan Tavern and the county clerk's office to further emphasize just how "inactive" the town had become, summarized thusly:

> Perceiving the smoke issuing from the kitchen chimney of a house of entertainment, we entered and stalking unchecked through the halls and public rooms penetrated at length to the kitchen

where we found an old black woman, the cook. Master, she said, was at home, but asleep upstairs
and she didn't dare to arouse him, didn't like to be woke up [...] From the Sleepy Tavern [Swan
Tavern] we went to the clerk's office to see an MS plan of the town and works. There we saw a
man, obese and drowsy, in slippers and shirtsleeves, sitting in an arm chair with his feet on
another—asleep. Uncle Dick, who knew him, pinched him awake, calling him by name, He was
civil and amiable offering to show us all the ancient deed books and gave us a sight of the plan,
but evidently thinking he had something valuable, declined to allow us to copy it.[65]

Due to this inactivity, he and his uncle, Richard Randolph, "had their views and retrospections"
all to themselves:

There were the British earthworks still complete in form and profile, a little abraded by time
and weed-grown. Here we picked up bullets and bones as from a recent battlefield and saw
things nearly as they were in 1781, nearly seventy years ago. In the village were the ruins of
Gov. Nelson's house [this was obviously reference to the Thomas Nelson House rather than the
William Nelson (1711–1772) House] and other houses still bearing the marks of cannon shot, the
perforated walls unrepaired and the brick-and-mortar rubbish lying where it fell.[66]

Strother continued:

On a green plateau overlooking the York River was the surgeon's headquarters where are still
quantities of bones and skulls, and iron bullets. Lafayette revisiting this country in 1824 landed at
this spot received by Watkins Leigh — and it was proposed to erect a monument commemorative
of the surrender but like all such things in Virginia, it ended in talk. It is difficult, however, to
determine a specific location from this information. Lafayette, it is known, landed in Yorktown
on the beach at the point which projects into the river just below the southeast limits of the town
[where the present beach picnic area is located]. He lodged in the 'Governor Nelson House,' and
most of the battlefield festivities took place in the area near the site of British Redoubt No. 10.[67]

When prolific American historian and author Benson John Lossing (1813–1891) was in Yorktown
in 1848 [well before his 1866 observations were made regarding the town's street names],
he toured the area with William Nelson [a descendant of the famed Yorktown Nelson clan]
and "visited the lines of entrenchments cast up by the British on the south and east sides of
the town. They extend in irregular lines from the river back to the sloping grounds in the
rear of the village, toward the 'Pigeon Quarter,' as it was termed, in the form of a figure five."
Evidently Lossing saw substantial parts of the line. "The mounds vary in height, from six
to twelve and fifteen feet, and being covered by a sward[68], may remain so for half a century
longer. The places of redoubts, the lines of the parallels, and other things connected with
the Siege, are yet visible."[69] Further, Lossing commented specifically on the still-existing
works on the edge of the bluff near Cornwallis Cave: "It [the cave] is almost directly beneath
the termination of the trench and breastworks of the British fortifications, which are yet
prominent on the bank above." This comment and his sketch of the works indicate that he

was in large part making reference to the French modification [relocation] of the British line in the southeast sector. In this event nothing other than traces would have remained where the original British positions had been.

> The angle of the works in the Lossing sketch appears more like the angle that the French would have made at British Redoubt No. 5 as they turned it sharply to the river. Clearly no Hornwork like the British had in this sector is shown. Then, too, if this assumption is accepted, the roof and chimneys of what obviously is the Governor Nelson House fall into a correct perspective.[70]

To all who have researched these descriptions, it would seem highly significant that a land survey in 1848 involving this general area noted the "old redoubt" as extending rather closely beyond the "Eastern boundary Y. Town." This surely was on the line of the shortened French earthworks. Nothing was noted farther to the south and east to indicate anything other than existing entrenchments. Remarkably, this is the same survey that notes four trees, about where the Second Parallel ran on the left of the road coming south out of Yorktown, which supposedly marked the location of Lord Cornwallis' surrender.[71] In an article from the March 2, 1852 *Richmond Daily Republican* there is yet another description of the works that followed a visit to the colonial town. Yorktown itself was noted as "a small place, with some thirty-five or forty dwellings" and this description:

> The battleground [...] still exhibits abundant traces of the eventful siege. The remains of British works, comprising the line which surrounded and defended the entire position, are still clearly visible. The embarkments have been considerably sunken by time, but not so much so as to prevent a clear conception of the whole line of defence. They must have been works of a very strong and formidable character. Our friend and guide pointed out to us a hollow in the earth still visible, caused by a shell thrown from the American side. The remains of the British magazine, a heap of scattered bricks, are still to be seen.

A Confederate soldier who was stationed at Yorktown in the late spring and early summer of 1861, left two suggestive references to the old works existing at that time in an article that appeared in the July 1863 *Southern Literary Messenger*. He noted that in May 1861: "Col. Hill[72] commenced fortifying the lower line of Yorktown by retouching the old British works. Now such things would be considered as no defense at all; but then with our limited force, they were the best we could do." He also observed in reference to the Second Lawson Regiment: "Their camp was established in the field at the lower end of Yorktown, within the remains of the old works, which the French had stormed nearly a century before." Arguably, this is not very helpful when trying to figure the precise location of these old works, but the French-altered British line in this sector could satisfy such implication as there is—and to call all structures "the old British works" would be a natural development. This, however, would soon become academic since Confederate engineers would push across the Tobacco Road ravine to the original British alignment, perhaps guided by the topography as the British engineers had been, perhaps becoming clearer to us today that if there were any visible evidences of the British line here they would have been slight indeed, and nothing would have been left in view when the massive Civil War works were completed.[73] This being true, Lossing was correct when he noted on June 3, 1866, while "visiting objects of interest in the vicinity" of Yorktown that: "The old British line of circumvallation had been covered by the modern [Civil War] works."[74] This was noted, too, on "A Plan of Yorktown and Vicinity, showing the Historical Sites of 1781 and the Celebration Grounds of 1881," which delineated the Confederate line around Yorktown and captioned it: "Confederate Line of Works around Yorktown in 1862 [now standing] on the site of the British 1781." United States Army colonel Robert Jay Arthur (1886–1970), writing in *The Two Sieges of Yorktown 1781 and 1862*, published on October 17, 1927, by Fort Monroe's Coast Artillery School Press, and taking into account what was on the mapping, could have been correct only in part when he wrote of the Civil War works: "Yorktown itself was entirely enclosed by strong earthworks which were substantially those thrown up by Lord Cornwallis in 1781, renewed and strengthened."[75]

When Union major general George McClellan, in his advance up the Peninsula in early April 1862, came to a halt in front of the Confederate line hinged on Yorktown, he found the town to be now only a village, tightly ringed with massive earthworks. Yorktown was the York River anchor to the Confederate line that extended across the Peninsula from the York to the James rivers. To the southwest of Yorktown, a line supported by two heavy positions—the Red and White Redoubts—continued to the headwaters of the Warwick River and then along the river. The Warwick flowed toward the James River and constituted a considerable natural obstacle. Two dams along the river, one at Wynne's Mill three miles from Yorktown, and another at Lee's Mill another two and a half miles downstream, deepened the waters and made a crossing even more difficult. In addition, the Confederates built three other dams to intensify this natural situation. Each dam [particularly that at Lee's Mill] was covered by earthworks and artillery. Then-major Robert Arthur, of the United States Army Coast Artillery School at Fort Monroe, Virginia, in brief fashion later described these works, writing in his book *The Two Sieges of Yorktown 1781 and 1862* (1927):

> The three bastioned fronts facing the direction of the approach [south and southeast] had parapets about fifteen feet in thickness, with ditches eight to ten feet deep and about fifteen feet in width at the top of the scarp. West of town the parapets were about eighteen feet in thickness and the ditches about ten feet in depth. About fifty-six heavy guns were mounted in the batteries along the line and along the water front, and were amply provided with traverses and magazines for their own protection and that of their ammunition.[76]

Civil War operations during the Peninsula Campaign changed the landscape in and around Yorktown due largely to the improvement in ordnance that made it necessary for the 1862 earthworks to be more massive than those constructed in 1781. Batteries and gun positions also needed to be larger, with differing shapes and even contours. When superimposed on any existing remains from the Revolutionary War, the latter were either in essence destroyed, or fully covered. Again, it was not unusual in the least that the Civil War line generally followed that of the British, since it was largely a matter of topography and advantageous position in each instance. This was true, as has been pointed out, even in that area to the southeast beyond old British Redoubt No. 5.[77] In its study of the overlapping of the 1781 British lines and the 1862 Confederate lines, the park service made these observations that bear repeating:

1. On the northwest side of town, both lines followed on the inner side of Buckner Street, and the 1862 line seems not to have crossed the street into the area where British Redoubt No. 1 was located. The Civil War line, however, turned the corner of the bluff and ran downstream without the break at the corner that the earlier line seemingly had. Town Lots 10-12 and 16 surely were involved, as were Lots 13-15 and possibly 9 inland from Main Street.

2. On the inland side of Main Street, the Confederates erected a sizeable position that embraced all of the site of British Redoubt No. 2 and the indented corner of the British line in this locality. It also probably encompassed the site of the British battery between No. 2 and Main Street, and possibly even the battery site to the south of No. 2. Most of this would have been beyond the original town limits, although Lots 15 and 21, and even 20, may have been involved.

3. The two lines appear to have been on like courses in that section between lines extended from Ballard Street and Nelson Street. Here the heavy Civil War works obliterated, or obscured, the sites or lines of the older British Redoubts Nos. 3 and 4 and the batteries associated with them. All would have been in the area of the Gwyn Read development.

4. In the section between lines extended from Nelson Street and the south corner of the original town survey, the Civil War line curved inland toward Main Street, but not to the same pronounced degree as did the old British line. In this area there was likely involvement with Lots 55, 59, 63, 67, and 71, as well as with more of the Gwyn Read development area. About at the edge of town there was a fortified break in the line that would allow needed egress and ingress from and to the town area. Just beyond this there was an inner trench that seemingly followed the direction of the shortened line built by the French late in 1781. It probably was this French line itself.

5. From this point around the head of the Tobacco Road ravine and on to the river, the Confederate and British lines seemed to be generally on the same line, even though the earlier line had been leveled after the siege of 1781. In 1862 the projection of the line out along the old York-Hampton Road was a stubby one, without the pronounced elongation of the old British Hornwork. There was also a pointed projection of the line about where the long west face of the Hornwork had been.

6. Curving east of this area, the Civil War line was flattened out with two battery projections, the second one probably on the site of British Redoubt No. 6 and its adjacent battery.

7. On or over the site of British Redoubt No. 7, the Confederates advanced a massive pointed projection of their line for more artillery placements. The line then curved to the cliffs above the river.

8. At the cliff edge and facing riverward, the Confederates installed another battery, which from all indications, violated the sites of British Redoubt No. 8 and its adjacent water battery.

9. All of the high bluff sites in Yorktown which overlook the York were brought into use for more Confederate artillery. The section running from the Church area upstream, toward and across where Ballard Street eventually opened to the water, was used for a large redoubt — battery complex which probably involved Lots 16, 22, 28, 34, and 40. The cliff edge from Read Street around to the Great Valley became the site of another elongated position for four thirty-two-pounder cannons. Here Lots 84 and 85 became involved. The bluff between the Great Valley and that down which the Comte de Grasse now runs likewise became a battery position above a hot shot battery on the waterfront below. Lots 76 and 77 would have been partly used in this construction. Between the Comte de Grasse Street ravine and that down which Tobacco Road runs just beyond the town limits, was still another fortified battery position. This area, on and behind the present Yorktown Monument, surely involved Lots 80 and 82 and the high ground between them, as well as the cliff edge.[78]

The study further notes that these works were abandoned by the Confederates when they evacuated Yorktown in the early days of May 1862, and there is little to suggest that the Union forces altered them in any appreciable manner while they occupied Yorktown. Fighting was moving to other areas and would not return to Yorktown. The works remained and are those that today give a besieged appearance to the town. Two gates through which there was entry into, and passage from, Yorktown were a part of the Confederate, and then of the Union, encircling entrenchments of Yorktown. The sally port on the west was across Main Street, just inside of where Buckner Street crosses.[79] The other gate was to the south where the highway passes today on old Main Street extended [an extension formerly called Monument Road]. These gates or passages were noted as still in use several years after the Civil War had ended, a fact known through the observations, once again, of travelers. Margaret Newbold Thorpe (1842–1915), a teacher sent to Virginia by the Friends' Association of Philadelphia and Its Vicinity for the Relief of the Colored Freedmen, who worked out of Fort Magruder near Williamsburg, made a visit to Fort Monroe during the 1867 Christmas season, returning by way of Yorktown. She observed that "[...] at Slabtown we saw the Union Cemetery; we entered Yorktown by one gate, pass the old Cornwallis Headquarters, go out through the opposite gate, took McClellan's famous corduroy road and so on to Fort Magruder.[80]

Some of the visual highlights from Yorktown's past are gone. Gone is the windmill that was a point of reference on the high cliff overlooking Yorktown Creek in the eighteenth century. This cliff is still known as Windmill Point. The colonial fort in mid-century presided from this so-called "Fort Hill" over the waterfront, protecting the town and harbor. This "Fort Hill" was the bluff extending towards the river beyond Grace Episcopal Church on the west side of Read Street. The old town pier, of timber and crib construction, was located down river between Read Street and the Archer House-Cornwallis Cave area.

Many important reminders of Yorktown's eighteenth-century past still exist. On Main Street is the Thomas Nelson House, the Georgian manor-style home of Thomas Nelson Jr.

built by his grandfather, Thomas "Scotch Tom" Nelson in the early eighteenth century, it is the most prominent of the remaining structures of that period. Nearby is the Dudley Digges house, built in the mid-eighteenth century by Yorktown lawyer Dudley Digges (1723–1790), who held several important positions in Virginia's colonial and state government. Also, along Main Street is the custom house, where taxes were collected on imported and exported goods passing through the port, and the Session–Pope–Sheild, Pate and Mungo Somerwell houses. On nearby streets are Grace Episcopal Church and the Edward Smith and Captain John Ballard houses. Reconstructed eighteenth century buildings, including the Swan Tavern, also help preserve Yorktown's historical atmosphere.

For all that remains intact, there is much about old Yorktown that is absent from the modern landscape. Gone altogether are many prominent homes while others, to include the Lightfoot mansion (originally known as the Mungo Somerwell House) built in c. 1710, purchased by Major General Philip Lightfoot II (1689 –1748)—popularly known as "The Merchant Prince"—and his family in 1716, remains standing near the corner of Ballard and Main streets, renovated over time to the point that it is nearly impossible to determine the correct construction date. Despite the vagaries of construction, the National Park Service has chosen to go with the name of the original property owner, though that seems to acknowledge a construction date of between 1700 and 1707, making it the oldest house in Yorktown. Of the three large Nelson family homes, gone is the home of Secretary Thomas Nelson (son of "Scotch Tom" and referred to by his title on the colonial council to distinguish him from his nephew) which stood on present-day Zweybrucken [Zweibrücken] Road. Some of its foundations are marked. Lord Cornwallis had his headquarters here at the beginning of the 1781 siege. The home of William Nelson (another son of "Scotch Tom" and father of Thomas Nelson Jr.) was a large H-shaped structure that stood across Main Street from Thomas Nelson Jr.'s mansion destroyed in the 1814 fire. Also, on Main Street, the home of Richard Ambler, a successful merchant who by marriage acquired extensive Jamestown holdings, next to the custom house garden is gone, having burned during the Civil War. But still surrounding the town are the earthworks first built by the British during the siege of 1781 and constructed over during the Civil War with Confederate fortifications during the second siege of Yorktown. From Yorktown Union major general George Brinton McClellan's Army of the Potomac launched an attack up the Peninsula to Richmond.

During the First World War, to support Atlantic defenses, the federal government in 1918 acquired about thirteen thousand acres for development into what famously became the United States Navy Mine Depot. This large installation straddled York, Warwick and James City counties and has since expanded and been developed as Naval Weapons Station Yorktown. Cheatham Annex, a facility which was developed over the former town of Penniman, is also included as part of the base. Other federal and military installations and one of the nation's most significant naval shipbuilders are also collocated or close to Yorktown, including the United States Coast Guard Training Center Yorktown that serves as a training school for the United States Coast Guard; Camp Peary, a nine thousand acre military reservation in York County, officially referred to as an armed forces experimental training activity (AFETA) under the authority of the Department of Defense; and the army base Fort Eustis and Newport News

Shipbuilding and Dry Dock Company, both in Newport News. Other major installations in the area are Naval Station Norfolk, located at Norfolk, and Langley Air Force Base, situated in Hampton.

Yorktown and the nearby area are significant to the early history of the United States. Colonial National Historical Park, which contains and preserves Yorktown National Battlefield and Yorktown National Cemetery, is located on the outskirts of town. The battlefield has many of the earthworks dug by the besieging American and French forces. The Yorktown Victory Monument—commemorating the victory, the alliance with France that brought it about, and the resulting peace with Great Britain after the war—is located just outside the current town. Designed by eminent New York architect Richard Morris Hunt (1827–1895), the monument was installed in 1884 and topped by a figure of *Liberty* sculpted by John Quincy Adams Ward (1830–1910). That element was destroyed by lightning on July 29, 1942. In need of a replacement *Liberty*, Norwegian-born, naturalized American sculptor Oskar Johan Waldemar Hansen[81] (1892–1971) was commissioned to fashion a new work, which was readied in 1956 and completed in time for the annual Yorktown victory celebration in 1957. In 1990, *Liberty* was again hit by lightning, suffering damage to the figure's hands and torso. Repairs were made that year and the lightning rod system first installed with Hansen's replacement *Liberty* upgraded.

Today, Yorktown is one of three sites of the Historic Triangle, which also includes Jamestown and Williamsburg as important colonial-era settlements. It is the eastern terminus of the Colonial Parkway connecting these locations. Of interest, one of Yorktown's historic sister cities is Zweibrücken, Germany, based on participation during the American Revolutionary War of the Royal Deux-Ponts Regiment, commanded by Comte Christian de Forbach [de Deux-Ponts] (1752–1817), son of Duke Christian IV of Deux-Ponts-Birkenfeld and Marianne Camasse, the countess Forbach. By decree of his father, dated March 30, 1775, he was granted the right to add to his name "von Zweibrücken."[82] Serving as his deputy commander was brother Comte Philippe Guillaume [later changed to Wilhelm] de Forbach[83] (1754–1807), later viscount of Deux-Ponts and finally baron de Zweibrücken. Both brothers were knights who served first in the French army and then in the Bavarian army. Comte Christian de Forbach's command was one of the four regiments that arrived at Newport, Rhode Island, with Comte de Rochambeau's expeditionary force in 1780, and that participated on the side of Americans in the Battle of Yorktown in 1781.

Into the twenty-first century, Yorktown remains popular as a destination in heritage tourism. Yorktown has distinct areas. Yorktown Village or Historic Yorktown is located close to the York River, near the George Preston Coleman Memorial Bridge that spans the river to Gloucester Point. The bridge carries U.S. Route 17, also known as the George Washington Memorial Highway, Yorktown's primary roadway, across the river. Historic Yorktown is comprised first of Water Street, a small strip along the beach of the river; it contains several small restaurants, a park, a hotel, a pier, and an antique shop. In May 2005 a building was constructed with more shops and restaurants, enhancing what is known as the Riverwalk section on the waterfront. Though Yorktown no longer appears as it did when it was an important eighteenth-century port city or when the British were trapped within its boundaries during the siege of 1781, it is still a place of national importance—a place where independence for the United States of America was won.

We are reminded that our history and heritage need not be recalled by physical remnants of the past. During his October 16, 1931 visit to the sesquicentennial celebration at Yorktown, then New York governor Franklin Delano Roosevelt (1882–1945) recalled that Virginia and sister states won the right to self-government on Yorktown's fields. "It was from the banks of my native Hudson that Washington and Rochambeau marched to end the War of the Revolution and to make possible the inauguration of our first president and the establishment of constitutional democracy," he told the assembled crowd. "I like to dwell not on the surrender of an army under a brave leader but rather on the genesis, as a result of this conflict, of a new concept of liberty for the human race—an ideal," he continued, "which quickly made itself felt among our allies of France and our mother peoples of the British Isles, and spread at last throughout the greater part of the civilized world." He offered, in closing, that the institutions of liberty and of friendship among nations have been often challenged. "They are challenged today. To these forces of despair, of discouragement, of despotism, of chaos and of war we can make no surrender. It is fitting that here we should renew our faith in the everlasting rightness, in the power to survive, of the fundamentals of self-government which were born a century and a half ago. In the normal development and sure progress of these truths," he declared, "lie the hope and the safety of the days to come."[84]

1   The Virginia General Assembly, often described as the oldest continuous law-making body in the New World, dates to the establishment of the Virginia Governor's Council and the House of Burgesses at Jamestown on July 30, 1619. At different times it may have been also called the Grand Assembly of Virginia. The General Assembly met in Jamestown from 1619 to 1699, when it moved to Williamsburg, Virginia, and met in the colonial capitol building. The body became the General Assembly in 1776 with the ratification of the Virginia Constitution. The government was moved to Richmond in 1780 during the administration of then-governor Thomas Jefferson, the future third president of the United States.

2   Thomas Ballard was the second son of Colonel Thomas Ballard of James City County. The younger Thomas Ballard was, therefore, probably born in York County in or about 1655, and reared at his father's home at Middle Plantation, which later became part of Williamsburg. That he eventually returned to York County was due to his parent's wise choice of his godfather in Major Robert Baldrey. Baldrey had come to Virginia in 1635, being then aged eighteen, had married, and had acquired a considerable plantation in York, where he was for years a justice of the peace. Ballard would inherit substantial property from Baldrey. He would also inherit the same from his father. Thomas Ballard Jr. was appointed a justice of the peace for York, and retained this honorable position until his death—and figures extensively in the contemporaneous York records as the feoffee in trust, with Joseph Ring, under the Act for Ports, passed by the Assembly in April 1691—through which important law Thomas Ballard became, with Ring, the founder of historic Yorktown. Ballard had also been chosen to represent York County in the Virginia House of Burgesses for the sessions beginning April 1, 1692, and March 2, 1692/3—and in the last-mentioned year he had a hand in founding yet another famous and enduring institution, when Ballard sold to the trustees of the proposed College of William and Mary a tract of land, inherited from his father, whereon the college buildings were afterward erected, and stand today. Ballard returned to the House of Burgesses for the session of 1696/7, and again for the sessions of September 28, 1698, of April 27, 1699, and of December 5, 1700, which last was prorogued to May 30 to August 14, 1702. He was again high sheriff of York in 1699; was for years one of the leading lawyers of Virginia, and was long an officer of the York militia, ranking as captain in 1693, and being commissioned lieutenant colonel on June 3, 1699, Edmund Jennings being then made colonel and commander-in-chief, and William Buckner, afterward Ballard's son-in-law, major. The Ballards of Virginia: https://ballardofvirginia.com/about/the-children-of-thomas-ballard-of-james-city-county-virginia/

3   The Tidewater region is a geographic area of southeast Virginia and northeastern North Carolina [lower Tidewater], part of the Atlantic coastal plain. Portions of Maryland facing the Chesapeake Bay are also given this designation. The area gains its name due to the effects of the shifting tides on local rivers, sounds and the ocean. The area is generally flat and low and composed of tidal marsh and large expanses of swamp. Much of the area is covered with pocosin and the higher areas are used for agricultural farmland. Geographically, in North Carolina and Virginia the Tidewater area is the land between the Suffolk scarp and the Atlantic Ocean. The Hampton Roads area is considered part of the greater Tidewater region, which is the land east of the Fall Line—the escarpment where the Piedmont and Atlantic coastal plain meet in the eastern United States—the natural border with the commonwealth's Piedmont region. To reiterate, Hampton Roads, the rest of the Virginia Peninsula, the Middle Peninsula, the Northern Neck and the Eastern Shore are part of this greater Tidewater region.

4   The three-thousand-mile Captain John Smith Chesapeake National Historic Trail, which includes Yorktown, traces the exploratory voyages Smith conducted from 1607 to 1609 on the Chesapeake Bay and along several major rivers. The trail includes parks, museum sites, driving tours, and water trails that align with Smith's historic voyage routes and offer opportunities for recreation and discovery.

5   After the Virginia Company of London lost its proprietary charter in 1624, the colony was taken over by the English Crown, and became a crown colony. Governors were appointed by the ruling monarch to oversee the interests of the Crown. During the interregnum period from 1649–1660, when England came under commonwealth rule and the protectorate rule of Oliver and Richard Cromwell, those governments appointed Virginia's governors. Captain John West was acting crown governor in the place of Governor Sir John Harvey, who was in his post from 1628 to 1639 but largely absent due to suspension and impeachment by the House of Burgesses—needless to say, he was highly unpopular in the Virginia colony.

6 Utie, later of the Virginia Council [House of Burgesses], first patented one hundred acres in 1624 on Chippokes Creek in Surry County. The captain was the burgess for plantations between Archer's Hope and Martin's Hundred, October 1629; for Hogg Island, 1629/30; member of the council from 1631 to 1635, with the title of captain, and in 1632 he received six hundred acres for planting at Kiskiack. He settled at the mouth of King's Creek, and called his home Utimara. One of the first justices of York County, the court was frequently held at his place. Utie was married to the former Ann Longworth (1570–1593).

7 Lee obtained from the York court a certificate for two hundred and fifty acres of land in 1647, due him for the importation of five persons to the colony.

8 History informs that in the mid sixteenth and early seventeenth centuries the Algonquian-speaking Kiskiack tribe, one of the original six tribes of the larger Powhatan Confederacy, was located near the south bank of the York River. Present-day Yorktown developed a few miles to the east of this location. The Kiskiack had built permanent villages, made up of numerous long houses or yihakans, in which related families resided. The Kiskiack were generally among the most hostile toward the English colonists who took up residence at Jamestown from 1607 and it was this tribe that participated in the Indian Massacre of 1622 in the hope of driving out the English from the banks of the James River. It is known that by 1649, the Kiskiack had settled along the Piankatank River, where the English granted their werowance Ossakican a reservation of five thousand acres. Two years later, the Kiskiack traded this land for equal acreage further upriver. The Kiskiack last appeared in historical records as participants in the 1676 Bacon's Rebellion. By the early seventeenth century, the Powhatan Confederacy had expanded to some thirty tributary tribes.

9 Department of the Interior/National Park Service. Division of History. Office of Archaeology and Historic Preservation. Yorktown and the Siege of 1781 [Charles E. Hatch Jr. historical handbook series number fourteen] [first published 1954 and revised 1957]. https://www.nps.gov/parkhistory/online_books/hh/14/hh14c.htm

10 Martiau was dispatched to the Virginia colony by King James I to help build a fort at Yorktown, Virginia. He served as a burgess from Jamestown in 1623. His construction of a palisade around the Jamestown Fort protected settlers from death during the now famous Indian Massacre of 1622. He was also instrumental in constructing the palisades at Yorktown. He received land patents for bringing over more colonists from England. He settled on a one thousand three-hundred-acre plantation on the York River, his home built on a bluff overlooking a curve in the York River. He was married to the former Jane Berkeley (1591–1657). The couple's gravestones were discovered during street excavations that took place in Yorktown during the year 1931. That same year, an eleven-foot Vermont granite monument, with commemorative bronze plaque was erected near the site of Martiau's home and graveyard on Ballard and Buckner streets, in the village of Yorktown. The monument was erected by the Huguenot Society of Pennsylvania, in cooperation with the National [Federation of] Huguenot Societies and the Yorktown Sesquicentennial Commission. Five years later, in May 1936, the National Park Service exhumed Nicolas Martiau's body from the original grave on Buckner Street in the family cemetery. The park service concluded the body in grave number six was likely that of Nicolas Martiau. The marker inscription in the Grace Episcopal Church cemetery notes that Martiau and sixteen of his family members were reinterred from the family burial site on Buckner Street [upon his land Yorktown was founded]. The Martiau marker was dedicated on May 22, 1993.

11 Harvey's land was called York Plantation, consisting at first of seven hundred and fifty acres, and later known as Temple Farm. When Harvey went bankrupt, the land was acquired in 1644 by Colonel George Ludlow, who patented it and adjoined the tract to his other lands in 1646. When he died in 1656, this land was inherited by nephew lieutenant colonel Thomas Ludlow, who died in 1660. For a number of years, according to the October 1913 *William and Mary College Quarterly Historical Magazine*, it remained in the occupation of Reverend Peter Temple, who married Mary, Thomas Ludlow's widow, but in 1686 it was sold to Major Lawrence Smith, of Gloucester County. The property continued in Smith's family until 1769, when Robert Smith sold it to Augustine Moore, who married his sister Lucy Smith. In the Moore house, still standing, were signed, of course, in 1781, the articles of surrender by Lord Cornwallis.

12 Richard Townsend's land of six hundred and fifty acres lay west of Yorktown Creek and, of note, it was this land that was first considered to establish the College of William and Mary.

13 Smith left a will on August 8, 1700, and from pages 97 and 98 of *The Armistead Family 1635–1910* (1910) by Virginia Armistead Garber, it is known that the first major Lawrence Smith, of Abingdon Parish, Gloucester County, Virginia, was a man of great influence and estate. From this record, it is further known Yorktown's former York Plantation, later known as Temple Farm, was sold to him. He was surveyor for the Crown for the counties of York and Gloucester. In 1691 he laid out the town of Yorktown on the land of Benjamin Read [also transposed as Reade], and received fifty acres for the same. https://www.geni.com/people/Col-Lawrence-Smith/6000000003266326774

14 Hatch [1957], ibid.

15 Department of the Interior/National Park Service. Division of History. Office of Archaeology and Historic Preservation. Yorktown's Main Street. From Secretary Nelson's to the Windmill and Military Entrenchments Close in and around the Town of York. [Charles E. Hatch Jr. resource study] [March 1974]. Colonial National Historical Park, Virginia. https://www.nps.gov/parkhistory/online_books/colo/yorktowns_main_street/chap1-1.htm

16 Hatch [1974], ibid. https://www.nps.gov/parkhistory/online_books/colo/yorktowns_main_street/notes.htm#1-1-3

17 Hatch [1957], ibid.

18 Hatch [1974], ibid.

19 Lot 30, a half-acre of land on the north corner of the intersection of Church and Main streets had a prominent location next to the courthouse and near the parish church in Yorktown. Though it first conveyed to a John Rogers in 1691, he sold it to Thomas Mountfort, the surveyor, in 1706. Rogers regained ownership of it in September 1710—indicating that Mountfort may well have been deceased—and sold it again to John Wills. Records indicate that Mountfort died in or about February 24, 1708/9.

20 Hatch [1974], ibid.

21 Ibid.

22 From Gloucester County records from other Virginia counties, it is known that Matthews and his wife Ann, of York County, conveyed to Edmund Tabb, of Gloucester County "one Lott or half acre of Land on the main street that runs back of Yorktown." This sale took place on June 6, 1748. Patrick Matthews died on February 15, 1762.

23 Hatch [1974], ibid.

24 Buckner was deputy surveyor for Stafford County, Virginia, in 1691, and a justice of the peace for York County in 1694. He was also an officer of the militia, for at a meeting of the court of claims for York that occurred on October 11, 1697, he was called Captain William Buckner, and in subsequent years was given the rank of major. In the years 1698 and 1699, he was a member of the House of Burgesses, and during these sessions took an active role in the revision of laws governing the colony. Buckner was again a member of the assembly in 1714, and from 1708 to 1716 held office as deputy surveyor general for the College of William and Mary. Buckner married Catherine Ballard, the daughter of Colonel Thomas Ballard (1630–1689), of York County, who was clerk of York County for many years after 1652, was burgess for James City County in 1666, member of the council in 1675, and speaker of the House of Burgesses in 1680 and 1682. He was also high sheriff of York County.

25 Hatch [1974], ibid.

26 Ibid.

27 Berthier worked at the Hotel de la Guerre [the French ministry of war] as early as 1768 under his father, Lieutenant Colonel Jean-Baptiste Berthier (1721–1804), an officer in the Corps of Topographical Engineers. Even as a boy, he was instructed in military art by his father, a skill he continued as he joined the army at the age of seventeen. By 1770, he was a lieutenant. Berthier joined Comte de Rochambeau's army in Newport, Rhode Island, and served until 1783 [during his service with Rochambeau he would see Yorktown], when he joined the service of Frederick the Great. He returned to France on the general staff of the Hotel de la Guerre, obtaining the rank of lieutenant colonel in 1789 and colonel in 1791. In 1789, during the French Revolution, Berthier joined the Versailles militia and was named chief of staff where he virtually commanded the National Guard at Versailles. When France declared war on Austria in 1792, Berthier became marshal de camp in the French army. He was relieved of his command after the overthrow of the king because of his sympathies for the royal family. Three years later, in 1795, after the Reign of Terror, Berthier was reinstated in the army as general and chief of staff to the Armies of the Alps and Italy. The following year he held the same position under Napoleon Bonaparte. He later became the commander in chief of the Army of Italy for a short time before rejoining Napoleon. He was a signatory of the Treaty of San Ildefonso on October 1, 1800, by which Spain ceded Louisiana to France. He then rejoined Napoleon, who named Berthier the first Marshal of the Empire in 1804. For his role in the Battle of Wagram on July 6, 1809, he was granted the title of Prince of Wagram. Berthier was with Napoleon in the field for the invasion of Russia, and he remained with the army as it wasted away to nothing. After Napoleon's exile to Elba, Berthier was at the head of the delegations welcoming back King Louis XVIII to Paris. In 1814, Berthier was made a Peer of France and a Commander of the Royal Order of Saint-Louis. Upon the return of Napoleon, Berthier, as Captain of the King's Bodyguard, joined the royal family in exile in Belgium for a time before removing to his family in Bamberg. While at his residence in Bamberg, Berthier either jumped out of the window or was forced out of the window and fell to his death. His coffin lay in state in the cathedral on June 5, 1815, before receiving an escort to Duke Ludwig Wilhelm's castle at Banz.

28 Gwyn Read, the eldest son of Benjamin Read and his wife, the former Mary Gwyn Read (1672–1731), was the developer of the property and it was much of this property that would be deeded in 1691 to form the present site of Yorktown.

29 Hatch [1974], ibid.

30 Ibid.

31 Historic Yorktown: https://www.nps.gov/york/learn/historyculture/historic-yorktown.htm

32 Edward Digges, an English barrister and colonist who served as colonial governor from March 1655 to December 1656, first emigrated to Virginia in 1650 and it was just then that he bought the West plantation of one thousand two hundred and fifty acres near Yorktown. He invested heavily in planting mulberry trees and promoting the silk industry of the colony, in recognition of which he was appointed auditor-general of Virginia. But Digges was far more successful with tobacco than silk. He became especially well known for growing "E.D." tobacco, a sweet-scented variety that brought an unusually high price in London.

33 Charles Cornwallis, first marquis Cornwallis, largely also known as Earl Cornwallis from 1762 to 1792, was in addition to his military duties, a colonial administrator.

34 *Notes on the State of Virginia*: https://web.archive.org/web/20130829133128/http://etext.virginia.edu/etcbin/toccer-new2?id=JefVirg.sgm&images=images/modeng&data=/texts/english/modeng/parsed&tag=public&part=all

35 Hatch [1974], ibid.

36 Keyes saw action in the Peninsula Campaign as a brigadier general. After the Seven Days Battles, Major General George Brinton McClellan (1826–1885) promoted all his corps and division commanders to the rank of major general—all but Keyes—who remained a brigadier general. When the army returned to Washington, D.C., in early August 1862, McClellan left Keyes and one of the two Fourth Corps divisions behind on the Peninsula as part of General John Adams Dix's Department of the James. President Abraham Lincoln nominated Keyes for promotion to the grade of major general, United States Volunteers, on March 12, 1862, and he assumed this new rank that May 5. In addition to the Fourth Corps, Keyes commanded the Yorktown District, VII Corps, and the division at Suffolk.

37 Hatch [1974], ibid. https://www.nps.gov/parkhistory/online_books/colo/yorktowns_main_street/chap1-2.htm

38 Ibid.

39 Ibid.

40 In his will, John Buckner Jr. wrote: "[...] I give unto Griffin Stith my six Lotts in York Town my wind mill with the Lott of ground it stands on & my warehouses under the Hill to him and his heirs [...]"

41 Hatch [1974], ibid.

42 The smock mill is a type of windmill that consists of a sloping, horizontally weather boarded or thatched tower, usually with six or eight sides. It is topped with a roof or cap that rotates to bring the sails into the wind.

43 Peale took artistic license in his depiction of the mill.

44 Hatch [1974], ibid.

45 Ibid.

46 The Royal Welch repulsed two French assaults on the Fusiliers redoubt following French bombardment at point blank range. Before the French could launch a third assault, the heavily outnumbered British force was ordered to surrender by their commander major general Lord Charles Cornwallis. The British were required to surrender their weapons and Regimental Colors. The Royal Welch Colors were safely spirited away by two young officers. In the present, the Royal Welch Fusiliers redoubt can be found on the bluff above the Yorktown river opposite the entrance to the Yorktown Victory Center on the west side of the old town [the Yorktown Battlefield National Park is on the southeast side of Yorktown]. The redoubt is currently a little overgrown but still accessible to the public with great views of the river and the French lines, located just under one thousand feet away. A bronze memorial plaque can be found inside the redoubt on the rampart facing the French lines. The painting depicts the successful American assault on the British redoubt No. 10 at the eastern end of the British line.

47 Hatch [1974], Ibid.

48 Hatch [1957], ibid.

49 Benjamin Harrison V, of Charles City County, Virginia, was a planter and merchant, Founding Father and signer of the Declaration of Independence. He was governor of Virginia from 1781 to 1784. His direct descendants include two United States presidents—his son, William Henry Harrison (1773–1841) and great-grandson, Benjamin Harrison (1833–1901).

50 Chevalier de la Valette had been in America as an officer with the army of General Jean-Baptiste Donatien de Vimeur, Comte de Rochambeau (1725–1807). Born in Montfort-l'Amaury, Yvelines department, France on June

5, 1731, he was nominated brigadier general on December 5, 1781, for distinguished conduct at the capture of York [Yorktown] (as a lieutenant colonel).

51   Hatch [1974], ibid. https://www.nps.gov/parkhistory/online_books/colo/yorktowns_main_street/chap2-4.htm

52   After the surrender, the Articles of Capitulation of Cornwallis, listing men, guns and accoutrements, were given to Colonel Charles Dabney at a dinner with George Washington, where the general instructed him with regard to his duties at the October 19, 1781 capitulation. In January 1782, a board of state officers consolidated remnants of all state line units into Charles Dabney's Virginia State Legion. The reformed legion numbered about two hundred and twenty-five officers and men who garrisoned at Richmond, Hampton and Yorktown for almost two years after the surrender. In September 1782, Dabney put down a small mutiny, probably brandishing his trademark large bore rifle that was inscribed with his name. The legion was disbanded in April 1783 and Colonel Charles Dabney received the thanks of the United States Congress for distinguished service, becoming a charter member of The Society of the Cincinnati, his membership certificate signed by General George Washington.

53   Hatch [1974], ibid.

54   Griffin, a surgeon to Virginia forces during the Revolutionary War, was captured and imprisoned by the British and held on a ship at anchor in the York River during the siege of the town.

55   Hatch [1974], ibid.

56   Hatch [1974], ibid. https://www.nps.gov/parkhistory/online_books/colo/yorktowns_main_street/chap2-5.htm

57   Ibid.

58   Benjamin Henry Latrobe was hired by President Thomas Jefferson (1743–1826) in 1803 to fill the position of Surveyor of Public Buildings, with the principal responsibility of constructing the Capitol's south wing. He was also responsible for work at the President's House and the Navy Yard. After the south wing was completed in 1807 Latrobe began reconstructing the interior of the north wing. Construction funds were withheld after 1810, and Latrobe's public employment came to an end. After the two wings were damaged by fires set by British troops in 1814, Latrobe was rehired to oversee the restoration work. During this period, he worked only on the U.S. Capitol and had no responsibilities for other government buildings. Latrobe's employment contract was signed with the commissioners on April 18, 1815, and he resigned on November 20, 1817. He left at the U.S. Capitol some of the greatest interiors in the history of neoclassicism in America, including the Hall of the House (now National Statuary Hall), the Old Senate Chamber and the Old Supreme Court Chamber. He is honored as the second Architect of the Capitol. [From the Architect of the Capitol: https://www.aoc.gov/architect-of-the-capitol/benjamin-henry-latrobe]

59   Hatch [1974], ibid.

60   Ibid.

61   Ward, born in Culpeper County, Virginia, in 1826, was a lawyer who joined the Confederate States Army as a lieutenant. In the last chapter of his life, he was a circuit court officer. He died in Richmond, Virginia, on July 2, 1896, and is interred in Hollywood Cemetery.

62   Hatch [1974], ibid.

63   Ibid.

64   During the Civil War, Strother joined the army as captain and assistant adjutant-general, became colonel of the Third West Virginia cavalry, and resigned in September 1864. In 1865, he received the brevet of brigadier general of volunteers.

65   Hatch [1974], ibid.

66   Ibid.

67   Ibid.

68   A sward is an expanse of short grass.

69   Hatch [1974], ibid. https://www.nps.gov/parkhistory/online_books/colo/yorktowns_main_street/chap2-5.htm

70   Ibid.

71   Ibid.

72   At the outbreak of the Civil War, Daniel Harvey Hill (1821–1889) was made colonel of the First North Carolina Volunteers—the Bethel Regiment—at the head of which he won the Battle of Big Bethel, near Fort Monroe, Virginia, on June 10, 1861. Shortly thereafter, he was promoted to brigadier general and commanded troops in the Richmond area. By the spring of 1862, he was a major general and division commander in the Army of Northern Virginia. He participated in the Yorktown and Williamsburg operations that began the Peninsula Campaign and led a division with great distinction in the Battle of Seven Pines and the Seven Days Battles.

73   Hatch [1974], ibid.

74 Ibid.

75 Ibid.

76 Hatch [1974], ibid. https://www.nps.gov/parkhistory/online_books/colo/yorktowns_main_street/chap2-6.htm

77 Ibid.

78 Ibid.

79 A photograph of that sally port was taken during the Peninsula Campaign by a Mathew Brady photographer and is included in II—The Siege of Yorktown.

80 Hatch [1974], ibid.

81 Before coming to the United States, Hansen served as a merchant seaman and later served in the United States Army. In the late 1930s and into the 1940s, he built a home and artist studio on property near Ashcroft, located just outside of Charlottesville, Virginia. Hansen is most associated with the design of many of the sculptures on and around the Hoover Dam.

82 Louis XVI granted him the title of marquis but on January 4, 1792, the Palatine Count Charles Augustus finally granted him the title of Chevalier de Deux-Ponts.

83 Philippe Wilhelm, commonly called Guillaume de Deux-Ponts, would go on to become a general in the Bavarian army.

84 Franklin D. Roosevelt Presidential Library: The Master Speech Files, 1898, 1910–1945. Series 1: Franklin D. Roosevelt's Political Ascension, File No. 443, October 16, 1931. http://docs.fdrlibrary.marist.edu/browse.cgi

I

REVOLUTIONARY BEGINNINGS

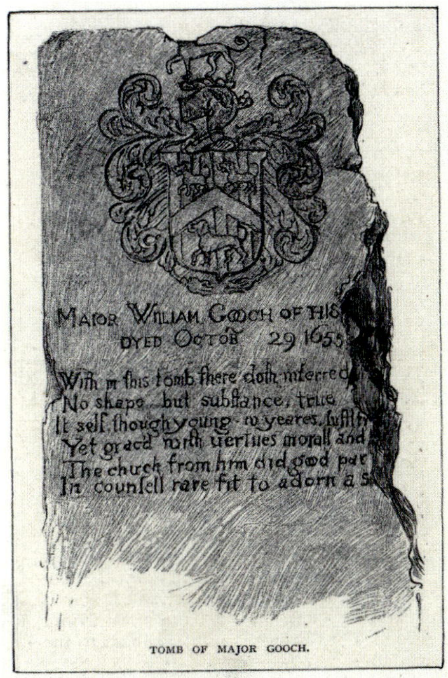

TOMB OF MAJOR GOOCH.

The grave of Major William Gooch (1626–1655) is documented as the first decorated tombstone in the English colonies and the second oldest legible stone in Virginia. Gooch, who was a burgess from York County, was appointed to the council in March 1655, the year he died at the age of twenty-nine. He is believed to be the William Gooch listed in Burkes' *Peerage* who died in 1655 and was the uncle of Sir William Gooch (1681–1751), first baronet and lieutenant governor [the colony's chief administrator just then, which has often led to him being called the governor] of Virginia from 1727 to 1749. On the land around Gooch's tomb was established the first settlement on the York River—variously called York, Old York and York Village—near Wormley Creek before 1635. A church was built at York Village roughly three years later. The village was abandoned by the end of the eighteenth century. The site is located on the United States Coast Guard Reserve Training Center and marked by a small park. The wood engraving of Gooch's flat stone with decoration and inscription was published in 1880 by Henry Howe (1816–1893). The carved armorial decoration probably indicates English workmanship. When the gravesite was added to the National Register of Historic Places on January 18, 1974, it was noted that it was protected by a concrete and iron cage, and shielded from the weather by a wooden roof structure. Simple linear earthworks dating from the Civil War were also visible east of the grave. *New York Public Library*

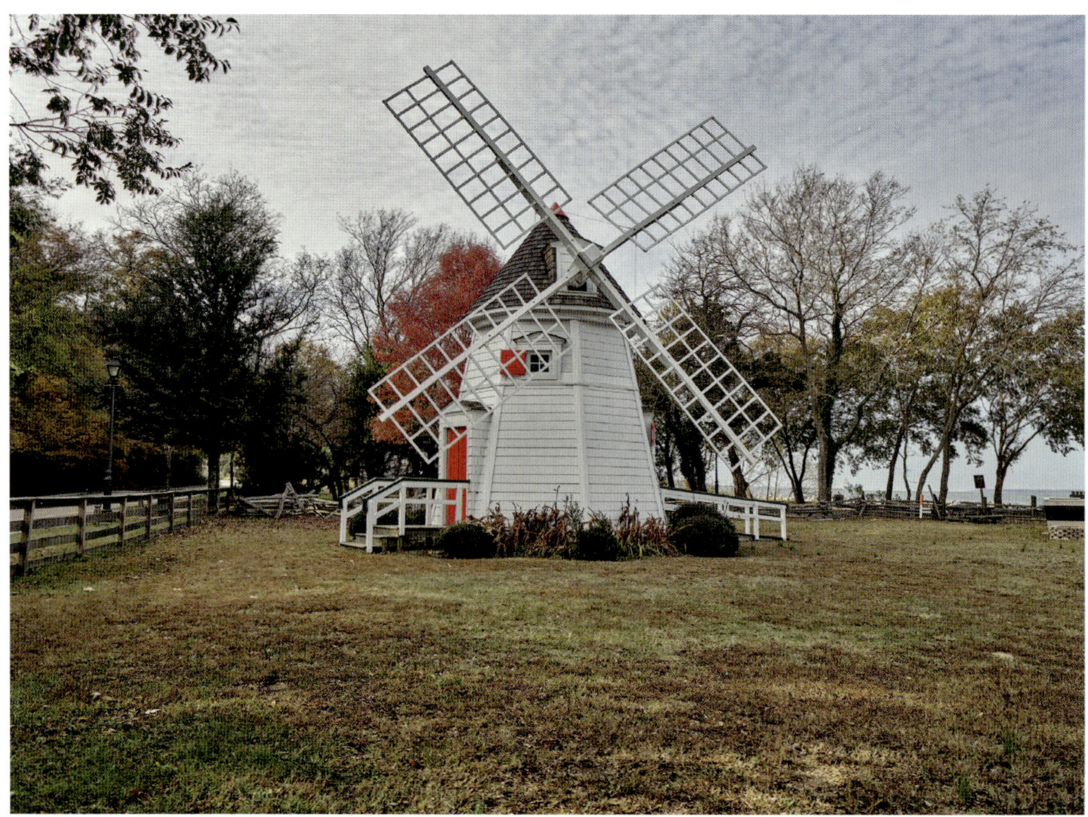

A replica of William Buckner's 1711 mill, which had ground corn over the course of two centuries and importantly served as a beacon on the York River, was recreated using historical paintings, engravings and sketches to guide the design of the new structure. Construction of Buckner's replica windmill as shown in this Carol M. Highsmith November 21, 2019 photograph, was started in April 2008 and finished early October 2011. This fully functional replica was built in Seaford, Virginia, by more than 100 volunteers over the course of three years. Each of their names is engraved on a commemorative stone plaque that is mounted inside the mill. In the fall of 2011, the windmill was disassembled and relocated to its present site in time for the tercentennial anniversary of the construction of the original. The Yorktown windmill was dedicated on October 19, 2011. The new Buckner windmill, situated today next to the Watermen's Museum on Water Street, stands less than 100 yards from where the original structure was built. *Library of Congress*

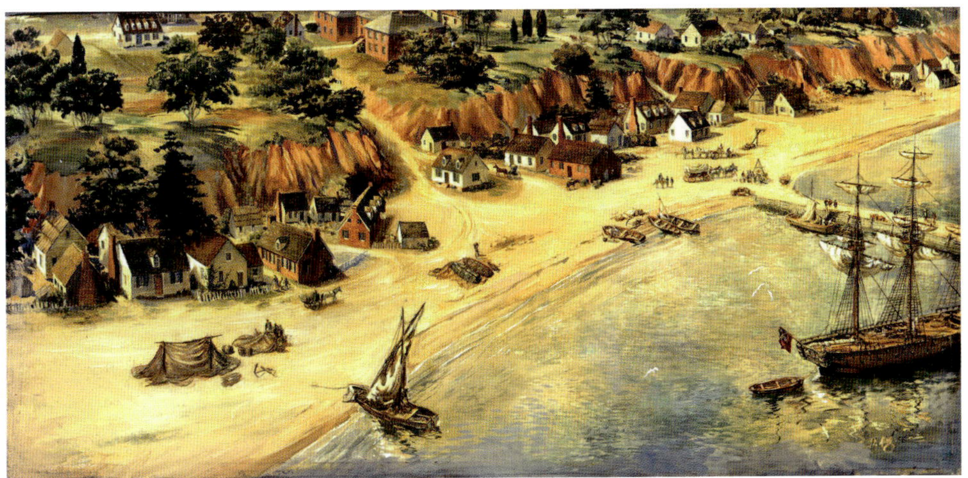

By the middle of the eighteenth century, Yorktown was the busiest seaport in the Chesapeake Bay region, whose wharves, docks and warehouses would attract the attention of the British army when they needed supplies in the summer of 1781. Renowned artist Sidney Eugene King (1906–2002) painted this piece in 1956, one of one hundred and eighty-five paintings he would do for the Department of the Interior/National Park Service. King's commission to paint a series of outdoor murals for the semiseptcentennial of Jamestown [1607–1957] led also to his paintings of Yorktown. He illustrated a commemorative book of his paintings that was presented to Queen Elizabeth II and President Dwight David Eisenhower during the Jamestown celebration. The Jamestown and Yorktown paintings are considered his best work. King's paintings famously tell America's story in accurate depictions of defining moments and most especially the colonial period. *National Park Service*

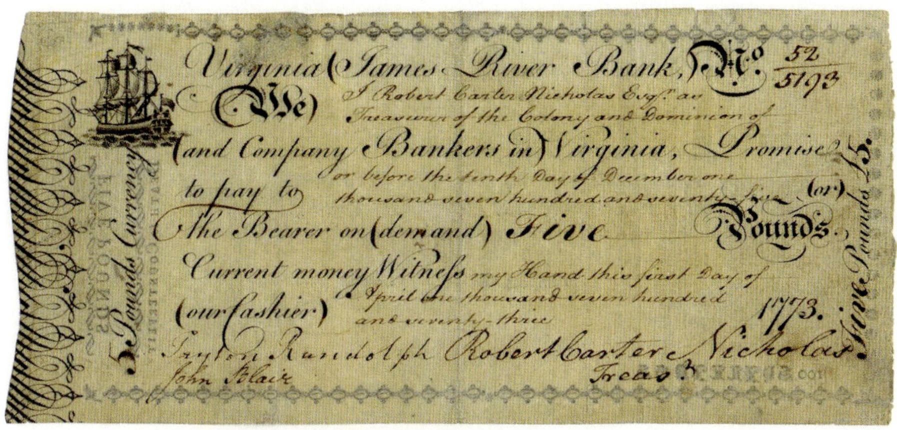

This James River Bank note adapted by the Virginia government for use as official currency is on display at the American Revolution Museum at Yorktown. Issued in 1773, the note was signed by Peyton Randolph (1721–1775), Virginia planter and first president of the Continental Congress; John Blair Jr. (1732–1800), lawyer, member of the Virginia House of Burgesses, Founding Father and associate justice of the Supreme Court of the United States, and Robert Carter Nicholas (1728–1780), lawyer, also a member of the House of Burgesses and before his death, a patriot. *Jamestown-Yorktown Foundation*

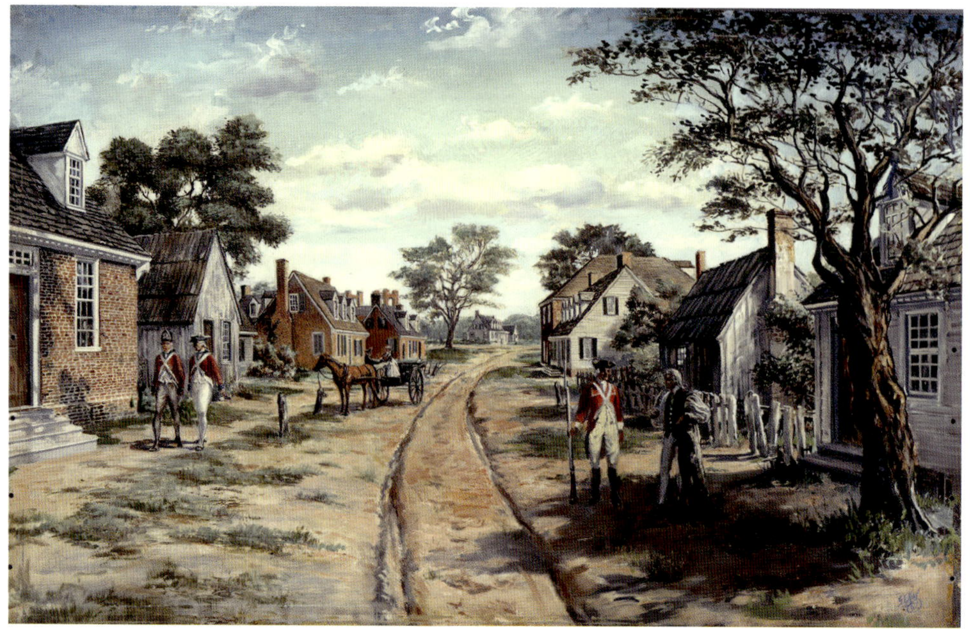

The scene in this Sidney King painting, completed in 1957, depicts eighteenth-century Main Street in Yorktown, looking east. Identifiable buildings include (left to right) the houses of Mungo Somerwell, Cole Digges, Charles Cox, and Dudley Digges and the custom house (right side, far end). *National Park Service*

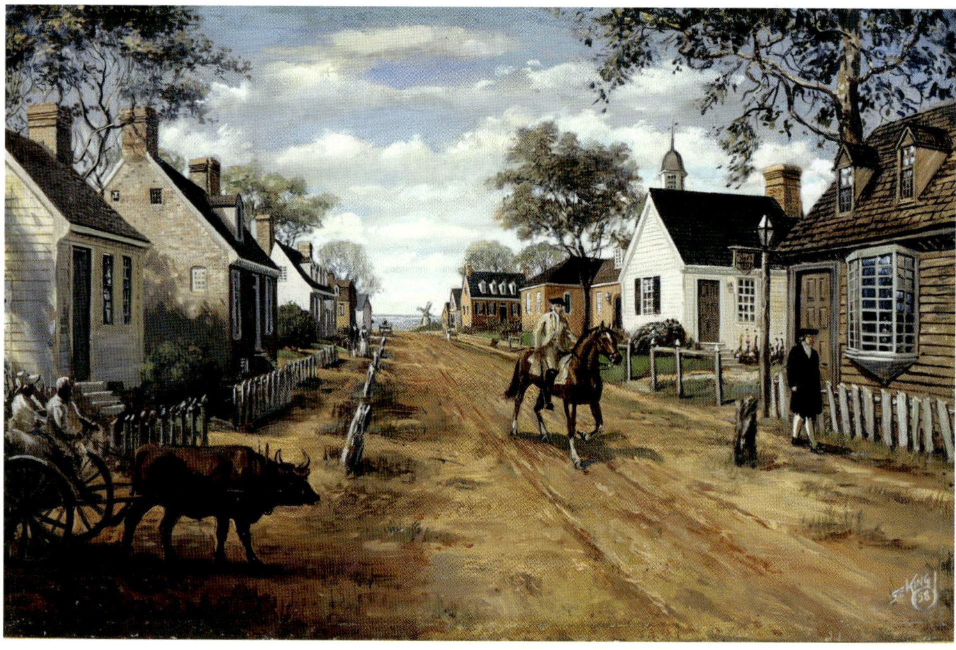

Sidney King painted eighteenth-century Yorktown's Main Street looking west the following year, in 1958. The scene includes Corbin Griffin's medical shop, the York County courthouse, Swan Tavern and the windmill. *National Park Service*

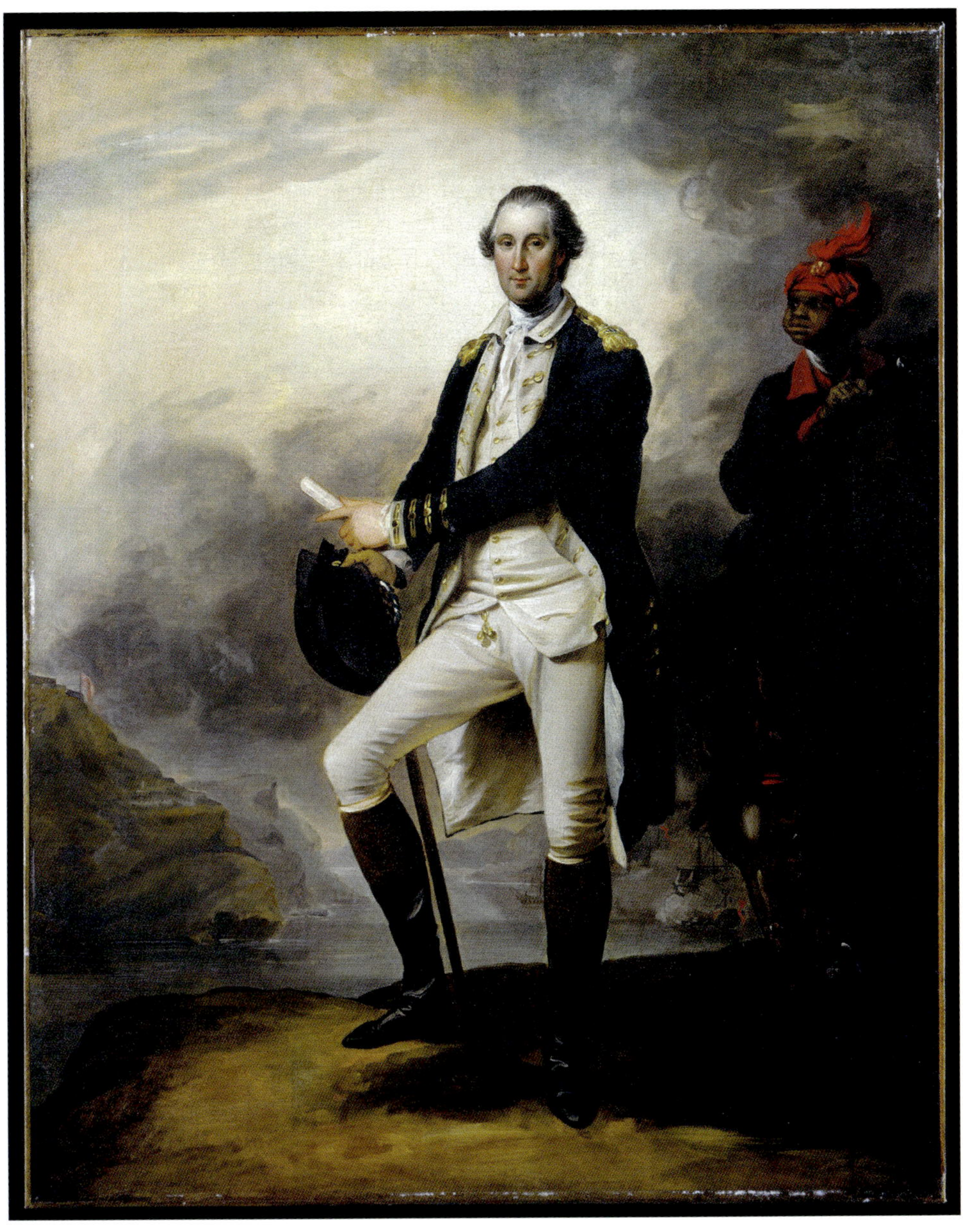

Artist John Trumbull's oil-on-canvas of George Washington (1732–1799) was completed in 1780 and is part of the permanent collection of the Metropolitan Museum of Art, New York City, New York. Trumbull (1756–1843) has been called "the painter of the Revolution" for his significant historical paintings rendered during the America's war for independence but also in the decades that followed it. As a soldier during the war, he sketched what he witnessed firsthand, to include the Battle of Bunker Hill. He was subsequently appointed second personal aide to General George Washington, and in June 1776, deputy adjutant-general to General Horatio Gates. He resigned from the Continental Army the following year over a dispute regarding his officer commission. *Metropolitan Museum of Art*[1]

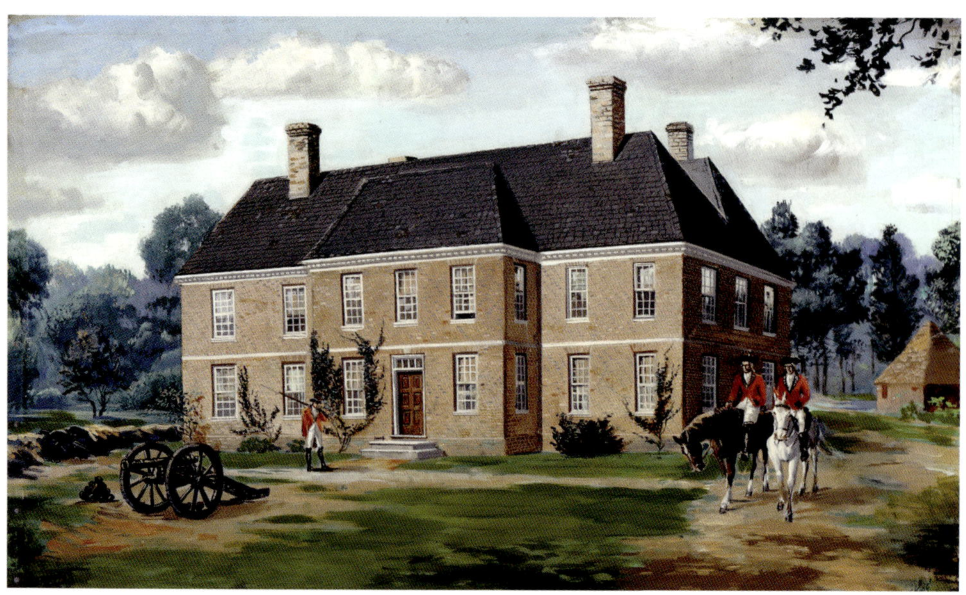

The home of Secretary of the Colonial Council of Virginia Thomas Nelson (1716–1782) [shown in this 1957 Sidney King painting] was initially used as the headquarters of Major General Charles Edward Cornwallis V, Lord Cornwallis (1738–1805) due to its proximity to the siege lines. Nelson was the younger of two sons of Thomas "Scotch Tom" Nelson (1677–1745), the first of the Nelson family in Yorktown. The high quality of Nelson's residence is known from the description provided by then lieutenant general François-Jean de Beauvoir, Marquis de Chastellux (1734–1788), who was with Rochambeau and the French army during the siege in 1781: "He [Secretary Nelson] lived at York, where he had built a very handsome house, from which neither European taste nor luxury was excluded; a chimney-piece and some bass reliefs of very fine marble, exquisitely sculptured, were particularly admired. [The house] was built on an eminence, near the most important fortifications, and in the most agreeable situation in town […] it soon drew the attention of our bombardiers and cannoneers and was almost entirely destroyed." Chastellux continued: "Mr. Nelson lived in it at the time our batteries tried their first shot and killed one of his negroes at a little distance from him; so that Lord Cornwallis was soon obliged to seek another asylum."[2] The house came under fire and would not survive the siege. But though in ruins, it remained what those who saw it—even years later—an impressive structure. Isaac Weld (1774–1856), an Irish topographical writer, explorer and artist, who came upon it in 1796, reported: "There is one house in particular, which stands in the skirt of the town, that is in a most shattered condition. It was," he recalled, "the habitation of a Mr. Neilson [sic], a secretary under the regal government, and was made the headquarters of Lord Cornwallis when he first came to the town; but it stood so much exposed, and afforded so good a mark to the enemy, that he was soon forced to quit it. Neilson [sic], however, it seems, was determined to stay there till the last, and absolutely remained till his negro servant, the only person that would live with him in such a house, had his brains dashed out by a cannon shot while he stood by his side; he then thought it time to retire, but the house was still continually fired at, as if it had been headquarters." Weld described the walls and roof pierced in innumerable places, and at one corner a large piece of the wall torn away but even in this state, he would opine, "it is still inhabited in one room by some person or other equally fanciful as the old secretary. There are trenches thrown up around it, and on every side are deep hollows made by the bombs that fell near it."[3] *National Park Service*

Opposite above: The Battle of the Virginia Capes [September 5, 1781] is the subject of this oil on canvas painted by Vladimir Zvegintzov in 1962, and shows the French fleet (left), commanded by Vice Admiral François Joseph Paul de Grasse (1723–1788), Comte de Grasse, engaging the British fleet (right) under Rear Admiral Sir Thomas Graves (1747–1814) off the mouth of Chesapeake Bay. *Continued on next page*

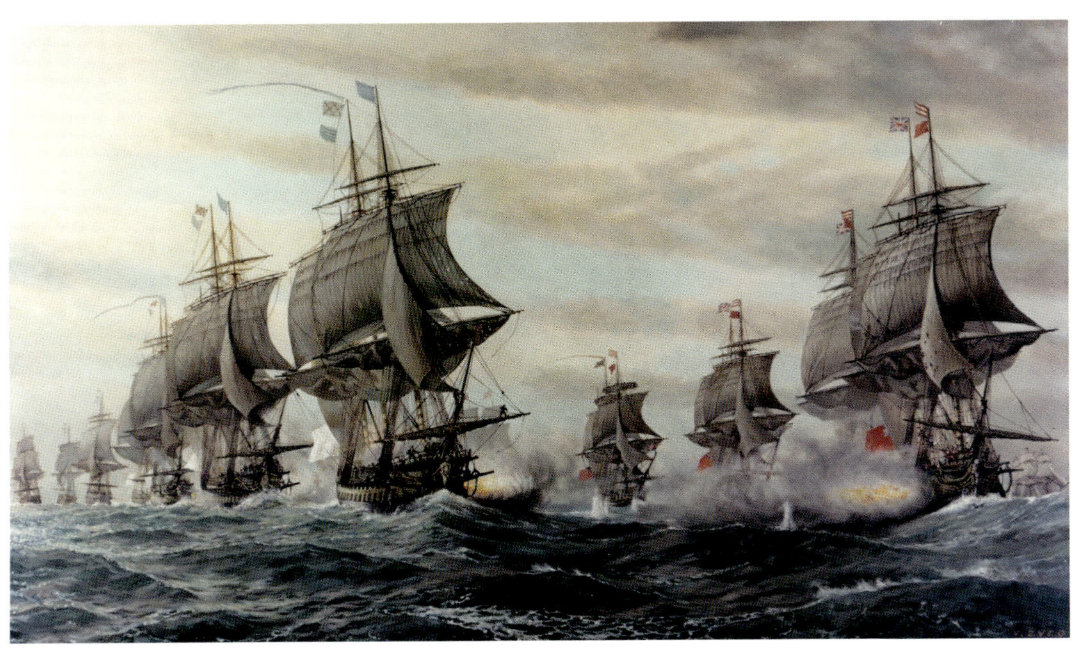

What remains of the original *Betsy* lies on the bottom of the York River just beyond the end of the pier located along Yorktown's Riverwalk. *The Betsy* was a two-masted brig, originally built as a coal collier that became one of more than a dozen vessels deliberately scuttled or sunk by the British in September 1781 just off the Yorktown waterfront. *The Betsy* was sent to the river's bottom that September 16. Starting in 1982, the Virginia Department of Historic Resources archaeologists excavated parts of the ship as well as hundreds of other artifacts. Much of the ship's hull and framing had survived after more than 200 years. Among the artifacts recovered from the 175-foot-long brig were weapons, rigging, barrels, a cannon carriage, and personal objects from the captain's cabin. This

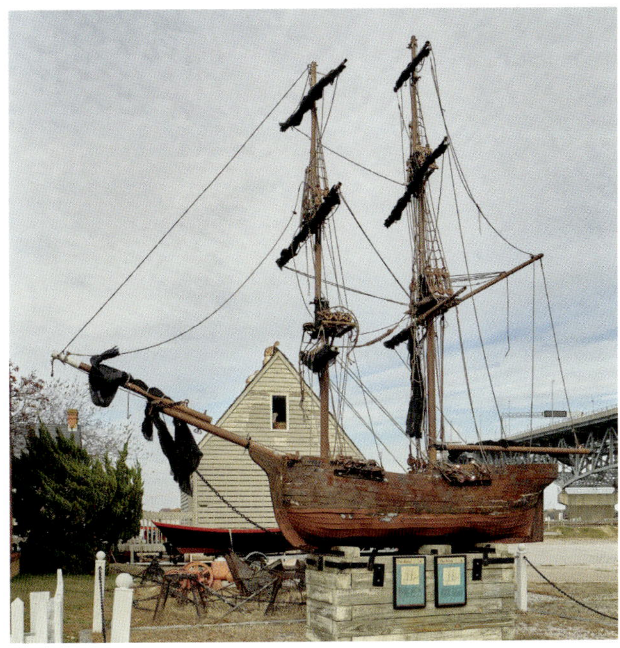

model replica of *The Betsy* on Riverwalk Landing next to the Watermen's Museum, photographed by Carol Highsmith on November 21, 2019, was built entirely from recycled materials. *Library of Congress*

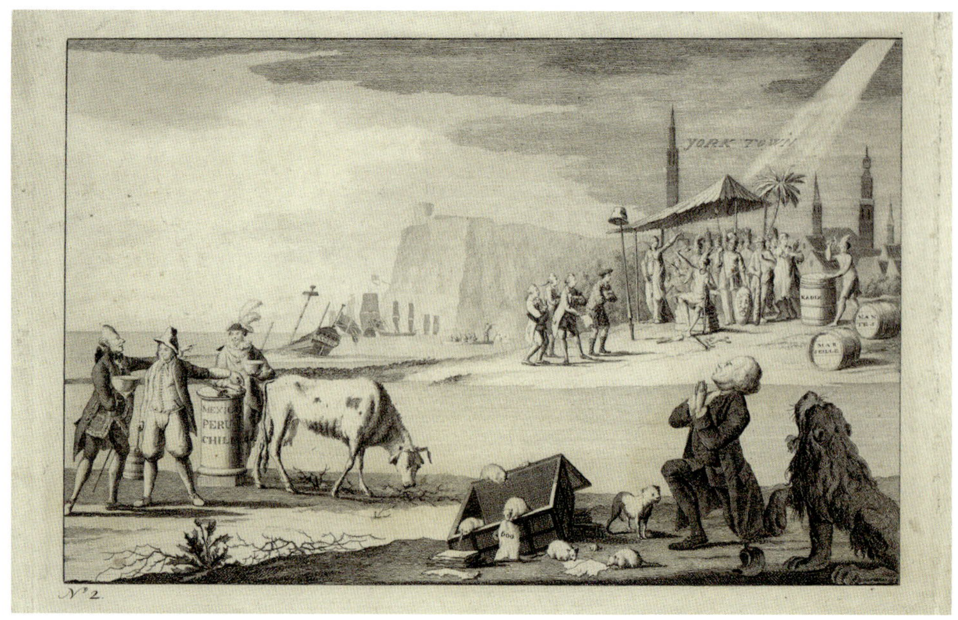

Published in 1781, this cartoon shows "America" receiving the surrender of Lord Cornwallis in the background, while an emaciated cow representing "English commerce" is robbed of her milk by France, Spain, and Holland in the left foreground. On the right a frock-coated Englishman begs, as does the British lion, whose paw has been injured by a broken teapot. *Library of Congress*

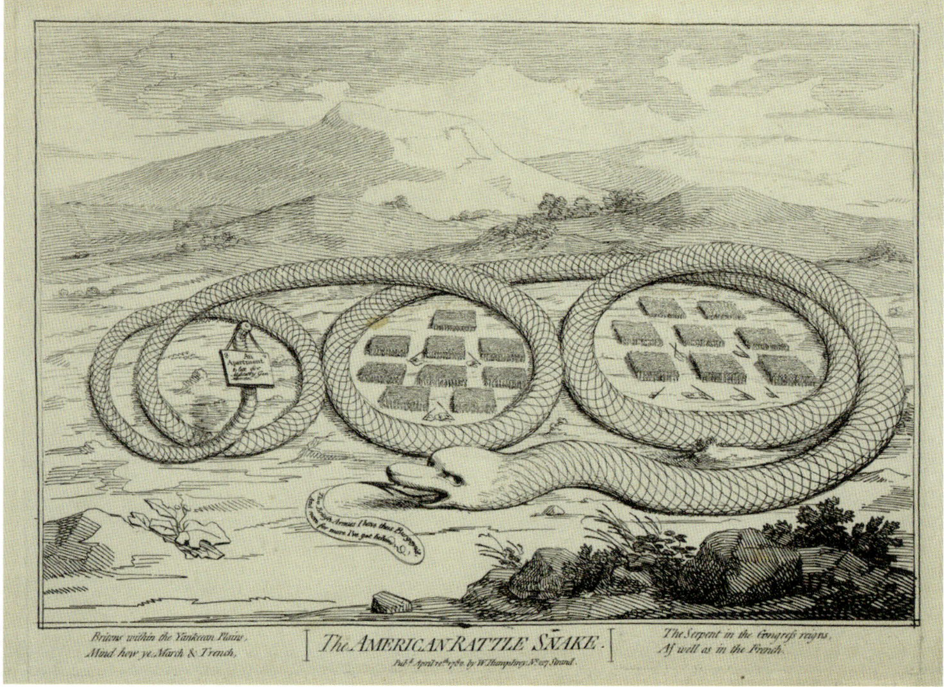

This print *The American Rattle Snake* by artist James Gillray (1756–1815) (shown here) was published by London printer William Humphrey (1745–1810) on April 12, 1782. *Continued on next page*

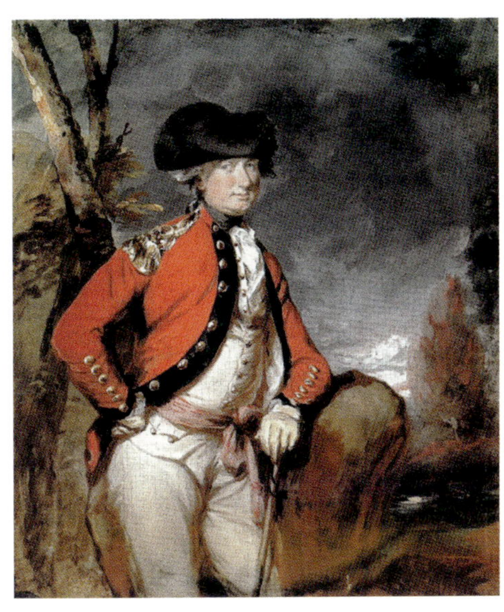

Right: A portrait of Major General Charles Edward Cornwallis V, Lord Cornwallis, commander of British troops at the 1781 siege of Yorktown, by British painter Daniel Gardner (1750–1805) is on exhibit at the American Revolution Museum at Yorktown. The portrait dates to the 1780s. *Jamestown-Yorktown Foundation*

Below: The tents that comprised the headquarters of General George Washington during the siege of Yorktown (and which are shown in this 1958 Sidney King painting) were set up behind the American and French lines. *National Park Service*

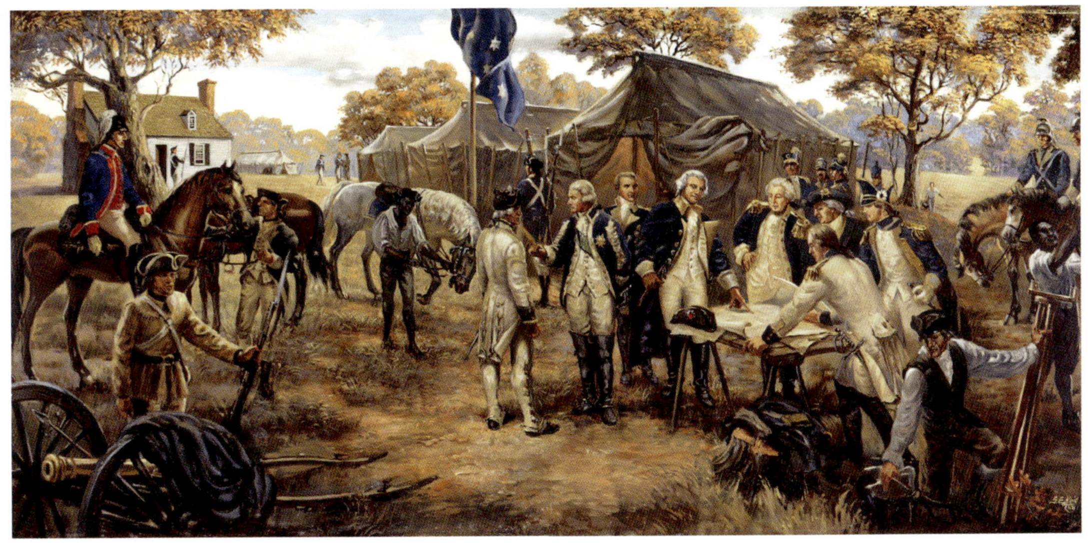

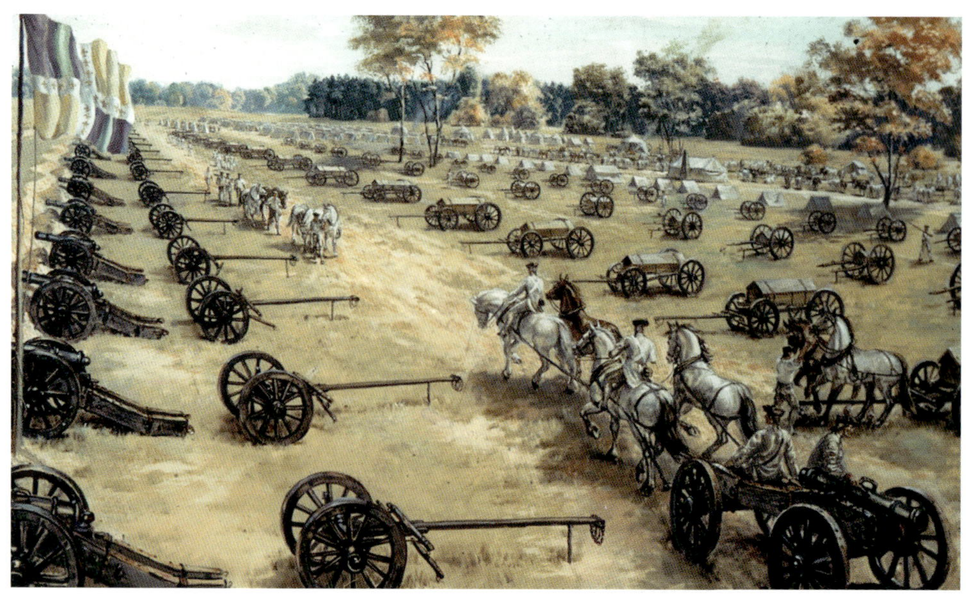

Sidney King painted this scene of French artillery stored behind the Allied lines prior to the siege of Yorktown, also in the same time frame as others shown herein. *National Park Service*

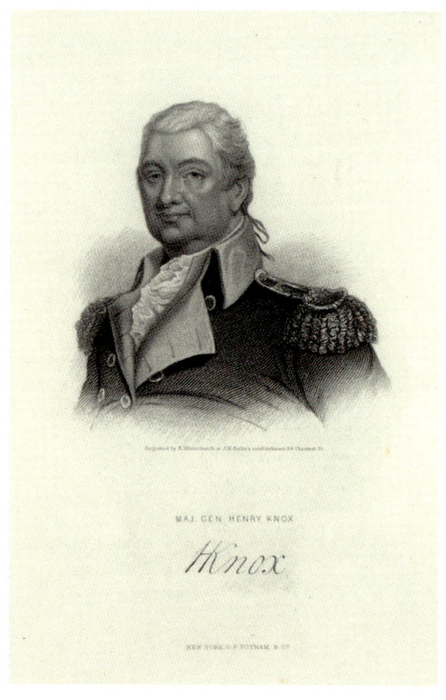

In 1781 Continental Army major general Henry Knox (1750–1806) accompanied General George Washington's forces south and participated in the decisive siege of Yorktown. He was personally active in the field, directing the placement and aiming of the artillery. Of interest, Knox and the artillery established a winter cantonment at Pluckemin [a hamlet of Bedminster, New Jersey]. There Knox established the Continental Army's first school of artillery and officer training. This facility is considered the precursor to the United States Military Academy at West Point, New York.[5] Knox also served as the first secretary of War in George Washington's cabinet. The Robert Whitechurch (1814–1876) stipple engraving of Knox (shown here) was printed by John McGoffin Butler of Philadelphia and published after Whitechurch's death by G. [George] P. [Palmer] Putnam and Company of New York in 1880. *New York Public Library*

Opposite above: Louis Charles Auguste Couder (1789–1873)'s oil-on-canvas painting *Bataille de Yorktown* [Siege of Yorktown] was painted in 1836. The painting hangs in the Galerie des Batailles at the Palace of Versailles, France. Couder, though born in London, was a French painter. In this scene, Marshal of France[6] and General Jean-Baptiste Donatien de Vimeur, Comte de Rochambeau (1725–1807) [pointing] and General George Washington give last orders before an attack in October 1781.[7]

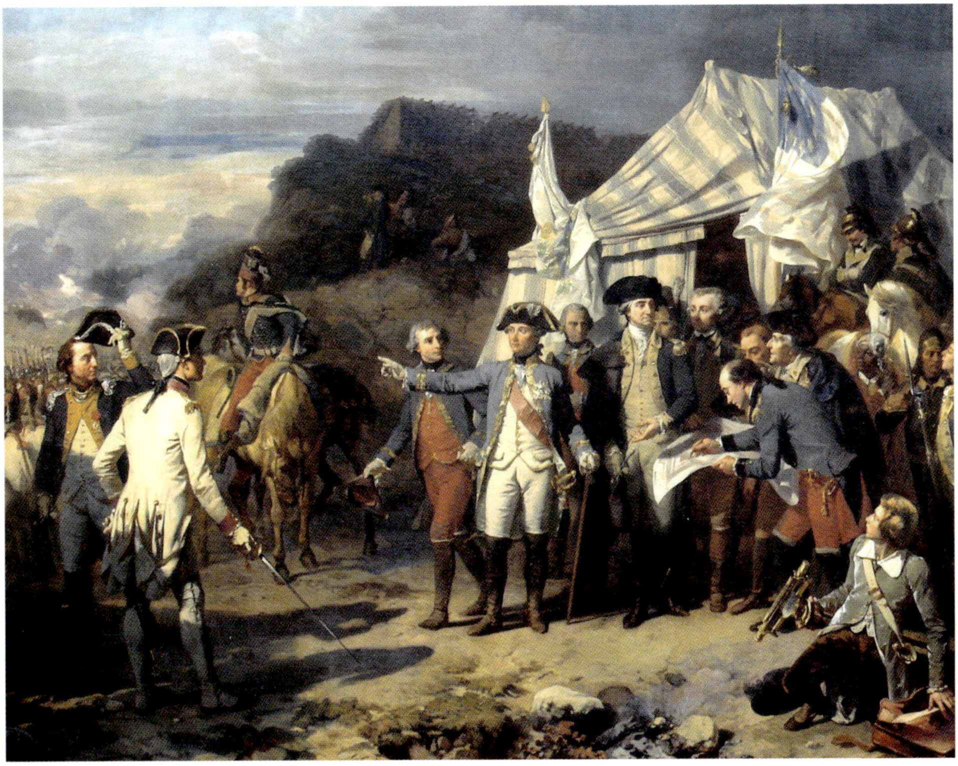

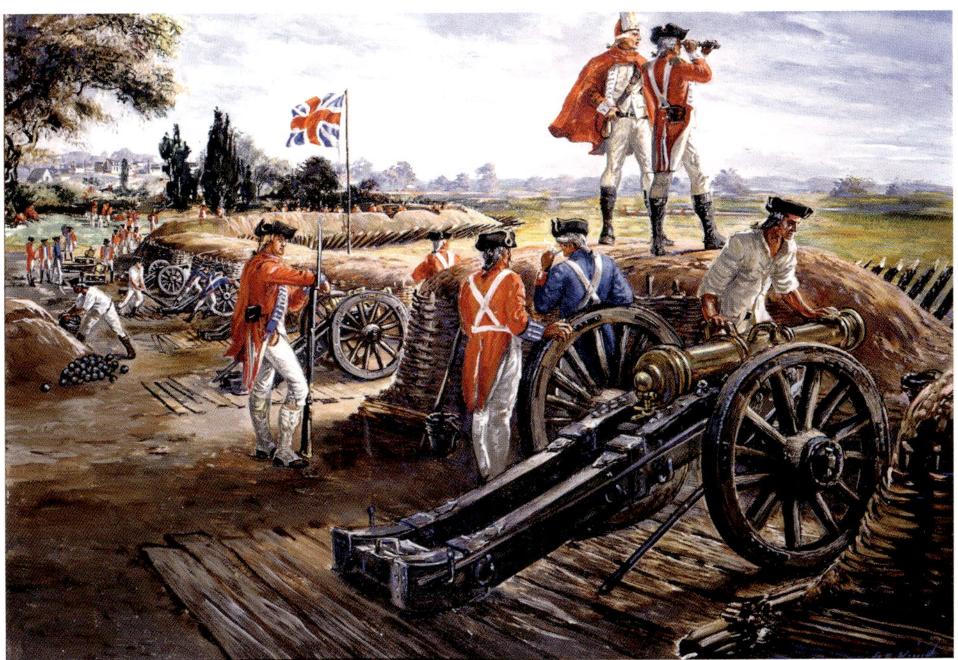

In this Sidney King painting, British officers surveyed the Allied lines from their artillery position on the outskirts of Yorktown. *National Park Service*

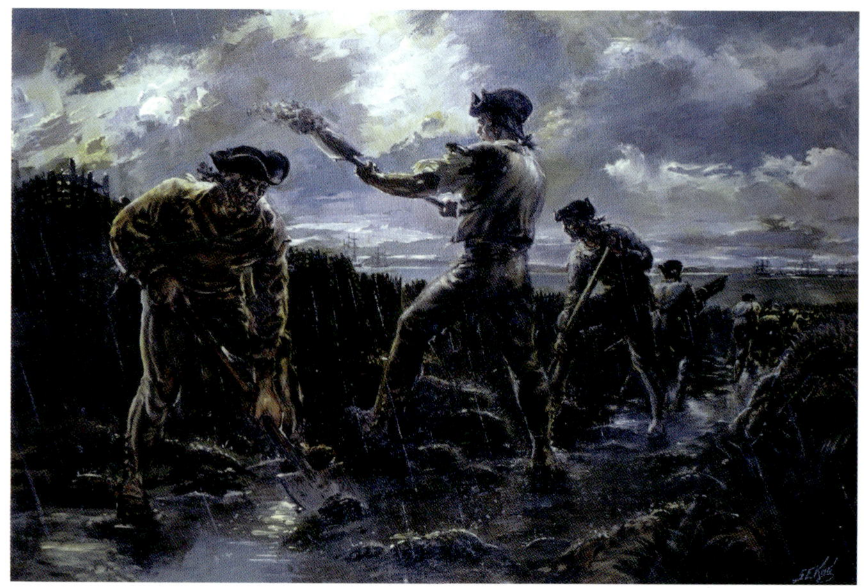

In order to escape detection by British troops, much of the construction of fortifications by American and French troops was done under cover of darkness. Sidney King painted this scene as part of his park service commission. *National Park Service*

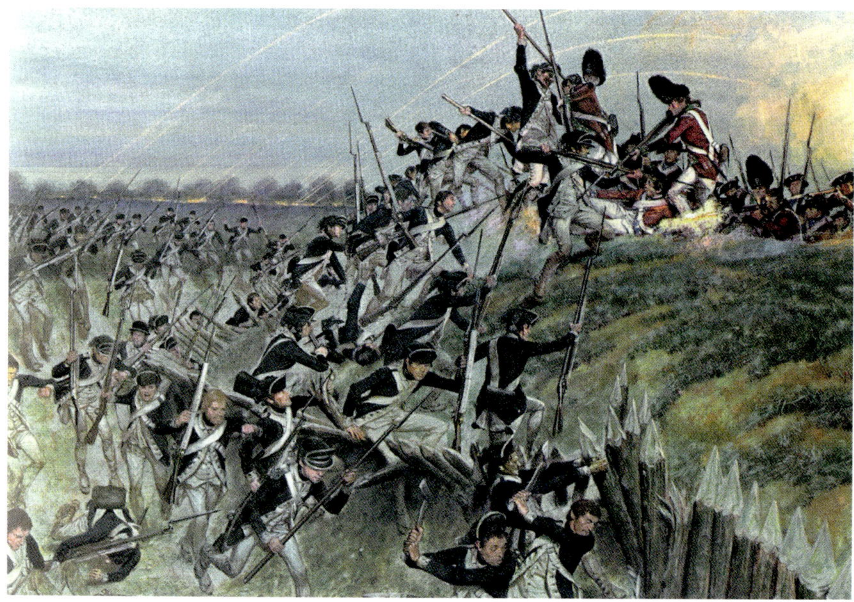

In order to complete the second siege parallel in front of the British fortifications surrounding Yorktown, General George Washington ordered the seizure of two British redoubts near the York River. The French were assigned the first—Redoubt No. 9—and the American Light Infantry under Lieutenant Colonel Alexander Hamilton (1757–1804) the second—Redoubt No. 10. On the evening of October 14, 1781, as covering fire of shot and shell arched overhead, the French and Americans moved forward. The Americans, with unloaded muskets and fixed bayonets, did not wait for sappers to clear away the abatis, as the French did, but instead climbed over and through the obstructions. *Continued on next page*

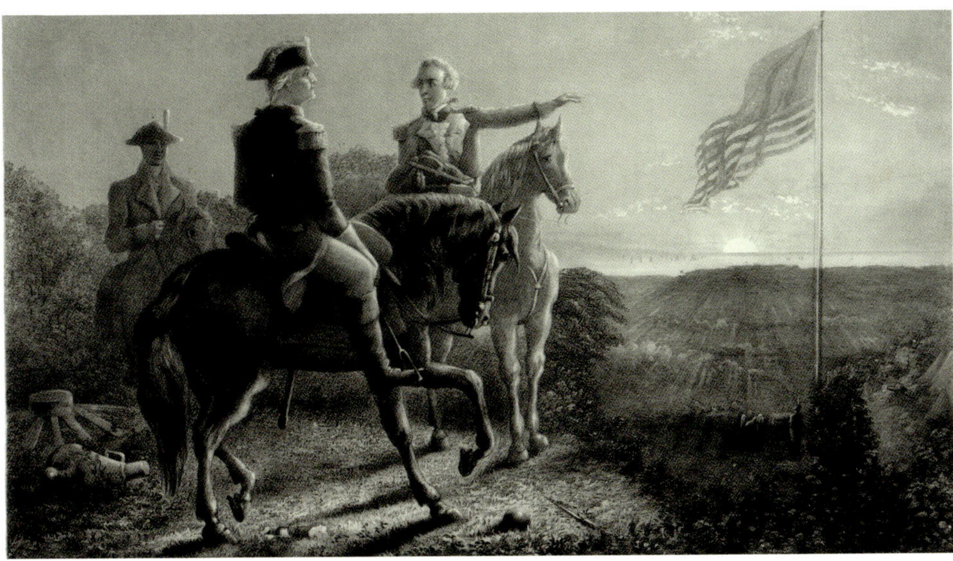

The morning of the British surrender at Yorktown, shown in this rendering titled *The Dawn of Peace*, was a moment to contemplate the cost of victory. This work was designed and engraved by A. Gilchrist Campbell, of New York, who published it on December 31, 1881. *Library of Congress*

William Nelson (1711–1772), of Yorktown, Virginia, president of the dominion of Virginia, is shown in this portrait by an unknown artist, derived from a watercolor copy by Charles H. Sherman, of New York, dated 1883. Nelson, a planter, politician, and colonial leader was the acting royal governor of Virginia from 1770 to 1771, was the son of Thomas "Scotch Tom" Nelson and the older brother of Thomas Nelson (1716–1782). In the early stages of the American Revolution, William Nelson was an active supporter of the colonial cause and his son, planter, soldier[9] and statesman Thomas Nelson Jr. (1738–1789), went on to represent Virginia in the Continental Congress, sign the Declaration of Independence and was governor in 1781. Thomas Nelson Jr. is regarded as one of the United States' Founding Fathers. Of note, Nelson had the suffix "Junior/Jr." added to his name to distinguish himself from his uncle, who was also named Thomas. *New York Public Library*

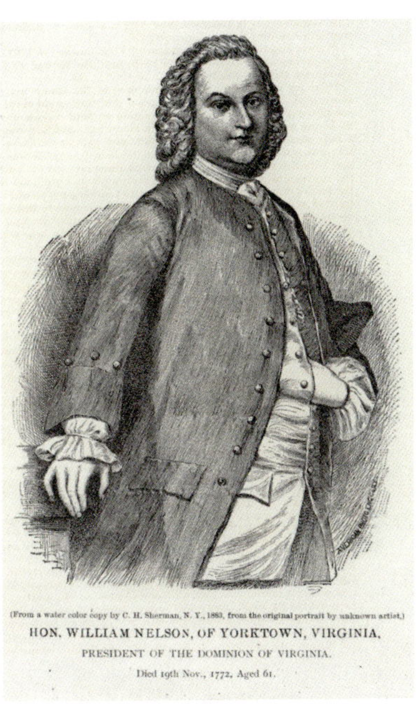

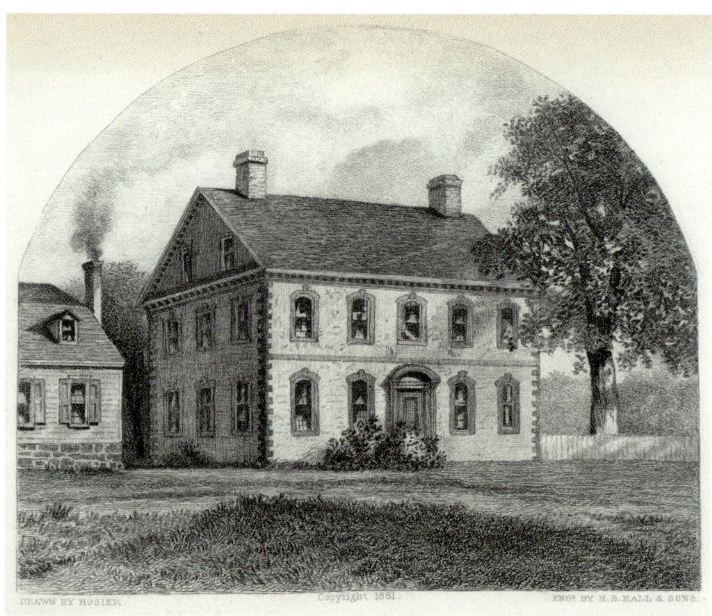

This is the Nelson House from an Abraham Hosier (1830–1883) engraving printed by Henry Bryan Hall[10] (1808–1884) and Sons, engraver, and published in 1880 by Henry Howe (1816–1893). Built by Thomas "Scotch Tom" Nelson in or about 1730 at the strategic location at the head of the so-called Great Valley, a principal connection between the town proper and the waterfront where he quickly developed interests, and later occupied by Thomas Nelson Jr., his grandson, this structure was damaged during the siege of Yorktown. Thomas Nelson Jr. was arguably Yorktown's most famous son as one of the signers of the Declaration of Independence. But it was Nelson's grandfather Thomas "Scotch Tom" Nelson who established the Nelson family in Yorktown, arriving from England in 1705. Historical records inform that he soon became a prosperous and influential merchant. Elder son William Nelson inherited the family business and went on to accumulate extensive land holdings throughout the colony. William also became a powerful politician, serving as both president of the Governor's Council and as acting governor. Thomas Nelson Jr., inherited the family business on the death of his father, William, and his wife, the former Lucy Grymes (1743–1830), continued to live in the house for more than thirty years after her husband's death and it remained in the Nelson family until 1908. *New York Public Library*

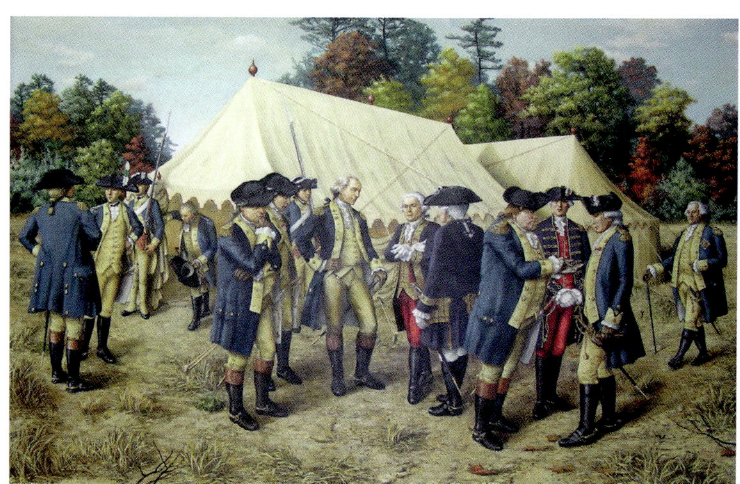

General George Washington and his senior staff are shown at the headquarters tents in Yorktown. The artist of this work is unknown. *National Park Service*

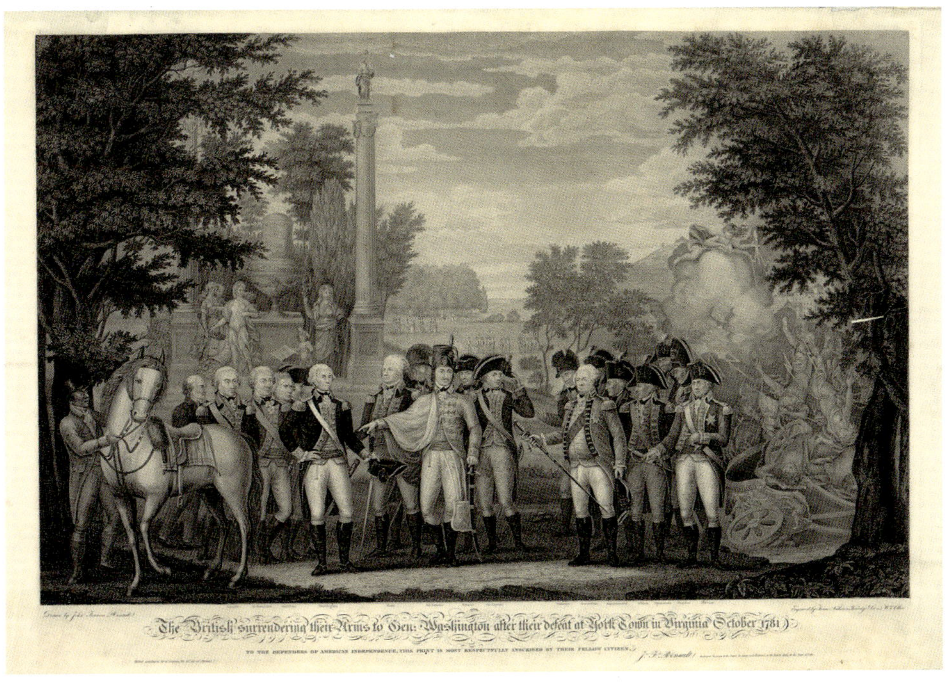

This perspective of the British surrendering their arms to General George Washington after their defeat at Yorktown, Virginia, on October 19, 1781, was drawn by Frenchman John Francis Renault and engraved by Tanner, Vallance, Kearny and Company and William Allen. The engraving was published on January 28, 1819. The print shows British officers on the right, with Lord Cornwallis presenting his sword, and French and American officers, center and left, with George Washington holding his hat in his left hand. Officers present (from the left) have been identified as Continental Army major general and Washington's second in command at Yorktown Benjamin Lincoln (1733–1810); French nobleman and army lieutenant general Jean-Baptiste Donatien de Vimeur, Comte de Rochambeau (1725–1807); Continental Army lieutenant colonel Alexander Hamilton (1757–1804); Washington; Continental Army major general Henry Knox; French brigadier general Armand Louis de Goutant Biron, Duc de Lauzun (1747–1793); Continental Army brigadier general Thomas Nelson Jr. (1738–1789); French aristocrat and military officer Marie Joseph Paul Yves Roch Gilbert du Motier, Marquis de Lafayette (1757–1834) [known simply as Lafayette in the United States]; British army lieutenant colonel [also later knighted and eventually ranked as a general years after his service in the former colonies] Banastre Tarleton (1754–1833), also known as "Bloody Ban," "The Butcher," and "The Green Dragoon"; British major general and aristocrat Charles Edward Cornwallis V, first Marquess Cornwallis [known as Lord Cornwallis] (1738–1805); British army lieutenant colonel Robert Abercrombie (1740–1827), who went on to a distinguished career in the British military; Major General Charles O'Hara (1740–1802), who represented the British at the surrender of Yorktown; British naval captain Thomas Symonds (1731–1792), famous as the commanding officer of the HMS *Charon* and who is remembered as the most senior naval officer present at the end of the siege of Yorktown; British lieutenant colonel Thomas Dundas (1750–1794), and British army lieutenant colonel George Waldegrave, fourth Earl Waldegrave, Viscount Chewton (1751–1789). The allegorical scene on the right, behind the British, depicts Discord, a female figure, wearing a liberty cap and floating on clouds, sending lightning bolts to up-end people and a chariot. On the left, behind American and French officers, Prosperity stands next to Cornucopia, with Justice and others in attendance, next to a tall pillar topped with Liberty holding a staff crowned with a liberty cap. The narrative reads: "To the defenders of American independence, this print is most respectfully inscribed by their fellow citizen, Jn. [John] Fcis. [Francis] Renault, assistant secretary to the Count de Grasse, and engineer to the French army, at the siege of York[town]." *Library of Congress*

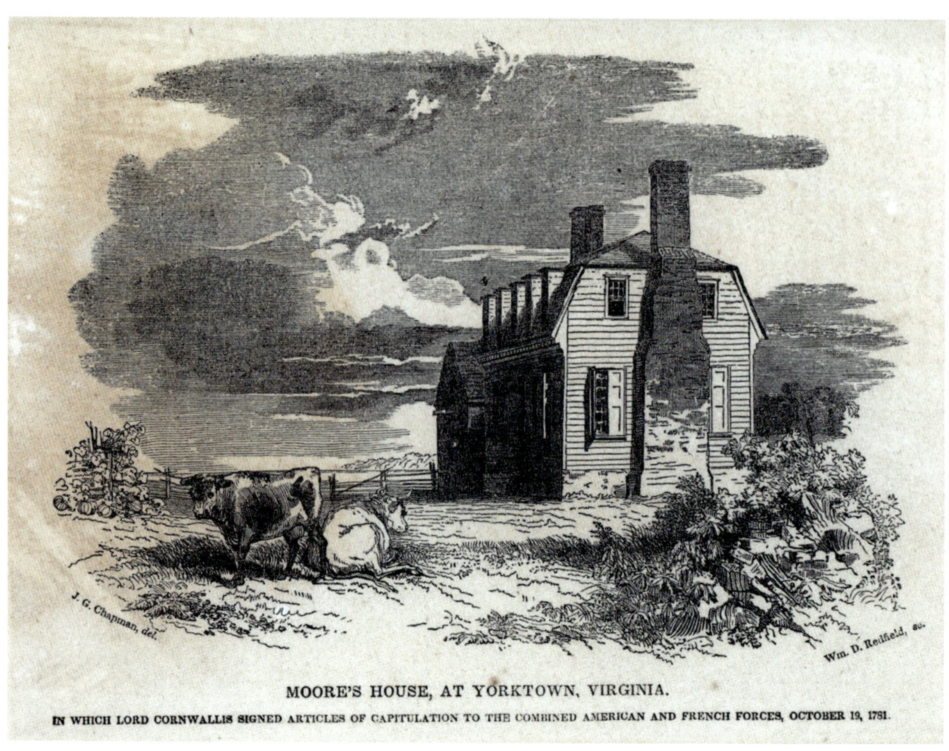

MOORE'S HOUSE, AT YORKTOWN, VIRGINIA.

IN WHICH LORD CORNWALLIS SIGNED ARTICLES OF CAPITULATION TO THE COMBINED AMERICAN AND FRENCH FORCES, OCTOBER 19, 1781.

William Dobson Redfield (1816–1838) of New York made this wood engraving of the Augustine Moore House, where Lord Cornwallis surrendered. The work was later published by Henry Howe in 1880 as part of his retrospective of Virginia history. The house was erected in or about 1725 on a five-hundred-acre tract called Temple Farm, which also included a dam and grist mill. The land was originally granted to the crown governor of Virginia, John Harvey (1581–1646), who held office from 1628 to 1639, and was known as the York Plantation at that time. Lawrence Smith II later built what is today known as the Moore residence on Temple Farm and the home remained in the family until 1754, when his son, Robert Smith, sold it to his brother-in-law, Augustine Moore (1730–1788), to avoid financial crisis. Augustine Moore and his family fled to Richmond to avoid the siege of Yorktown. Cornwallis requested a cease fire on October 17, 1781, and chose the house as the site for surrender negotiations, likely due to its neutral and convenient location. Washington's and Cornwallis' representatives met at the house the following day, where they negotiated the Articles of Capitulation. A rough draft was delivered to Washington's headquarters that night, where he made only minor changes. The revised articles were agreed to and signed on October 19. The house later passed to Hugh Nelson[11] (1768–1836) in 1797 following the deaths of merchant Augustine and his wife, the former Lucy Smith (1736–1797). *New York Public Library*

Marshal of France Jean-Baptiste Donatien de Vimeur, Comte de Rochambeau (1725–1807), French nobleman and army lieutenant general, is shown in this engraving that dates to the early nineteenth century. During the Revolutionary War he served as commander in chief of the French Expeditionary Force [code named *Expédition Particulière*] that embarked from France to reinforce George Washington's Continental Army in the thirteen colonies' bid to win independence from Great Britain. Rochambeau commanded a force of five thousand five hundred men. The logistical maneuvering and siege of Yorktown was Rochambeau's greatest military achievement. The importance of the victory at Yorktown is often overlooked by French military history because it greatly benefitted his allies, the Americans, and not France itself. *New York Public Library*

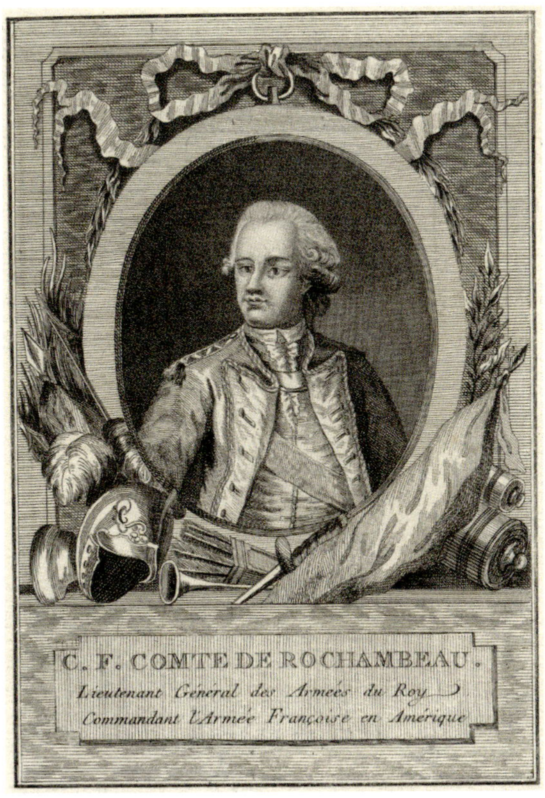

This replica memorial statue to Jean Baptiste Donatien de Vimeur, Comte de Rochambeau was erected in the southwest corner of Lafayette Square in Washington, D.C. French sculptor Joseph Job Fernand Hamar (1869–1943) was selected to work on the statue, which was dedicated by President Theodore Roosevelt on May 24, 1902. The park in which the statue is situated is directly north of the White House on H Street between Fifteenth and Seventeenth Streets Northwest. Hamar's original version of this statue was unveiled in Vendôme, France in June 1900. *Daderot*[12]

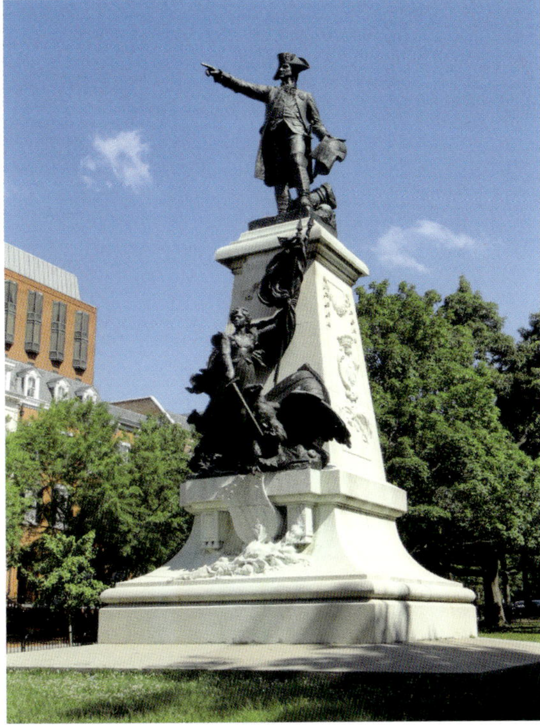

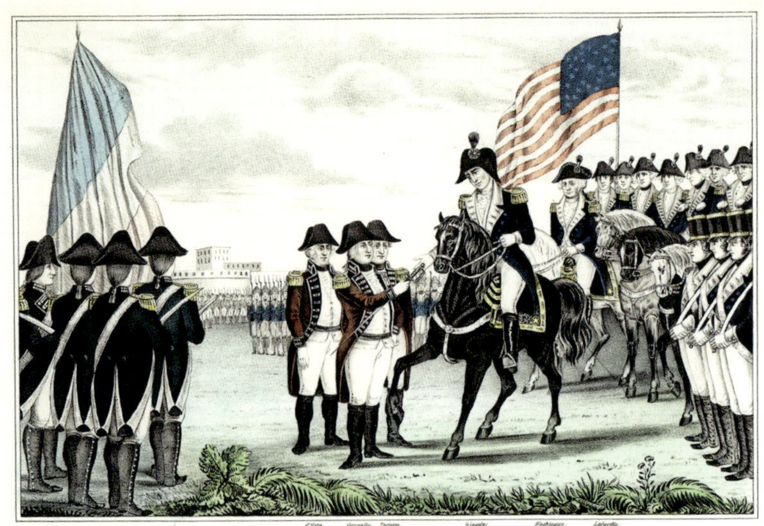

This hand-colored Nathaniel Currier (1813–1888) lithograph of the surrender of Lord Cornwallis was published on August 26, 1846. The print shows British major general Charles O'Hara, surrounded by French and American soldiers handing his sword in surrender to Continental Army major general Benjamin Lincoln. Nathaniel Currier, a lithographer, headed the company Currier and Ives with James Merritt Ives (1824–1895), also a lithographer but importantly the firm's bookkeeper and business and marketing manager, the latter at which he excelled. The company was America's longest running printing establishment, publishing over seven thousand images covering a span of seventy-three years. *Library of Congress*

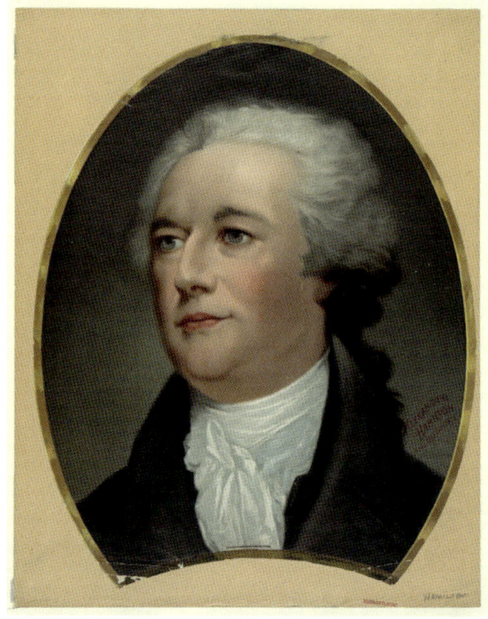

Present at the siege of Yorktown and the British surrender that followed was Lieutenant Colonel Alexander Hamilton, who played a major role in the American Revolution. As the senior aide to George Washington, he was dispatched on many missions to convey war plans to Washington's generals. As an American statesman and one of the nation's Founding Fathers, he was an influential interpreter and promoter of the United States Constitution as well as the founder of the nation's financial system, the Federalist Party, the United States Coast Guard, and the *New York Post* newspaper. He would become the first secretary of the Treasury, and authored the economic policies of Washington's administration. Hamilton is shown in this Knapp Company chromolithograph published in 1896 from a painting made in 1792 by John Trumbull. *Library of Congress*

Eighteenth-century English artist Joshua Reynolds (1723–1792) painted this oil-on-canvas portrait of Lieutenant Colonel Banastre Tarleton in the uniform of the British Legion, wearing what came to known as the Tarleton helmet in 1782. The original canvas is 92.9 inches by 57.1 inches and hangs in the National Gallery, located in central London. Tarleton's cavalrymen were called Tarleton's Raiders and the green uniform he wore (shown here) was the standard attire for the British Legion formed in New York in 1778. According to a 1911 account by Hugh Chisholm, after the British surrender at Yorktown, senior British officers were asked to dinner by their American captors[13]—all but Tarleton, whose reputation for ruthlessness led to his being so detested by Continental Army officers that the thought of breaking bread with him was out of the question.[14]

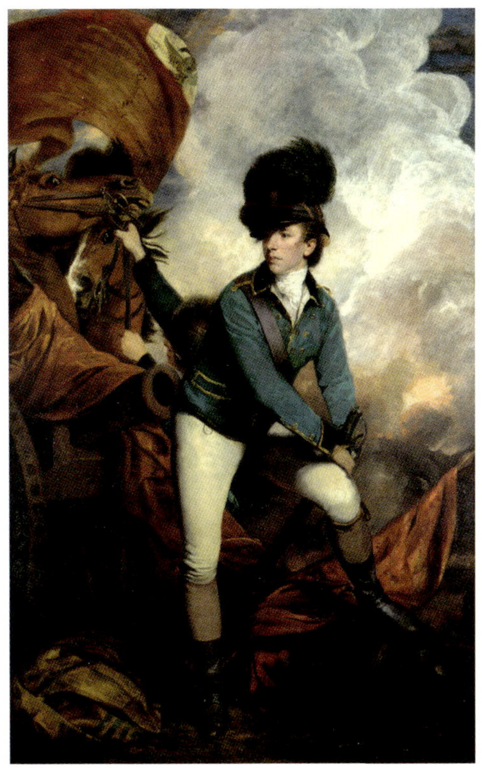

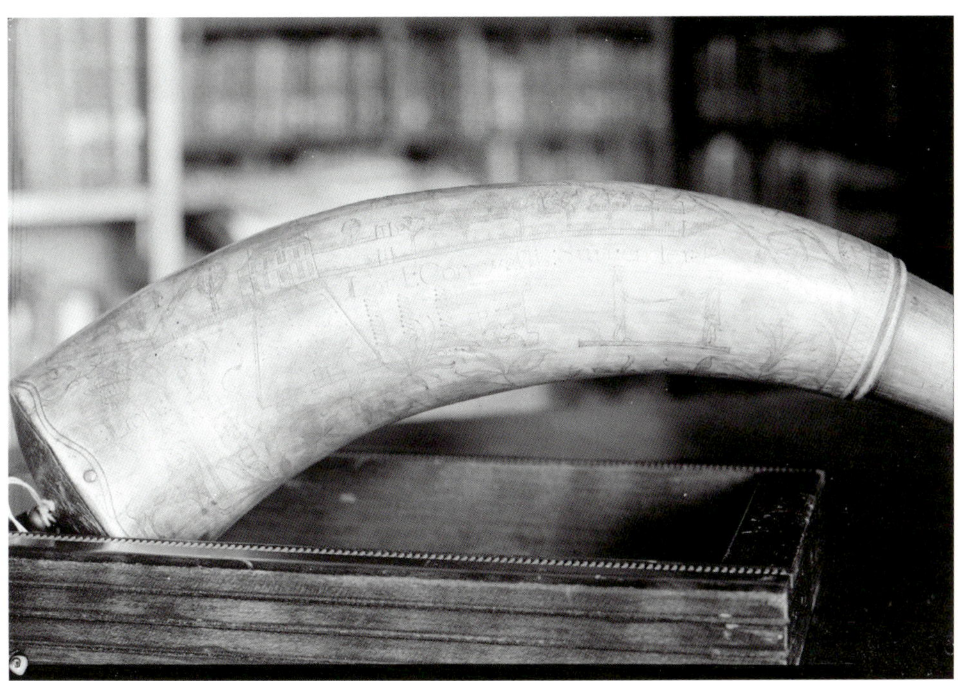

This powder horn is covered in carving that documents the surrender of Lord Cornwallis to George Washington at Yorktown and dates to the period. *Library of Congress*

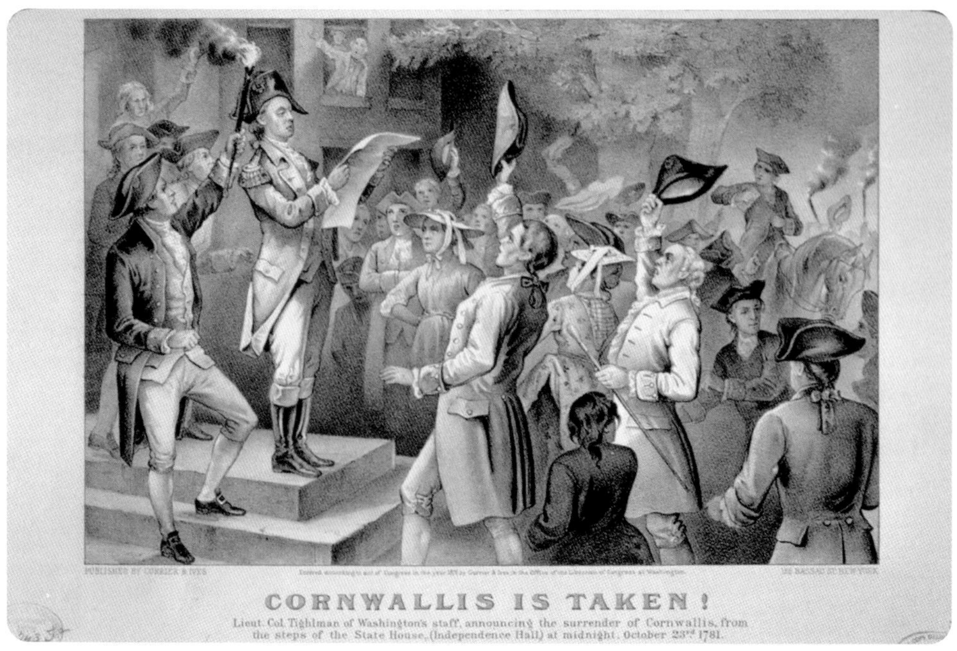

"Cornwallis is taken!" Continental Army lieutenant colonel Tench Tighlman (1744–1786), of George Washington's staff, is shown in this Currier and Ives print, published in 1876, announcing the surrender of Cornwallis from the steps of the statehouse [Independence Hall] at midnight [or shortly thereafter on October 24, 1781. Tilghman was born on Maryland's Eastern Shore, the oldest son of James Tilghman, a lawyer and loyalist to the British crown. Parting ways with his family, this patriot joined a militia unit in 1775 and that unit joined the American army the following year. Shortly thereafter, Tilghman was selected as aide-de-camp to Washington on the general's staff, a position he held until the end of the war. The backstory to this Currier and Ives lithograph bears repeating. Upon the signing of the Articles of Capitulation at Yorktown, Tilghman was sent with a dispatch to the president of the Continental Congress. *Continued on next page*

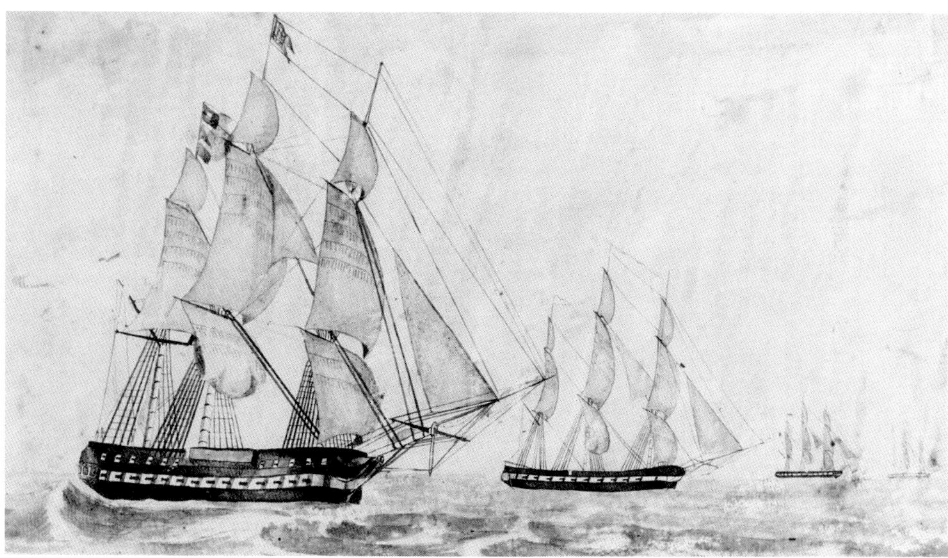

Continued from previous page: Tilghman sailed down the York River on October 20 and then up the Chesapeake Bay, reaching the Eastern Shore the evening of October 22. Tilghman rode horseback day and night, stopping for a fresh horse wherever he could find one. In the early morning hours of October 24, sick with chills and fever, he rode into Philadelphia. In no time, his news spread throughout the city. Tilghman left the army in 1783, but his health was failing. He died in 1786 at the age of forty-two.[15] *Library of Congress*

Opposite below: The first United States Navy ship to be named for the town of Yorktown, where the climactic battle of the Revolutionary War was fought in the fall of 1781, was this sixteen-gun-sloop, laid down in 1838 by the Norfolk Navy Yard and launched in 1839. The USS *Yorktown* was commissioned on November 15, 1840, Commander John Henry Aulick (1791–1873), in command. *Yorktown* departed Hampton Roads on December 13, 1840, bound for the Pacific Squadron. This watercolor by Gunner William H. Myers, of USS *Cyane*, shows the squadron's ships sailing in line abreast between 1842 and 1843. The ships are (left to right) USS *United States*, USS *Cyane*, USS *Saint Louis*, USS *Yorktown* and USS *Shark*. On May 2, 1846, *Yorktown* departed Porto Praya, Cape Verde, and returned to the east coast of the United States, reaching Boston on May 29. There, on June 9, the sloop was once again decommissioned. Subsequently recommissioned at Boston, she sailed on November 22, 1848, for her second deployment with the African Squadron. Still engaged in hunting down slave ships, *Yorktown* cruised along the African coast, carefully observing each ship she encountered for any sign of the illicit traffic in human flesh. On September 6, 1850, she struck an uncharted reef at Isle de Mayo in the Cape Verde Islands. Although the ship broke up in a very short time, not a life was lost in the wreck. *Naval History and Heritage Command*

ENDNOTES

1 John Trumbull [CC0], via Wikimedia Commons [This file was donated to Wikimedia Commons by as part of a project by the Metropolitan Museum of Art.]

2 Department of the Interior/National Park Service [Historic Resource Study]. Yorktown's Main Street. Part 1 – From Secretary Nelson's to the Windmill. Prepared by Charles E. Hatch Jr. [March 1974] https://www.nps.gov/parkhistory/online_books/colo/yorktowns_main_street/chap1-3.htm

3 Ibid.

4 Christopher Gadsden (1724–1805) was the principal leader of the South Carolina patriot movement during the American Revolution and a soldier and politician from that state. He was a delegate to the Continental Congress and a brigadier general in the Continental Army during the war. He was also a merchant.

5 Brooks, Noah. *Henry Knox – A Soldier of the Revolution: Major General in the Continental Army, First Secretary of War Under the Constitution, Founder of the Society of the Cincinnati, 1750–1806.* New York: G. P. Putnam's Sons, 1900.

6 This is a French military distinction, rather than military rank, that is awarded to generals for exceptional achievement. The title has been awarded since 1185, though it was briefly abolished from 1793 to 1804 and also briefly dormant from 1870 to 1916. A Marshal of France displays seven stars on each shoulder strap. A marshal also receives a baton, a blue cylinder with stars, formerly fleurs-de-lis during the monarchy and eagles during the First French Empire. The baton bears the Latin inscription of *Terror belli, decus pacis,* which translates "terror in war, ornament in peace."

7 Auguste Couder stock photo [Public domain], via Wikimedia Commons

8 Heise, Kenan, "Hugh McBarron, military illustrator," *Chicago Tribune,* April 23, 1992. http://articles.chicagotribune.com/1992-04-23/news/9202050940_1_paintings-military-history-illustrations

9 Thomas Nelson Jr. fought with the Virginia militia during the siege of Yorktown.

10 Henry Bryan Hall emigrated from England to New York in 1850 and established the firm of H.B. Hall and Sons, and in the process set up an extensive practice as an engraver and publisher of portraiture.

11 Hugh Nelson was the son of Thomas Nelson Jr. He graduated from the College of William and Mary in 1780. He served in the Virginia Senate from 1786 to 1791, and in the Virginia House of Delegates from 1805 to 1809

and 1828 to 1829. He was speaker of the Virginia House of Delegates from 1807 to 1809. He was elected as a Democratic-Republican to the twelfth and to the five succeeding Congresses and served from March 4, 1811, until his resignation on January 14, 1823, having received an appointment in the diplomatic service. Nelson was appointed by President James Monroe as the United States minister to Spain on January 15, 1823, and served until November 23, 1824. He died at his home Belvoir, in Albemarle County, Virginia, on March 18, 1836.

12 By Daderot (Daderot) [CC0 or CC0] [public domain], via Wikimedia Commons

13 Chisholm, Hugh, ed. "Sir Tarleton Banastre." *Encyclopedia Britannica* [Eleventh Edition]. Volume 26. Cambridge, United Kingdom: Cambridge University Press, 1911.

14 Joshua Reynolds stock photo [Public domain], via Wikimedia Commons

15 National Park Service [Lieutenant Colonel Tench Tilghman] https://www.nps.gov/york/learn/historyculture/tilghmanbio.htm

II

THE SIEGE OF YORKTOWN

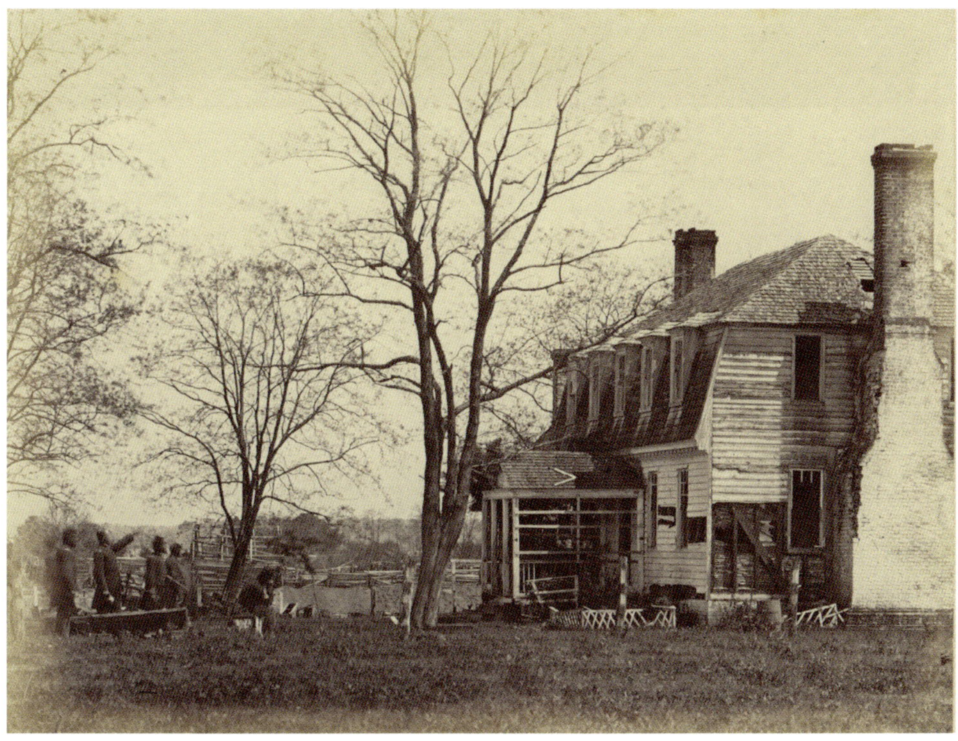

The Augustine Moore House (shown here) remained in the Moore family until 1797, when it passed to the son of Thomas Nelson Jr., Hugh Nelson, after the death of both Augustine and his wife Lucy. Thereafter, the house changed hands many times. During the Civil War 1862 Peninsula Campaign, military action around Yorktown caused considerable damage to the house. Juxtaposed between Confederate lines in Yorktown and the Union forces on Wormley Creek, the house was within easy range of shell fire. Later, foraging soldiers stripped away siding and other usable wood for fuel. The house remained derelict until 1881 when much needed repairs and some additions were made in preparation for the Yorktown centennial celebration of the allied victory over British forces. Alexander Gardner (1821–1882) took this photograph of the Augustine Moore House in May 1862. The picture was not printed until later, when it appeared in *Gardner's Photographic Sketch Book of the War*, published in Washington, D.C., by Philip and Solomons as volume one, number fifteen, in 1866. *Library of Congress*

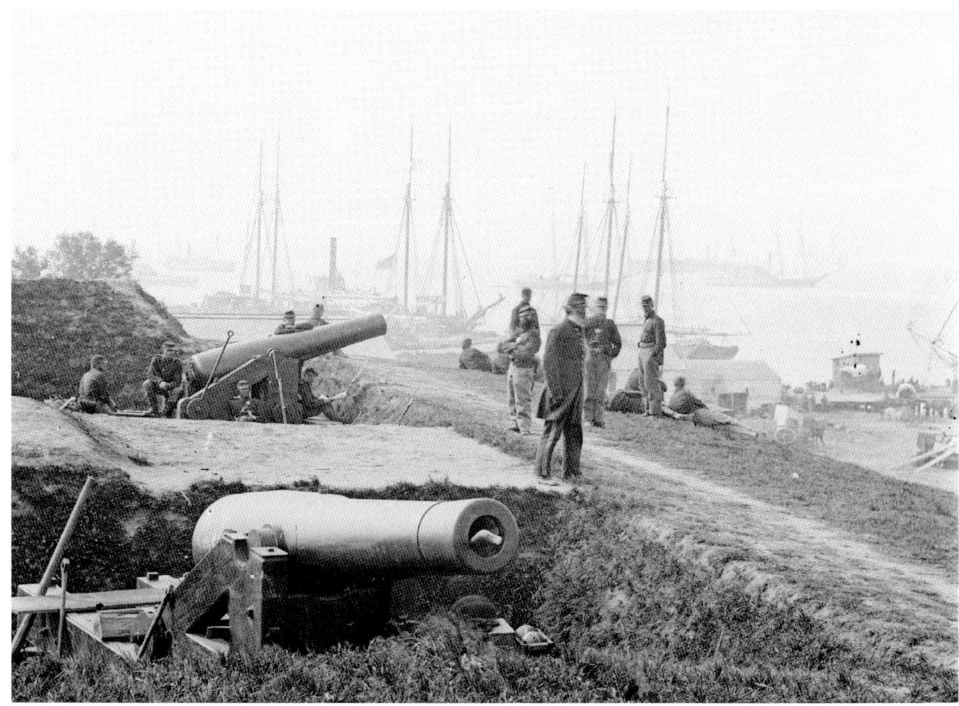

The Battle of Yorktown [also called the siege of Yorktown] was fought from April 5 to May 4, 1862, as part of the Peninsula Campaign. Marching from Fort Monroe, Union major general George Brinton McClellan's Army of the Potomac encountered Confederate major general John Bankhead Magruder's small Confederate force at Yorktown behind the Warwick Line. McClellan (1826–1885) suspended his march up the Peninsula toward Richmond, having deemed Yorktown worthy of a siege operation, convinced that Magruder (1807–1871) had mounted formidable defensive works and troop strength from Lee's Mill to Yorktown. This confusion about Magruder's actual troop strength and the presence of the Confederate ironclad CSS *Virginia* and heavy rebel batteries mounted along the York River led to McClellan's decision to use a land approach to Yorktown, where Confederate forces waited along a defensive line that could effectively block the full width of the Peninsula if he had the ability, which Magruder did not, to properly man all of his defensive works. This 1862 photograph shows a Confederate battery mounted with eight-inch Columbiads, the Yorktown fort and landing in the background. *Library of Congress*

Opposite above: This photograph shows Union soldiers and supplies including gun carriages, mortars and tons of shot and shell ready to be taken up river for federal operations against Richmond, at the lower wharf at Yorktown, Virginia. The picture was taken in May 1862, and already the dismantling of both the Confederate and the federal forts had begun. Steamships in the distance—one of which is identifiable as the steamer *Robert Morris*—transported the siege train for the First Connecticut Artillery to and from White House Landing, the federal supply point for White House, an eighteenth-century plantation on the Pamunkey River in New Kent County, Virginia. Troops of the Army of the Potomac under the command of Major General George B. McClellan burned White House to the ground on June 28, 1862, as they retreated during the Seven Days Battles. The house was rebuilt after the war but burned to the ground again in 1875, at which time no further attempts were made to reconstruct it. Of note, White House was the home of Martha Dandridge Custis (1731–1802) and Daniel Parke Custis (1711–1757) after they were married in 1750; Martha Custis took George Washington as her second husband in 1759 and they moved to his farm at Mount Vernon in Fairfax County, Virginia, overlooking the Potomac River. *Library of Congress*

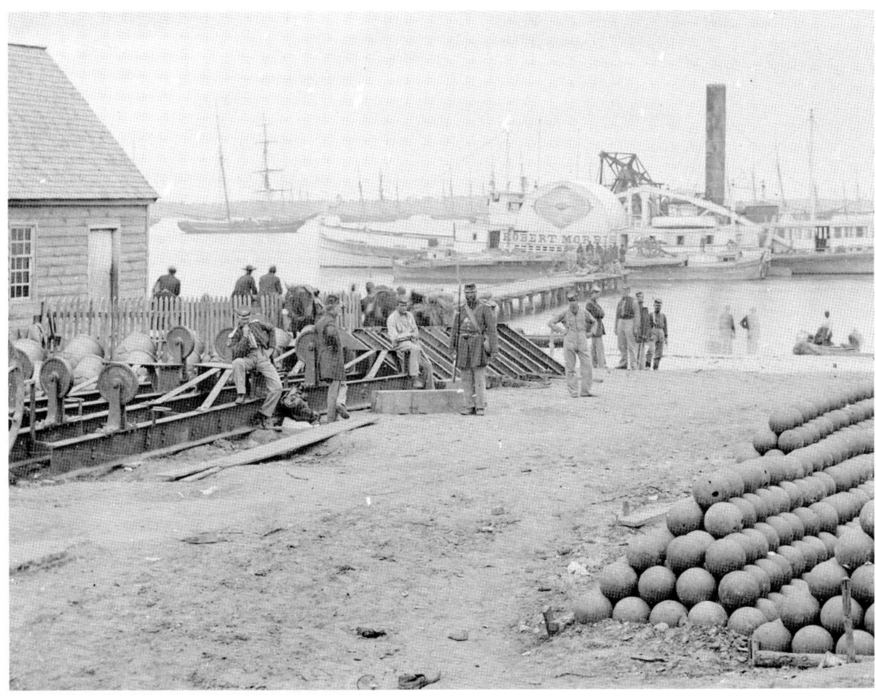

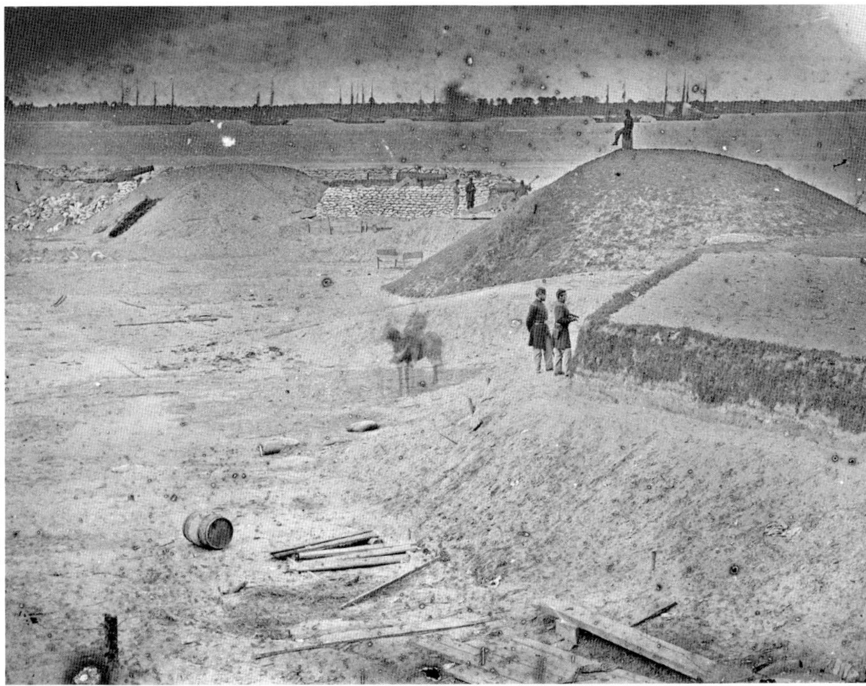

The former Confederate water battery (shown here, foreground) overlooking the York River at Yorktown was Magruder's strongest defense against McClellan, intended to keep federal forces from taking the town so easily. The battery was photographed in May 1862 after the Confederate defenders were in retreat. *Library of Congress*

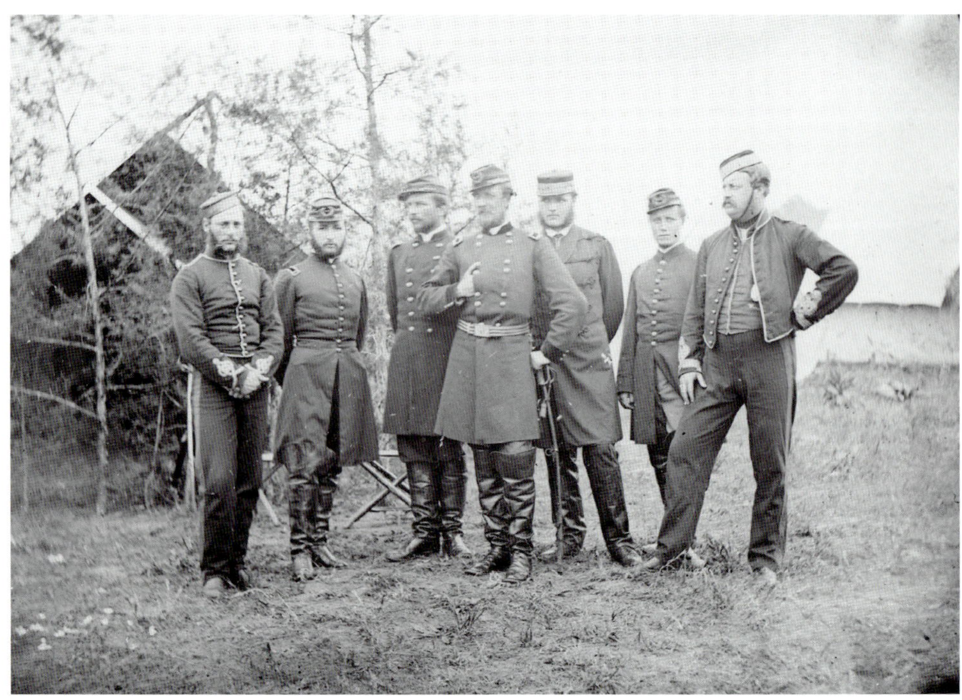

Union brigadier general William Farquhar Barry (1818–1879) (center) posed with British officers and two French noblemen in this picture taken at Yorktown in June 1862. Federal officers were often flanked by European commanders who followed them into camp, showering much attention on their respective hosts. Barry was McClellan's chief of artillery and in that capacity organized ordnance for the Army of the Potomac, to include the breadth of the Peninsula Campaign. *Library of Congress*

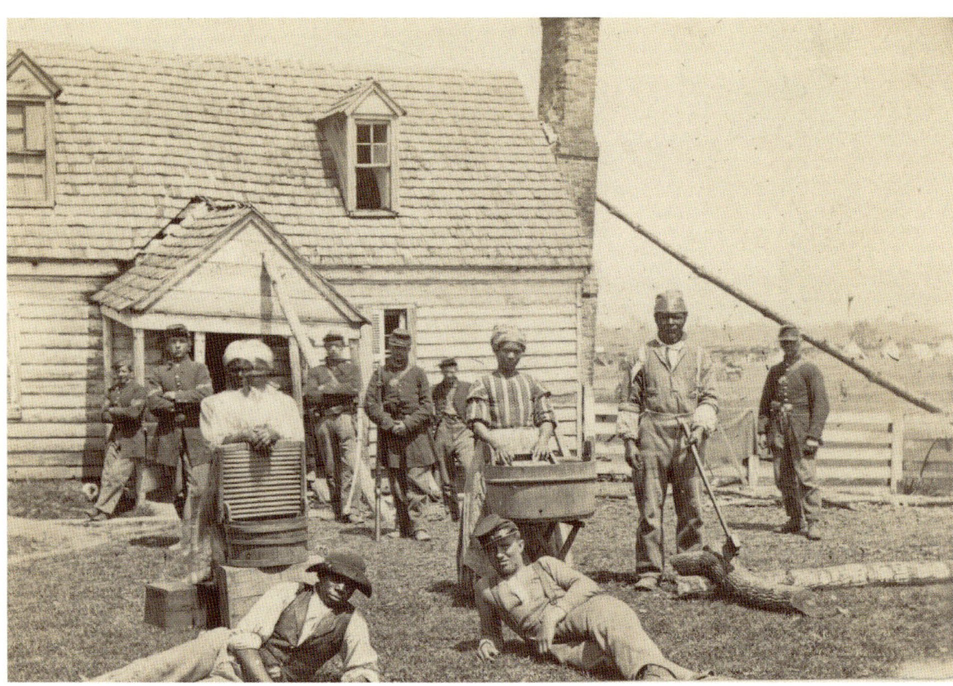

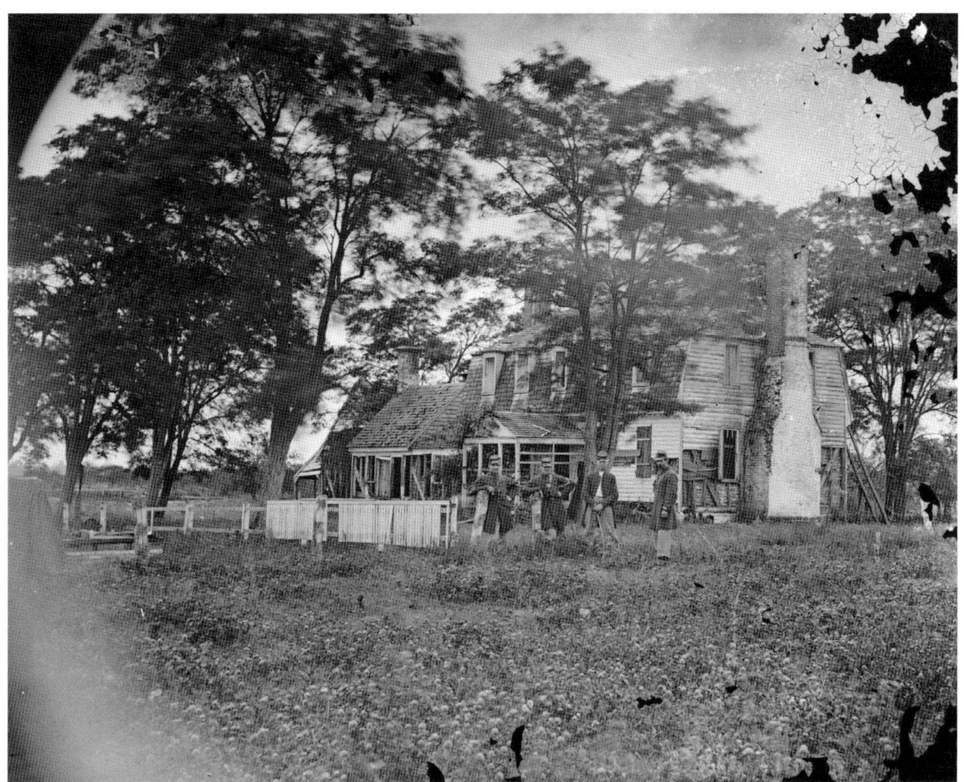

The Augustine Moore House was photographed by James F. Gibson's fellow Mathew Brady photographer George Norman Barnard (1819–1902) during the Peninsula Campaign March–July 1862. Those are federal troops standing in the foreground. Barnard was among Brady's initial corps of photographers sent into the field to photograph the battlefields of Northern Virginia, Peninsula, including Bull Run and Yorktown, and also Harper's Ferry. This was the scene of Yorktown's only surrender when British forces signed the Articles of Capitulation on October 19, 1781. Near here, too, many Continental Army troops are buried. *Library of Congress*

Opposite below: This James Forbes Gibson (1828–1905) photograph shows a group of African American refugees [also called contrabands] with Union soldiers in front of Allen's farmhouse [this was Lafayette's Revolutionary War headquarters before the Battle of Yorktown and is sometimes also called Lafayette House] near Williamsburg Road in May 1862. During the Peninsula Campaign, this had become Union major general Fitz John Porter's headquarters. Porter (1822–1901), a career army officer, came from a family prominent in American naval service; his cousins were Commodore William David Porter (1808–1864), Admiral David Dixon Porter (1813–1891), and David Glasgow Farragut (1801–1870). The II and III Corps of Union major generals Edwin Vose Sumner (1797–1863) and Samuel Peter Heintzelman (1805–1880), respectively, can be seen camped in the background. Gibson, who arrived on the Peninsula in April 1862, was arguably the least known of the Civil War photographers but also among the best documentarians of the war. He took some sixty photographs at Yorktown, where federal forces blanketed the historic town for almost a month. The skirmishing on the Williamsburg Road on June 29, 1862, was part of the Allen's farm [Peach Orchard] engagement of the Seven Days Battles [Peninsula Campaign]. *Library of Congress*

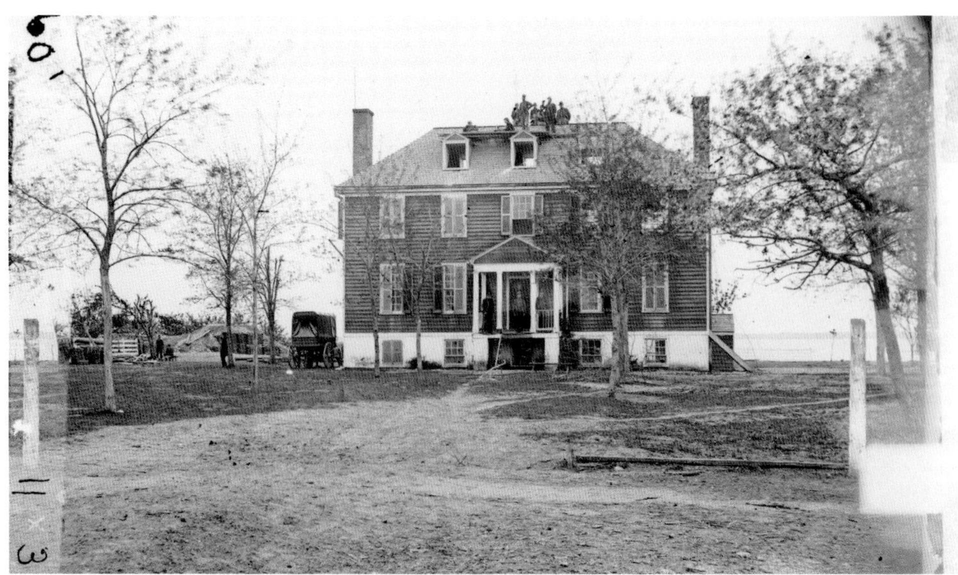

The home of Confederate colonel Benjamin Lyons Farinholt (1839–1919) is shown here with part of federal battery number one visible left in this May 1862 James Gibson photograph. Farinholt was born in Yorktown to Richard Lyons Farinholt (1799–1857) and the former Anna Martha Virginia Pierce (1811–death date unknown); he was married to his cousin, Lelia May Farinholt (1842–1927). The colonel saw action in most of the major engagements of the Civil War. Federal troops occupied the house at the time this picture was taken and are seen up on the roof and standing in the doorway. *Library of Congress*

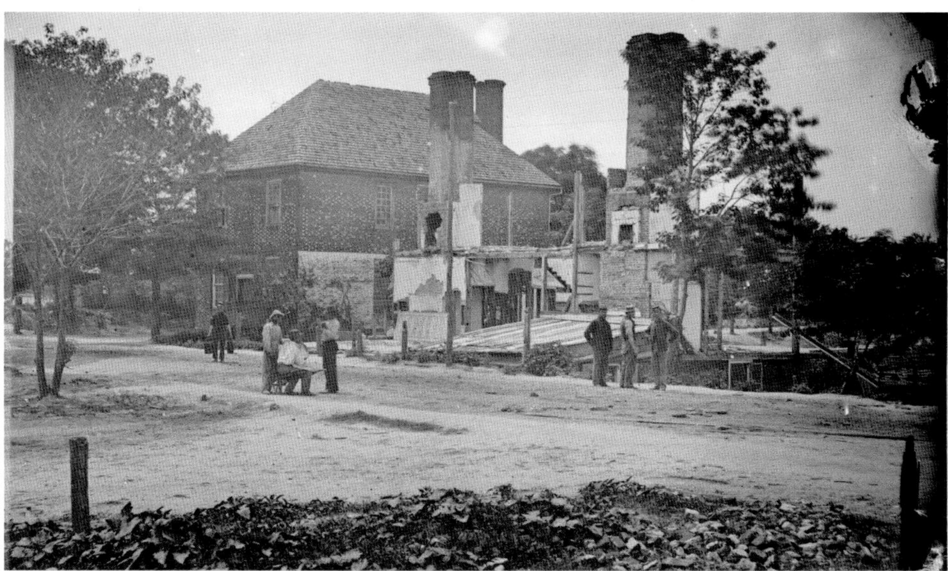

This exterior view of Yorktown's old custom house was taken in June 1862 by George Barnard and later published by Gardner's Gallery, of Washington, D.C., as a part of its *Photographic Incidents of the War* stereograph series. During the Peninsula Campaign, the custom house was used by Confederate major general John Bankhead Magruder as his Yorktown headquarters. During the subsequent federal occupation of the town, the wood-frame residence next-door to the custom house (shown here) was destroyed by fire. *Library of Congress*

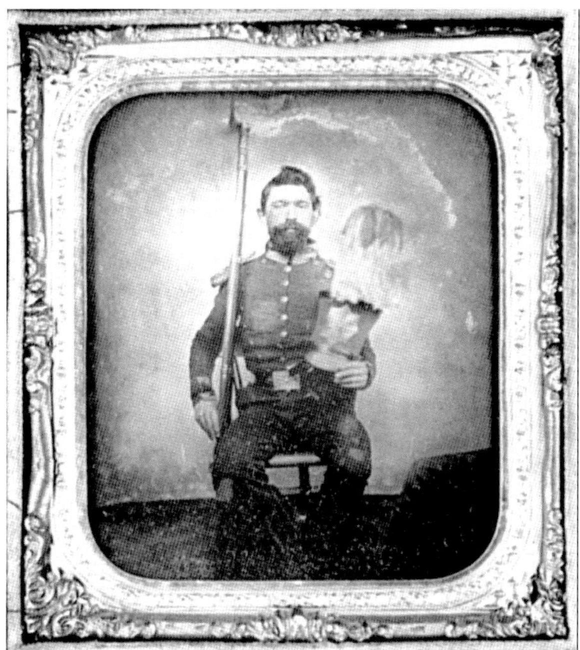

Private Andrew Fletcher Skidmore (1830–1862), of the Mount Vernon Guards, Company E, Seventeenth Virginia Infantry, Confederate States Army, was killed at Yorktown on May 2, 1862. He was born in Alexandria, Virginia, to Jesse (1790–1854) and Sarah Boyd (1789–1865) Skidmore. *Library of Congress*

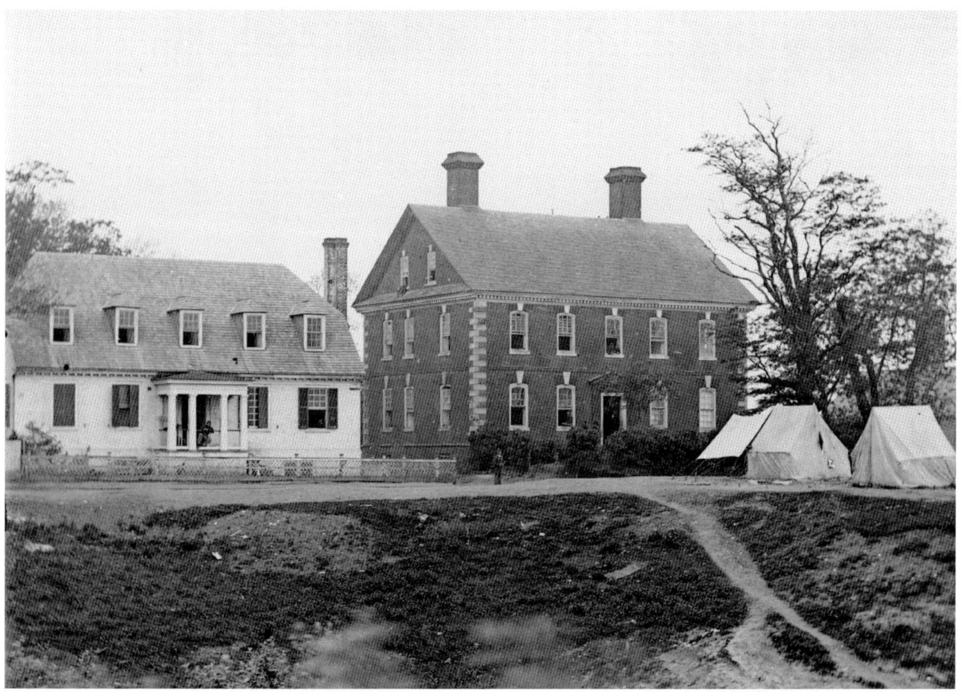

The Thomas Nelson House [York Hall] (right) was used by Confederate major general John Bankhead Magruder as a hospital during the Peninsula Campaign. Dorothea Lynde Dix (1802–1887), superintendent of Union army nurses during the war, set up a hospital in the house after the Confederate withdrawal. The Brady studio took the picture in May 1862. The Sessions-Pope-Sheild House is the residence to the left. *Library of Congress*

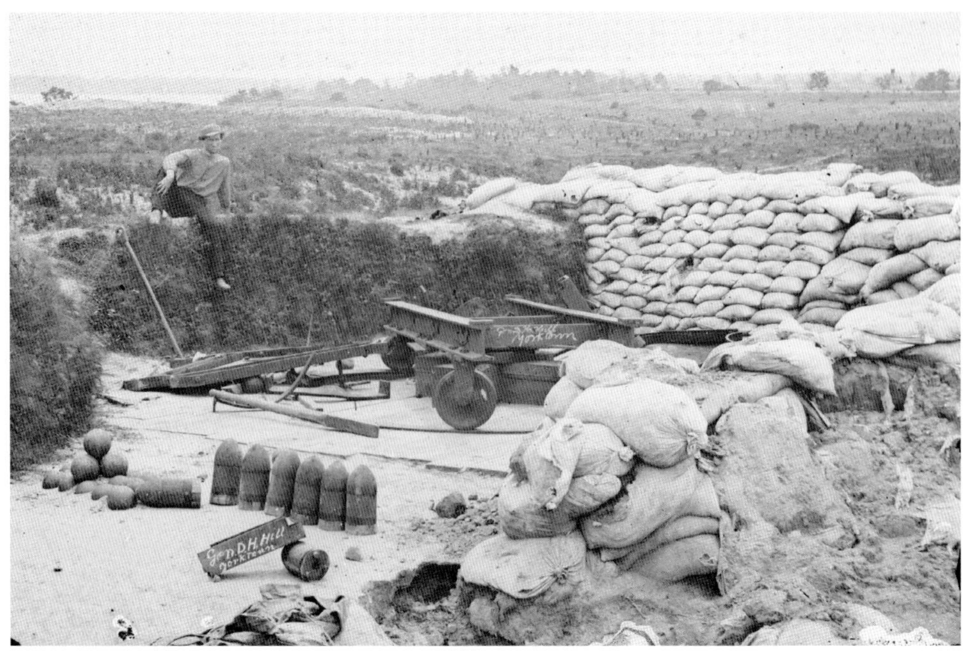

The rampart of this former Confederate shore position (shown here) with McClellan's battery number one in the distance, shows just how much Confederates liked to name their cannons after their generals. On the remnants of gun carriage and ammunition box (foreground) the gun was named for Major General Daniel Harvey Hill (1821–1889). The picture was taken in June 1862 by George Barnard. Hill's brother-in-law was Confederate lieutenant general Thomas Jonathan "Stonewall" Jackson (1824–1863), and a close friend of Lieutenant General James Longstreet (1821–1904) and General Joseph Eggleston Johnston (1807–1891). Hill participated in Magruder's Yorktown and Williamsburg operations, and as a major general just then, led a division in the Battle of Seven Pines and the Seven Days Battles. *Library of Congress*

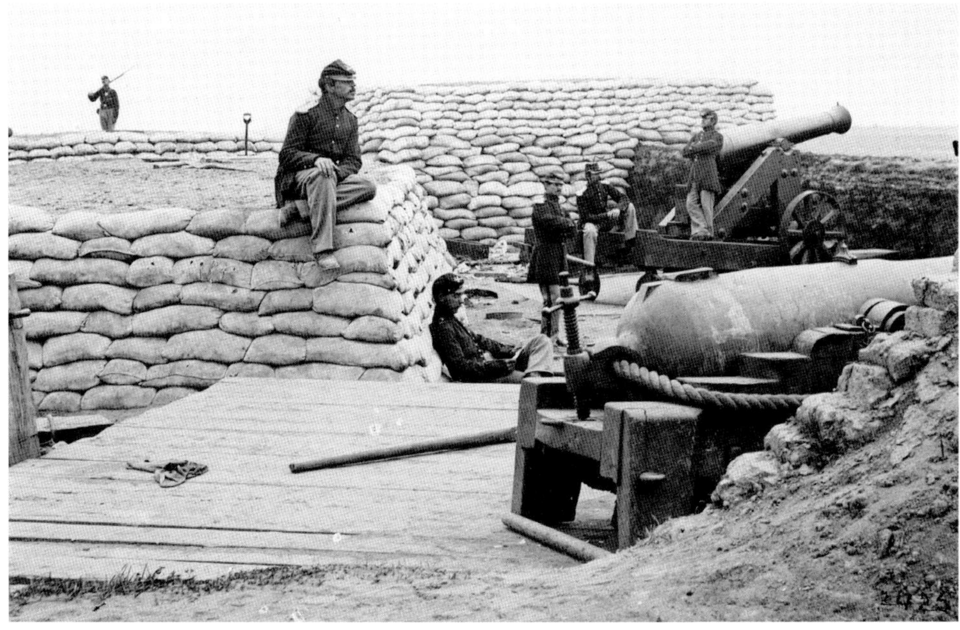

Opposite below: Federal soldiers are shown inside a two-gun Confederate battery—protected with sandbags—in entrenchments just south of Yorktown during the Peninsula Campaign. The near gun is a navy thirty-two pounder and the far gun is a twenty-four-pounder siege piece. More than three thousand pieces of naval ordnance fell into the hands of the Confederates early in the war through the ill-advised and hasty abandonment of Norfolk Navy Yard by the federals. Many of these guns did service at Yorktown and subsequently on the James River against Union forces. *Library of Congress*

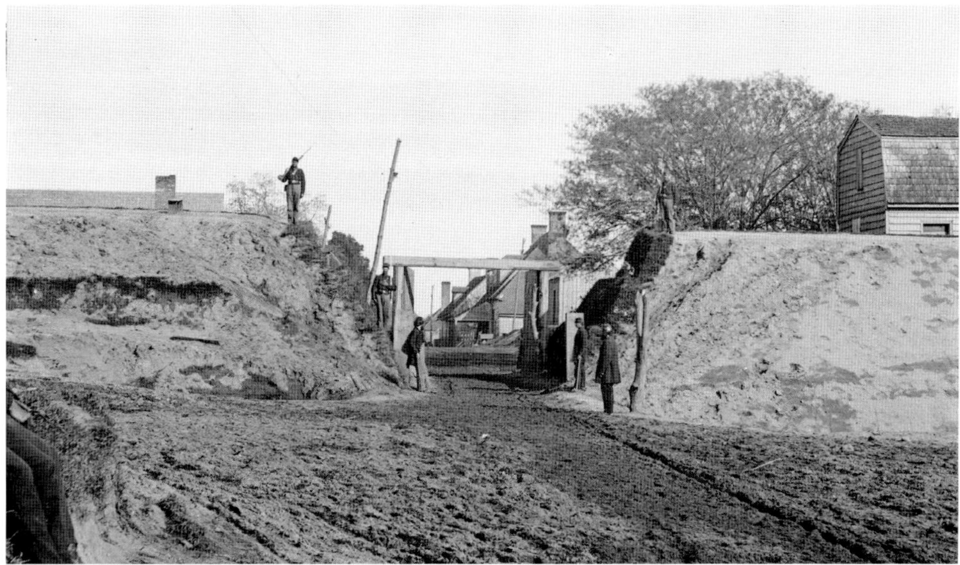

The sally port in the center of the southwestern point of Yorktown entrenchments was photographed in 1862. This structure commanded the road leading past Yorktown to Williamsburg, upon which the Confederates fell back as McClellan advanced after the evacuation. This view looks into the town and toward the river. The advancing federals entered the city from the other side. The inhabitants, who had first hidden in their homes, flocked to the street corners as regiment after regiment swept into the town with colors flying and bands playing. Out through this gate the detachment marched in pursuit of the retreating Confederates, who made a strong stand at Williamsburg. *Library of Congress*

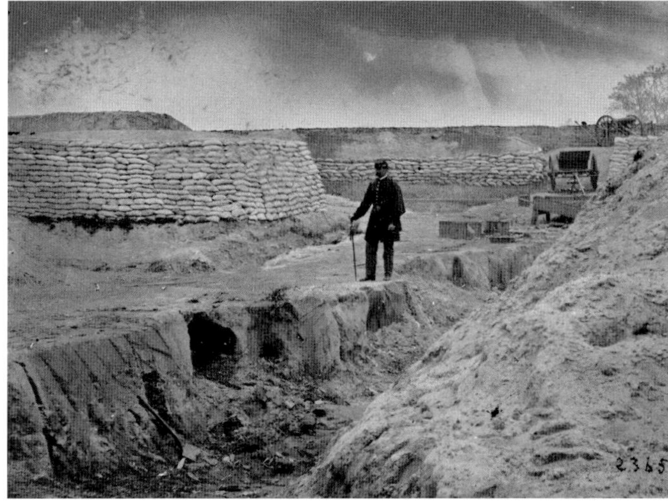

The ditch (foreground) dug by Lord Cornwallis in 1781, was deepened by Confederate general John Bankhead Magruder in 1862, the year this picture was taken. *Library of Congress*

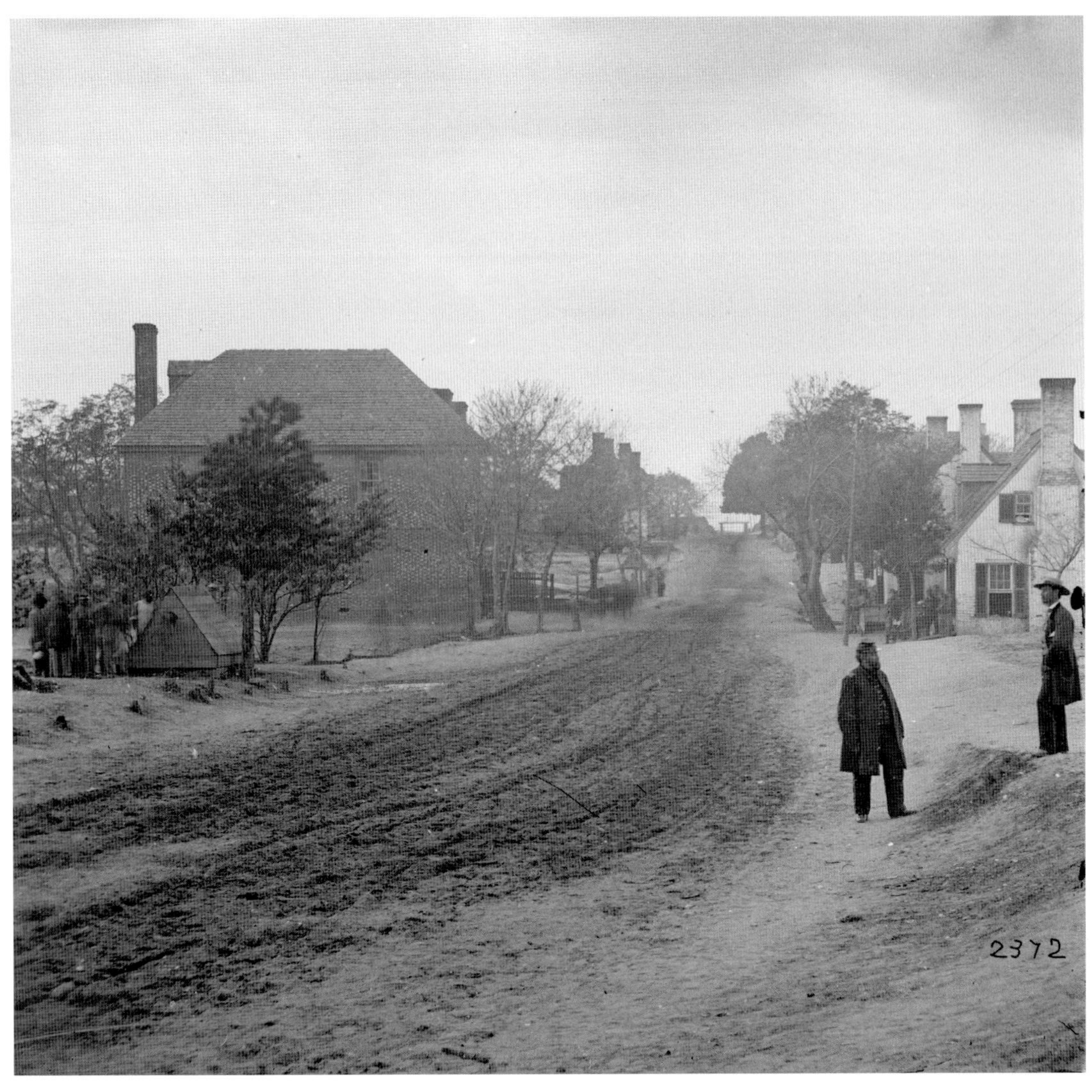

This Main Street Yorktown scene, looking west, was photographed in 1862 by a Mathew Brady field photographer. The two-and-a-half-story custom house, built on Lot 43 by Richard Ambler (1690–1766), a merchant and the customs collector, in 1721 and used by him as a storehouse, is on the left and the Thomas Pate House is across the street. Both structures stand at the corner of Main and Read streets. Colonel Thomas Pate (1650–1703)[1] built a home on Lot 42 in Yorktown shortly after 1700. Pate, who first emigrated to the Virginia colony in 1672 to take over a family-run 2,100-acre tobacco plantation in Gloucester County, would hold a number of civil and military positions there, to include his duties as a member of the House of Burgesses in 1684. Nathaniel Bacon, leader of Bacon's Rebellion, died in Pate's Gloucester County home in 1676. Pate was appointed collector of the plantation duty for the Virginia colony in 1684, and in or about 1690, he began ferry operations across the York River to what became the port city of Yorktown, primarily for the export of tobacco to England. Four years later, in 1694, he owned an ordinary [an inn] in Yorktown and he built his home there, across from the custom house. As such Pate's house is the second oldest surviving home in the town. It was among the properties added to Colonial National Historical Park on the purchase of the George Preston Blow (1860–1922) estate by the federal government in October 1968. The house is architecturally important and contributes significantly to the Main Street scene in the key Custom House — Nelson House — Grace Episcopal Church section. *Library of Congress*

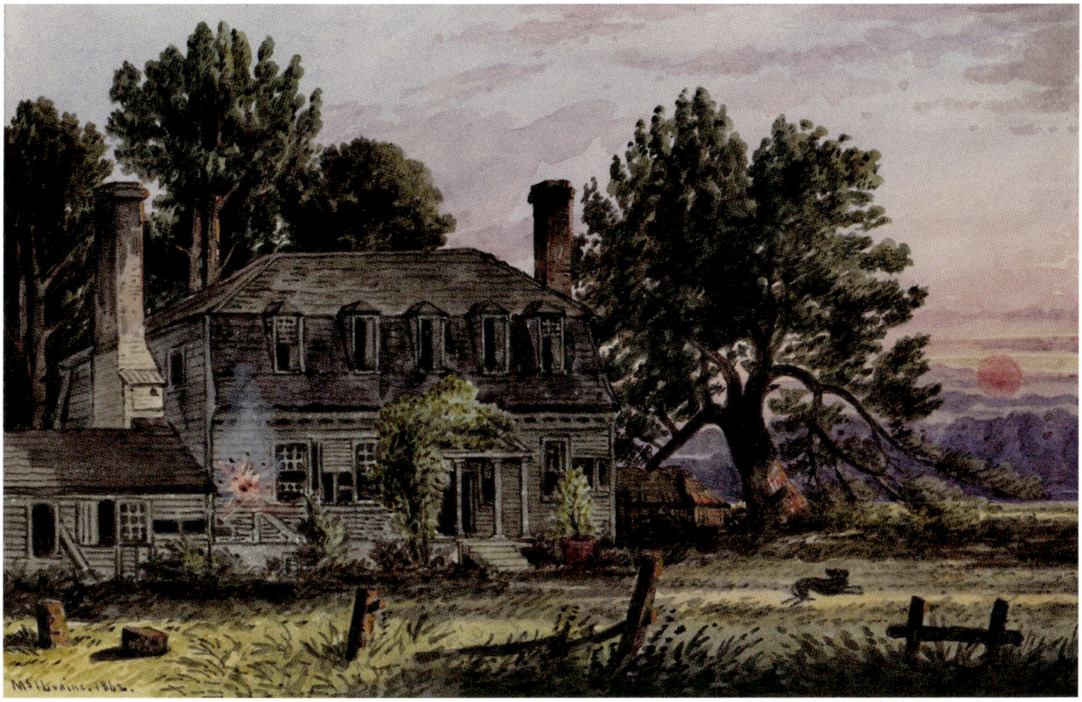

Watercolorist William McIlvaine Jr. (1813–1867) painted the Augustine Moore House in 1862 during the Peninsula Campaign. The illustration shows the house being hit by a shell, with the sun low on the horizon. In the second watercolor of the rear of the house, McIlvaine included a group of Zouaves in the foreground pointed to the heavy damage inflicted by federal artillery. *Library of Congress*

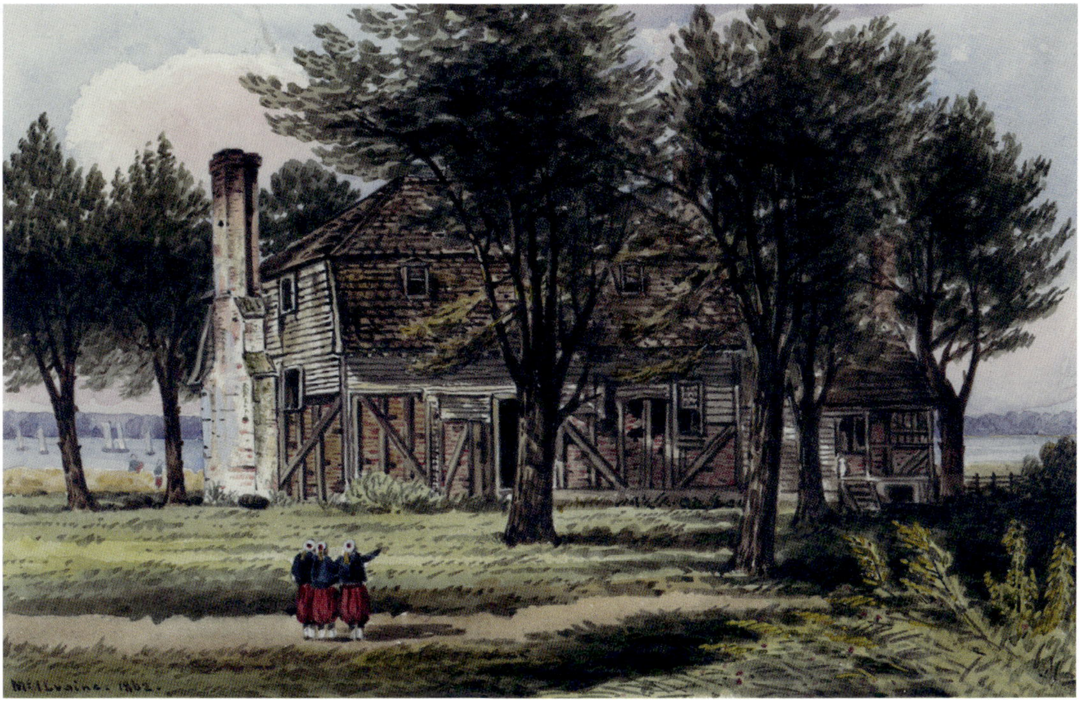

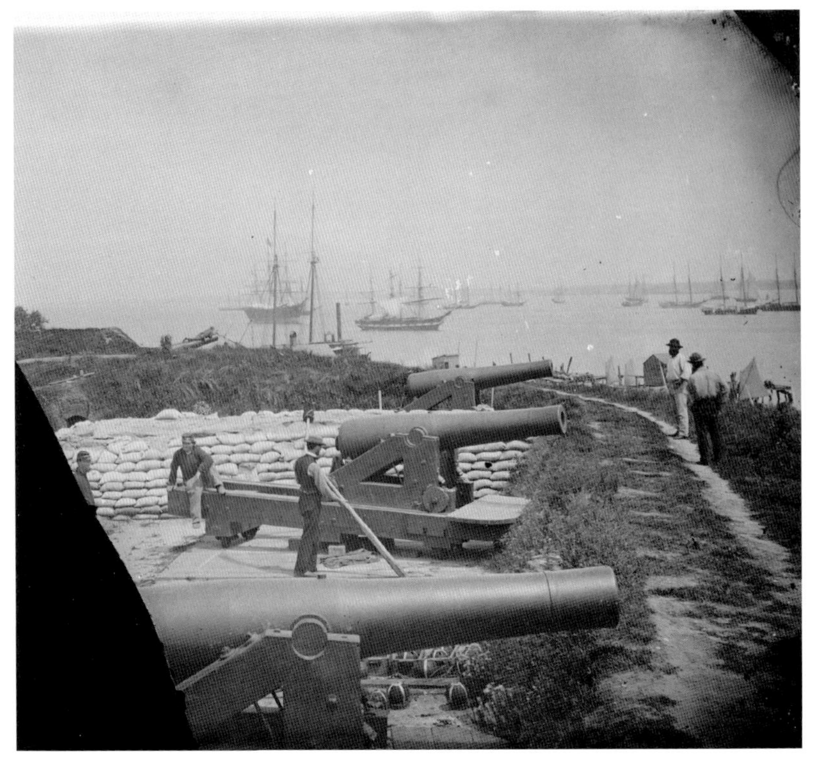

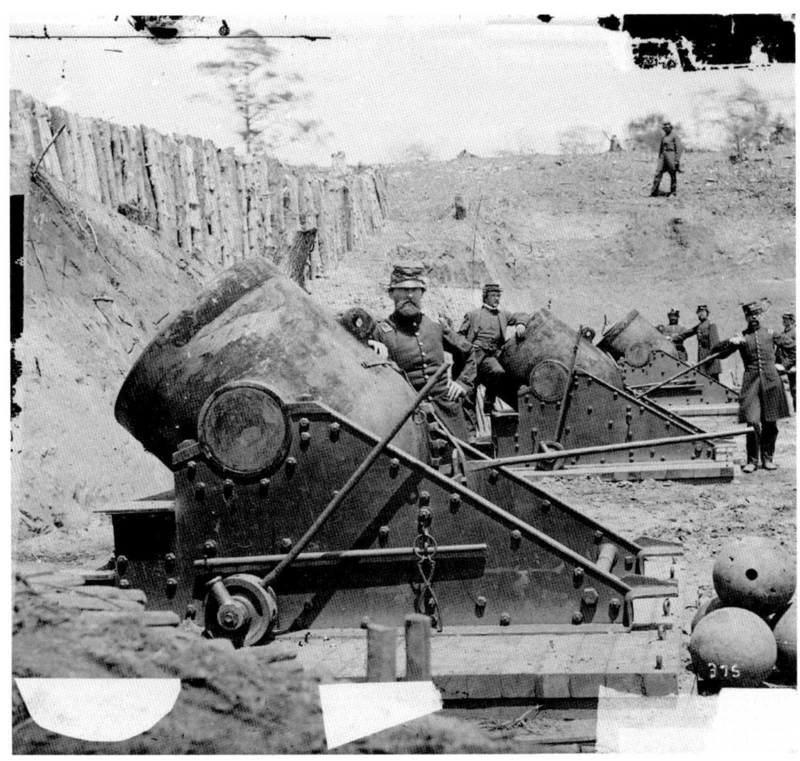

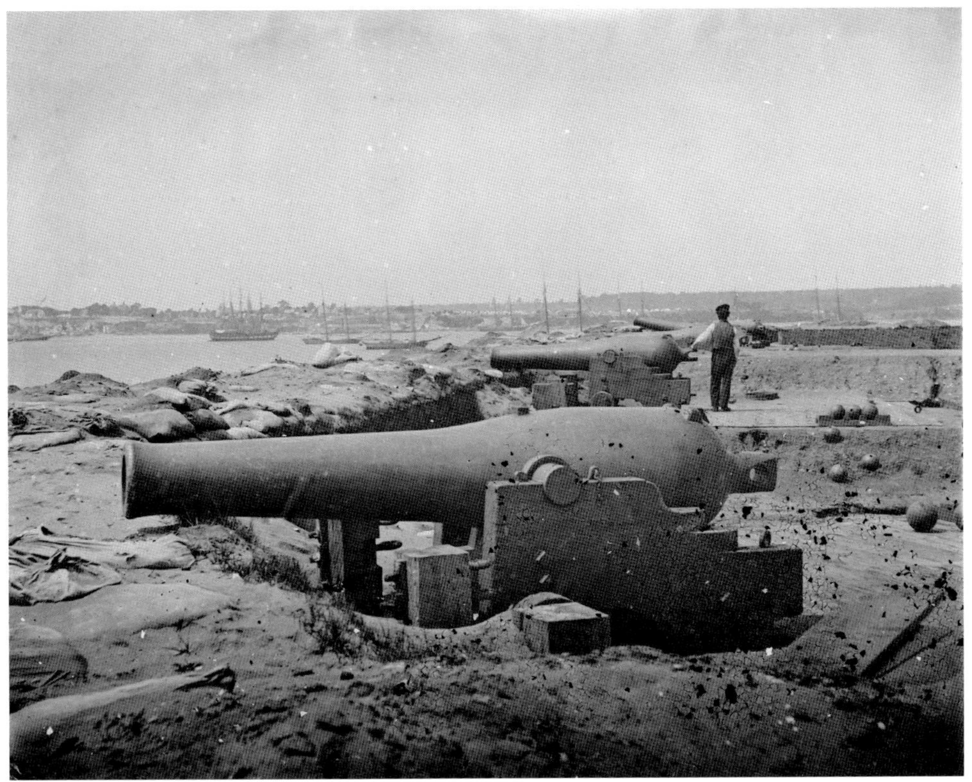

A Confederate water battery mounted with a Dahlgren eleven-inch smooth bore naval gun was photographed by George Norman Barnard (1819–1902) at Yorktown in May 1862, after rebel forces had pulled back and federal troops occupied the emplacements. For the studio of Mathew Benjamin Brady (1822–1896), Barnard shot an historic series of images of the battlefields from the First Bull Run campaign, of soldiers in camp, and of the aftermath of the Union's siege of Yorktown. Though his tenure with Brady was brief, Barnard's work, especially his photographs taken at Yorktown, are of a quality that became his trademark. *Library of Congress*

OPPOSITE PAGE:

Above: Looking north up the river, four of the five eight-inch Columbiads composing part of what had been Confederate battery Magruder are visible in this June 1862 photograph. The grape-shot and spherical shells, which had been gathered in quantities to prevent the federal fleet from passing up the river, were abandoned on the hasty retreat of the Confederates, the guns being spiked. The vessels in the river are federal transport ships, with the exception of the frigate just offshore. *Library of Congress*

Below: This close-up photograph of the south end of federal battery number four, mounting ten thirteen-inch seacoast mortars, each weighing twenty thousand pounds, was photographed by James F. Gibson in May 1862. Officers of the First Connecticut Heavy Artillery posed around the mortars, which were positioned on the right bank of Wormley Creek. The battery, one of fifteen planted to the south and southeast of Yorktown, never fired a shot. *Library of Congress*

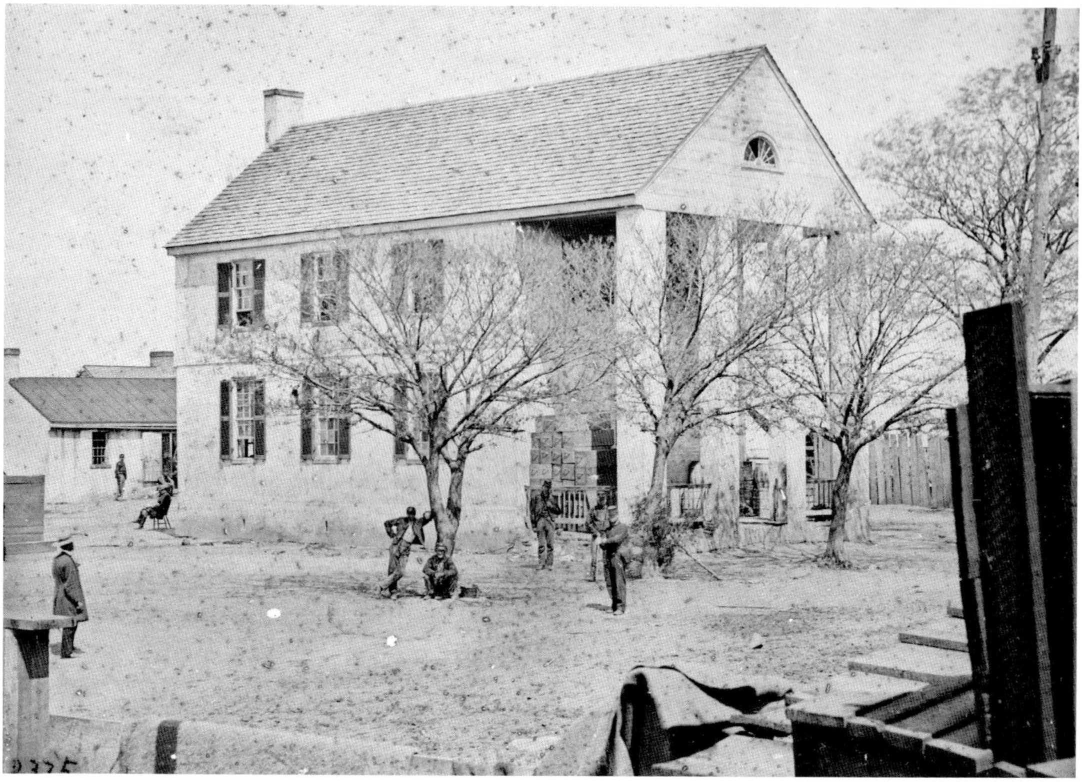

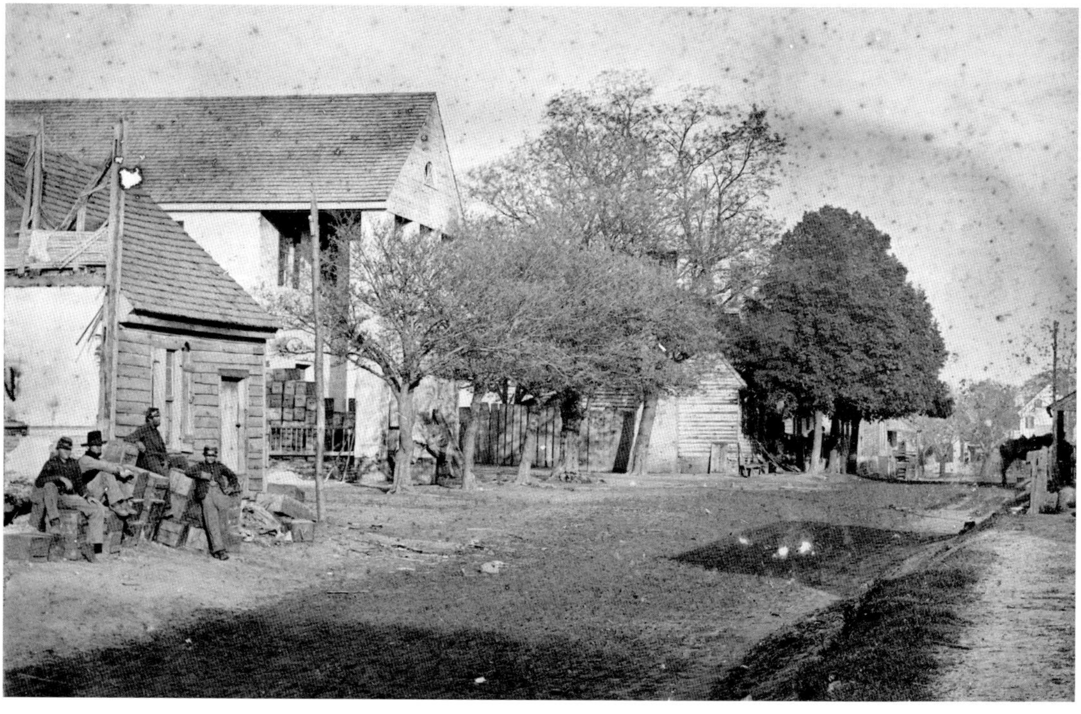

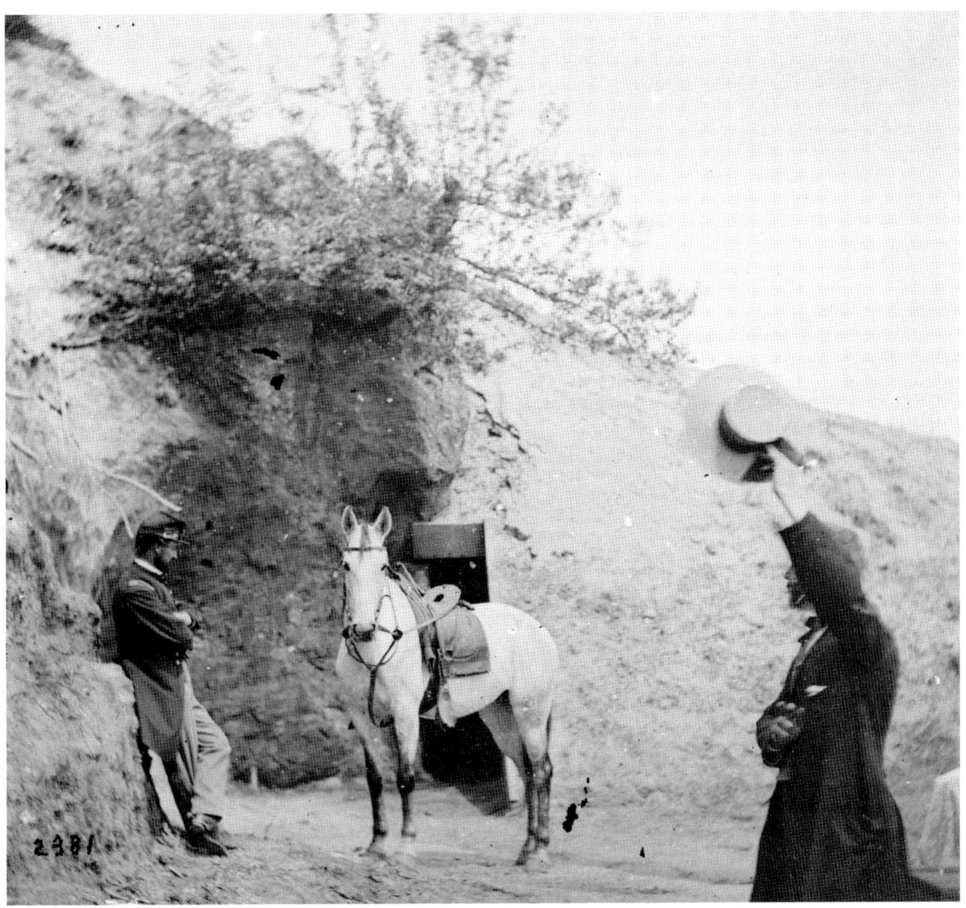

Cornwallis Cave[3], a natural cave in a marl cliff, was used as a powder magazine by the Confederate army but was occupied by federal troops when this picture was taken by a Mathew Brady photographer in 1862 during the occupation of Yorktown. Union captain Sanford Harvey Perkins' (left) is shown with a "Secesh" horse, which he procured from Lelia May Farinholt (1842–1927), of Yorktown, whose husband was Confederate colonel Benjamin Lyons Farinholt. Perkins (1829–1874), who joined up with the First Connecticut Heavy Artillery and then transferred to the Fourteenth Connecticut Infantry on June 7, 1862, ended the war as a lieutenant colonel. He was severely wounded in the neck at Fredericksburg, Virginia, on December 13, 1862. *Library of Congress*

Opposite page:

Above: The Yorktown courthouse, located on Main Street and occupied by federal troops, is shown in this 1862 photograph. The town's 1737 jail is located just behind the courthouse. *Library of Congress*

Below: In this street view of the courthouse, pictured during the Union occupation in 1862, shows federal troops to the left. During a fire that swept Main Street the following year, the courthouse was destroyed. The federal garrison had packed it full of ammunition and powder and it caught fire and exploded on December 16, 1863, in a series of what were described as violent blasts that went on for almost three hours and could be heard for miles outside the town. Also lost was the old jail and the Swan Tavern.[2] *Library of Congress*

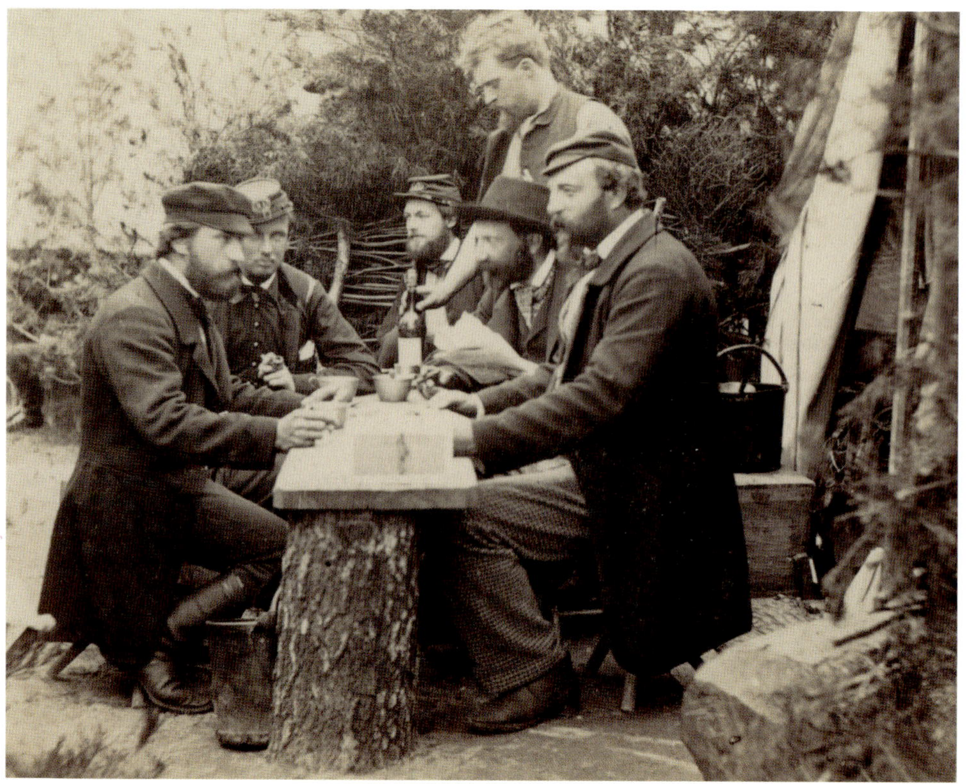

François Ferdinand Philippe Louis Marie d'Orleans, Prince de Joinville (1818–1900) (seated foreground left), the son of Louis Philippe I (1773–1850), King of the French from 1830 to 1848, and Maria Amalia of Naples and Sicily, served with great distinction in the French navy, attaining the rank vice admiral; he was also a noted writer and artist. When his father lost his throne in 1848 the prince fled France with his family for Claremont in Surrey, England. He failed in an attempt seven years later to become a second so called "prince president" of France. At the outbreak of the American Civil War in the spring of 1861 he traveled to Washington, D.C., and placed the services of his son and two of his nephews at the disposal of Abraham Lincoln's war department. The following year the prince accompanied Major General George B. McClellan in the Peninsula Campaign, which he documented in a book titled *Campagne de l'Armée du Potomac* published in 1862. Of interest, the prince's son Pierre (1845–1919) entered the United States Naval Academy on October 15, 1861, and received an honorary appointment as an ensign in the United States Navy on May 28, 1863, and served on the frigate USS *John Adams*. He was granted a leave of absence by the navy effective January 1 of the following year, resigned on May 30, 1864, and returned to France the following month. In this May 1, 1862 James Gibson photograph, the prince is joined at lunch in Camp Winfield Scott, Yorktown vicinity, by his nephews, the brothers Louis Philippe Albert d'Orleans, Comte de Paris and Robert Philippe Louis d'Orleans, Duc de Chartres (1840–1910), and friends. *Library of Congress*

Opposite above: Louis Philippe Albert d'Orleans, Comte de Paris (1838–1894) [also called Prince Philippe of Orleans] (left) and Robert Philippe Louis d'Orleans, Duc de Chartres, right, brothers and the nephews of Prince de Joinville, are shown here wearing the Union uniform in their capacity as aides to Major General George McClellan, which lasted the breadth of the Peninsula Campaign before both resigned and Louis Philippe returned to England two years later. Louis Philippe wrote a seven-volume *Histoire de la guerre civile en Amérique*, an important reference work on the war. On the deaths of his grandfather and father, Louis Philippe was the pretender to the French throne. *Library of Congress*

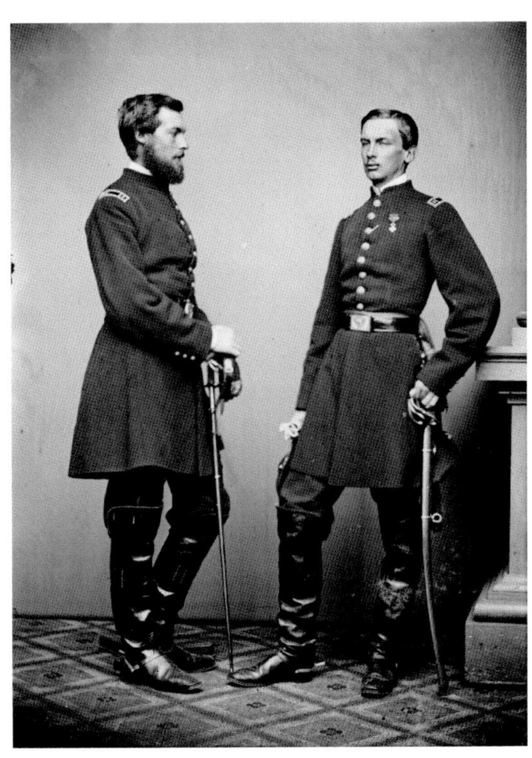

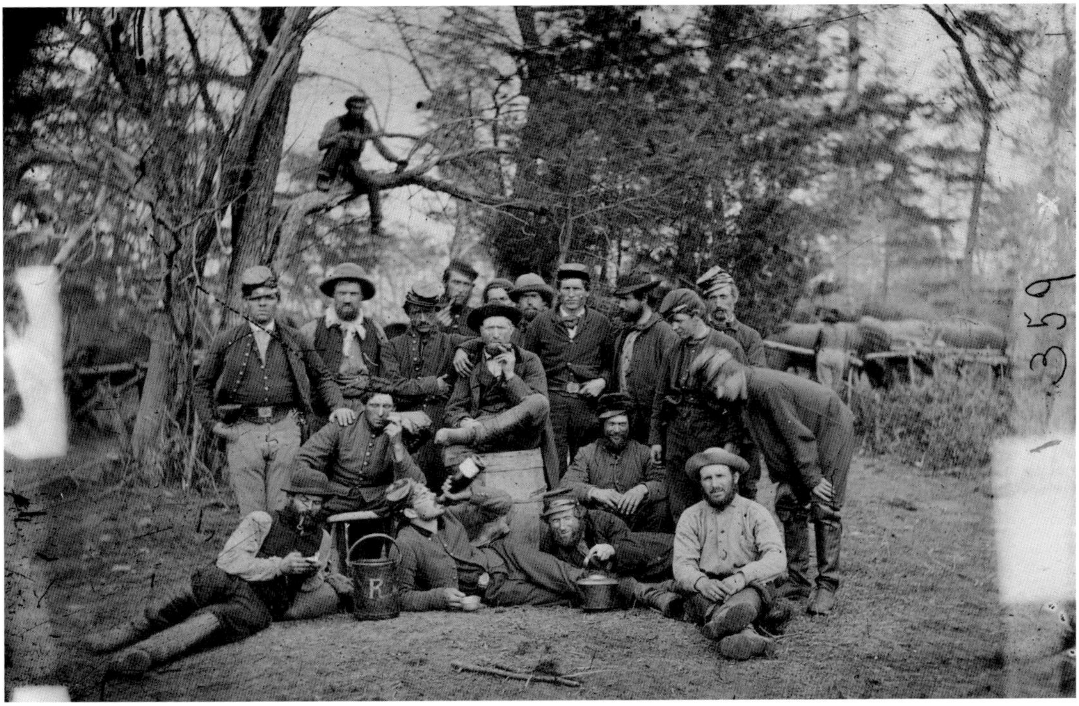

The men shown here, photographed by James Gibson on May 3, 1862, at Camp Winfield Scott near Yorktown, were the servants of staff officers. They were called the "beef killers" of the army. *Library of Congress*

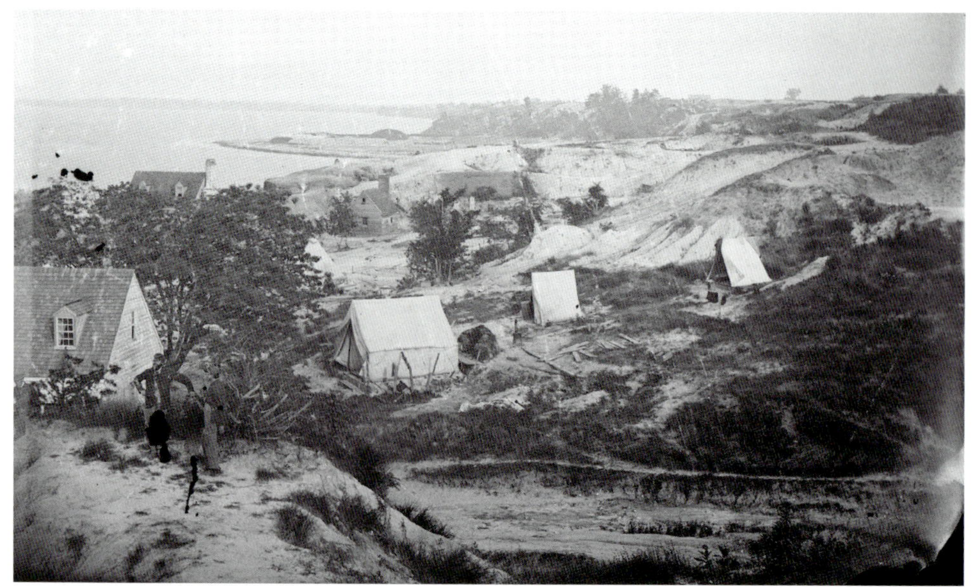

This view of Yorktown and a former Confederate water battery was taken from Cornwallis Cave in June 1862 by George N. Barnard. *Library of Congress*

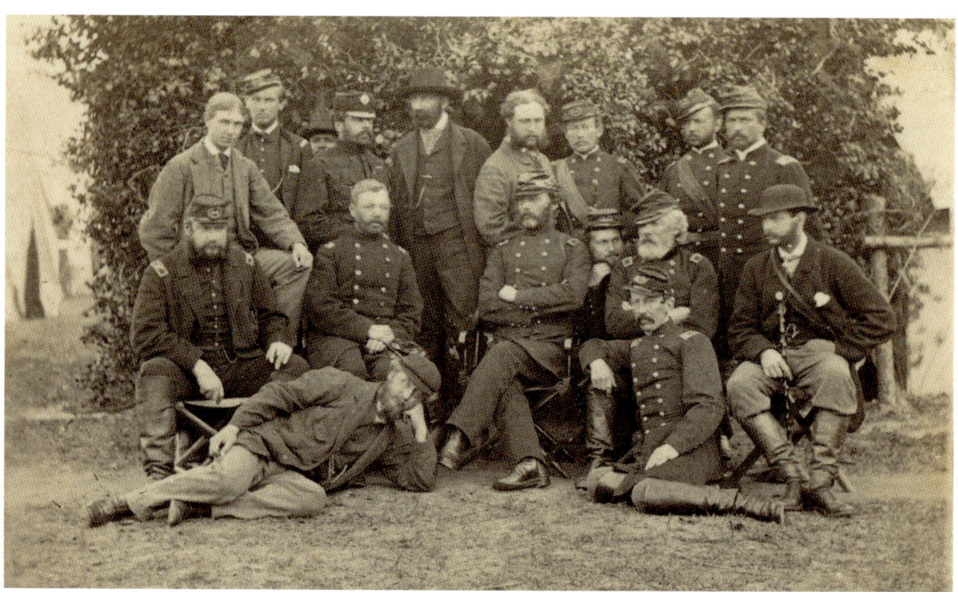

Brigadier General Randolph Barnes Marcy (1812–1887) (seated center), chief of staff to his son-in-law Major General George McClellan, posed with some of his officers and a few civilians at Camp Winfield Scott near Yorktown on May 2, 1862. James Gibson took the photograph. *Library of Congress*

Opposite page: The First Connecticut artillery park was encamped at the former quarters of the Louisiana Tigers when these pictures were taken in May 1862 by Mathew B. Brady. In the broad horizontal view, the artillery parked at the rear of the lower wharf was by no means all that McClellan deemed necessary to overcome the resistance at Yorktown. In the center are Parrott guns. *Continued on next page*

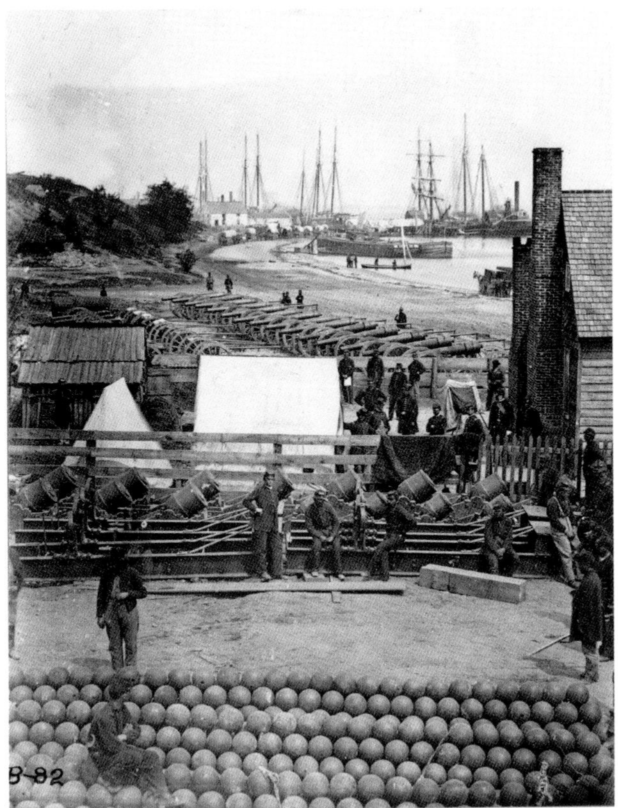

Continued from previous page: In the background, at the upper wharf, are the transports ready for the embarkation of the troops and loading of armament. The small mortars in the foreground were known as cochorns. They could be lifted by half a dozen men and transported by hand to any part of the entrenchments. The cochorns' range was only a few hundred yards but with small charges they could quite accurately drop shells at almost a stone's throw. During the siege of Petersburg, they were used by both armies. Here, too, were troops and artillery (bottom photograph) ready for the forward move. *Library of Congress*

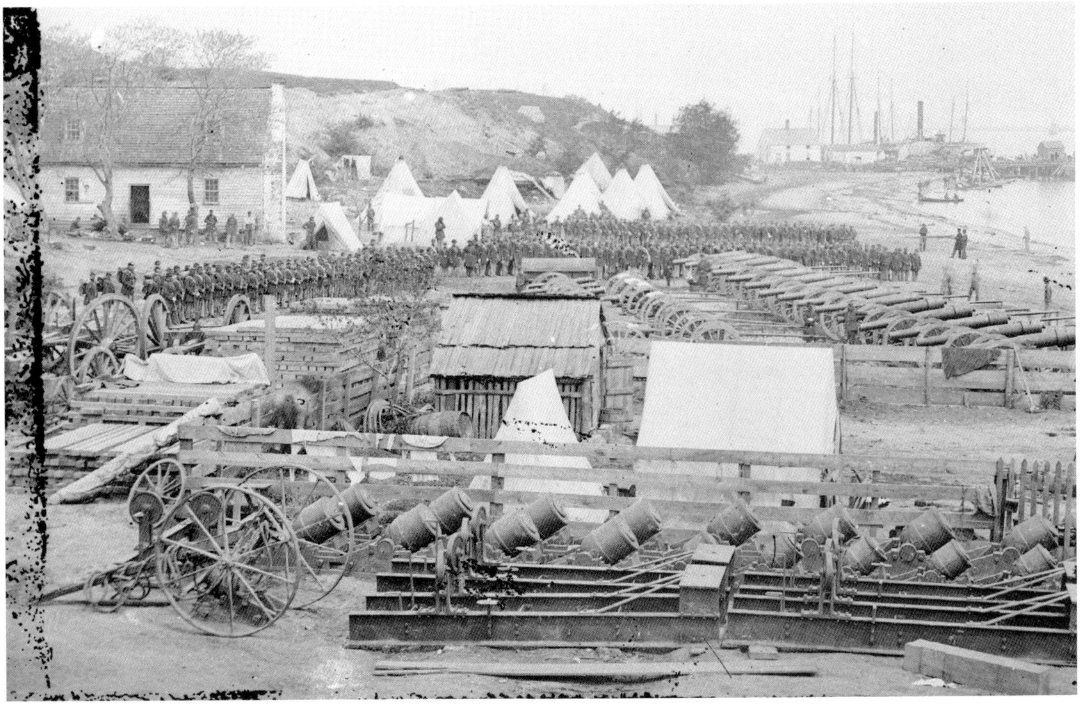

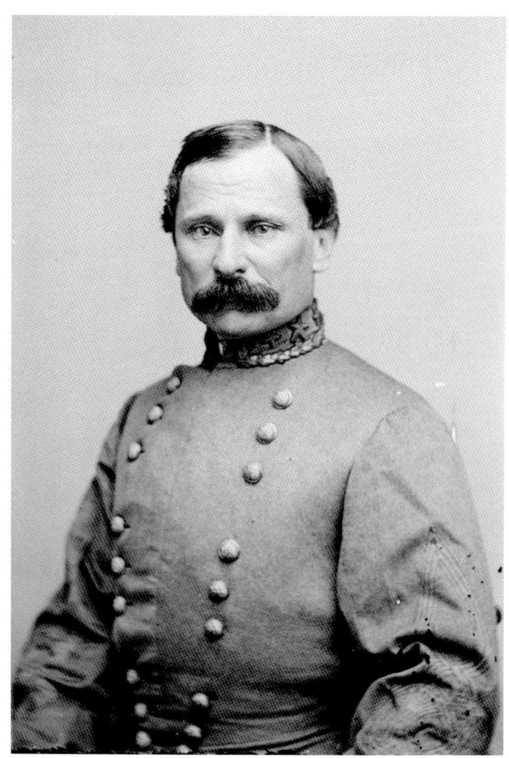

Confederate major general Cadmus Marcellus Wilcox (1824–1890) was present during combat actions during the Peninsula Campaign and is shown in this late war portrait. Wilcox, born in Wayne County, North Carolina, and who moved to Tennessee at the age of two, had been, like most of the rebel army's general officers, a former career United States Army officer before the outbreak of the Civil War. At the time of his participation in the Peninsula Campaign, Wilcox was a brigadier general in command of a brigade of troops from Alabama and Mississippi under Major General James Longstreet's I Corps. *Library of Congress*

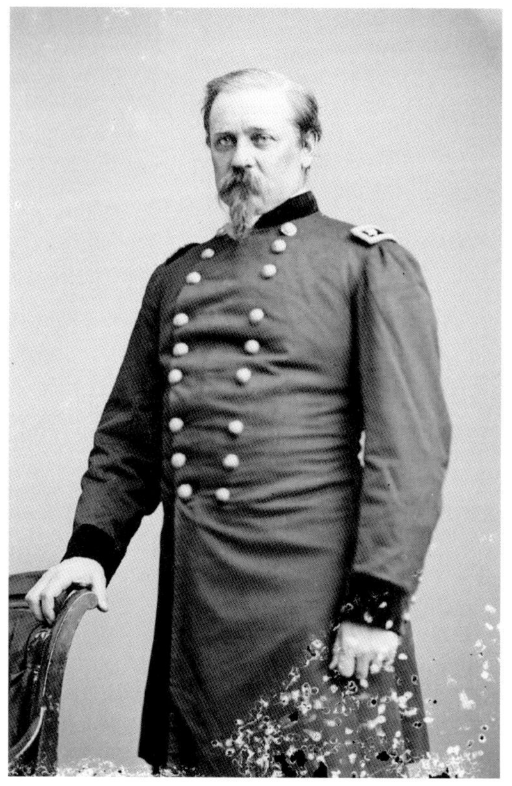

Brigadier (later Major) General William Farrar "Baldy" Smith (1824–1903), a key figure for the federal side at Yorktown, was the commander of the so-called "Bloody" Sixth during the Peninsula Campaign, and later the IX and XVIII Corps over the progress of the war. Smith was remarkable for attracting the extremes of glory and blame, praised on the one hand for his gallantry in the Seven Days Battles and the Battle of Antietam but demoted for insubordination after the disastrous defeat at the Battle of Fredericksburg. He is shown in this Mathew Brady photo, taken after his promotion to major general. *Library of Congress*

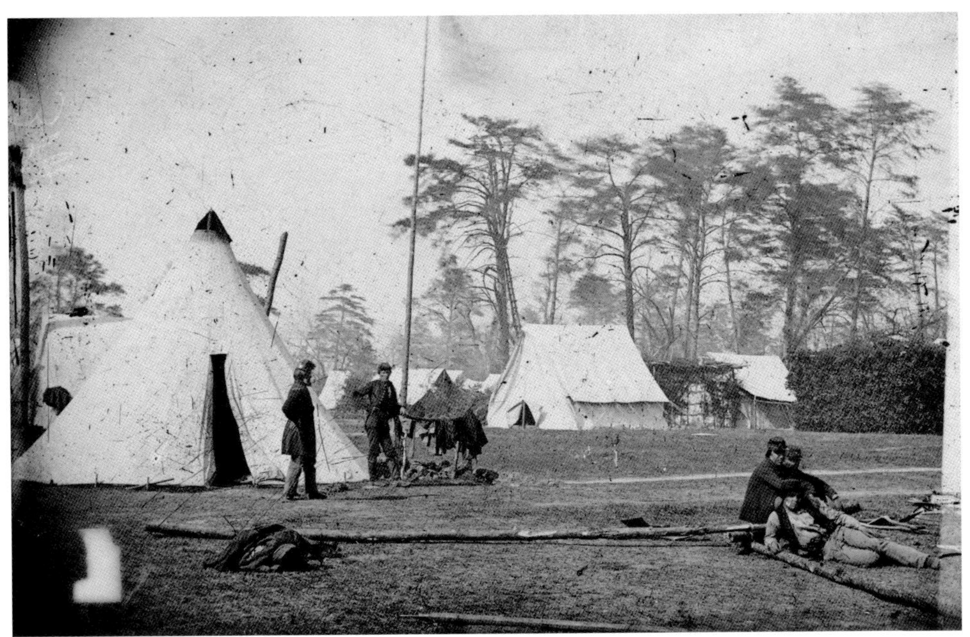

Major General George McClellan's tent inside the bounds of Camp Winfield Scott, was photographed by James Gibson in May 1862. The camp, near Wormley Creek, was McClellan's headquarters before Yorktown. He was a stickler for neatness and in this camp his orderlies wore white gloves and the horses were remarkably well fed. *Library of Congress*

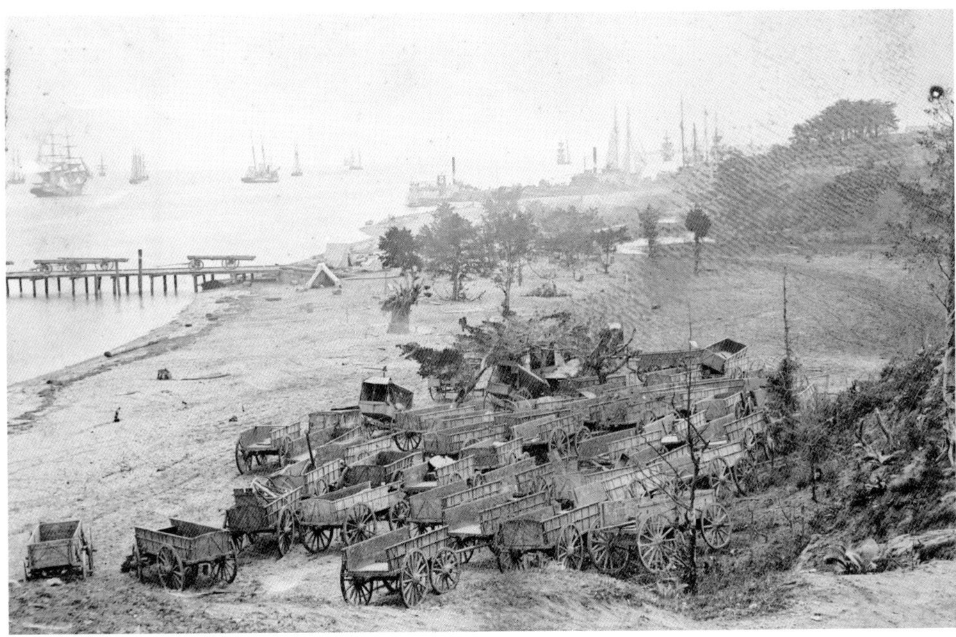

During the Peninsula Campaign, a Mathew Brady photographer took this picture of the federal wagon park. To keep the troops well outfitted, McClellan's army repositioned 1,150 wagons, 15,000 horses and tons of equipment and supplies from Northern Virginia to the Peninsula, beginning on March 17, 1862. *Library of Congress*

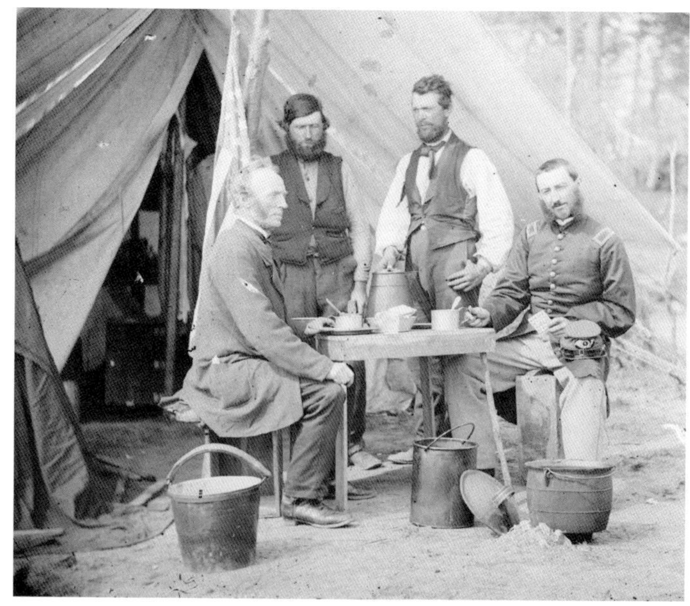

Shown in this James Gibson photograph, taken in front of the photographic tent at Camp Winfield Scott in May 1862, is photographer George Barnard (standing right). *Library of Congress*

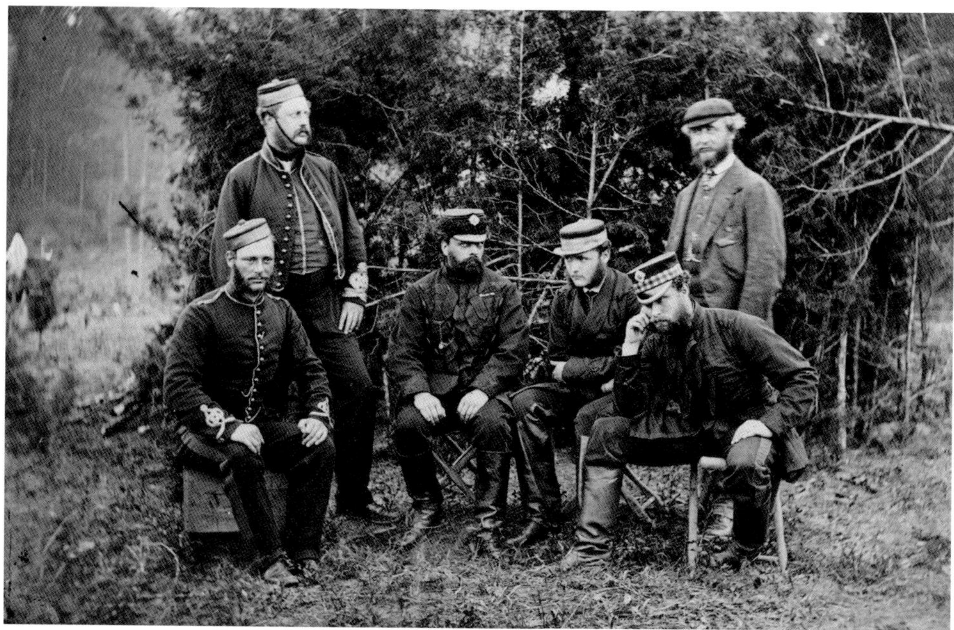

During the Peninsula Campaign, this group of British military officers was photographed by James Gibson in May 1862 bivouacked at Camp Winfield Scott. Foreign and British officers were largely present in federal camps during the Peninsula Campaign to observe and advise their American counterparts and not to engage in combat. On May 13, 1861, within a month of the outbreak of America's Civil War, Queen Victoria issued a proclamation declaring the United Kingdom of Great Britain and Ireland's neutrality in the Americans' domestic conflict. Foreign enlistment[4] in the American Civil War largely favored the Union, which successfully recruited more volunteers from overseas. But as the war progressed, this did not keep British and other European citizens and businesses from secretly funding and supplying armament to fighting for the South. *Library of Congress*

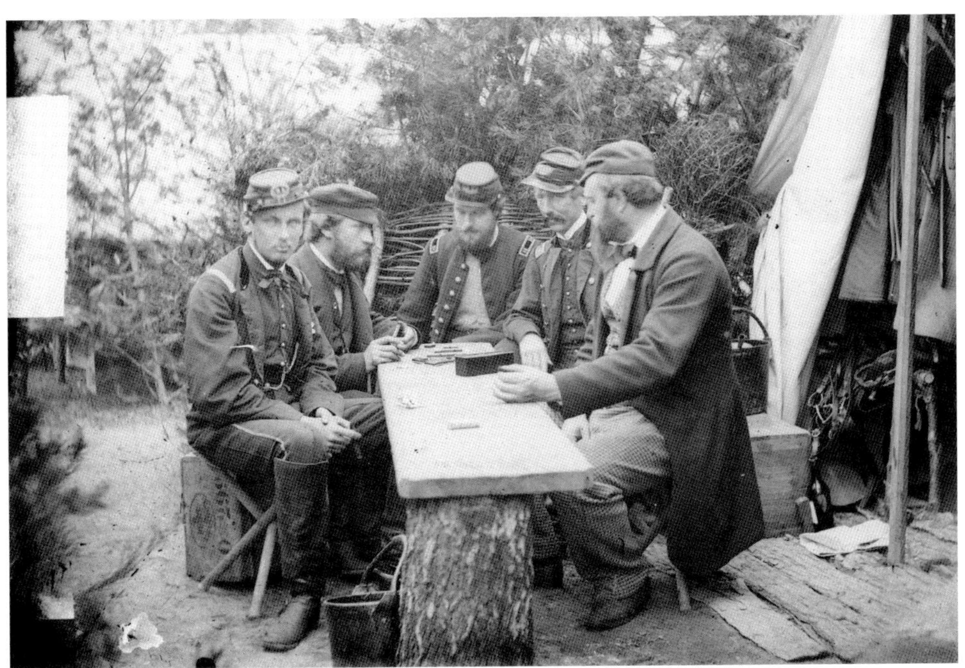

From the left, Duc de Chartres, Prince de Joinville, Comte de Paris and two unidentified friends were photographed by James Gibson playing dominoes at a mess table at the headquarters in Camp Winfield Scott on May 3, 1862, on the day Yorktown fell. Dominoes was one of many diversions taken up by soldiers in Civil War camps, none so popular as letter writing. In July 1861 one Virginian observed: "Everybody is writing who can raise a pencil or sheet of paper."[5] Letters home were important expressions of soldiers' experiences and their feelings about the war and day-to-day life. *Library of Congress*

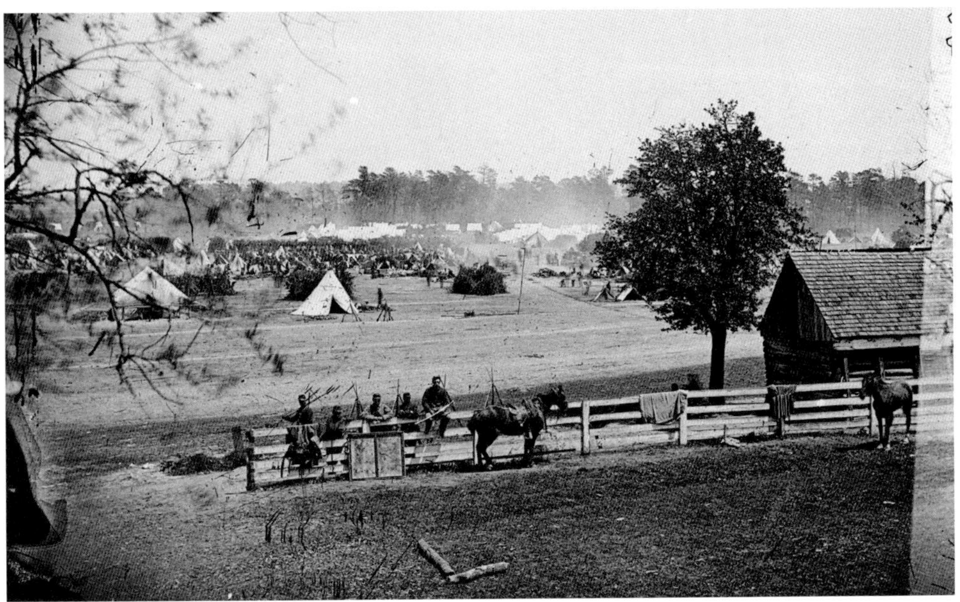

Camp Winfield Scott, headquarters of Union major general George Brinton McClellan, was photographed by James Gibson on May 7, 1862. The camp was located in the vicinity of Yorktown. *Library of Congress*

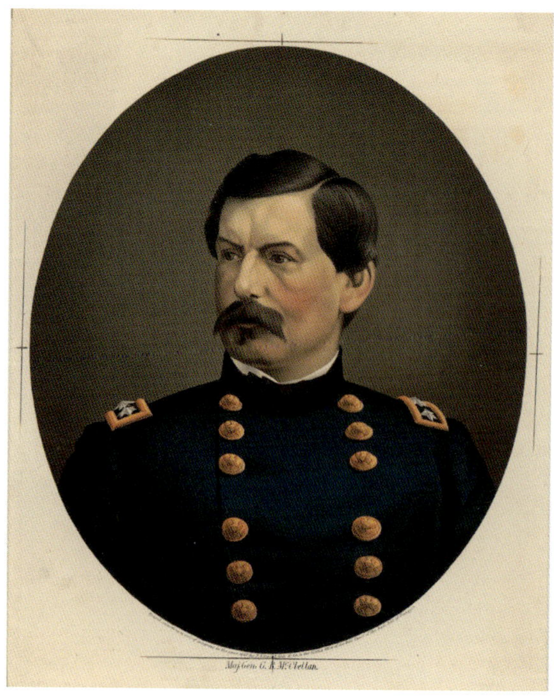

This portrait of Philadelphia-born major general George Brinton McClellan (1826–1885) was published in 1867 by Peter Stephen Duval and Son, lithographers. McClellan, a civil engineer, was a graduate of the United States Military Academy at West Point and served with distinction in the Mexican-American War (1846–1848), as did many of his future Union and Confederate counterparts. Between the wars, he left the army to work in the railroad industry. With the outbreak of the Civil War he was appointed a major general and put in charge of the Army of the Potomac in the Eastern Theater. For a brief period—November 1, 1861 to March 11, 1862—he was the fourth commanding general of the United States Army. McClellan's focus on planning and preparation hindered his ability to move decisively against aggressive opponents in rapidly evolving battlefield environments and he consistently overestimated the strength of Confederate forces, just as he did at Yorktown and throughout the Peninsula Campaign, which was flawed and failed. President Abraham Lincoln would go on to replace him as general-in-chief of the United States Army with Major General Henry Wager Halleck (1815–1872), who, in turn, would be replaced on March 9, 1864, by General Ulysses S. Grant [born Hiram Ulysses Grant] (1822–1885). French-born Duval (1804–1886) was the most prominent Philadelphia lithographer of the nineteenth century. *Library of Congress*

Opposite above: George Barnard took this picture of an exploded [thirty-two-pounder navy gun] in a Confederate battery located southeast of Yorktown in June 1862. Confederate aeronaut [balloonist] captain John Randolph Bryan (1841–1917), a Gloucester County, Virginia native, Virginia Military Institute graduate and aide-de-camp to Major General John Bankhead Magruder, was borrowed by General Joseph E. Johnston in the spring of 1862 and sent up in a balloon on more than one memorable occasion to map McClellan's positions around Yorktown looked down on this battery on his reconnaissance of federal positions. The gun shown here was exploded by the Confederates on Major General David Harvey Hill's rampart. Although the Confederates abandoned two hundred pieces of ordnance at Yorktown, they were able to render most of it useless before leaving. Hill succeeded in terrorizing the federals with grape-shot, and some of this was left behind. After the evacuation the ramparts were overrun by Union trophy seekers. The soldier resting his hand on his musket is one of the Zouaves whose bright and novel uniforms were so conspicuous early in the war. This site was directly on the line of the British fortification of 1781. *Library of Congress*

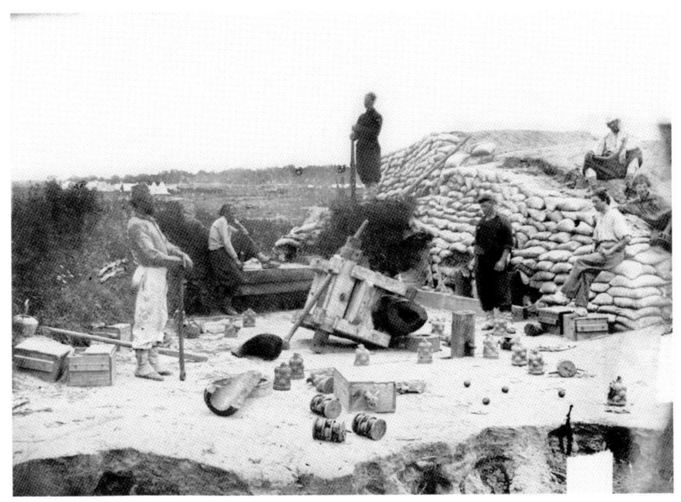

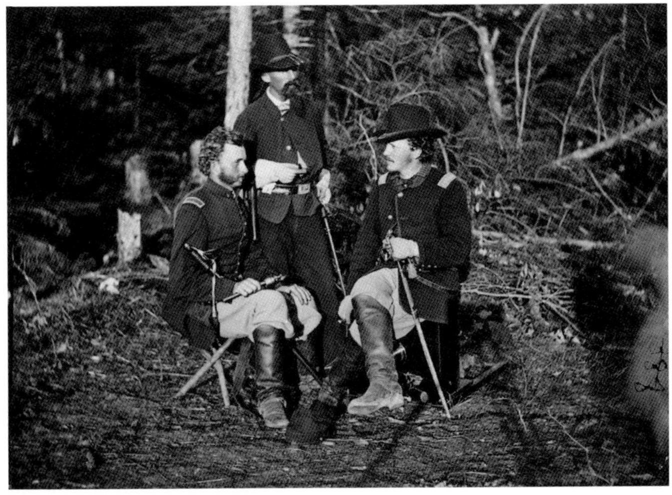

During the Peninsula Campaign, James Gibson took this picture of (left to right) Union first lieutenants William Graham Jones (1837–1863), George Armstrong Custer (1839–1876), and Nicolas Bowen (1837–1871). Jones served in the Army of the Potomac under General Andrew Porter and participated in the Peninsula Campaign. But on June 24, 1862, Jones was appointed as lieutenant colonel of the Seventy-First Pennsylvania Infantry and fought at the Battles of Fair Oaks, Peach Orchard, and Malvern Hills. He resigned his commission to become aide-de-camp to Major General Edwin Vose Sumner and served at the Battles of Antietam and Fredericksburg. In October 1862, Jones was appointed as colonel of the Thirty-Sixth Ohio Volunteer Infantry to replace the late colonel Melvin Clarke who fell at Antietam and sent to West Virginia to join the regiment. The regiment was attached to Turchin's Brigade in the XIV Corps under Major General George Henry Thomas (1816–1870). On September 19, 1863, Jones died at the Battle of Chickamauga in Georgia and fell behind enemy lines. He was initially buried in a soldier's grave on the battlefield and was later removed to Spring Grove Cemetery, in his native Cincinnati, Ohio, in December 1863. Custer served in the Fifth Cavalry Regiment and participated in the siege of Yorktown from April 5 to May 4, 1862, where he was also an aide to Major General George McClellan. Less than a week before the Battle of Gettysburg [July 1–3, 1863], Custer was brevetted to brigadier general at the age of twenty-three. Bowen was a topographical engineer. After the war Bowen was put in charge of Fort Columbus, Governor's Island, New York harbor. *Library of Congress*

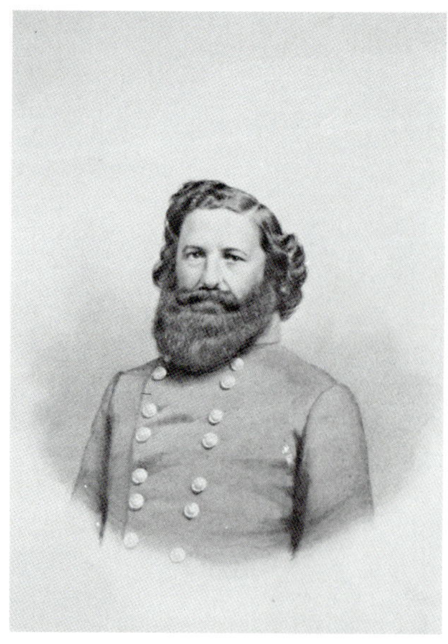

Brigadier General Lafayette McLaws (1821–1897) covered Major General John Magruder's retreat from Yorktown. This picture was taken between May–August 1862. As a lieutenant colonel, back in 1861, McLaws played a key role in the construction of the Williamsburg Line, four miles of defensive works across the Virginia Peninsula, which later played a crucial role in the Battle of Williamsburg during the Peninsula Campaign. McLaws was promoted to major general of the I Corps on May 23, 1862. Of interest, McLaws Circle, part of Anheuser-Busch's 2,900-acre Kingsmill development near Williamsburg, Virginia, begun in the early 1970s, was named in his honor. *Library of Congress*

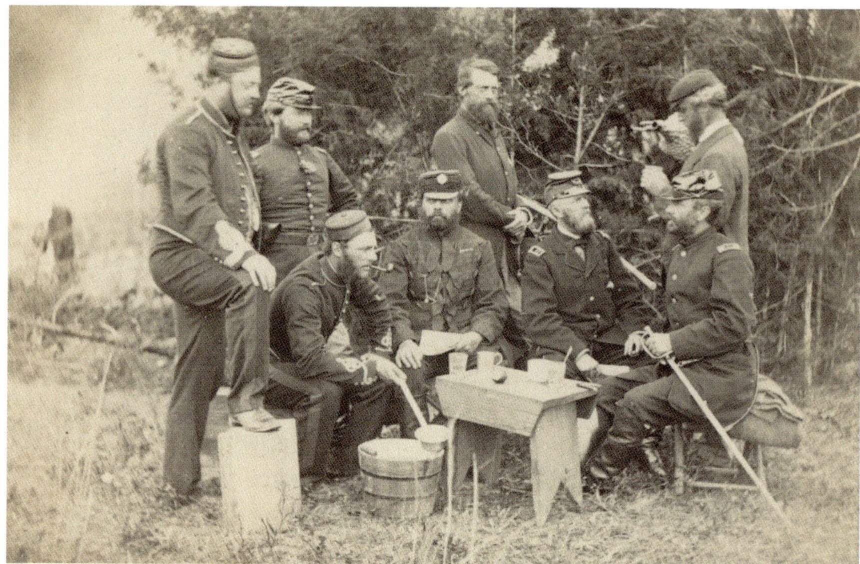

Union major general George Stoneman Jr. (1822–1894) (standing center, hat in hand) posed for this picture, taken by either James Gibson or George Barnard, with English officers and members of Stoneman's staff as they took refreshment at Camp Winfield Scott in May 1862. Stoneman, who stood six-foot-four-inches, was a cavalry officer, trained at West Point, where his roommate was Thomas Jonathan "Stonewall" Jackson (1824–1863), later the famed Confederate lieutenant general who played a prominent role in nearly all military engagements in the Eastern Theater of the war until his death. Before the Peninsula Campaign, Stoneman was adjutant to Major General George McClellan and after McClellan became commander of the newly-formed Army of the Potomac, he assigned Stoneman as his chief of cavalry, and he was promoted to brigadier general of volunteers on August 13, 1861. Historical narrative informs Stoneman had a difficult relationship with McClellan as he wanted to use the cavalry as a raiding and combat force, while McClellan merely envisioned it as an extension of the army signal corps. *Continued on next page*

Continued from previous page: As a matter of record, the Army of the Potomac's cavalry performed poorly in the Eastern Theater during the spring and summer of 1862 [to include the Peninsula Campaign], being soundly outgeneraled and outfought by Confederate cavalry. Of note, Stoneman moved to California after his postwar army service ended and from 1883 to 1887 he served as the fifteenth governor of that state. *Library of Congress*

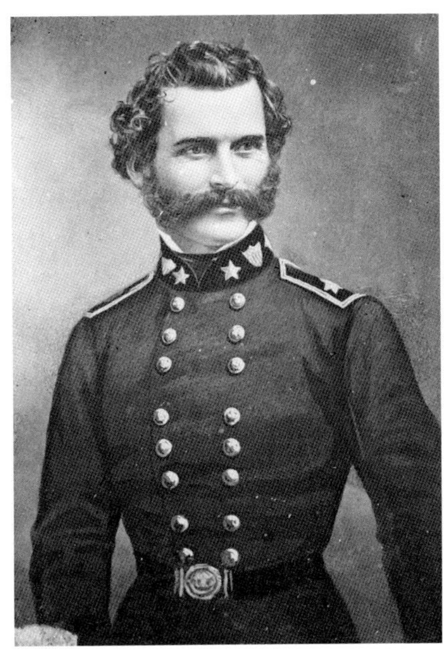

Confederate brigadier general and New Bern, North Carolina native Gabriel James Rains (1803–1881) was one of Major General David Harvey Hill's brigade commanders. In retreat, he planted hidden shells on the roads out of Yorktown that were rigged to explode if stepped on. Back then, they were not called antipersonnel mines or improvised explosive devices but rather "torpedoes" or "infernal machines" for the death they wrought. Rains was considered the pioneer of antipersonnel mines, what many, even his peers, believed was a terrible weapon. This picture of Rains, a graduate of the United States Military Academy at West Point, was taken in his United States Army uniform and at the height of his pre-Civil War service to the nation. *Library of Congress*

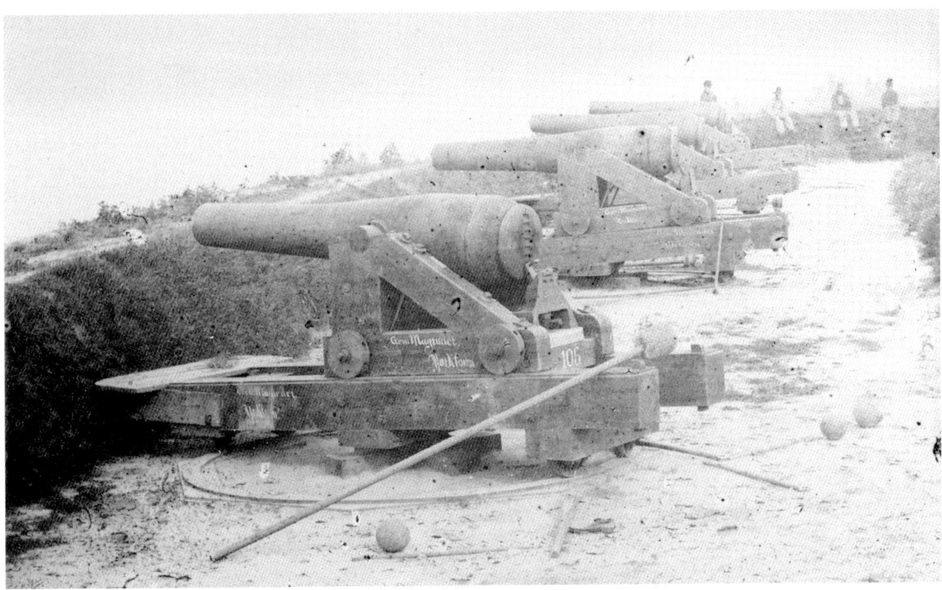

Confederate water battery Magruder, with Rodman smooth-bore siege guns, was photographed by George Barnard in June 1862. The gun carriages bear Magruder's name and the place "Yorktown." *Library of Congress*

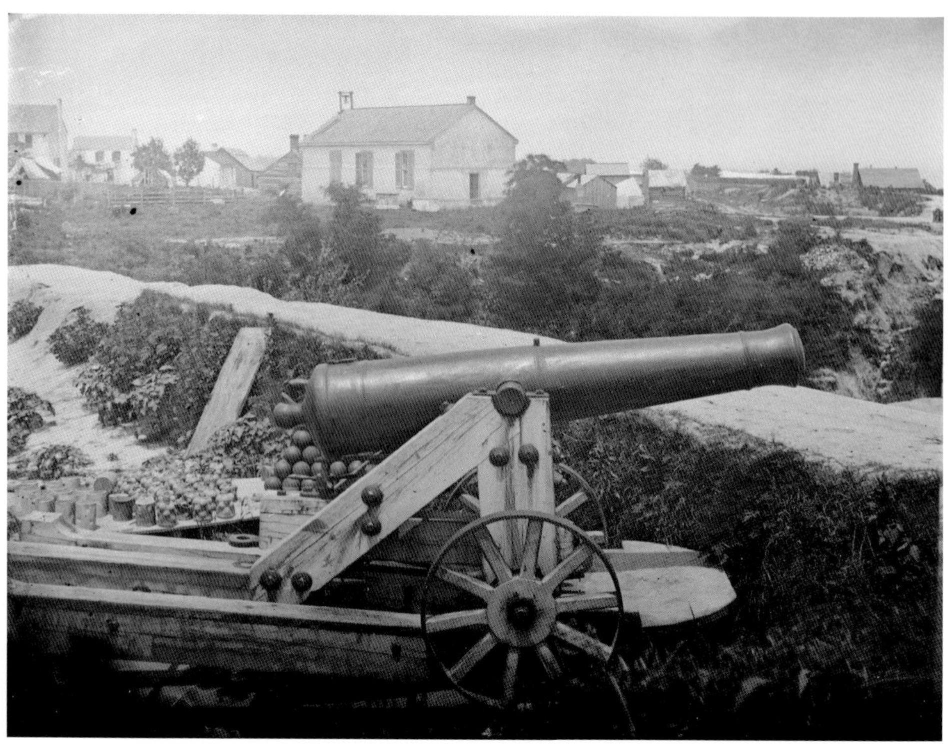

This photograph, taken by George Barnard on July 1, 1862, shows a Confederate naval gun (foreground) [in a battery] and in the background, Grace Episcopal Church, one of the few surviving colonial structures built of marl, although the marl walls of this structure were covered with stucco in the mid-nineteenth century. Built in 1697 and called the York-Hampton Parish Church, the rectangular building is fifty-five feet nine inches by twenty-eight feet eight inches. This church was the third parish church of York Parish, which had been created in 1638. The first two churches were built in or about 1642 and 1667, respectively, and were located two miles below Yorktown at the old York settlement. In 1706 York Parish merged with Hampton Parish to form York-Hampton Parish. Evidence dating construction of the third sanctuary building to 1697 is royal governor Francis Nicholson's pledge recorded in the county order book dated November 26, 1696, of twenty pounds sterling toward the erection of a brick church, provided the church be built within two years. Instead, the church was built of marl slabs from the cliffs above the York River. The building received a twenty-nine-foot north wing in the eighteenth century, giving it a T-shape with a steeple. During the Revolutionary War it was used as a magazine by Lord Cornwallis and it was then that it lost its windows and pews. In the War of 1812, it was used as a stable. The original structure was gutted by the Great Fire of 1814 and was not restored for another thirty-four years, at which time it was rebuilt, this time in a Greek Revival style without the original north wing and the walls stuccoed; the name was also changed just then to Grace Episcopal Church. During the Civil War, it was recorded that federal troops purportedly built a signal tower on the roof but this is unlikely where it was built. Sketches and photographs taken of the church indicate that the tower was actually built adjacent to the church's north wall, free standing and not attached to the building. The interior, used as a hospital, suffered extensive damage, and the colonial churchyard was demolished. In the foreground of the photograph, to the left are arranged loads of canister [tin cans filled with lead or iron balls] and stands of grapeshot, clusters of a dozen or more larger iron projectiles fired like a scatter-load from the cannon. The church, like the battery, overlooks the York River. Note also that there is a bell rack with a mounted bell but no evidence of a tower on or near the structure. *Library of Congress*

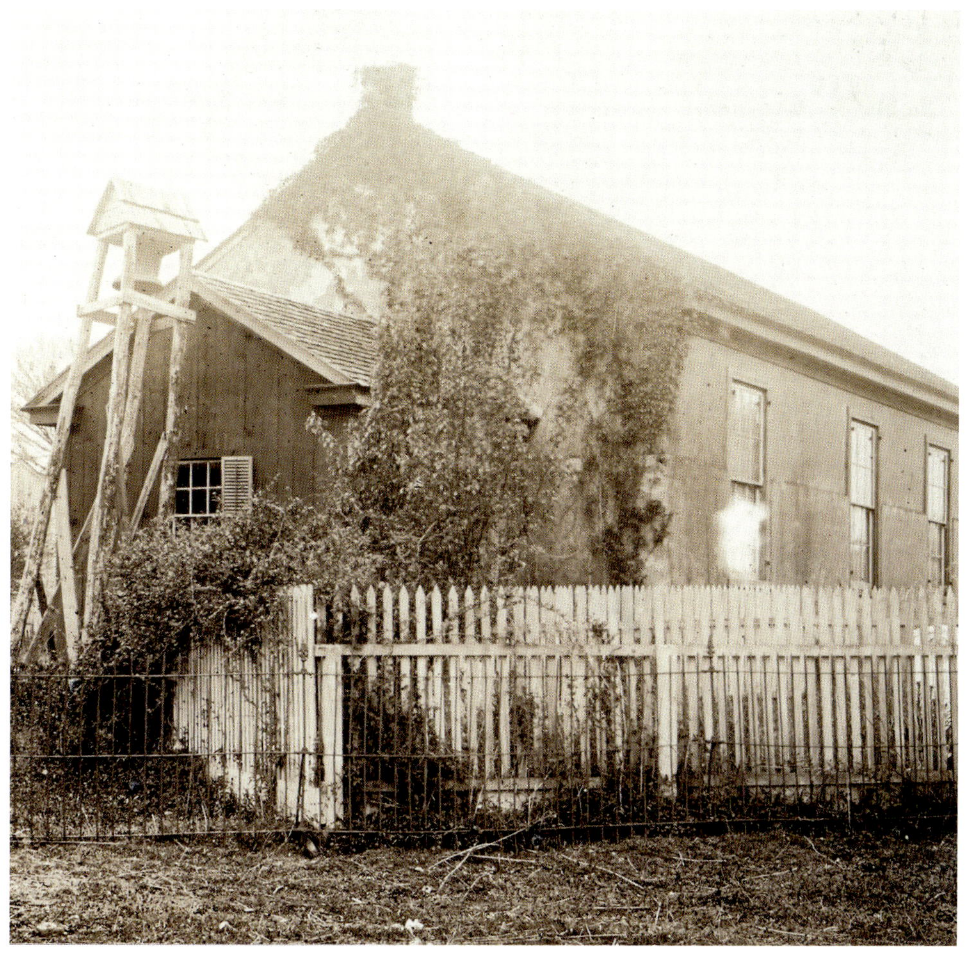

This Keystone stereoview of Grace Episcopal Church, restored for worship soon after the war and by some estimates as early as 1870, shows the east end of the building with the chimney stack above the roof and the door opening removed and the building extended. The bell tower, rising from the ground, stood free behind the church and did not reach as high as the peak of the church roof. This was erected to accommodate the bell, which had been returned to Yorktown by the Hooks Smelting Company. The picture is dated by this tower. On July 11, 1889, the bell was hung on this crude scaffold in the churchyard and rung for service. There are three windows evident on the north side. More than a decade before this picture was taken, the Reverend Alexander Yuille Hundley (1848–1890) came to the church in 1877 as deacon and within two years became rector. He remained with the parish for six years but by then had just a little over two dozen communicants left on the rolls. The church was listed as vacant seven years after Hundley's arrival and it would be the Reverend Alexander Marshall Overby (1840–1925) of Williamsburg's Bruton Parish Church who came over just one Sunday in the month at the beginning of 1884. Near the end of the decade, in 1888, the church was beginning to come back and by 1893 had twenty-five active families. Still the building was in poor condition and in need of work inside and out, evidenced by what can be seen in this photograph. *Keystone-Mast Collection, University of California Riverside/California Museum of Photography*

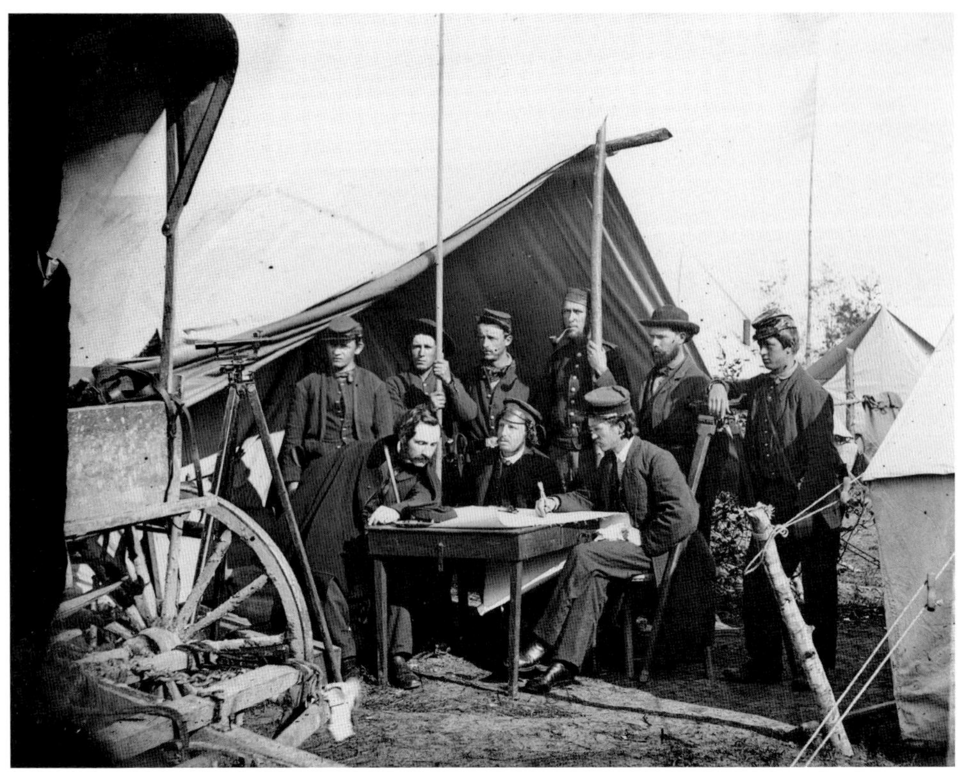

James Gibson took this picture at Camp Winfield Scott on May 2, 1862, of the topographical engineers[6] posed in front of one of their tents. Surveying instruments are set up left and right. The two men seated center and right are most likely Frederic William Dorr (1830–1893) and John Walter Donn[7] (1835–1905). The officer seated to the left is William Henry Paine (1828–1889) who invented the steel tape reel worn by the man standing (and leaning) on the survey instrument (right). Standing second from right appears to be Allan Pinkerton (1819–1884), a Scottish-American detective and spy, best known for creating the Pinkerton National Detective Agency. Donn was first assigned to duty with Brigadier General George Archibald McCall (1802–1868), who served in the Peninsula Campaign and was wounded and captured at Frayser's Farm in June 1862, operating with Dorr and Cleveland Salter Rockwell (1837–1907) in the topographical survey work required during the war. Donn later recalled that while at Fort Monroe and the Peninsula, he and the others had been put on the official staff of Major General Andrew Atkinson (1810–1883), chief topographical engineer, United States Army Corps of Engineers. "Arriving at Old Point Comfort we were directed to reconnoiter the whole country lying between the [Old] Point and Yorktown. In the meantime, the army passed on and sat down before the enemy's line of works. Having completed all the work in the rear of the army our next duty was to approach the line of Confederate works as nearly as possible and study and determine its general form, and position. The ground was traversed in this way from the York to the Warwick River and thence to the James."[8] Donn would also opine that when the Confederates evacuated Yorktown that he, Dorr and the others continued their work up the Peninsula generally in advance of the army and without escort to secure a larger measure of safety [no shooting]. After the war, Paine settled in Brooklyn and worked as a consulting engineer on many projects of the New York Bridge Company to include the Brooklyn Bridge, for which he logged fourteen patents pertaining to cable railway work, notably a cable gripping apparatus that was called the Paine grip. *Library of Congress*

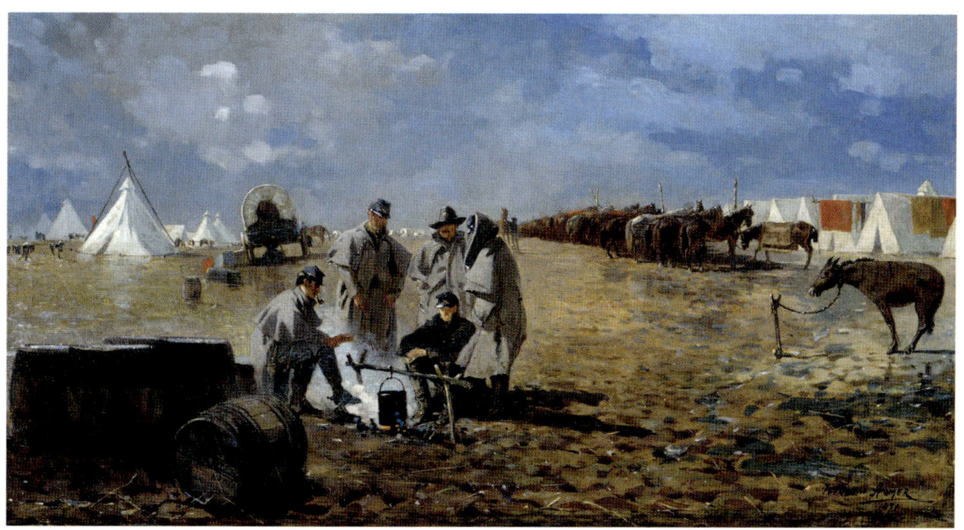

A Rainy Day in Camp [also known as *Camp near Yorktown*], painted by Winslow Homer (1836–1910), is shown here. Homer completed this painting, his last major scene of life at the front, six years after the Civil War ended, using studies he had made during the siege of Yorktown, Virginia, in April and May 1862. The red cloverleaf above Homer's name on the overturned barrel in the left foreground was the insignia of the First Division of the II Corps of the Army of the Potomac, of which the Sixty-First New York Volunteer Infantry—the unit to which the painter was assigned—was a part. One critic remarked that the bedraggled mule at the right "tells the whole story" of the miserable conditions at Yorktown. The original painting resides at the Metropolitan Museum of Art.[9]

Sergeant James Daniel Gardner [also spelled Gardiner] (1839–1905) was born in Gloucester, Virginia, where he worked as an oysterman before enlisting in the Union army from Yorktown on September 15, 1863. He joined Company I of the Thirty-Sixth Regiment United States Colored Troops as a private. At the Battle of Chaffin's Farm, on September 29, 1864, Gardner's regiment was among a division of black troops assigned to attack the Confederate defenses at New Market Heights. The defenses consisted of two lines of abatis and one of palisades manned by Brigadier General John Gregg's[10] Texas Brigade. The attack was met with intense Confederate fire and over half of the black troops were killed, wounded or captured. During the assault, Gardner advanced ahead of his unit into the Confederate fortifications and according to his Medal of Honor citation "shot a rebel officer who was on the parapet rallying his men, and then ran him through with his bayonet." The day after the battle, Gardner was

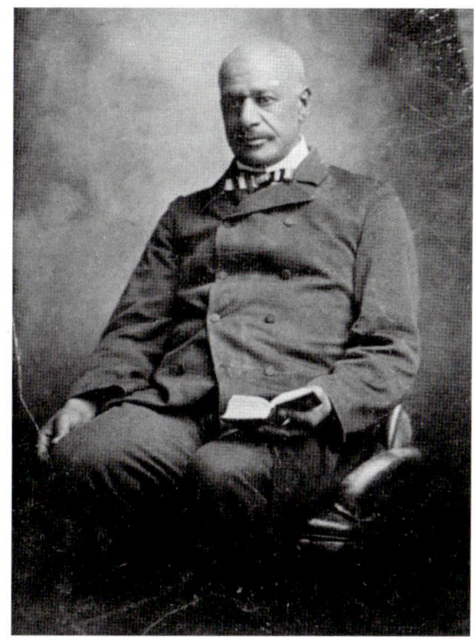

promoted to sergeant and several months later, and three days before the war ended, on April 6, 1865, he was awarded the Medal of Honor for his actions that day at the Battle of Chaffin's Farm. A memorial commemorating Gardner was unveiled on May 6, 2006, outside the Gloucester County Courthouse. The picture of Gardner shown here was taken in his later years. *Library of Congress*

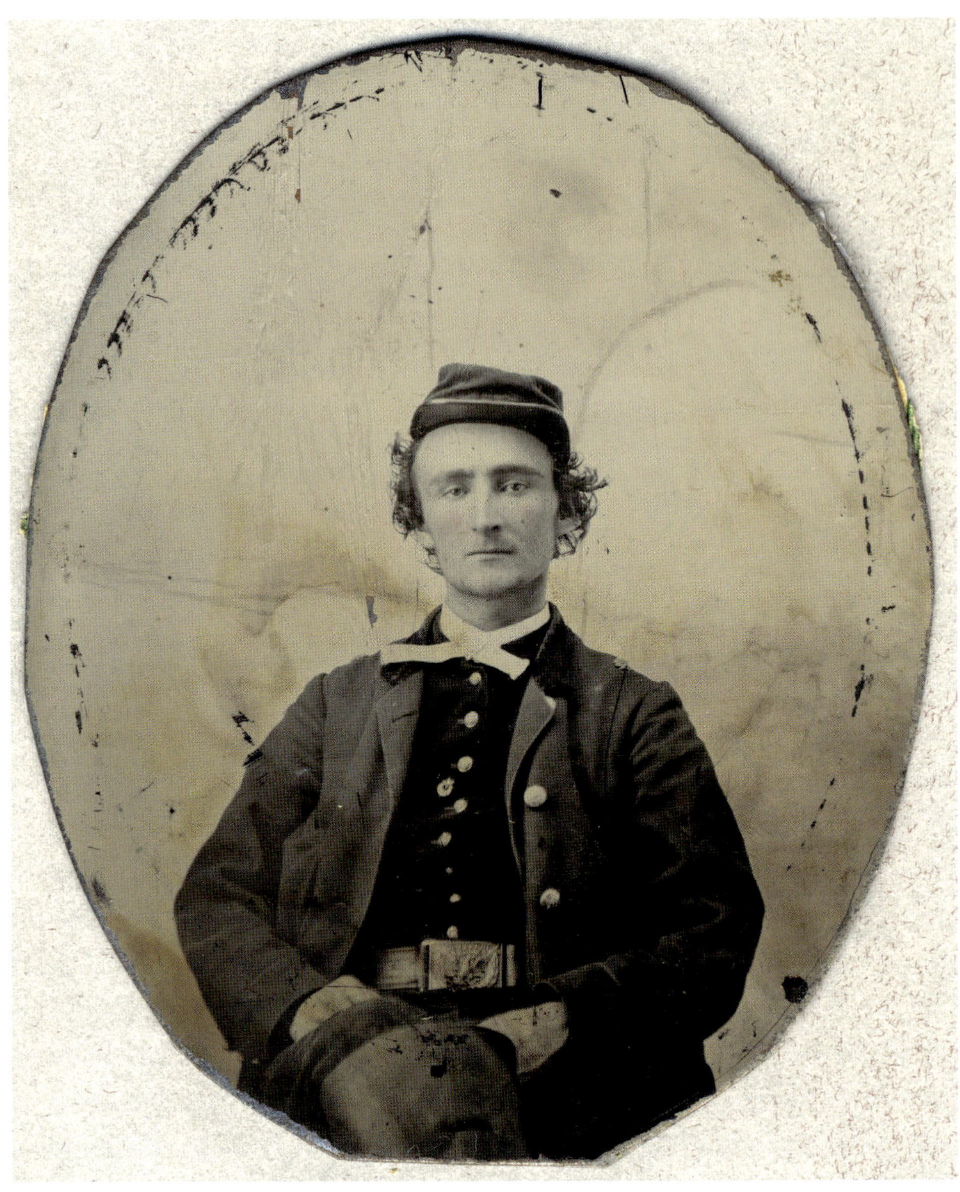

This oval tintype portrait of Ionia, Michigan native and Union major James Harvey Kidd (1840–1913) was taken at Yorktown, Virginia, in February 1864. Kidd served under Brigadier General George Armstrong Custer and was wounded three times. Custer recommended he be promoted to colonel in command of the Sixth Michigan Cavalry, and that December he led his cavalrymen in raids on the Shenandoah Valley, destroying millions of dollars of Virginians' property. He was brevetted to brigadier general on June 15, 1865, for his actions in the Shenandoah Valley and mustered out of the army on November 7 of that year. *Bentley Historical Library, University of Michigan*

ENDNOTES

1 Thomas and Elizabeth Early Pate's son Matthew married Anne Reade, paternal granddaughter of Colonel George Reade, who was a great-great-grandfather of General George Washington, the nation's first president, and his wife, the former Elizabeth de la Marteau.

2 Erickson, Mark St. John, "The Great Fire of 1814 left once-flourishing Yorktown in blackened ruins," *Daily Press*, March 1, 2014. http://www.dailypress.com/features/history/our-story/dp-the-great-fire-of-1814-left-yorktown-in-blackened-ruins-20140228-post.html

3 Cornwallis Cave, which is actually quite small, is located on Yorktown's Water Street on the York River shore.

4 There were a number of foreign citizens who became generals in the Union army: clearly, the Comte de Paris and his nephews; Irish-born Michael Corcoran (1827–1863), a brigadier general and close confidant of President Abraham Lincoln, killed at the First Battle of Bull Run; Włodzimierz Bonawentura Krzyżanowski (1824–1887), Polish-born American engineer, politician and Union army brigadier general; Irish-nationalist Thomas Francis Meagher (1823–1867), a United States Army brigadier general; Albin Francisco Schoepf (1822–1886), Polish-born Union brigadier general best known as the commanding officer of Fort Delaware, a wartime camp for Confederate prisoners of war; German-born revolutionary and an American statesman, journalist and reformer Carl Christian Schurz (1829–1906) who was a general in the Union army and later went on to represent Missouri in the United States Senate and became the thirteenth United States secretary of the Interior; Franz Sigel (1824–1902), a German military officer who became a Union major general; Philippe Régis Denis de Keredern de Trobriand (1816–1897), a French aristocrat, lawyer, poet and novelist, who came to the United States in his twenties and became a general in the Union army, and Ukrainian Ivan Vasyliovych Turchyn (1822–1901), better known as John Basil Turchin, a Union army brigadier general who led two critical charges that saved the day at Chickamauga and was among the first to lead soldiers up Missionary Ridge.

5 Robertson Jr., James I., "Notes on (Civil War) camp," *New York Times*, April 14, 2012. https://opinionator.blogs.nytimes.com/2012/04/14/notes-on-civil-war-camp/

6 Dorr, Donn and Rockwell were all appointed captains in the Union army during the war.

7 When twenty-five years of age he entered United States Coast and Geodetic Survey, and remained in its service until he died. During the Civil War, he was a member of the United States Army Corps of Engineers [Topographical Survey] and figured prominently in battles from the beginning of the war until its end.

8 National Oceanic and Atmospheric Administration (NOAA). War Record of J. W. Donn, including reminiscences of Frederic W. Dorr [July 1861 to June 1865] by John W. Donn, assistant, United States Coast Survey. http://www.history.noaa.gov/stories_tales/donn.html

9 Winslow Homer stock photo [Public domain], via Wikimedia Commons

10 John Gregg (1828–1864) was a judge, politician and brigadier general killed in action during the siege of Petersburg, Virginia, shot while leading a counterattack at the Battle of Darbytown and New Market roads. Gregg's widow, Mary Garth Gregg, traveled through the lines to retrieve his body and inter him at the Odd Fellows Cemetery in Aberdeen, Mississippi.

III

ONE CENTURY ENDS,
ANOTHER BEGINS

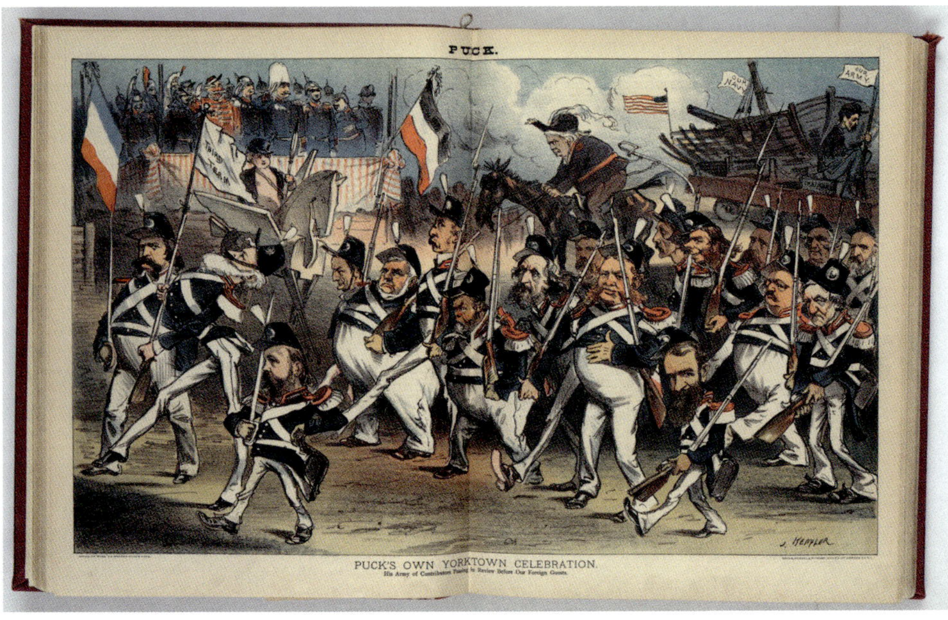

This print by artist Joseph Ferdinand Keppler (1838–1894) titled "Puck's own Yorktown celebration" shows Puck sitting on a wooden cut-out Pegasus reviewing a procession of soldiers made up of captains of business and industry, politics, the courts and the military, among whom are John Alexander Logan (1826–1886), a Union major general during the Civil War, Illinois congressman and United States senator; Roscoe Conkling (1829–1888), a New York congressman and United States senator, carrying a flag labeled "Third Term," who died before this work was published; Joseph Warren Keifer (1836–1932), an Ohio congressman and the thirtieth speaker of the United States House of Representatives, and a Union army brevetted brigadier general during the Civil War; William Maxwell Evarts (1818–1901), the twenty-seventh United States secretary of state and former attorney general and also a United States senator from New York; David Davis (1815–1886), a United States senator from Illinois (1877–1883) who was president pro tempore of the United States Senate (1881–1883), and associate justice of the Supreme Court of the United States (1862–1877); James Gordon Bennett Jr. (1841–1918), publisher of the *New York Herald*, who staged both the first polo match and the first tennis match in the United States, and also sponsored significant exploration around the globe; *Continued on next page*

John Kelly (1822–1886), of New York City, a congressman before Civil War and significantly a boss of Tammany Hall whose control of the same determined the course of the city's elections for a decade; Cyrus West Field (1918–1892), businessman and financier, who with other entrepreneurs created the Atlantic Telegraph Company and laid the first telegraph cable across the Atlantic Ocean three years before the Civil War; William Henry Vanderbilt (1821–1885), businessman and philanthropist—and the richest American after he took over his father's fortune in 1877; Jay Gould (1836–1892), a leading American railroad developer and speculator, one of the richest men of the Gilded Age; Samuel Jones Tilden (1814–1886), the twenty-fifth governor of New York and lawyer; Benjamin Franklin Butler (1818–1893), Civil War Union major general, lawyer and businessman who also served as a Massachusetts congressman and the thirty-third governor of that state; Reverend Thomas De Witt Talmage D.D. (1832–1902), preacher and divine equaled as a pulpit orator only by Reverend Henry Ward Beecher (1813–1887), the great abolitionist, shown here riding on horseback. Following the soldiers, in the background on the right, is a float showing an old soldier labeled "Our Army" and a decrepit ship labeled "Our Navy." In the background (left) is a reviewing stand for foreign guests with a French flag on one side and a German flag on the other. The work was published for the centennial of the American victory at Yorktown by Joseph Ferdinand Keppler and Adolph Schwarzmann (1838–1904), who started the English version of *Puck* in New York four years before this print was published on October 19, 1881. *Library of Congress*

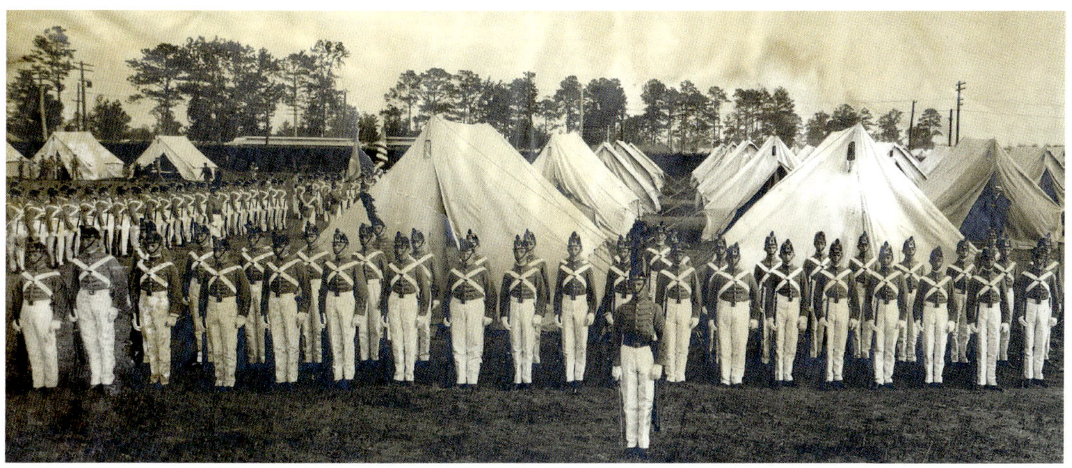

The Virginia Military Institute (VMI) Corps of Cadets participated in the Yorktown centennial celebration (shown here) on October 20, 1881. This photograph shows their encampment. *Virginia Military Institute*

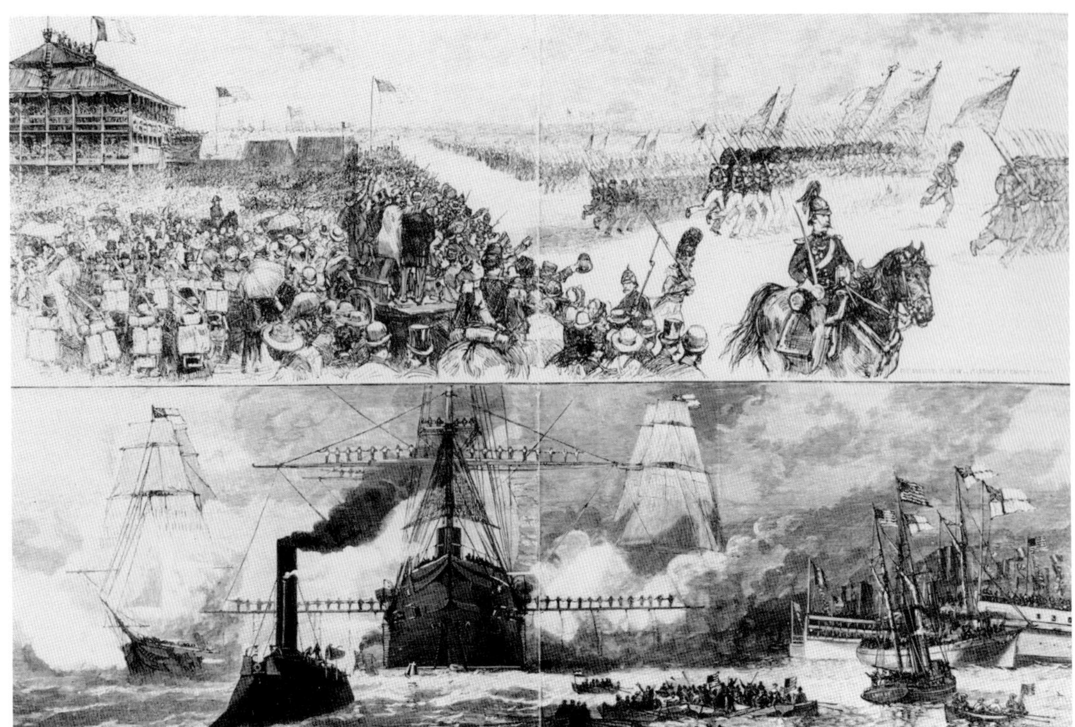

The Yorktown centennial events, showing military and naval reviews, is depicted in this line engraving after sketches by artist Julian Oliver Davidson (1853–1894), published in the October 29, 1881 *Harper's Weekly*. The military review, shown in the upper engraving, took place on October 20, with the naval review (lower scene) on the following day. In the naval review engraving, USS *Alarm* [1873], an experimental torpedo boat, is the vessel in the left center foreground. USS *Tennessee* [1865], a screw frigate, is in the center, with her yards and boat booms manned, and her guns saluting the British flag. The small civilian steamer *Lookout* belonging to Thomas Barker Ferguson (1841–1922), the Maryland commissioner of fisheries just then, and used by the United States Commission of Fish and Fisheries from 1878, is in the right foreground. *Naval History and Heritage Command*

Opposite page:

The commemoration of the American victory at Yorktown heralding the nation's independence was a nationally celebrated event. As illustration, a centennial banquet was held by the Chamber of Commerce of the State of New York at the world-famous New York City restaurant Delmonico's on November 5, 1881, in honor of "the guests of the nation." The souvenirs from that evening include a paper broadside and a silk mounted menu illustrated with the chamber of commerce's seal, a train and sailing ship made suitable for hanging. *New York Public Library*

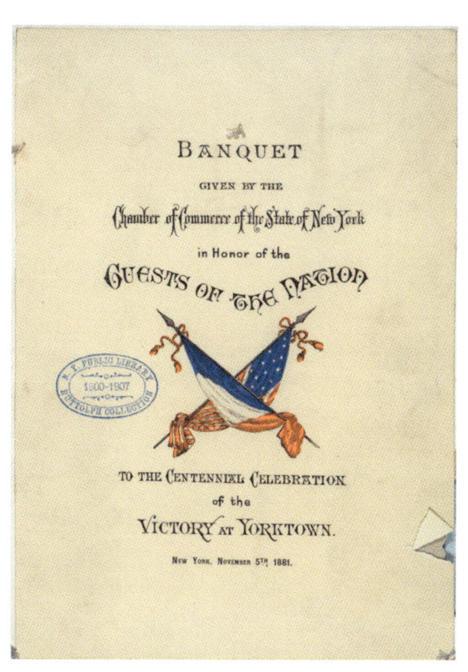
BANQUET
GIVEN BY THE
Chamber of Commerce of the State of New York
in Honor of the
GUESTS OF THE NATION
TO THE CENTENNIAL CELEBRATION
of the
VICTORY AT YORKTOWN.
NEW YORK, NOVEMBER 5TH 1881.

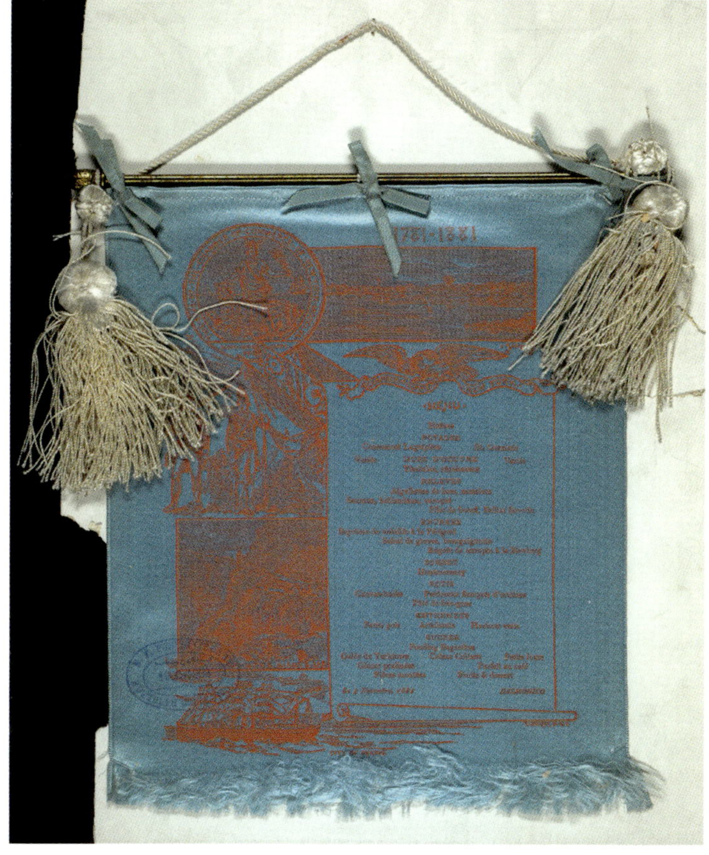

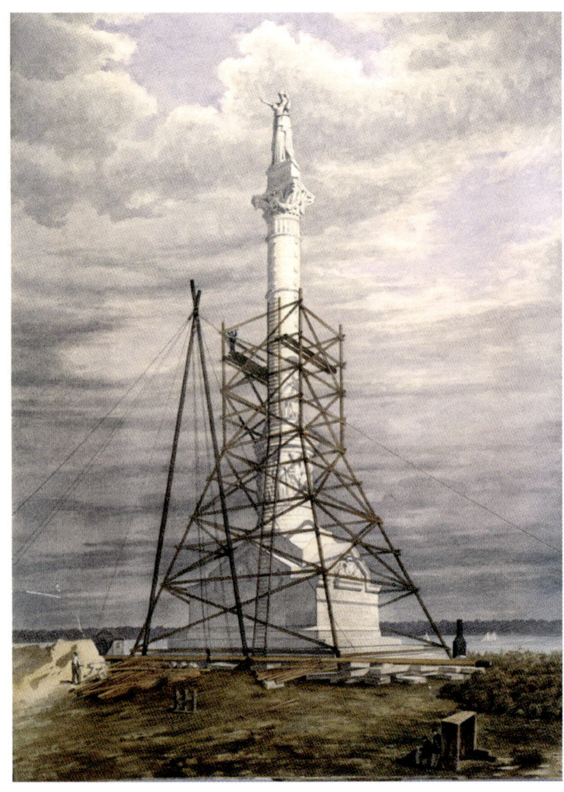

The Alliance and Victory Monument [hereafter the Yorktown Victory Monument] was designed by New York architect Richard Morris Hunt (1828–1895) in partnership with architect Henry Van Brunt (1832–1903) and sculptor John Quincy Adams Ward (1830–1910). The monument was nearing completion when the architects made this original architectural drawing in 1884, a watercolor on paper showing scaffolding in place. *Library of Congress*

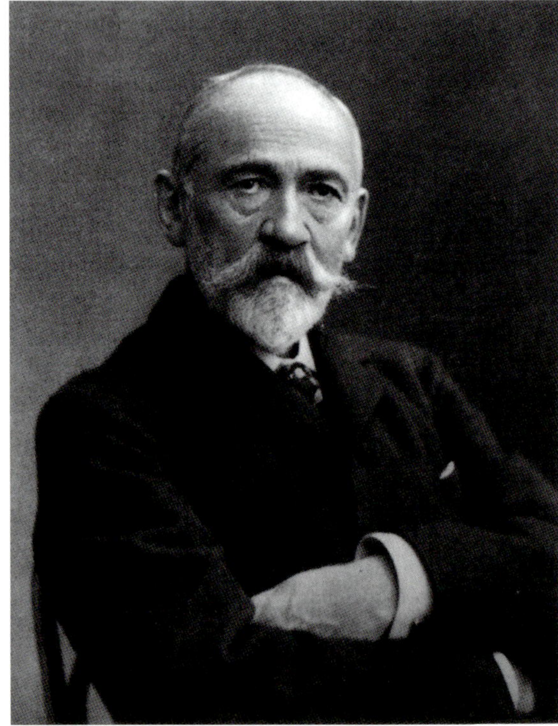

Sculptor John Quincy Adams Ward is shown in this photograph, taken in or about 1900. Ward's nineteenth century commissions for sculpture were largely limited to portrait busts and monuments—he excelled at both. *Archives of American Art*[1]

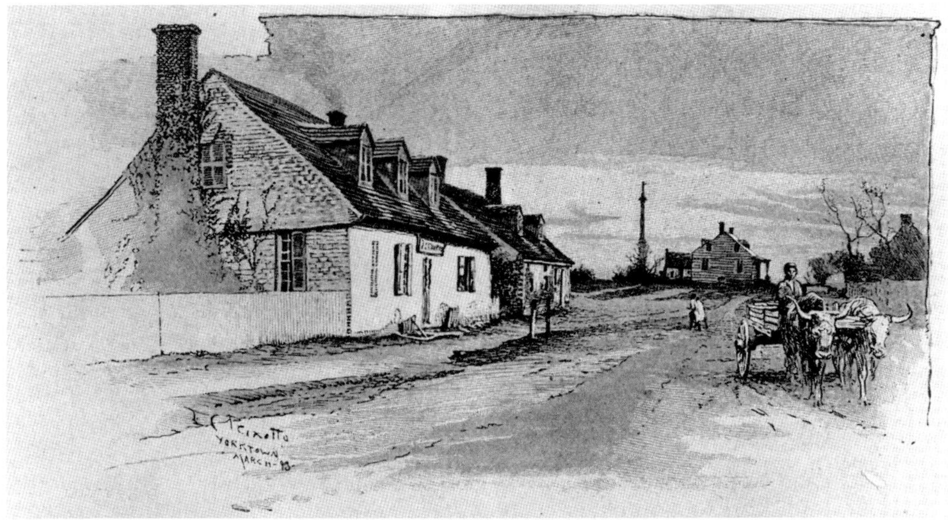

Main Street—principal street in Yorktown—is shown in this drawing by San Francisco native Ernest Clifford Peixotto (1869–1940), an artist, illustrator and author. The artwork is dated March 1893. In the distance is the monument constructed between 1881 and 1884 to commemorate the British surrender. Though known largely for his murals and also his travel literature, Peixotto's artwork regularly appeared in *Scribner's Magazine*. During the First World War, Peixotto served as a captain in the United States Army Corps of Engineers as an artist attached to the headquarters. Nearly one-and-a-half years after his death, he was buried in Arlington National Cemetery. *Naval History and Heritage Command*

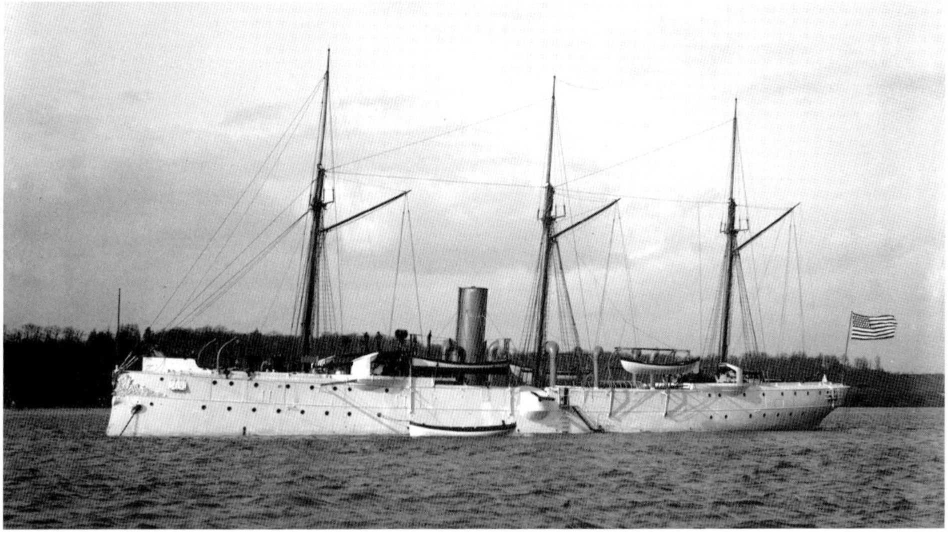

A Detroit Publishing Company photographer took this picture of the USS *Yorktown* (PG-1) in 1901. This second *Yorktown* was a steel-hulled, twin-screw gunboat laid down on May 14, 1887, at Philadelphia, Pennsylvania, by the William Cramp and Sons shipyard. The *Yorktown* was commissioned at the League Island [Philadelphia] Navy Yard on April 23, 1889; Commander French Ensor Chadwick (1844–1919)[2] was in command. The ship became the second naval vessel to be named for the town in Virginia where the climactic battle of the American Revolution was fought in the fall of 1781. *Yorktown* was placed out of commission at Mare Island on June 12, 1919. *Library of Congress*

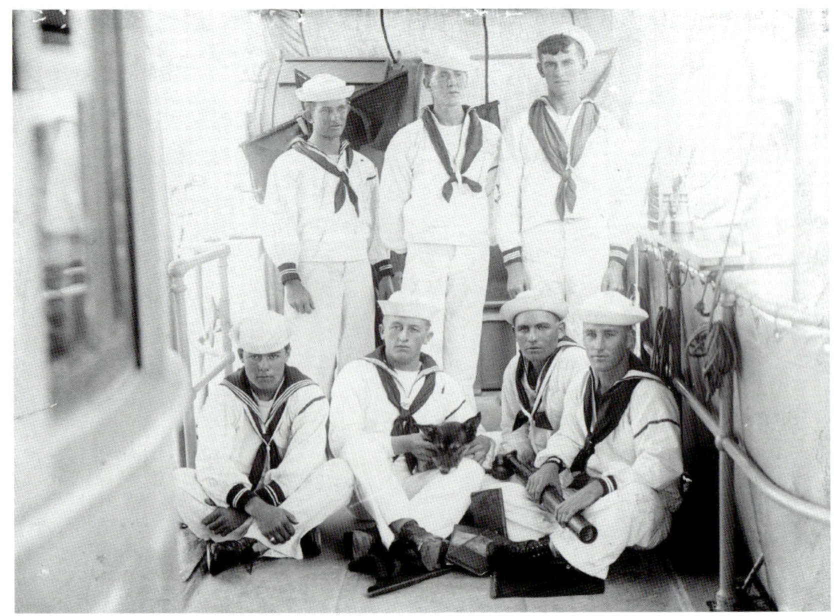

Ship's signal boys and quartermasters of the United States Navy's USS *Yorktown* (PG-1) are shown in this 1902 photograph. Abraham DeSomer (1884–1974), an enlisted man and later an officer [a lieutenant commander] in the United States Navy, is seated left in the bottom row. DeSomer received the nation's highest military decoration—the Medal of Honor—for actions during the American intervention at Veracruz, Mexico. He was on his initial sea duty on board *Yorktown* when the picture was taken. *Naval History and Heritage Command*

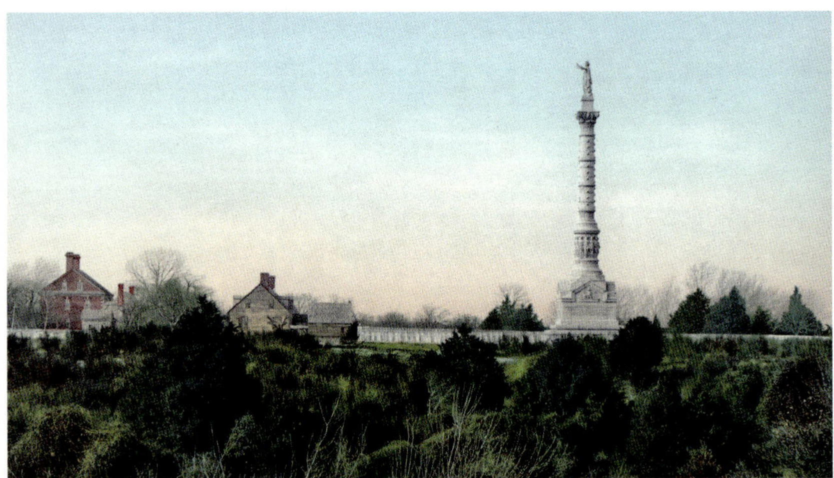

The Detroit Publishing Company published this photochrom image of the Yorktown Victory Monument in 1902. The Yorktown Victory Monument—commemorating the victory, the alliance with France that brought it about, and the resulting peace with Great Britain after the war—is located just outside the modern-day Yorktown. The monument was originally topped by a figure of Liberty sculpted by John Quincy Adams Ward (shown clearly here) but it was destroyed by lightning in 1942 and replaced in 1957 by sculptor Oskar Johan Waldemar Hansen. *Library of Congress*

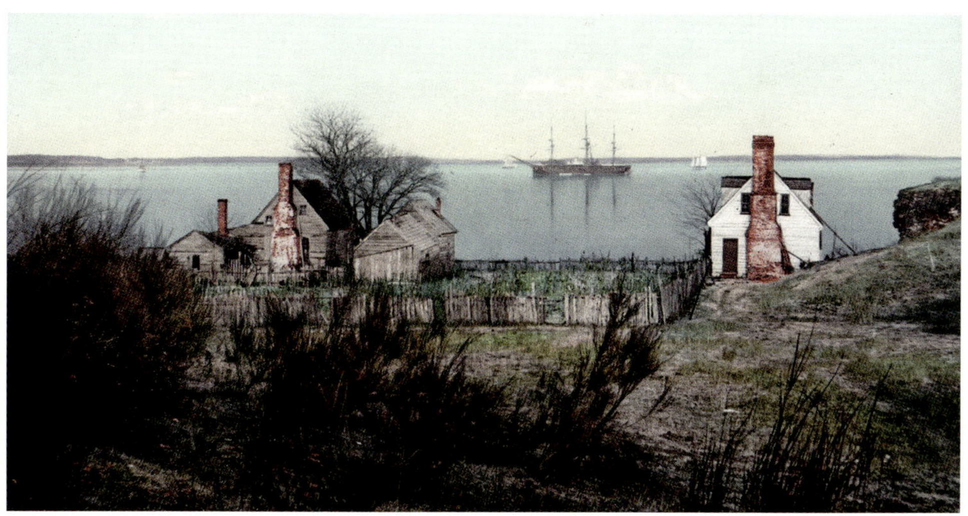

In 1903, a Detroit Publishing Company photographer took this picture of the Yorktown harbor, which was then made into a photochrom. The William Rogers House [later the DeNeufville House] is on the right. Rogers, a potter who set up his own pottery factory, lived in the house from in or around 1711. The fact that Rogers was making pottery at Yorktown was a break from British law that prohibited such practice, rather it insisted colonists purchase goods imported from England. The Rogers factory was supported by the royal governor of Virginia, who always referred to him as the "poor potter from Yorktown" so he would not be perceived as a threat to the imported English pottery business. Yet contrary to this description, Rogers was far from poor. He was making quality pottery on an industrial scale. The Rogers pottery was in operation from 1711 to 1760, as Colonial National Historical Park records indicate, long after Rogers' death in 1739. The original factory was found during an archeological dig in 1966 one block off Main Street near the Nelson House. *Library of Congress*

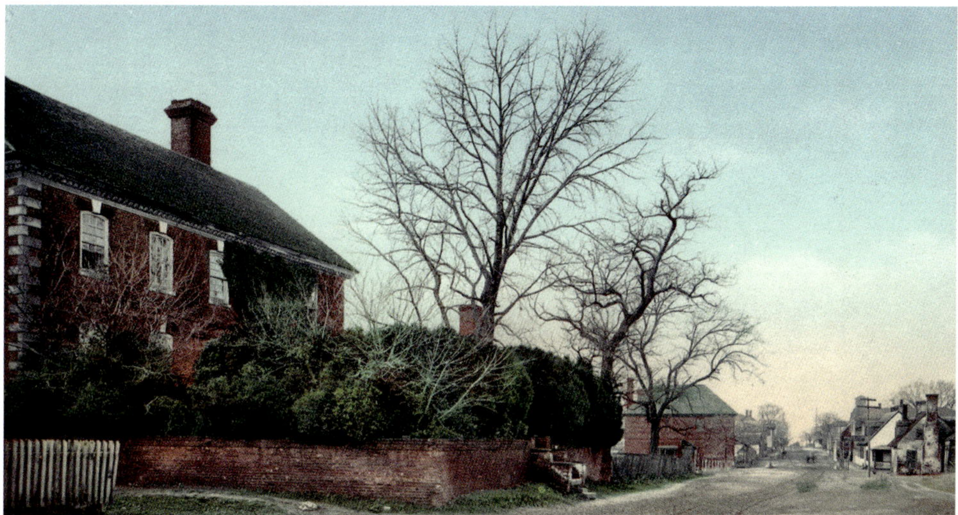

The Thomas Nelson House [later bought by Captain George Preston and Adele Matthiessen Blow] (left) and Main Street is shown in this Detroit Publishing Company photochrom, also taken in 1902. The home, famously also called York Hall, was just six years from passing out of Nelson family ownership. The custom house is visible (left) just beyond the house. *Library of Congress*

The cornerstone of the Yorktown Victory Monument was laid by "the order of the Ancient Free and accepted Masons" on October 18, 1881, "as the appropriate opening" for the Yorktown centennial celebration. The monument was erected using Hallowell Maine granite in its shaft, according to the design of the commissioned artists who followed the directions relative to emblems, inscriptions and symbols. The design of the monument included all of the elements originally specified by Congress in 1781 and repeated in 1880. An official report outlined these elements. The base carries an inscription on each of its four sides: one dedicates the monument as a memorial of victory; a second presents a succinct narrative of the first siege; a third commemorates the treaty of alliance with France, and the fourth tells of the resulting treaty of peace with England. The pediments, just over the inscriptions, carry emblems of nationality, war, the alliance

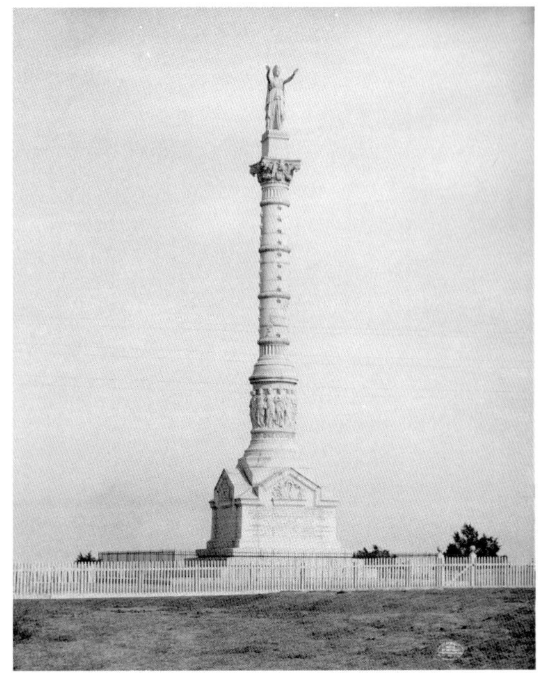

and peace. The podium is a symbol of the birth of freedom that carries thirteen female figures hand in hand in a solemn dance to denote the unity of the thirteen colonies. Beneath their feet is the inscription "One country, one constitution, one destiny." William Henry Jackson (1843–1942) took this picture of the Yorktown Victory Monument in 1903 for the Detroit Publishing Company. *Library of Congress*

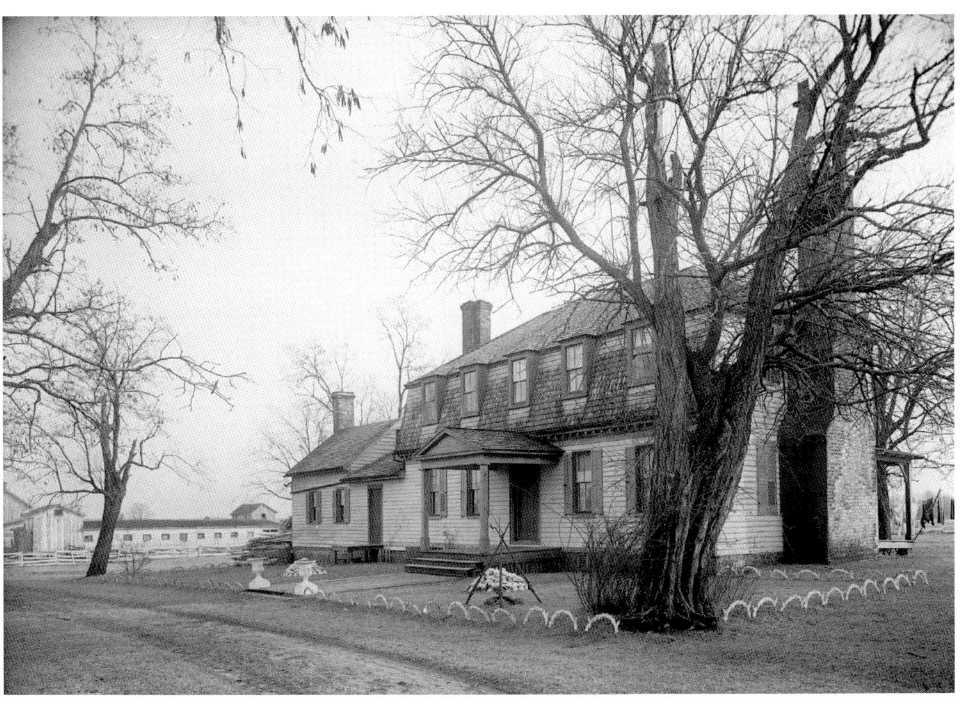

Opposite below: The Augustine Moore House, scene of the Articles of Capitulation that marked Lord Cornwallis' surrender to George Washington, was photographed by William Henry Jackson in 1903 for the Detroit Publishing Company. The house was refurbished just enough to house dignitaries during the centennial events. *Library of Congress*

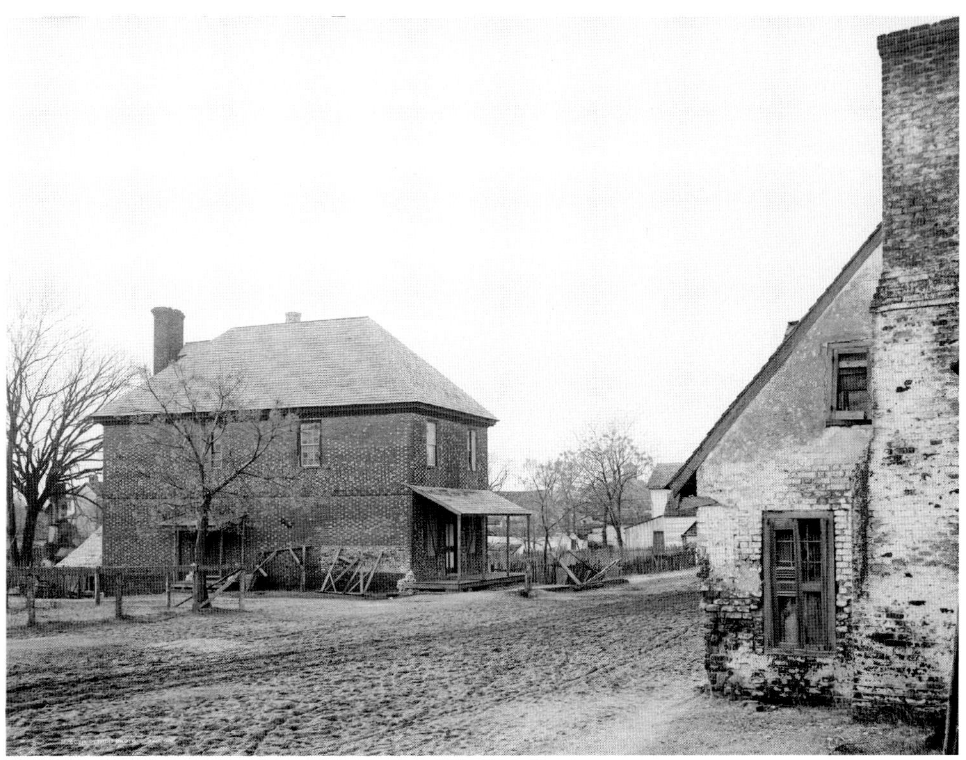

The first custom house in the United States (left), built in 1721 at Yorktown—just then the largest deep-water port between Charleston, South Carolina, and Philadelphia, Pennsylvania—by Richard Ambler (1690–1765), a merchant and one of the wealthiest men in Virginia, was actually a storehouse for goods. Ambler was the collector of import/export taxes for the port. The Colonial National Historical Park narrative indicates that it was used as a barracks at the beginning of the Revolutionary War. In 1778, it was sold by Ambler's wife, the former Elizabeth Jacquelin (1709–1756), to Thomas Wyld, who used it as an inn and storehouse until the fighting started at Yorktown. The British took it over as a barracks. After the English surrender, the French also used it as a barracks. In 1783, the Amblers regained the building in a lawsuit with Wyld, who had never paid for it in full. The Amblers had built a wooden house connected to the custom house, and this survived until the Civil War, when it burned down. After the war, it was sold to Daniel M. Norton [later McNorton] (1843–1918), a former slave-turned-physician, who used it as his medical office. His patients were also former slaves who settled in Slabtown, an area near Yorktown National Cemetery. Adele Matthiessen Blow bought the building in 1922 from McNorton's heirs and two years later it was restored by the Comte de Grasse Chapter of the Daughters of the American Revolution (DAR) under the leadership of Emma Leake Chenoweth (1861–1951). On October 24, 1924, the building was formally dedicated as the chapter's meeting house to include a museum documenting the building's and Yorktown's early history. William Henry Jackson took this photograph of the custom house for the Detroit Publishing Company between 1900 and 1906. *Library of Congress*

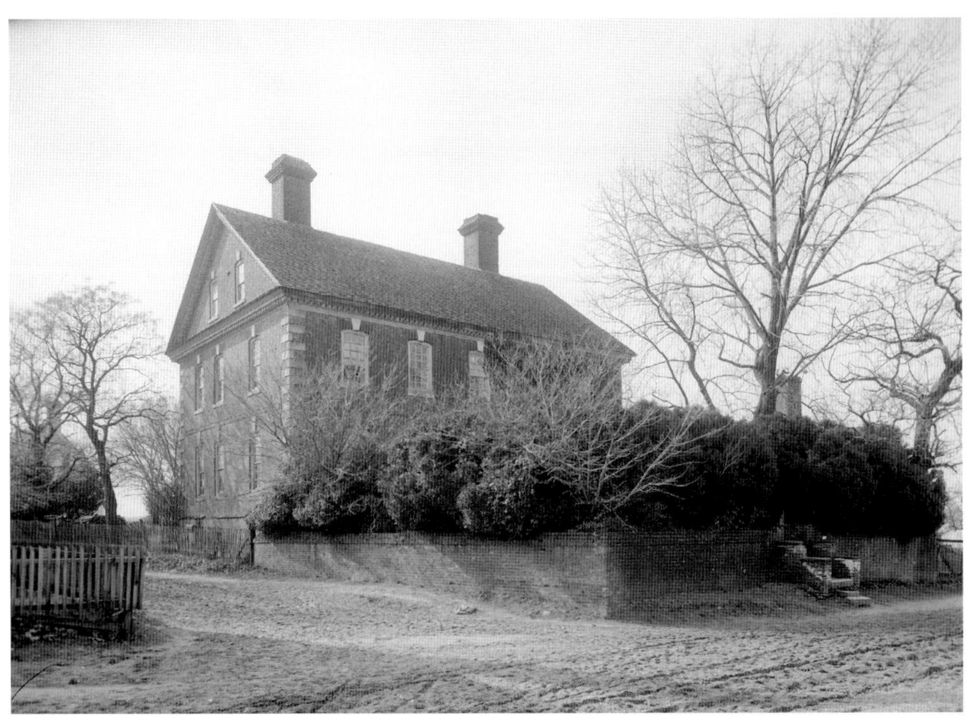

William Henry Jackson took this picture of the Thomas Nelson House between 1900 and 1906 for the Detroit Publishing Company. *Library of Congress*

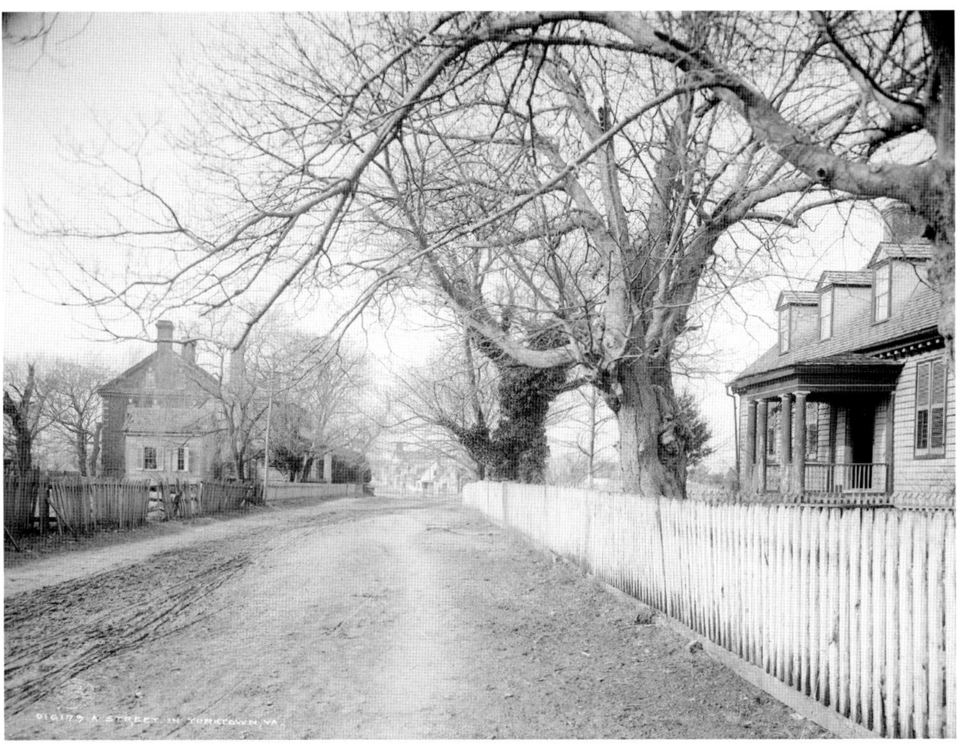

Opposite below: This photograph Yorktown's Main Street was taken by William Henry Jackson for Detroit Publishing Company in 1903. The Thomas Nelson and Sessions-Pope-Sheild houses [corner of Nelson and Main streets] are on the left. The Dudley Digges House [also called the West House] is visible in the foreground (right). Dudley Digges built this stately home in or about 1760 but it was damaged during the Revolutionary War siege of Yorktown and Digges moved to Williamsburg, where he died three decades later. The Dudley Digges House was restored in 1960 and all outbuildings now on the property were reconstructed by the National Park Service a decade later. The building is not open to the public but instead provides office space for the park service. *Library of Congress*

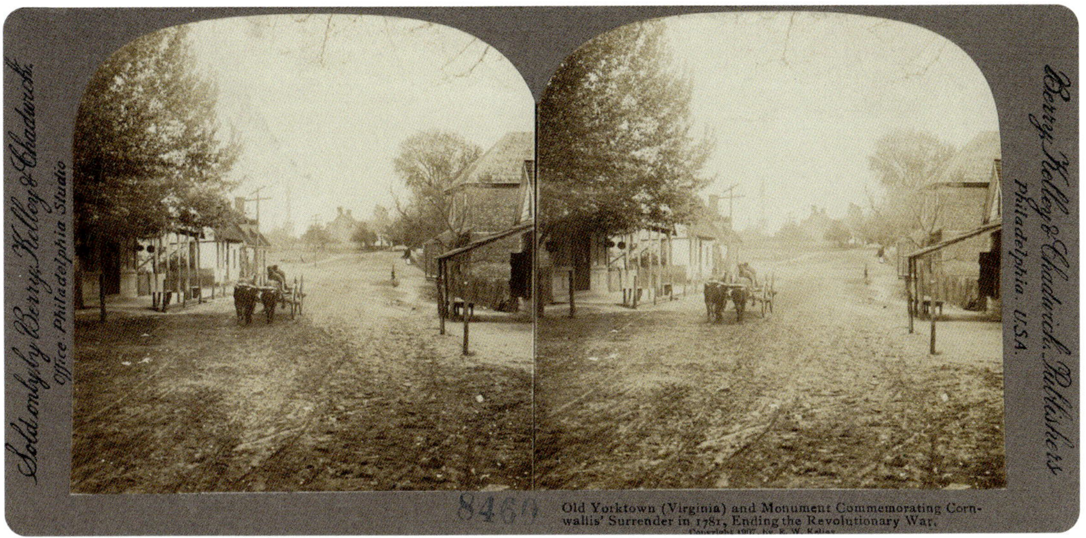

This picture of Yorktown's Main Street, taken in or about 1907, includes the Yorktown Victory Monument visible in the background (left). The brick custom house is on the right. The stereoview was published by Berry, Kelley and Chadwick, an early twentieth-century prolific publisher and retailer of stereoviews with locations in Philadelphia, Chicago, Dallas, and Atlanta. *Library of Congress*

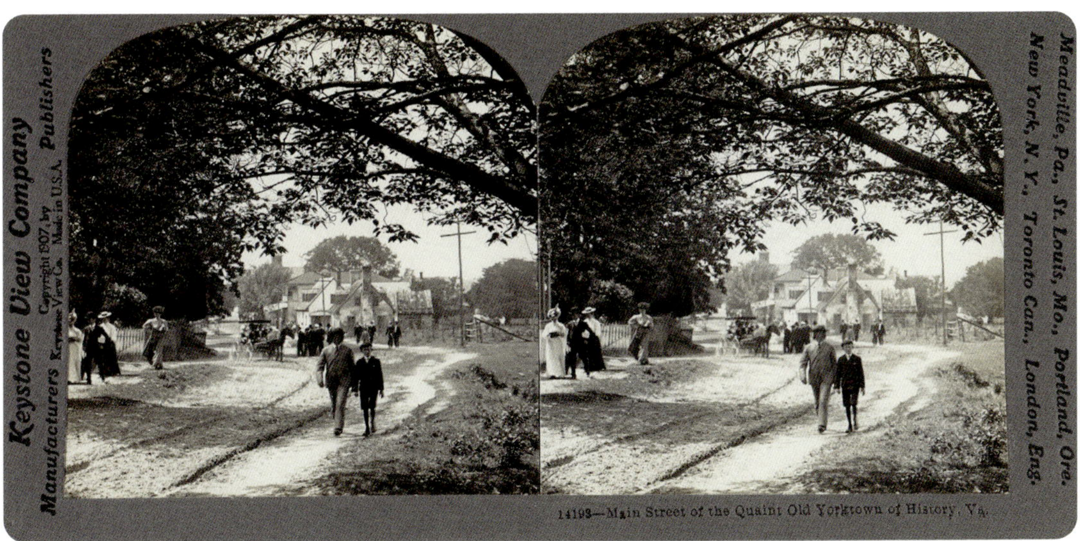

The Keystone View Company published this stereoview of Yorktown's Main Street in 1907. *Library of Congress*

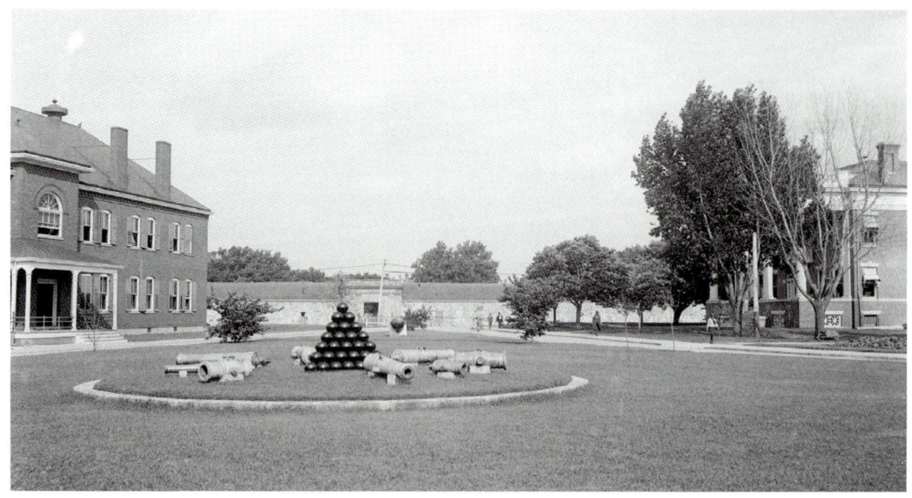

A Detroit Publishing Company photographer took this picture in 1908 of trophies captured from Lord Cornwallis at Yorktown in 1781, located at Fort Monroe's trophy park, which once occupied the southwest corner of the parade ground. Within the three angles of this park were three ten-inch siege mortars, each flanked by triangular piles of mortar shells. In the center was a brass mortar, which was originally used for firing stone, by having them placed in a basket prepared for this purpose. The use of the latter weapon had long since been abolished when this piece was put on display in the park. Surrounding this, on all sides, were rows of ten-inch mortar shells, and above these, a row of projectiles for the eight-inch rifle. The trophies consisted of three howitzers, manufactured respectively in 1829, 1740 and 1677: each having two handles, the handles of two of them being dolphins, and the third plain; two siege pieces, manufactured respectively in 1759 and 1767, the first of which bore a coat of arms with the inscription: "The Right Hon. George Sackville, Lt. General, and the rest, of the principal officers in His Majesty's Ordnance," and each having the dolphin handles like those aforementioned; two field pieces, one about three inches, and the other four inches in diameter. In addition to the mentioned inscription, each trophy had the English coat of arms and the following additional inscription [added after the British defeat]: "Surrendered at the Capitulation of Yorktown, Oct. 19, 1781."[3] Of note, this park existed until the Second World War when much of the artillery was turned to scrap. *Library of Congress*

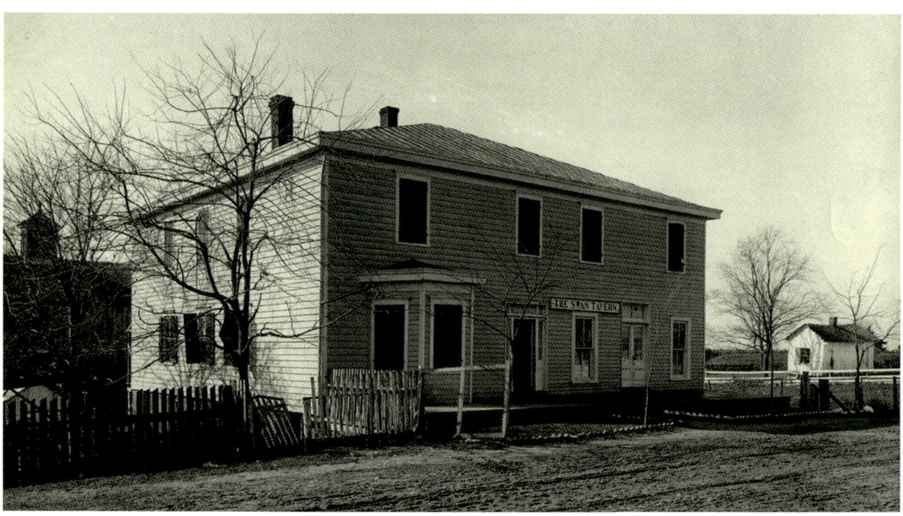

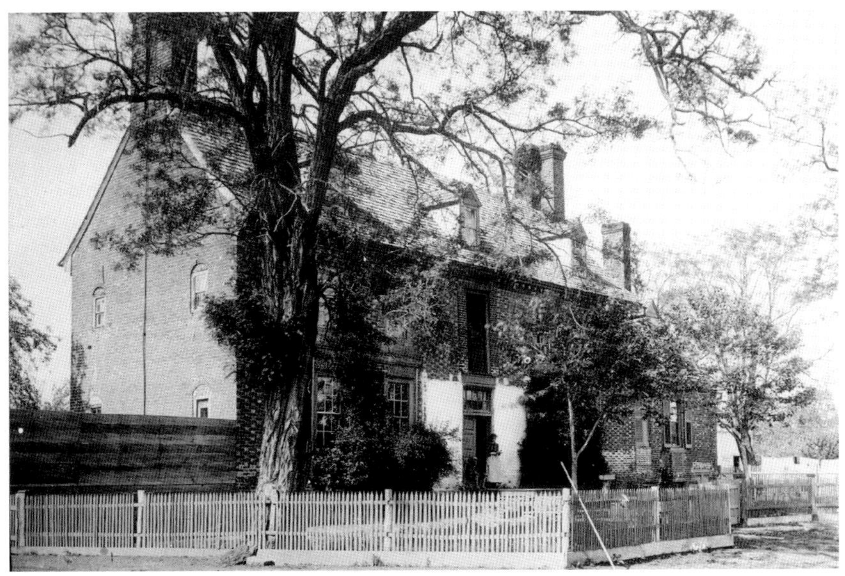

The seat of Ringfield Plantation on King Creek is located just off the Colonial Parkway some six miles out of Yorktown. Although it is within the confines of Naval Weapons Station Yorktown, the area is controlled by Colonial National Historical Park under the terms of a special use permit from the Department of the Navy. The parkway separates the grounds from the main body of the station as it does to much of the colonial glebe land tract for old Hampton Parish in York County. The land across this creek was first granted to Captain Robert Felgate (1578–1644) in 1630. Sixty years later it was acquired by Joseph Ring (1646–1703), a prosperous planter and one of the trustees of the Town of York when it was founded in 1691. Ring's plantation house stood for over two centuries approximately one mile to the west. The story of the Ringfield area covers a two-hundred-year span from frontier, through settlement and development into the plantation economy, then reversion to general nineteenth century farming, and finally into a sort of quiet sanctuary status in the property's later years. The house was built after 1692 and before 1698, and stood as a veritable landmark until it burned over two hundred years later. This picture of the Ringfield Plantation house was taken in or about 1910, and included in a later Historic American Buildings Survey (HABS). At the time of the fire, it had become the residence of the first inspector of ordnance in charge at the naval station. On October 5, 1920, the house was vacated when the officer moved to new quarters built at Indian Field. Two months later, on December 14, 1920, Joseph Ring's old house was destroyed by fire of incendiary nature. Thomas Tileston Waterman (1900–1951), in his annual HABS report for 1940 wrote: "Some writers claim that the house, Ringfield, was built in the middle of the seventeenth century. A photograph, however, taken before the fire shows a building that would appear to belong to the period of [about] 1700 rather than any earlier, though it might be later." When the elder Joseph Ring died in 1702/3 and left a particularly valuable estate behind, the trustees were recorded as Captain Matthew Page of Rosewell, and Edmund Bartlett [sometimes called Berkeley]. The size of Ring's fortune and his important family connections—his wife being a Mann of Timberneck Hall—suggest that he would have built a new house at the time he acquired the property. The two-story house, built of Flemish bond brick and shown in the picture, Waterman noted, would have been one of great importance of its period. "There seem to have been very few two-story houses such as Ringfield in the period up to 1725," observed Waterman, "either in brick or wood." *Library of Congress*

Opposite below: Harry Cowles Mann (1866–1926) took this photograph of the Swan Tavern in or about 1910. This is not the building that is the better-known Swan Tavern on Main Street across from the courthouse, a building that burned during the Civil War siege of Yorktown and that was not rebuilt until 1930, well after Mann took this photograph. *Amy Waters Yarsinske*

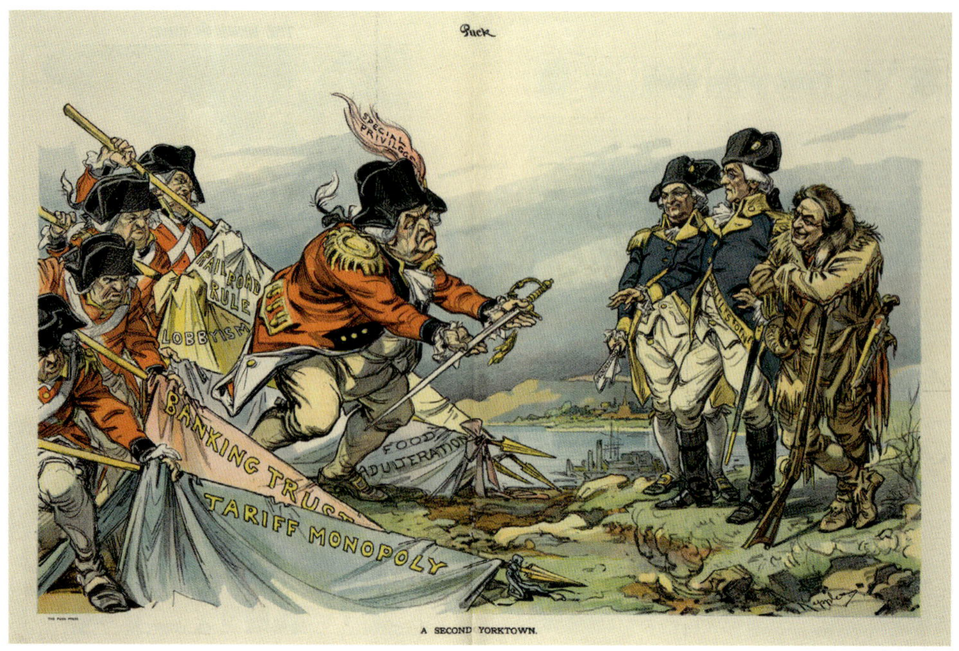

Titled "A Second Yorktown," this illustration published by the firm first established by Joseph Ferdinand Keppler and Adolph Schwarzmann [Keppler and Schwarzmann] in the February 21, 1914 *Puck*, shows a scene reminiscent of the surrender at Yorktown, a man portraying Lord Cornwallis labeled "Special Privilege" is shown offering his sword to President Woodrow Wilson (1856–1924) portraying George Washington, with William Jennings Bryan (1860–1925) on the right and Oscar Wilder Underwood (1862–1929) on the left. Standing behind the British officer are soldiers laying down their standards labeled "Monopoly," "Tariff," "Banking," "Food Adulteration," "Lobbyism," and "Rail Road Rule." The artist of this piece was Udo Joseph Keppler (1872–1956). *Library of Congress*

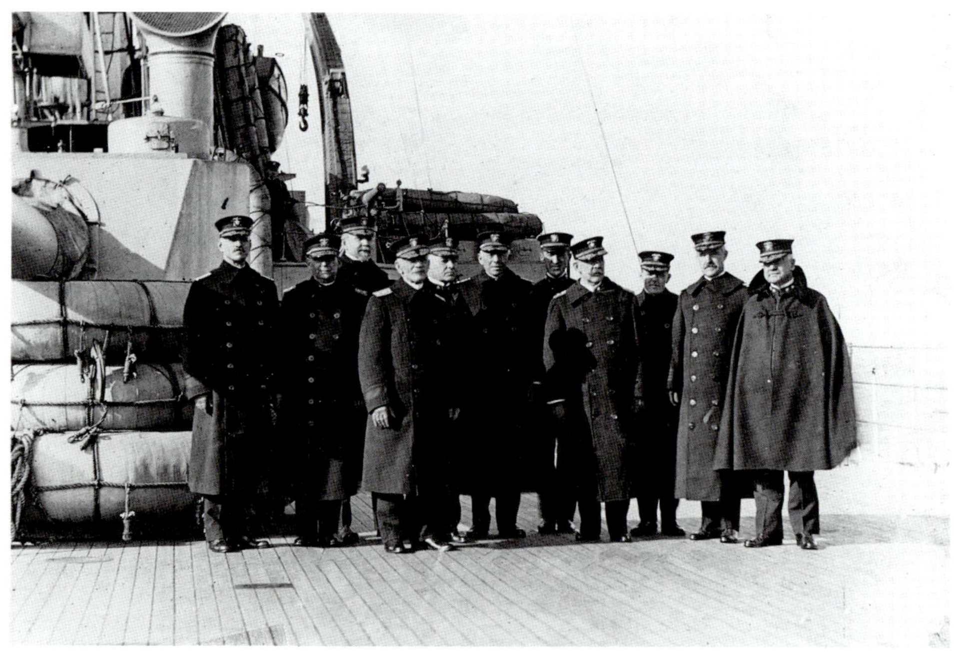

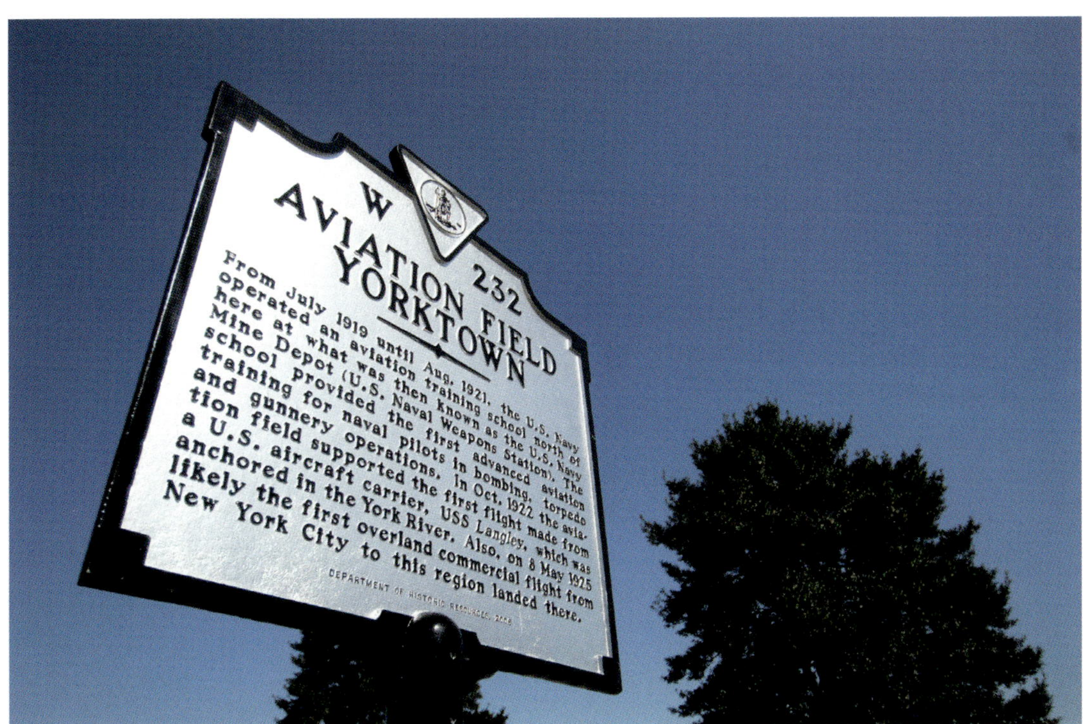

A historical marker for Aviation Field Yorktown was unveiled on October 3, 2006, during a dedication ceremony, sponsored by the Virginia Aeronautical Historical Society in Yorktown. The historic navy airfield was located there from July 1919 to August 1921, and supported the first flight made from the aircraft carrier USS *Langley* (CV-1). The picture shown here was taken by navy mass communication specialist seaman Mandy McLaurin. *United States Navy*

Opposite below: (Left to right) Rear Admirals Guy Hamilton Burrage (1867–1954), Clarence Stewart Williams (1863–1951), Carlo Bonaparte Brittain (1867–1920), William Alexander Marshall (1849–1926), William Rawle Shoemaker, and John Adrian Hoogewerff (1860–1933), and Commander Neil Ernst Nichols (1879–1943), Commodore Harry Phelps (1861–1919), Commander Allan Shannon Farquhar (1884–1966), Captain George Ralph Marvell (1869–1941), and Rear Admiral Thomas Washington (1865–1954) are shown in this December 1918 photograph taken at Yorktown, Virginia.[4] *Naval History and Heritage Command*

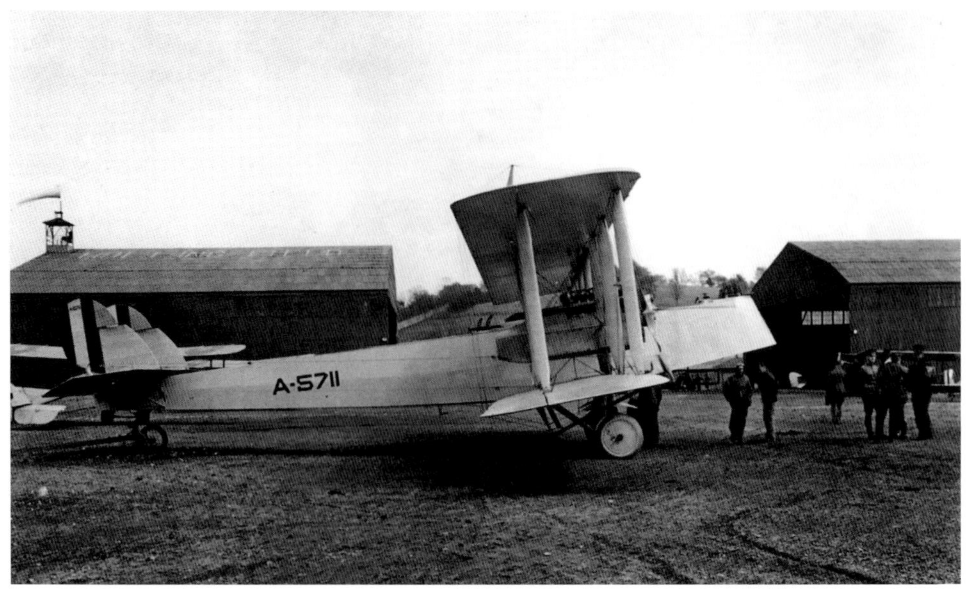

A Martin Bomber-Torpedo (MBT) [bureau number A5711], the first of two Martin bombers [the other was bureau number A5712] in this configuration procured by the navy, is pictured on the ground, probably at Marine Flying Field Quantico, Virginia. This aircraft was completed on January 9, 1920, and accepted by the navy on February 19, 1920. The aircraft was first assigned to Naval Air Station Anacostia in Washington, D.C., on April 23, 1920, and it was transferred to Yorktown, Virginia, on September 28, of that year. The aircraft's final assignment was Marine Flying Field Quantico, where it served from September 26, 1921, until December 28, 1922, when, on that day, it suffered a Lougerou crack that was determined beyond repair. The aircraft was stricken from the navy aircraft record on February 3, 1923. The navy bought eight improved versions of the MBT—the Martin Torpedo (MT)— designated bureau numbers A5713 to A5720. The latter eight aircraft were later redesignated TM-1s. *National Naval Aviation Museum*

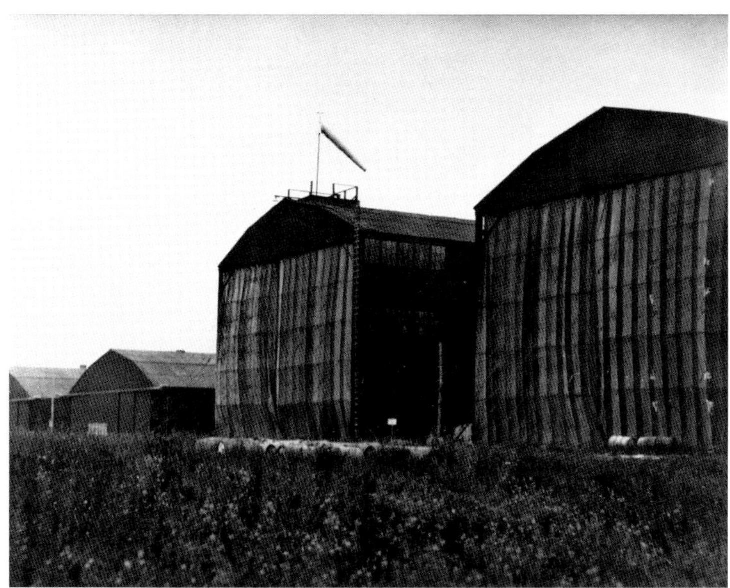

This close-up of the two large hangars at the aviation training school on the Navy Mine Depot Yorktown was taken in or about 1919. The hangars were originally designed to accommodate kite balloons. *Naval History and Heritage Command*

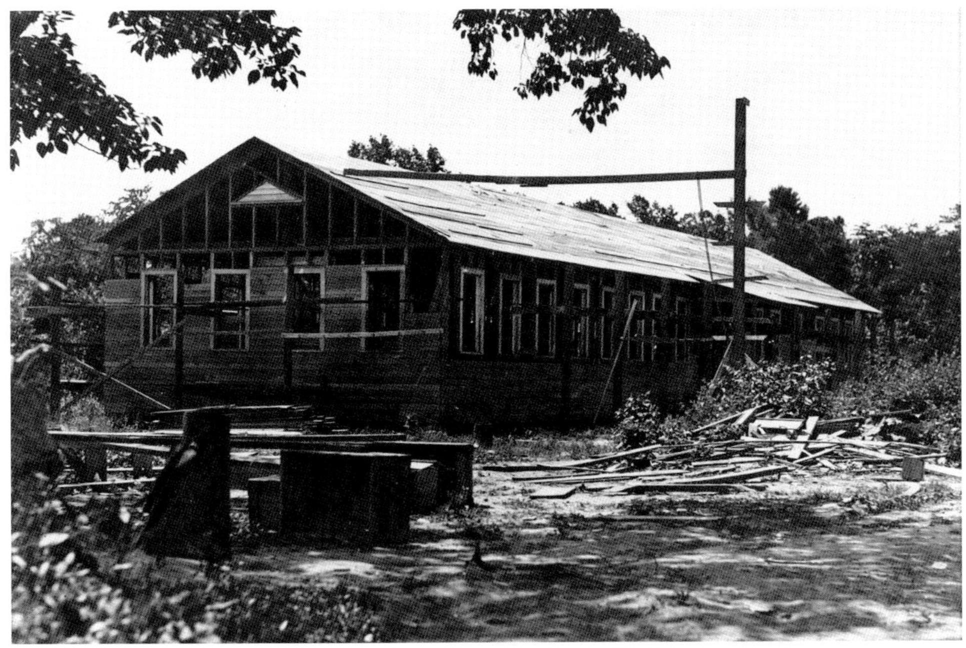

Buildings at the aviation training school, located at the Navy Mine Depot Yorktown are shown in this photograph taken in or about 1919. *Naval History and Heritage Command*

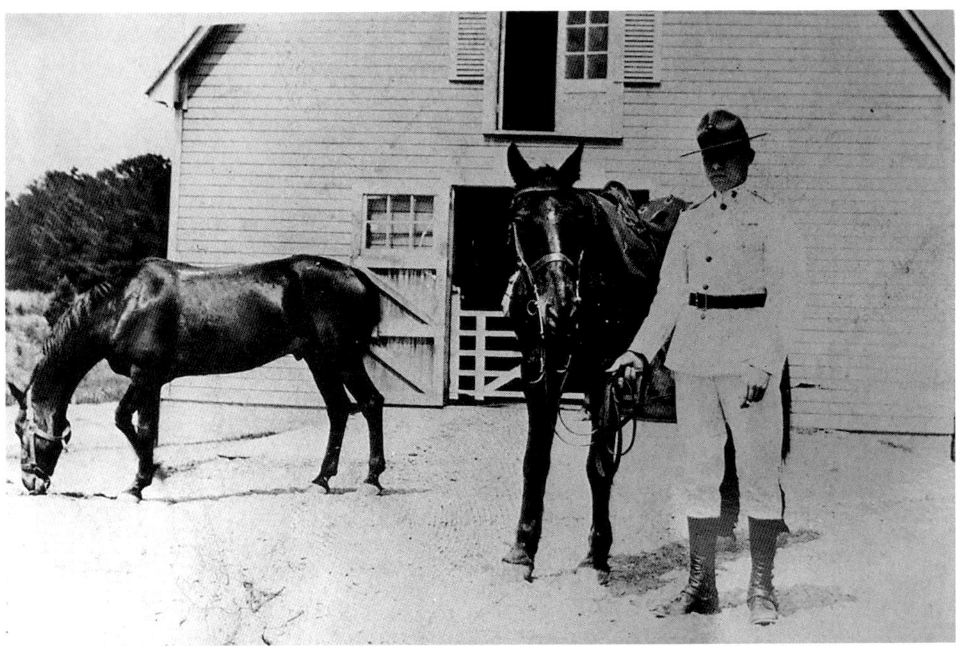

The United States Marine Corps patrolled Navy Mine Depot Yorktown and its perimeter in or about 1920. The mine depot at Yorktown became Naval Weapons Station Yorktown in 1958, when the navy expanded the mission of the base. Marines patrolled the base on horseback from 1918 to 1960, when the horses were replaced by motor vehicles. That change made the Naval Weapons Station Yorktown the last naval activity to use horse-mounted marines. *United States Navy*

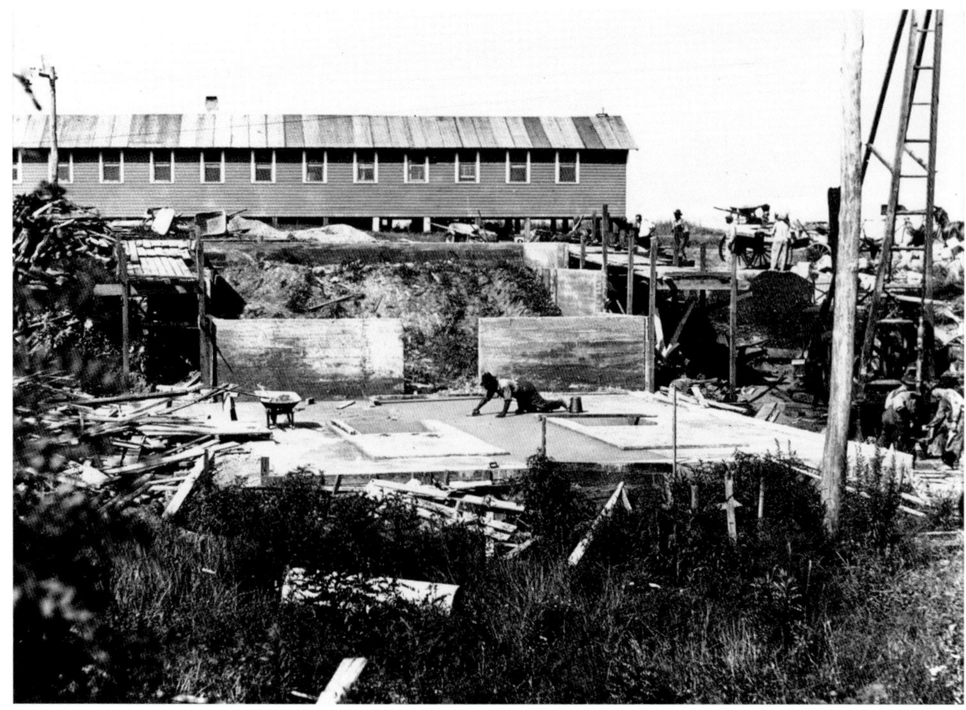

This was the aviation training school located on Navy Mine Depot Yorktown still under construction during the critical period it was used as a landing field for aircraft involved in the bombing of German vessels off the Virginia Capes in July 1921. The photographs shown here were taken by the United States Army Air Service Photographic School. *Naval History and Heritage Command*

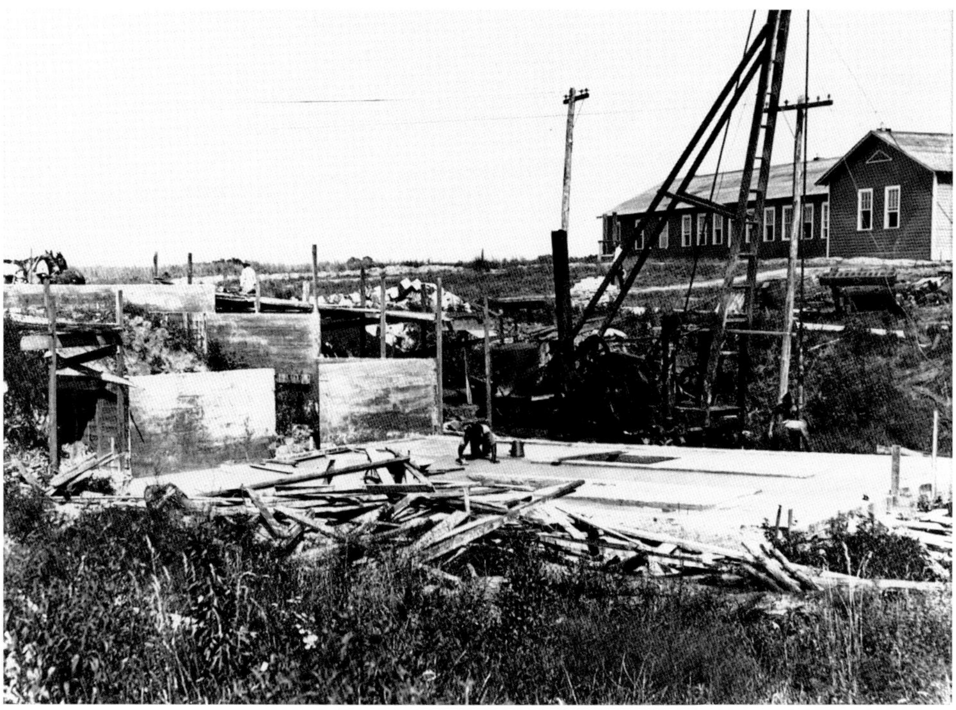

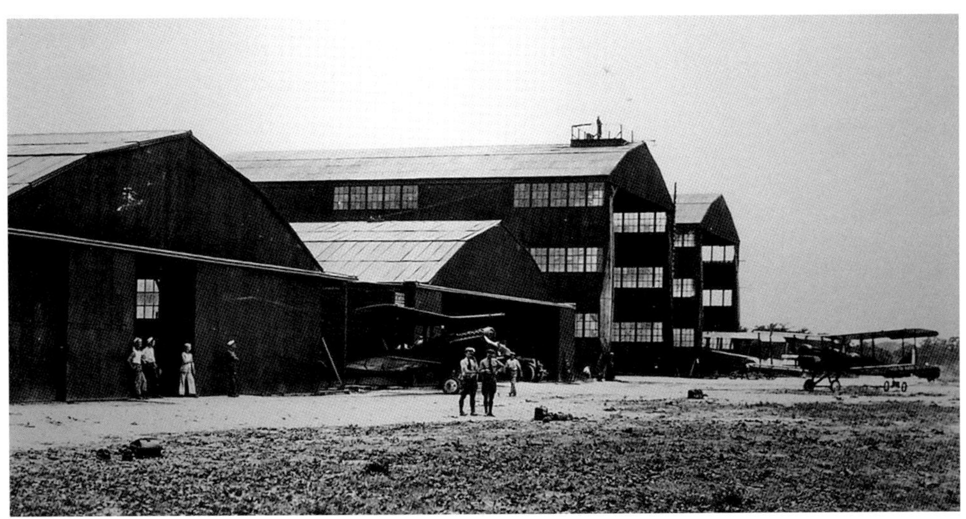

The aviation training school on Navy Mine Depot Yorktown was established after the First World War to provide the first advanced aviation training for naval pilots in bombing, torpedo and gunnery operations. This photograph of the aviation field hangars was taken in late spring 1921 looking southwest. Two De Havilland 4 [DH-4] series Liberty Plane two-seat aircraft are shown in this photograph. These aircraft were significantly flawed in their original configuration. The improved version was put out by De Havilland as the DH-4B. Forty-two DH-4Bs were transferred by the War Department to the navy and an additional eighty were rebuilt by the Naval Aircraft Factory also as DH-4Bs. Another improved version was produced as the DH-4B-1 and it, too, was transferred from the War Department to the navy. *United States Navy*

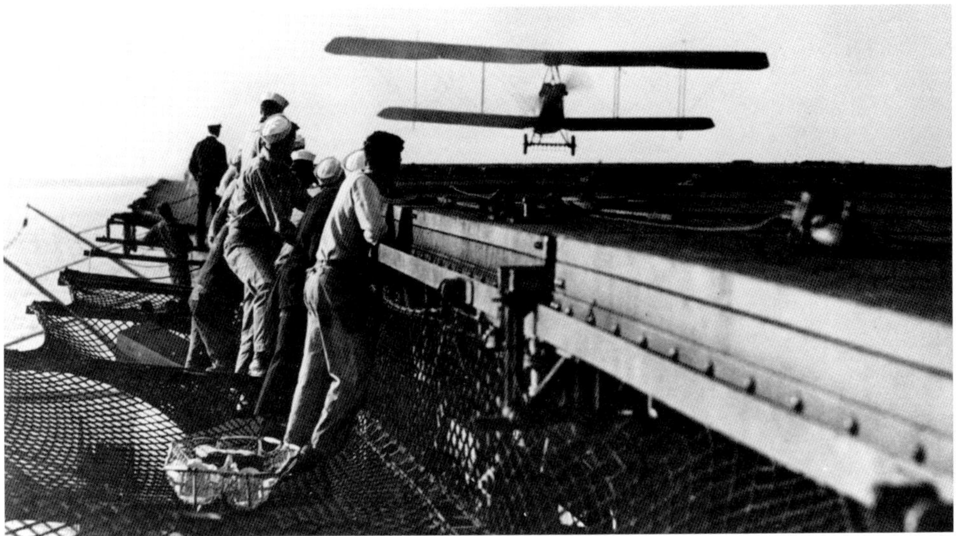

As the first American aircraft carrier, USS *Langley* (CV-1) was the scene of several seminal events in United States naval aviation. On October 17, 1922, while anchored in the York River, Lieutenant Commander Virgil Childers "Squash" Griffin [naval aviator number 41] (1891–1957) piloted the first plane—a Lewis and Vought VE-7—launched from an American aircraft carrier deck. Taken a little over a week later, on October 26, this Aeromarine 39-B piloted by Lieutenant Commander Godfrey de Courcelles "Chevy" Chevalier [naval aviator number 7] (1889–1922) made the first landing on the aircraft carrier (shown here). *Naval History and Heritage Command*

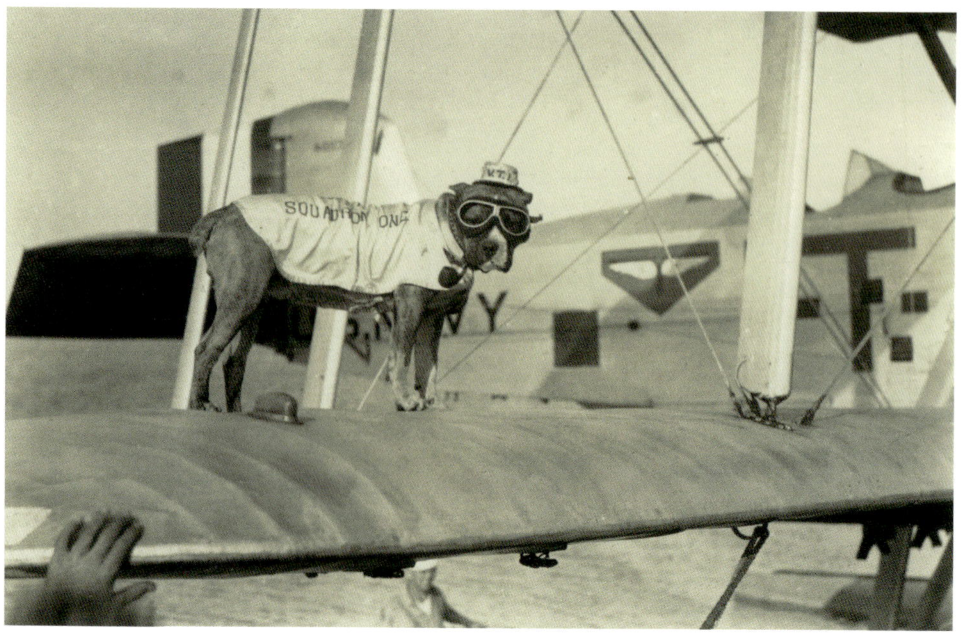

Navy Torpedo Squadron One (VT-1)'s mascot was ready to go flying when this picture was taken in or about 1929. On August 1, 1921, a First World War high-altitude bombsight mounted on a gyroscopically stabilized base was tested by VT-1, headquartered at Yorktown, Virginia, marking the successful completion of the first phase of Carl Lucas Norden's development of an effective high-altitude bombsight.[5] The squadron earlier came under the command of Lieutenant Harold Terry Bartlett [naval aviator number 21] [also pictured here], in July 1920, when he was tasked to get the squadron up and running at the Yorktown airfield. The VT-1 squadron insignia is on the fuselage of the aircraft. *Amy Waters Yarsinske*

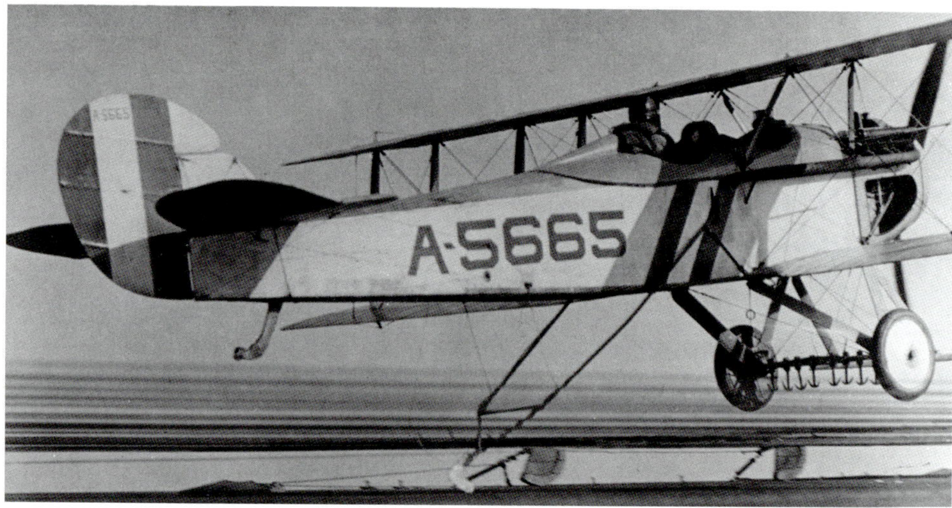

A Lewis and Vought VE-7 [bureau number 5665] aircraft piloted by Naval Aviation Pilot [Boatswain] Anthony Joseph "Tony" Feher [naval aviator number 95] (1883–1975) is shown landing on the USS *Langley* in this 1923 photograph. Feher became a naval aviation pilot in 1917. Feher, an enlisted pilot just then, would later retire after forty-three years of continuous service with the officer rank of commander. *Naval History and Heritage Command*

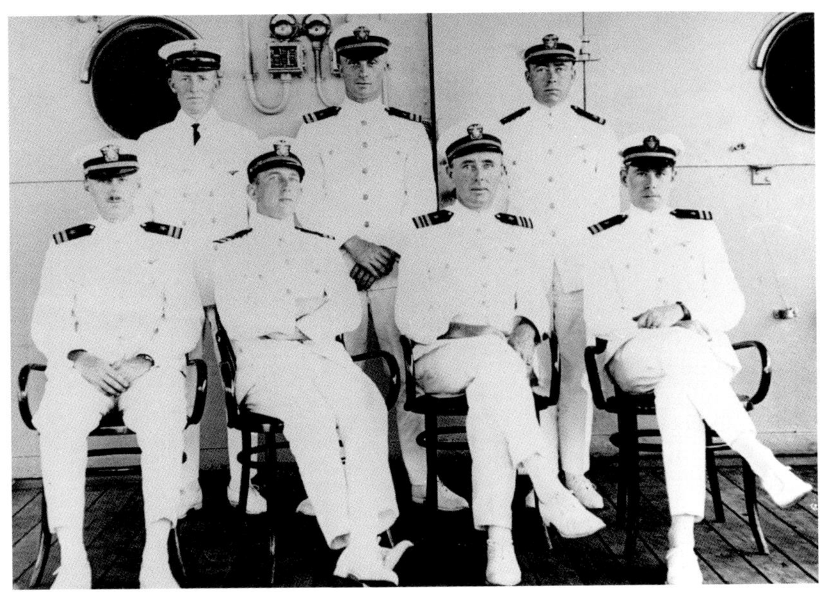

Seated (left to right) on board the USS *Langley* (CV-1), in or about 1922/3, were Lieutenant Alfred Melville "Al" Pride [naval aviator number 1119] (1897–1988), Lieutenant Wallace Myron Dillon [naval aviator number 2946] (1895–1965), Lieutenant Commander Virgil Childers Griffin, and Lieutenant James Roland Kyle Jr. [naval aviator number 2950] (1892–1925). Standing (left to right): Naval Aviation Pilot [Chief Petty Officer] Owen Milton "Sam" Darling (1897–1964), Lieutenant Braxton "Dusty" Rhodes [naval aviator number 2916] (1892–1966), Ensign Delbert Lawrence Conley [naval aviator number 1166] (1895–1957). Kyle, a native of Lynchburg, Virginia, was assigned to parachute school at Naval Air Station Lakehurst, New Jersey, at the time of his death—his parachute failed to open when he bailed out of a disabled aircraft. Darling was appointed a naval aviation pilot (NAP) in 1920 and later retired as a lieutenant. *National Naval Aviation Museum*

Harold Terry "Cueless" Bartlett [naval aviator number 21] (1887–1955) was a lieutenant when this picture was taken during the First World War. He was promoted to lieutenant commander and assigned to Yorktown as officer in charge of Fleet Torpedo Plane Division, Hampton Roads in 1920, and commanding officer of Torpedo Squadron One (VT-1), the navy's first torpedo plane squadron, in 1922, having directed construction of the squadron's base the previous year. Torpedo Squadron One (VT-1) was not a participant in the bombing of the obsolete battleship USS *Indiana* (BB-1) [renamed *Coast Battleship Number 1* after decommissioning] anchored off Tangier Island in the Chesapeake Bay, and subjected to aerial bombing tests conducted by the navy and executed by Bartlett, who took a squadron out of Naval Air Station Hampton Roads to hit it with dummy bombs. Explosive charges were set off at the positions where the bombs hit. Bartlett (shown here) was later the flight commander 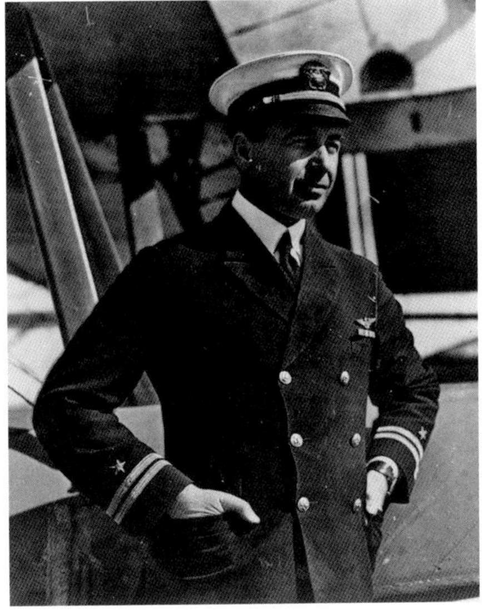 of the Naval Aircraft Factory PN-10 nonstop flight from Hampton Roads to the Canal Zone in 1926. The flight covered 2,060.9 miles. Bartlett was the recipient of the Navy Cross. *Naval History and Heritage Command*

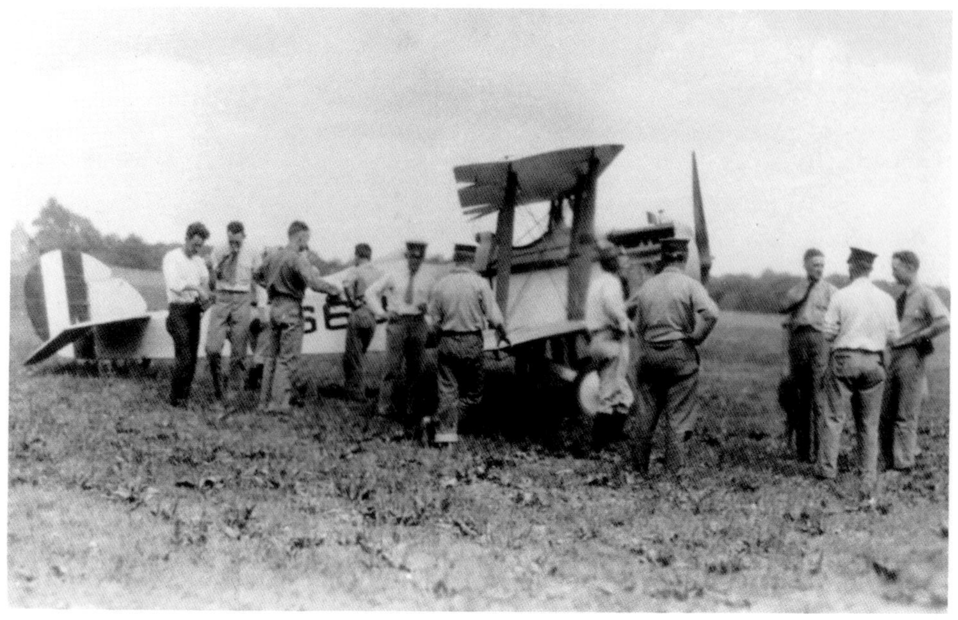

Navy personnel gathered around an early production Lewis and Vought VE-7 at the Navy Mine Depot Yorktown on June 8, 1921. The navy received the first VE-7 in May 1920 and production orders soon followed. The aircraft shown here was a two-cockpit trainer built as one of the first thirty-nine delivered to the navy. *National Naval Aviation Museum*

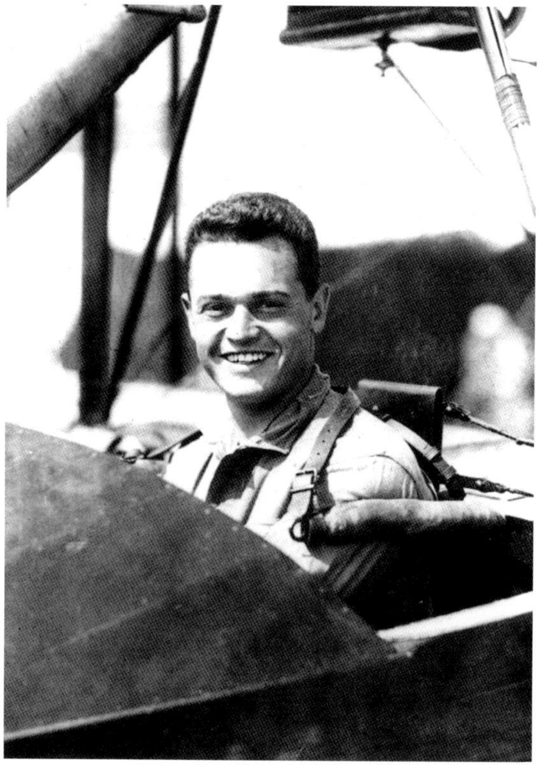

Lieutenant Commander Godfrey de Courcelles "Chevy" Chevalier (1889–1922) is shown in this early photograph, dating to in or about 1914. Less than a month after he made the first landing on an aircraft carrier in navy history when he touched down on the *Langley*, Chevalier died from injuries sustained in an airplane crash on the mudflats off the Hermitage estate in Norfolk's Lochhaven section on November 14, 1922. *National Naval Aviation Museum*

Opposite above: An Observation Squadron Six (VO-6) Vought VE-7 seaplane is pictured in flight in or about 1924. The vertical stabilizer on the seaplane version of this aircraft were larger than those on the landplane variant. On May 24, 1922, routine operations of catapults on board ship started when a VE-7 was successfully launched from the battleship USS *Maryland* (BB-46) off Yorktown, Virginia. *National Naval Aviation Museum*

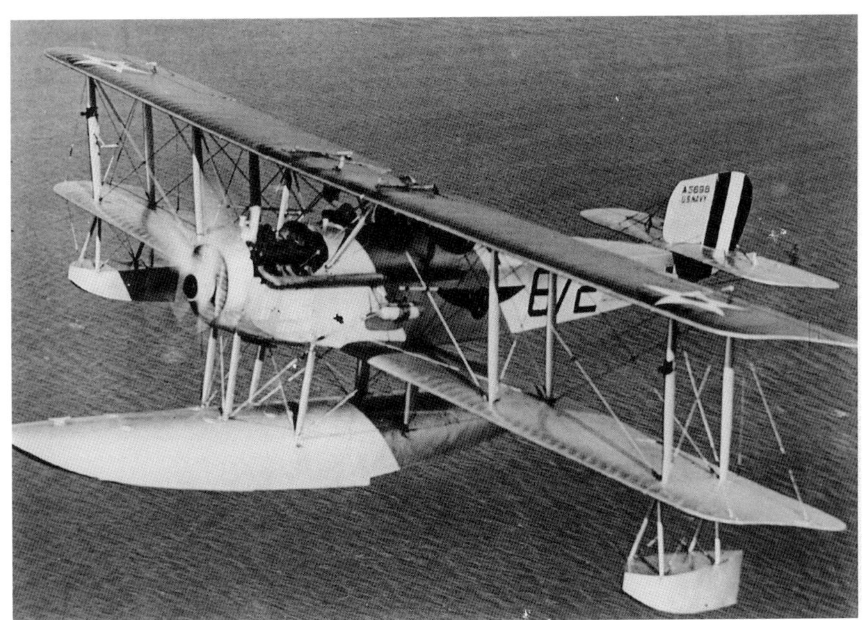

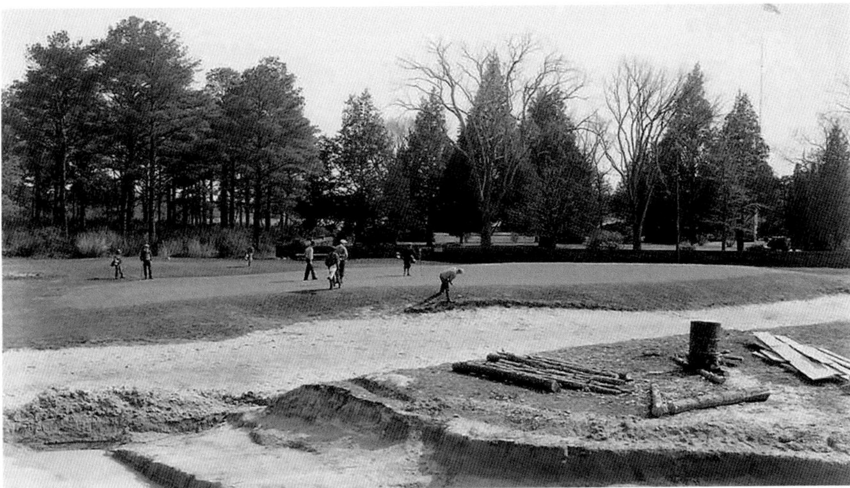

The Yorktown Battlefield was saved by an unlikely champion—the Great Depression. Prior to becoming part of the National Park system, the Yorktown Battlefield was part of the Yorktown Country Club. As an amenity to members, the eighteen-hole Riverview Golf Course was constructed around the earthworks that remained of the Revolutionary War and Civil War on the Yorktown Battlefield in 1926 and work was even begun on a large hotel. But the Stock Market crash three years later ended construction of the hotel and quashed plans for a second golf course on the footprint of the battlefield. Colonial National Monument was established the following year [now called the Colonial National Historical Park] and the National Park Service acquired the former country club property. According to published accounts, the first Yorktown Visitor Center stood on the site of the hotel.[6] According to the December 8, 2008 *National Parks Traveler*, there is a small area of raised ground close to the tree line near redoubts nine and ten that is actually the tee for one of the holes of the former golf course and those sweeping vistas across mowed fields were once fairways for the golfers. In this photograph, which dates to the period before the park service acquired the battlefield, a golfer approaches the green just outside the Yorktown National Cemetery. *National Park Service*

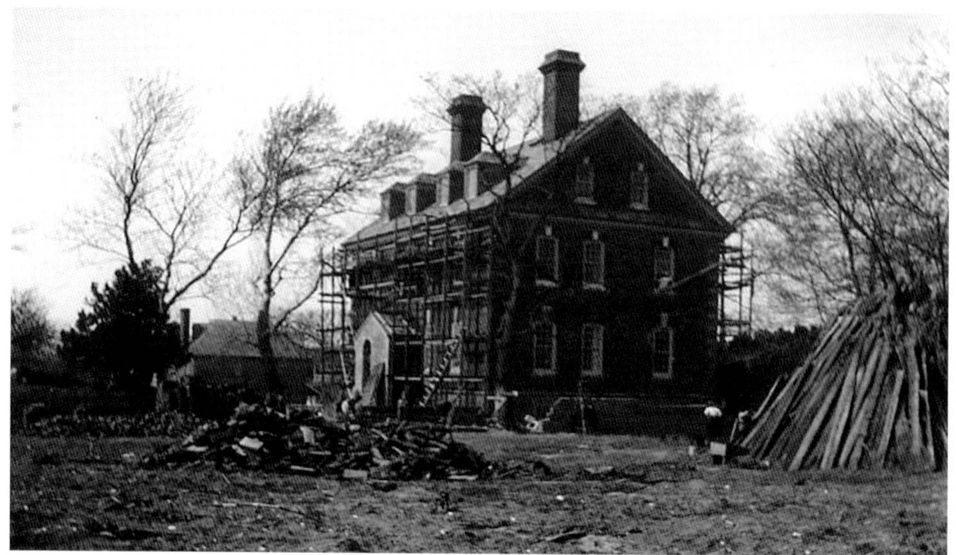

Baltimore architect Laurence Hall Fowler (1876–1971) took these pictures of exterior renovations to the Thomas Nelson House [also called York Hall] [Lot 52] after it was purchased by Norfolk, Virginia native George Preston Blow (1860–1922) and his wife, the former Adele Matthiessen (1867–1929), the daughter of industrialist Frederick Wilhelm Matthiessen in 1914. In the third photograph, the rear elevation of the Sessions-Pope-Sheild House is on the right and there is a dairy cow standing in the middle of what later became paved over Nelson Street. The Thomas Nelson House renovations were designed by Griffin and Wynkoop, architects, after the Blows bought it. *Johns Hopkins University*

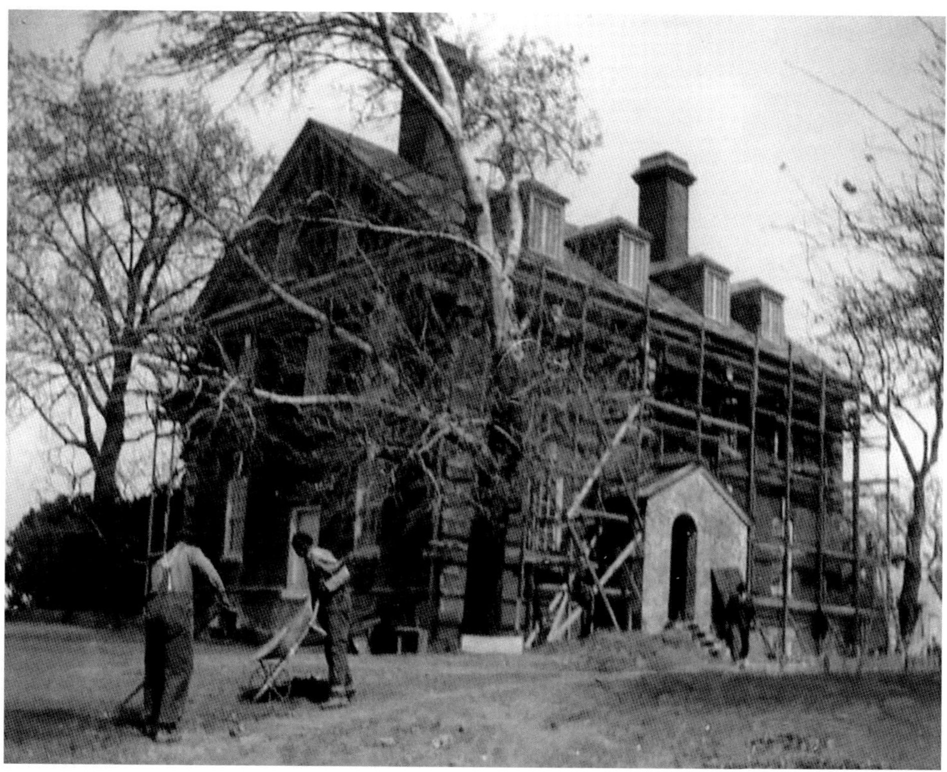

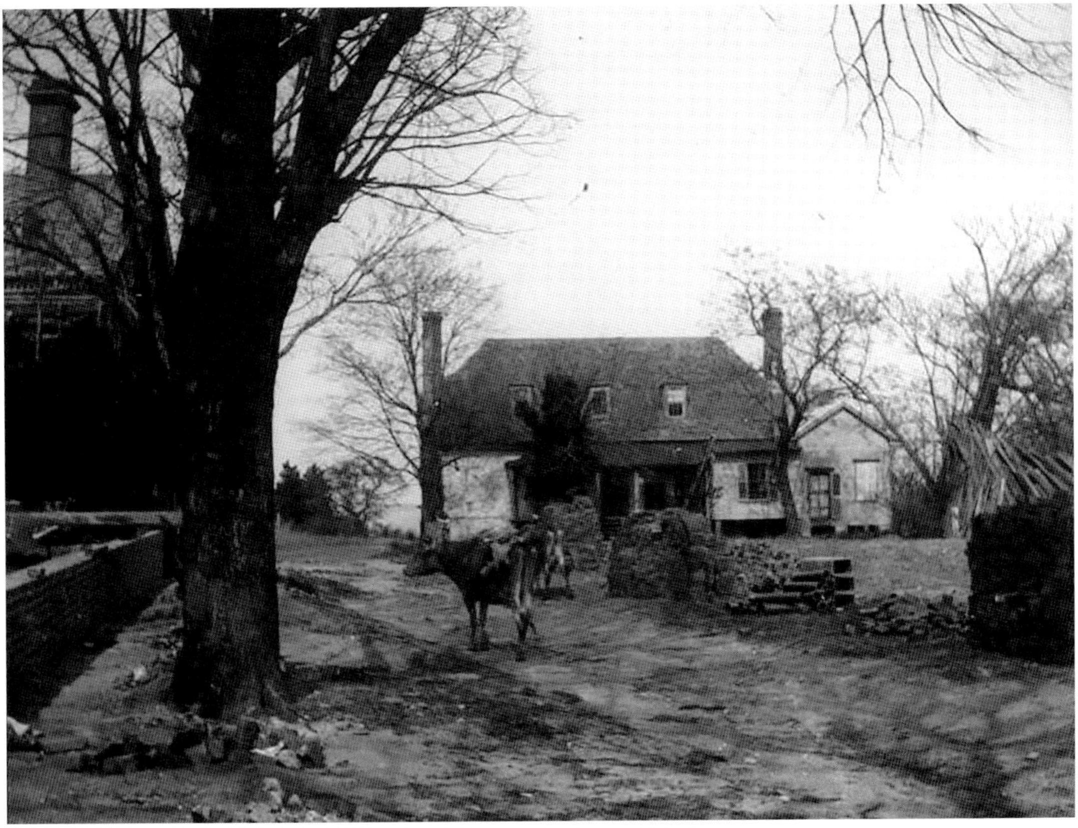

George Preston Blow was born in Norfolk, Virginia, on October 23, 1860, and admitted to the United States Naval Academy, Annapolis, Maryland, class of 1881. During his naval career Blow also established the United States Hydrographic Bureaus in Cleveland and Chicago and invented several naval devices including the depth-charge. Blow was promoted to lieutenant on February 22, 1894, and was assigned to the second-class battleships USSs *Texas* in 1895 and *Maine* the following year. He survived the explosion of the *Maine* in Havana Harbor on February 15, 1898. He was in command of tug USS *Potomac* (AT-50) which assisted in raising *Infanta Maria Teresa*, and later commanded USS *Vulcan*, an iron-hulled, schooner-rigged screw steamship, which attempted to tow the prize warship to the United States. He resigned his commission as a lieutenant on February 1, 1900, and served as president of the Western Clock Company, makers of Westclox [his wife's father owned the company] until his retirement in 1920. Blow died on November 20, 1922, in Washington, D.C., and is buried at Arlington National Cemetery as a lieutenant, United States Navy. This picture shows Blow as a midshipman. *Naval History and Heritage Command*

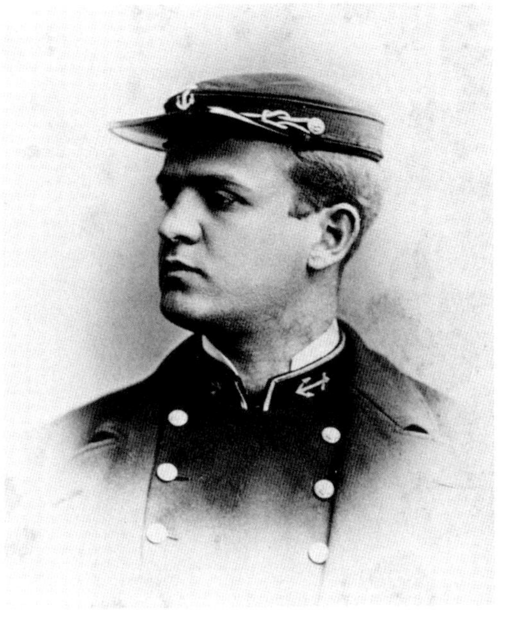

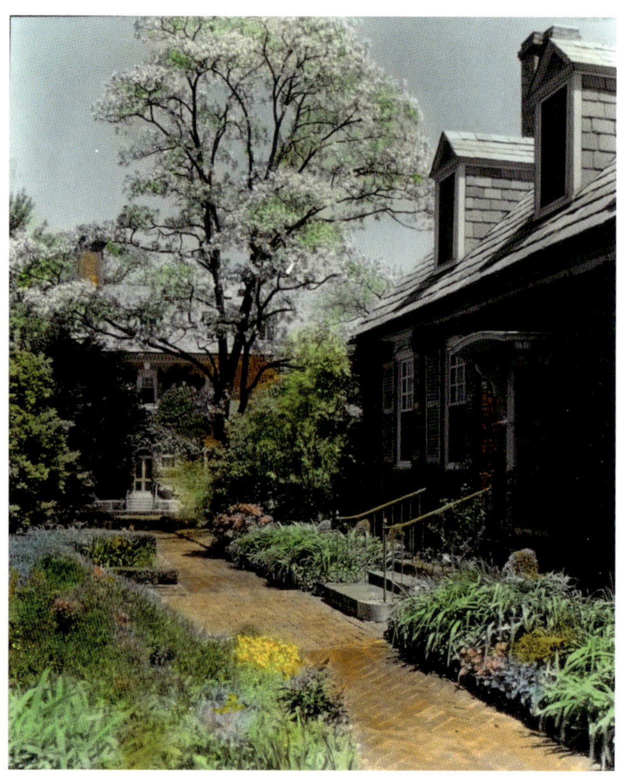

Renowned photographer Frances Benjamin Johnston (1864–1952) took photographs of the Thomas Nelson House [also called York Hall] fifteen years after the Blows purchased it, documenting the primary residence; the Edmund Smith House, which had become the Blows' guest house, and the Ballard House, a cottage the Blows fashioned into a "master kitchen" although it was historically far from it. Johnston also photographed the gardens around the property. She completed her work as part of the greater Carnegie Survey of Architecture of the South. When George Blow bought the Thomas Nelson House, he also acquired the Edmund Smith House (shown right in this magic lantern slide) [Lot 53], built in 1751 and left to Smith's daughter Mildred (c. 1732–1775), who married David Jameson (c. 1732–1793), a Yorktown merchant, scientist and statesman. The Smith-built residence was converted to a guest house for the York Hall estate in the early twentieth century and the entrance was changed to the garden front as seen in this Johnston photograph and the former street entrance was made into a window. At the time of the renovation, two gabled dormers were added to the two already opening on the west slope of the roof, thus matching the four original dormers on the street front. The windows are marked by segmental arches and stone sills and have architrave trim and nine-over-nine sash. The stacks of the two exterior end chimneys are slightly removed from contact with the house. *Library of Congress*

Opposite above: This was the door on the west side of the Thomas Nelson House owned just then by George Preston and Adele Matthiessen Blow and photographed by Frances Benjamin Johnston in 1929 as part of the Carnegie Survey of Architecture of the South. This door has since had the ornamentation above the door removed and it has been restored to the period of its original construction. *Library of Congress*

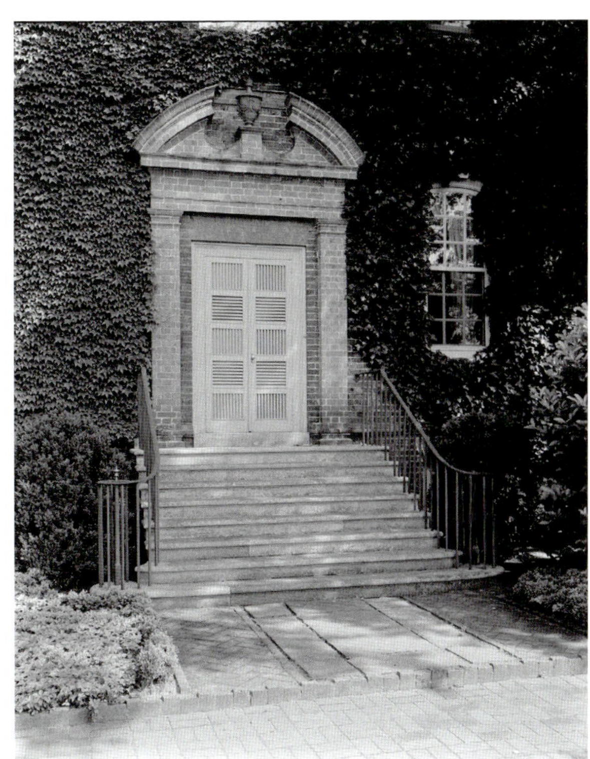

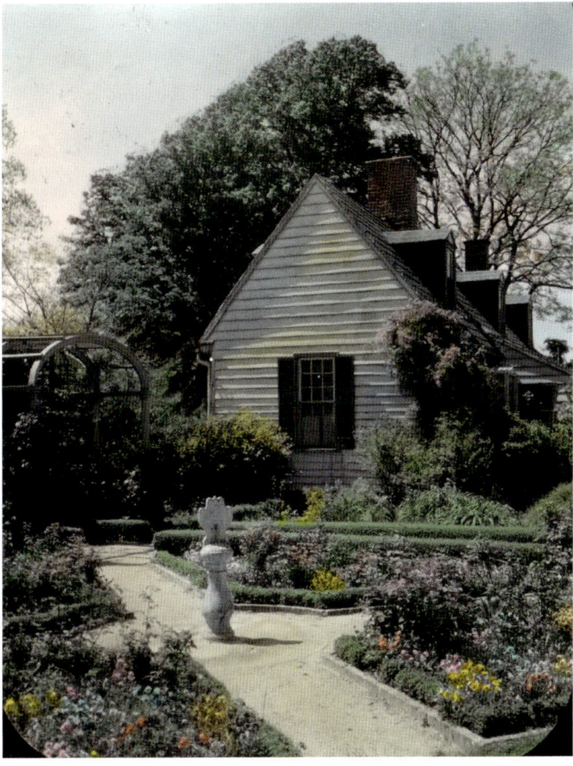

Below: Dubbed the "master kitchen" by Frances Benjamin Johnston, when she photographed the Thomas Nelson House and dependencies for the Carnegie survey in 1929, this structure was actually the Ballard House [Lot 54] [also called Pearl House], one of two homes—the other being the Edmund Smith House—that stand on the cross street east of the Thomas Nelson House on Nelson Street and therefore sequentially south of the Nelson residence. The Ballard House was constructed by Captain John Ballard (1700–1746) one year before his death. The five-bay rectangular frame structure was once covered by white beaded clapboards (shown here). The exterior-end chimney on the south end has a stack set out from contact with the gable, although the north chimney is within the frame of the house. Four gabled dormers open on the east slope of the steeply-pitched roof, and three on the west slope (shown here). A molded cornice is employed on the exterior. The doorway on the street façade is off center to the south; three bays extend north of the doorway. The first-floor windows have nine-over-nine sash and the dormers have six-over-six. *Library of Congress*

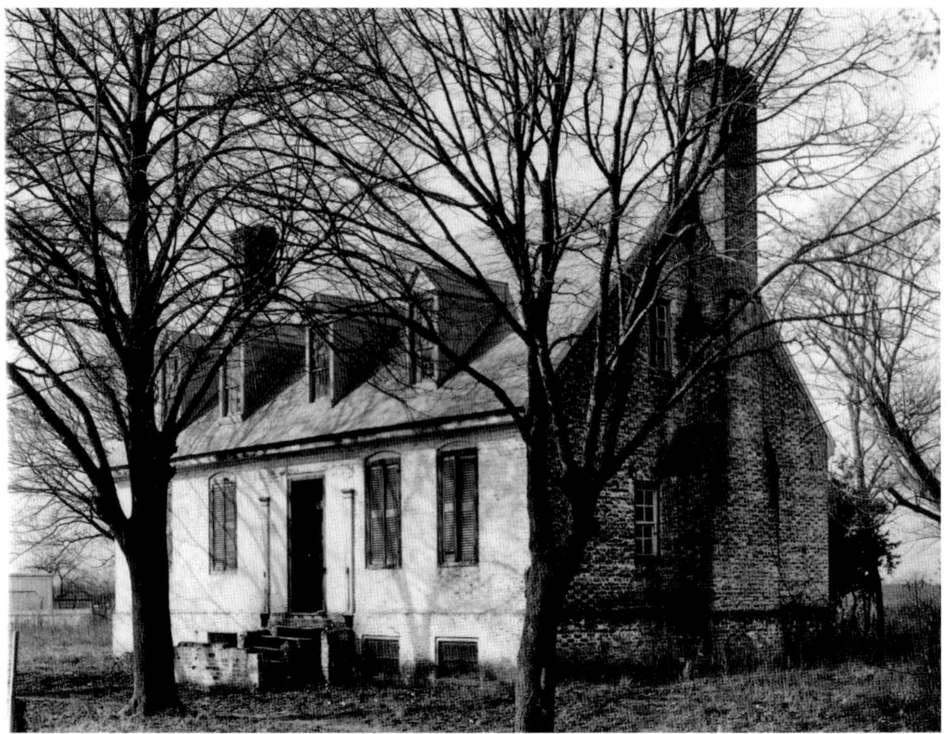

The Edmund Smith House (shown here as it looked before the Blows acquired it) was under construction when Smith died in early 1751. In his will, made on the preceding December 18, he had written: "I give and bequeath unto my daughter Mildred Smith my lot of land in York Town whereon I am now building. It is my will and desire that the house should be finished out of my estate." Likely for business reasons, David Jameson and his wife, the former Mildred Smith, conveyed the lot to James Tarpley, a Williamsburg merchant, on January 17, 1753. But nine months later, Jameson bought it back. Jameson, born in Essex County, Virginia, moved to Yorktown at least by June 1751 and had varied business and mercantile interests, to include the sale of lands, slaves, and indentured servants, with the settlement of estates, with freighting ships with cargoes, and periodically the management of lotteries. Lawrence Smith, Mildred's brother, apprenticed himself to Jameson to learn the merchant trade. David and Mildred Jameson made their home on Lot 53, though he came to own other property in the town. Three years after Edmund Smith died, Jameson acquired from Thomas Archer a twenty-eight-by-twenty-foot store [a storehouse] on the water side. Historical record suggests that it was near this place that Jameson's lower garden, mentioned in 1770, was located. Jameson was named to Patrick Henry's Privy Council in 1777 and four years later, in 1781, he became lieutenant governor under Thomas Nelson Jr. and when Nelson became ill and unable to attend to business it devolved to Jameson to carry on for a period of several weeks in August of that year. Mildred Smith Jameson died in 1778 at the age of forty-six and was buried in the Smith family cemetery on the old Ludlow Tract on Wormley Creek, then owned by Augustine Moore, who had married Lucy Smith, her aunt. Mildred's tomb carried the Jameson coat of arms featuring ships under sail with pennants and the Latin motto *vive ut vivas*, which translates "live that you may live." David Jameson was later active in the incorporation of Yorktown in 1787 following the enabling legislation of the Virginia General Assembly in 1785. After his death in 1793, the house and dependencies remained in the Jameson family until 1815, when the property was sold to Major Thomas Griffin, a prominent citizen of Yorktown, a veteran of the War of 1812 and politician. The photograph would date to in or about 1910 and was acquired by George Preston Blow in his research of the property prior to purchase. The house was acquired by the National Park Service in October 1968 and made part of Colonial National Historical Park. *Library of Congress*

The landscape around the Thomas
Nelson House was reimagined by
Richmond, Virginia landscape
architect Charles Freeman Gillette
(1886–1969) for the Blows. The gardens
of the home, fashioned by Gillette and
seen in Frances Benjamin Johnston's
photographs, no longer exists and
the house, minus the Blow additions,
is today a National Park Service site.
The boxwood garden designed by
Gillette and shown here exists today
only in photographs, this one taken
by Johnston as part of the Carnegie
survey. *Library of Congress*

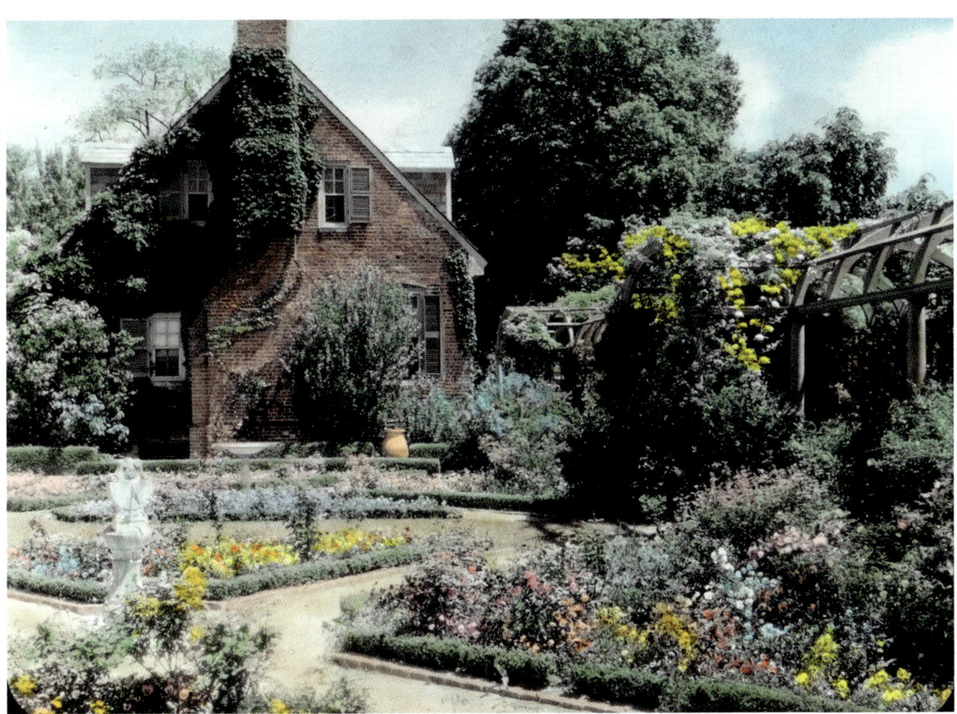

Charles Gillette designed this memory garden for the Blows, also shown in this Frances Benjamin
Johnston photograph. The Edmund Smith House—the Blows' so-called guest house—is in the background.
Library of Congress

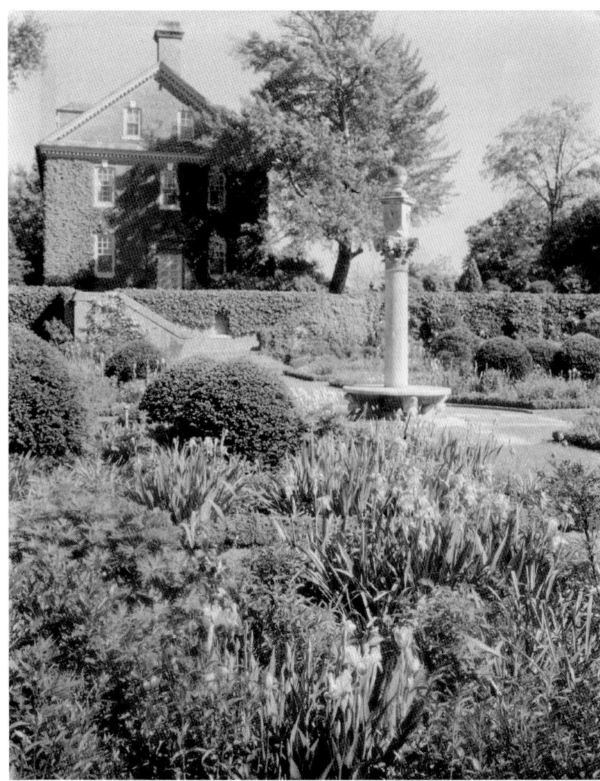

Frances Benjamin Johnston took this picture of the side garden designed for the Blows by Charles Gillette. *Library of Congress*

Opposite page: The Thomas Nelson House is a rectangular, two-story brick house, five bays wide (on the north façade) and three bays deep, with a generously proportioned dentil cornice, a broad gable roof with pediments on the ends and two interior chimneys with corbelled caps. The corners are quoined in stone; the window sills, lintels and keystones are also in stone. The original center doorway has simple gauged and rubbed brick piers, and the triangular pediment of rubbed and molded brick but before it was restored, the elaborate west doorway was a modern addition (shown in a previous Johnston photograph). The large hipped dormers of the house that were added in 1920 by the Blows have since been removed. The Blows made not only exterior errors in their renovation but also did a number of interior restorations that were later rectified. The interior of the Thomas Nelson House received an early restoration by George Preston and Adele Matthiessen Blow, which was photographed extensively by Frances Benjamin Johnston for the Carnegie survey. At the time it was documented by the National Park Service, the floor plan still retained a center hall with the smaller two rooms on the east separated by a small stair and two large square rooms on the west. This plan is repeated on the second floor. The entrance hall is paneled above and below the molded chair rail, and there is a fully developed cornice. The stair, ascending in three easy flights, retains its original treads, risers and stringer. Although all the rooms are paneled, the northeast room is the most elaborate. The walls are not only paneled but are marked off by a modified Corinthian order, composed of columns engaged three-quarters of their depth with capitals having single bands of tall acanthus leaves. Windows, doors and mantel are framed by this order. The marble mantel, as with all the others in the house, is a copy of the original. In the northwest room, fluted pilasters, which are Doric, although the capitals had been removed, flanked the windows, doors and mantels. The house has been part of Colonial Historical National Park since 1968. *Library of Congress*

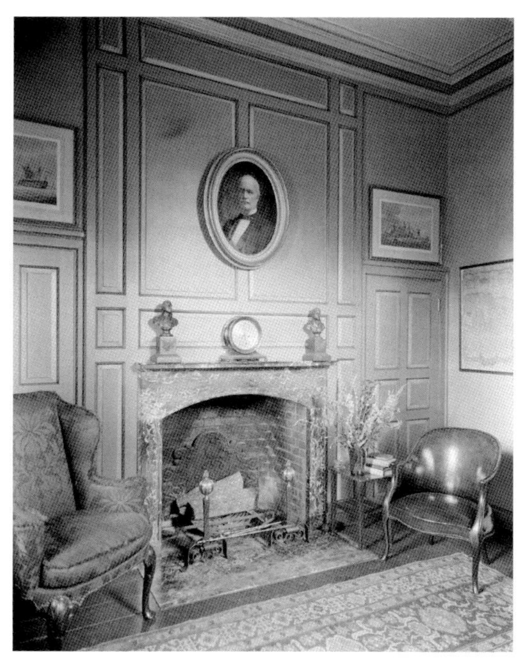

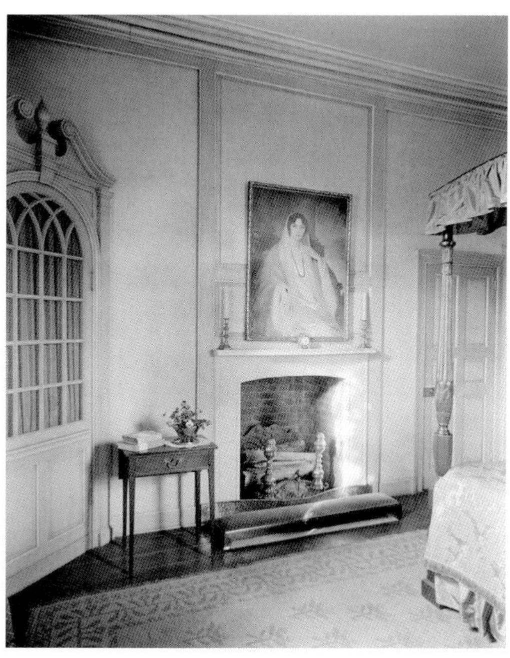

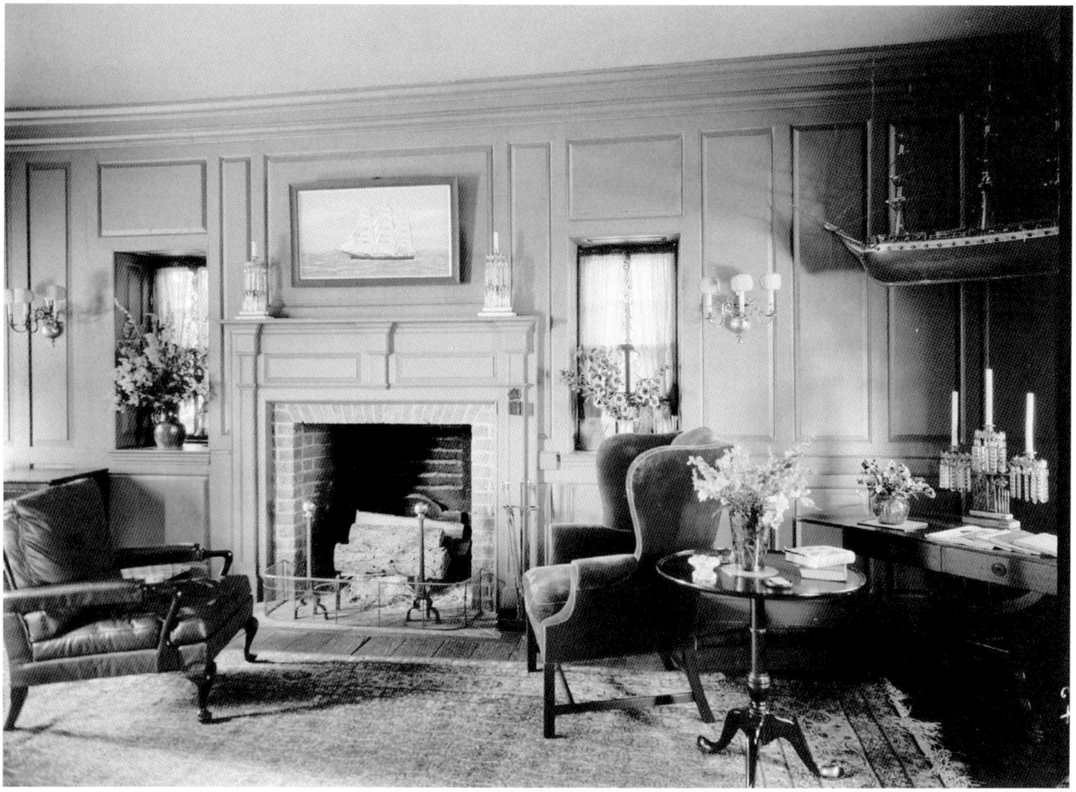

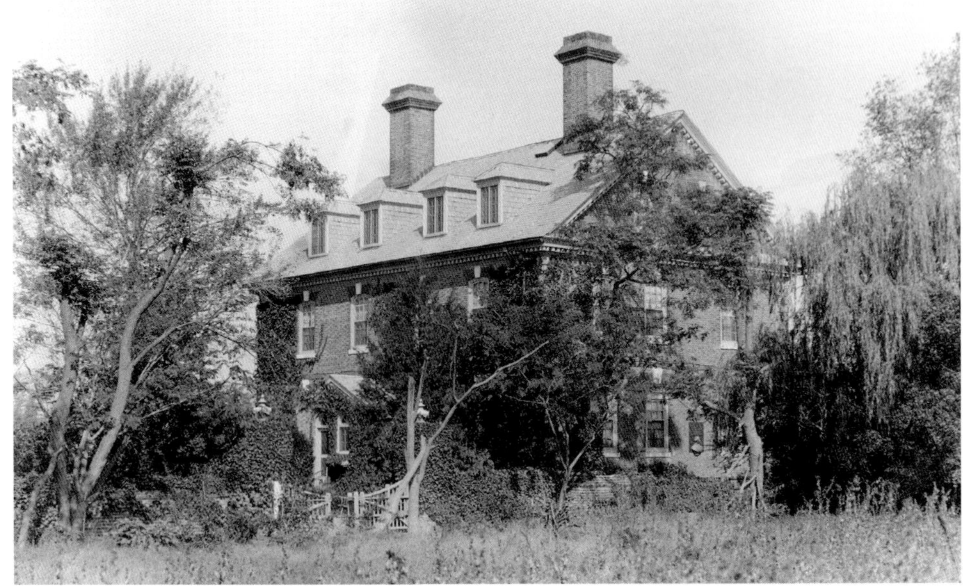

This photograph—and others that follow—of the Thomas Nelson House and surrounding property were collected by George Preston Blow. Many of these pictures, though not all, were taken in or around 1915 for the Blows as they assumed ownership but had not yet begun exterior and interior renovation of the house and dependencies on the lots directly south of the main house and fronting Nelson Street. Thomas Tileston Waterman documented the property for a Historic American Buildings Survey (HABS) on December 29, 1937, with an addendum filed November 7, 1940. The pictures he used for his report came from George Preston Blow. *Library of Congress*

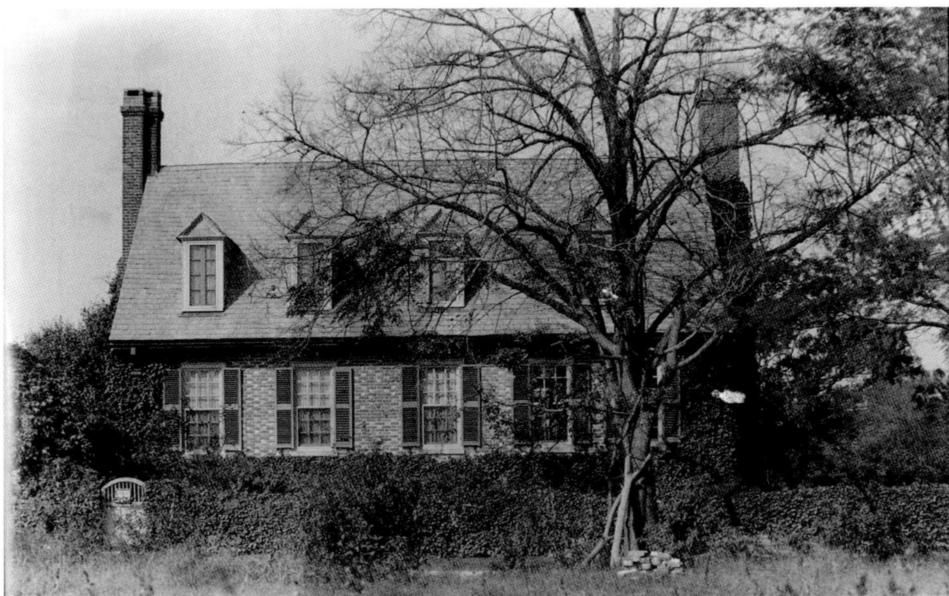

The Edmund Smith House on the grounds of the Thomas Nelson House [used by the Blows as a guest house] is shown here on the northeast front, looking from across the property. The picture was taken in or about 1915. *Library of Congress*

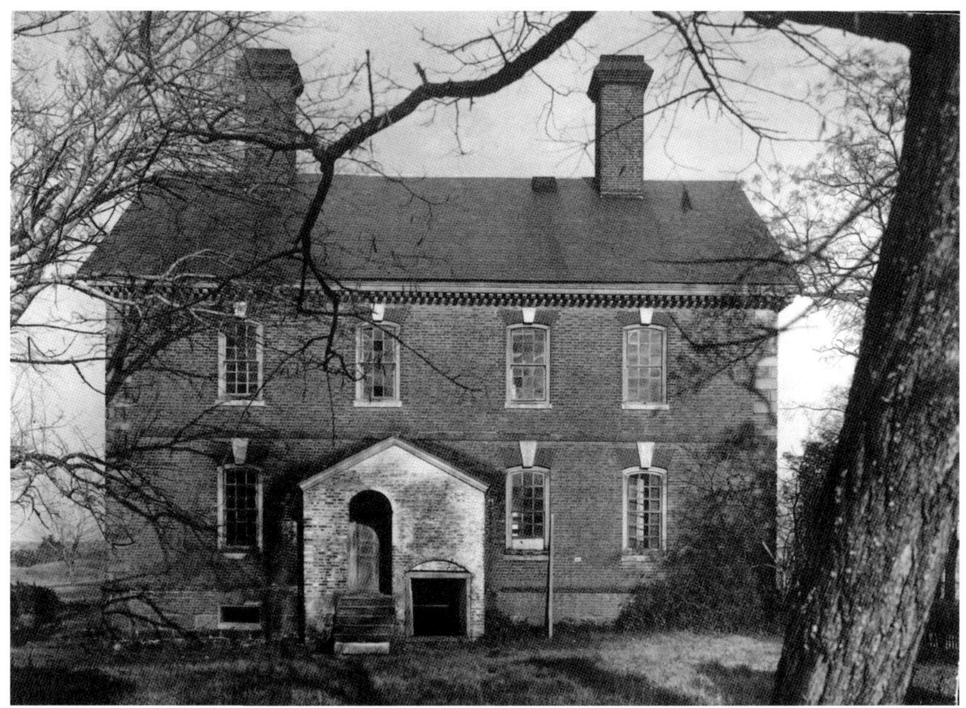

This is the southwest rear of the Thomas Nelson House as it looked in 1915, prior to George Preston and Adele Matthiessen Blow renovation. *Library of Congress*

The ruins of one of the Thomas Nelson House dependencies, located on the half-acre parcel [Lot 48], the south corner of the intersection of Main and Read streets and labeled as "the master kitchen" is shown in this photograph, taken looking south in 1915 and provided to Thomas Waterman for his HABS report by George Preston Blow. Thomas "Scotch Tom" Nelson acquired the property in 1709 just three years after he secured Lot 52 on which he would build his home. The half-acre had, in 1707, first gone to William Cary who forfeited it when he failed to build on the lot. This parcel would remain in the Nelson family for a number of generations in association with the Thomas Nelson House and that came to be the home of his grandson, Thomas Nelson Jr. This northwest side of the house would be used for part of the garden throughout the historic period of the house. *Library of Congress*

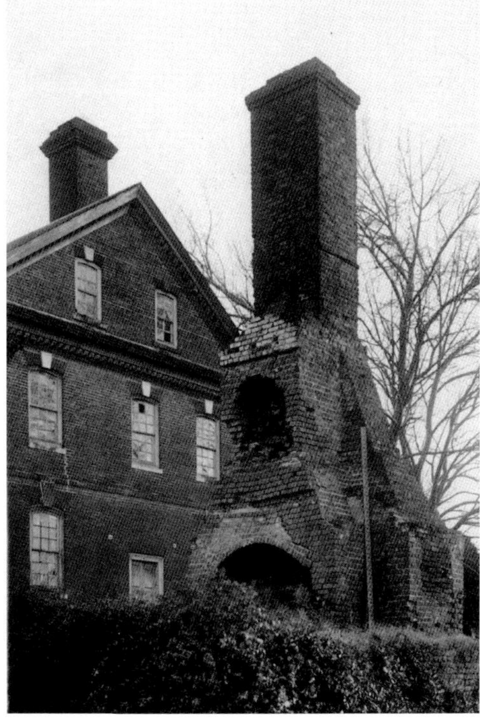

Endnotes

1 By Wilhelm (AAA Online Archives) [Public domain], via Wikimedia Commons.

2 Chadwick, who rose to the rank of rear admiral, became prominent in the naval reform movement in the post-Civil War era and is remembered for his major contributions to naval education. He was president of the Naval War College from 1900 to 1903.

3 George Germain, first viscount Sackville (1716–1785), Lord George Sackville [from 1720 to 1770] and Lord George Germain [1770 to 1782], was a British soldier and politician who was secretary of state for America in the cabinet of Frederick North, second earl of Guilford (1732–1792), also Lord North, during the Revolutionary War. In 1781, the confusion involving orders sent to Lord Cornwallis from General Sir Henry Clinton (1730–1795) contributed to the British loss at Yorktown. The news of Yorktown reached London on November 25, 1781, and the messenger went first to Germain's residence at Pall Mall. Germain thereafter informed other ministers and together they told Lord North what had happened. Germain was appointed the one to inform the king.

4 Rear Admirals Williams and Washington rose to the rank of admiral before retirement, and Burrage became a vice admiral. Rear Admiral Brittain, then chief of staff to Admiral Henry Braid Wilson Jr. (1861–1954), commander, Atlantic Fleet, killed himself on April 23, 1920, while the fleet was in Cuban waters. Commodore Phelps was struck and killed by an automobile in Norfolk, Virginia, on December 23, 1919, a year after the picture shown herein was taken. Farquhar retired as a rear admiral.

5 Carl Norden (1880–1965), an engineer, was born in Semarang, Java, a Dutch territory, as Carel Lucas van Norden. He emigrated to the United States in 1904 and along with Elmer Sperry, he worked on the first gyrostabilizing equipment for American ships and that effort soon spilled over to military contracts for Norden and Ambrose Sperry (1860–1930), an American inventor and entrepreneur. Development of the aircraft bombsight was a turning point in air warfare. Norden's bombsight was supposedly accurate enough to hit a one hundred-foot circle from an altitude of twenty-one thousand feet but under actual combat conditions, this accuracy was never achieved.

6 Burnett, Jim, "Did the Great Depression save the Yorktown Battlefield?" *National Parks Traveler*, December 8, 2008. https://www.nationalparkstraveler.org/2008/12/did-great-depression-save-yorktown-battlefield

IV

SAVING HISTORY

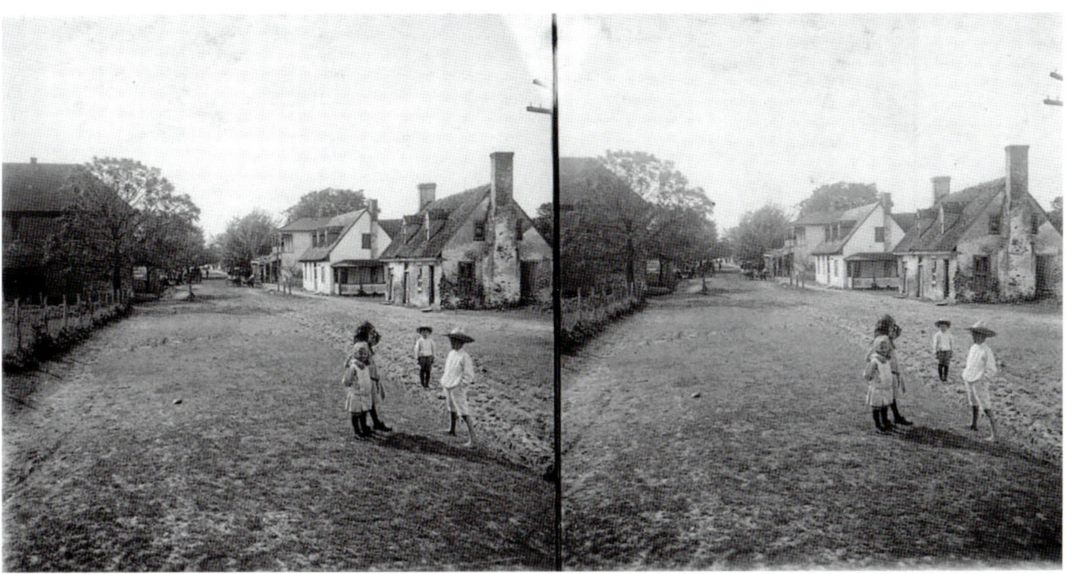

The children in this photograph, published as a Keystone stereoview, was taken in or about 1926 and shows Yorktown's Main Street looking northwest. The custom house is on the left. The Cole Digges House [also called the Thomas Pate House] [Lot 42] is in the foreground (right) and next to it is the Mungo Somerwell House [Lot 36], and the Medical Shop [Lot 30]. *Keystone-Mast Collection, University of California Riverside/California Museum of Photography*

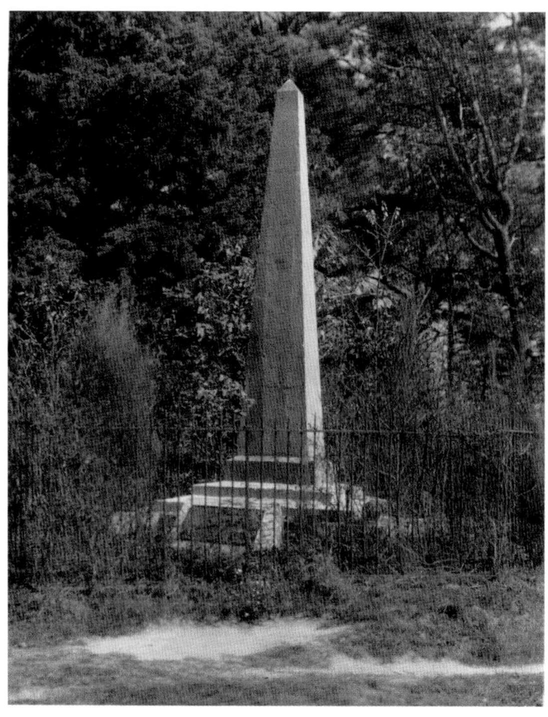

The exact spot where British general Charles O'Hara surrendered his sword at the 1781 siege of Yorktown went unrecorded on every map, including those demarcating the field in which the British army laid down its arms. Certainly, attempts were made to find it—none of them hitting the right spot until well after the 1981 bicentennial celebration. One notable attempt at the end of the nineteenth century was well intentioned but also wrong. Fourteen years after the erection of the Yorktown Victory Monument, Yorktown National Cemetery superintendent and former Union army first lieutenant John Washington Shaw (1837–1907) constructed a brick and concrete obelisk (shown here) less than a mile from the victory monument high on a bluff overlooking the York River adjacent to the cemetery; it was dedicated on October 19, 1895. After Shaw's death, the obelisk standing along Union Road remained in place but overgrown. When the location of his surrender marker was subsequently contested, the obelisk was broken up by the National Park Service, which dumped it in the woods off Allied Encampment Road, just off Goosley Road in 1934 or shortly thereafter. Shaw's marker lay broken up in the battlefield woods for nearly eighty years, according to an October 19, 2013 *Daily Press* article, before the park service transported it to a secure fenced maintenance yard earlier that fall. The actual surrender site was marked with a new wayside in 2005. *Amy Waters Yarsinske*

Opposite page: The Greek revival style Grace Episcopal Church, located on Lot 35 northeast of the courthouse on Church Street and north of the Mungo Somerwell House on Main Street, was returned to use as a house of worship in 1870. The bell of this church is inscribed "County of York, Virginia, 1725." The bell probably hung originally in the courthouse but is known to have hung in the church's belfry during colonial times. It is unknown when the bell broke but one belief is that fragments of it were carried off during the Civil War and not destroyed earlier in the Great Fire of 1814. The pieces were later found after the war and recast in Philadelphia in 1882 by the Hooks Smelting Company. But it is unknown how—or even when—the broken fragments of the bell found their way to a smelting company in Philadelphia. Henry Howe documented, in 1846, in fact, that the bell had survived the 1814 fire and was kept in safe custody while the church stood in ruins. "A magazine explosion during [Union major general George] McClellan's occupancy of Yorktown injured the belfry to the extent that the bell fell and was cracked. The broken bell was carried away to Philadelphia, where it finally came in the hands of a smelting company. At the time of the centennial [1881]," John Baer Stoudt wrote in 1932, "it was recast and presented to the church."[1] *Continued on next page*

Continued from previous page: Grace Episcopal Church also has the second oldest set of communion silver in Virginia. The chalice and flagon date to 1649/50 and are inscribed "Hampton parrish [*sic*] in Yorke County in Verginia [*sic*]." The flagon, attributed to London silversmith Thomas Garrett[2] from the incised maker's mark "T.G.," is believed to be the earliest English silver flagon in an American church. According to nineteenth-century Virginia Episcopal bishop William Meade (1789–1862), the silver was the gift of Colonel Nathaniel Bacon [the elder] (1620–1692), who had come to Virginia in 1653 and three years later represented York County in the Virginia House of Burgesses and the following year, joined the governor's council. The elder Bacon's plantation was situated on King's Creek. There is no extant record to substantiate the bishop's claim regarding Bacon's gift of the chalice and flagon. The belfry, western doorway and circular window date from a 1926 renovation. Frances Benjamin Johnston took this picture of the church in 1929 for the Carnegie Survey of Architecture of the South. *Library of Congress*

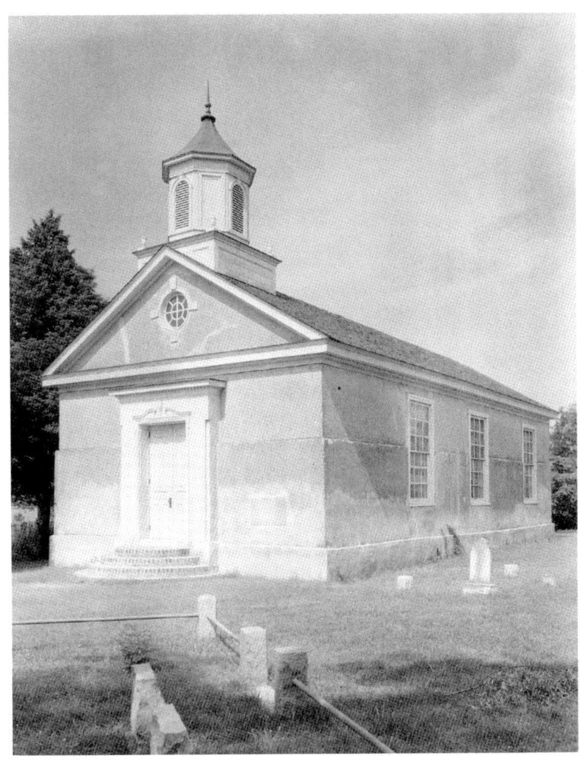

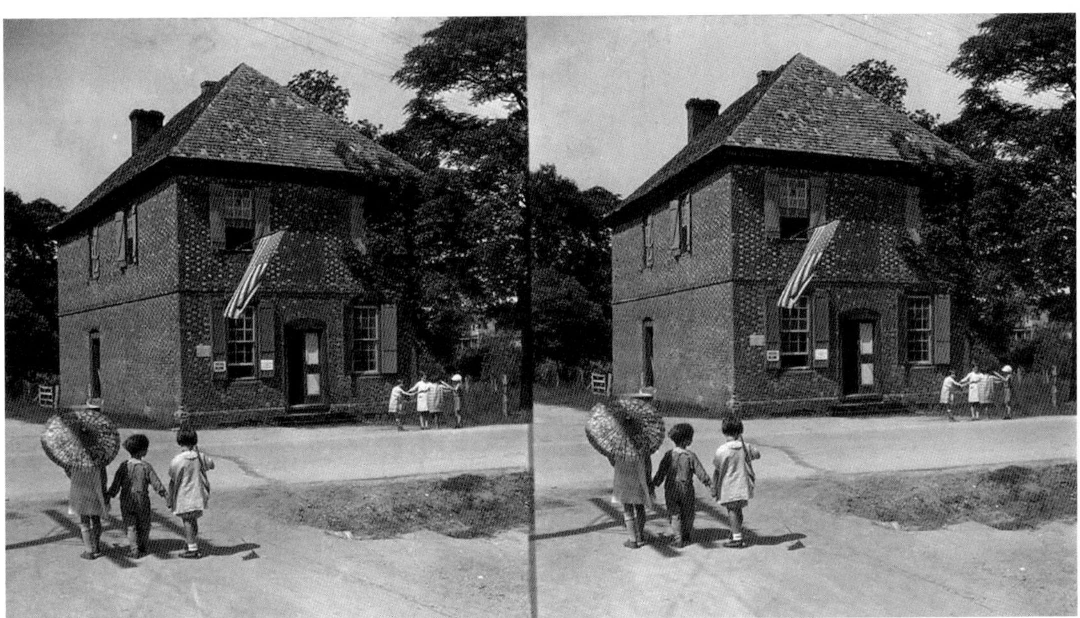

This Keystone stereograph view is looking southwest across the intersection of Main and Read Streets at the custom house in 1926, three years before the building underwent restoration. *Keystone-Mast Collection, University of California Riverside/California Museum of Photography*

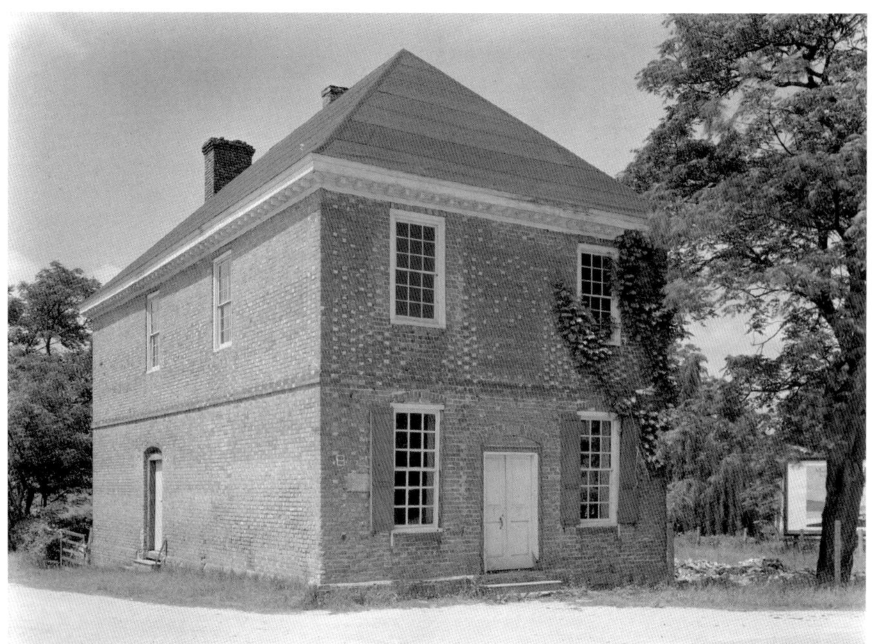

Frances Benjamin Johnston photographed the custom house at Main and Read Streets for the Carnegie Survey of Architecture of the South in 1929, the same year that Richmond, Virginia architect W. Duncan Lee (1884–1952) and contractor Edward Carpenter Wilkinson (1871–1956) began an ambitious restoration effort on the custom house, the expense of which was underwritten by Letitia Pate Whitehead Evans (1872–1953), a member of the Comte de Grasse Chapter of the DAR but importantly a businesswoman and philanthropist and the first woman to be on Coca-Cola Company's board of directors. Evans donated millions of dollars to more than one hundred and thirty organizations in Virginia and Georgia in her lifetime. Lee exercised sympathetic handling of the building and its fabric, both in the use of decoration and materials. His work on the building also reflected the influence of Colonial Revival style, spurred on by the advent of pictorial works illustrating colonial architecture and the resounding interest and success just then of the Colonial Williamsburg enterprise. Lee used lightly stained woodwork, which contributed to the popular notion that eighteenth century Virginia homes contained natural wood finishes. Additionally, because Lee's work on three of Virginia's most famous architectural structures— Colonial Williamsburg, Carter's Grove and Westover—he has been credited with popularizing the image of a "red-brick Colonial Virginia" and with creating architecturally balanced forms. The custom house, its dependencies and surrounding brick wall embody many of Lee's stylistic trademarks. Note the absence of the brick wall and kempt, terraced lawn in Johnston's photograph, taken before Lee and Wilkinson started their work. *Library of Congress*

Opposite page: Architect W. Duncan Lee's focus on the exterior of the custom house was to replace components that were too badly damaged to be salvaged, to include a new roof, a replacement dormer and the rebuilding of the brick chimney. A first-story window on the Read Street exposure was added and the original door and surround replicated and replaced. Lee also added the side porch and cellar entrance on the northwest wall. The areas around the windows on the front and rear walls were chopped in, as the masonry appears to be more random bond. The other three contributing resources were also products of the 1929 restoration and designed to complement the custom house architecture. Enclosing the southeast, rear and northwest side of the custom house property is a stately brick wall. Two brick dependencies—a kitchen and necessary—are located near the south and west corners of the lot, respectively. To maintain continuity Lee incorporated the rear walls of the two dependencies into the main structure. The wall, laid in a Flemish bond pattern, is corbeled with brick coping. *Continued on next page*

Continued from previous page: Virginia governor John Garland Pollard (1871–1937) rededicated the custom house on November 15, 1930, to "the memory and the spirit of the men and women who achieved American independence." In the years that followed, the custom house hosted a number of DAR activities as well as participating in the annual celebration of Yorktown Days held every October. Today, the old custom house still serves as the chapter meeting place for the Comte de Grasse Chapter of the DAR. The custom house stands today as one of the few surviving structures not only of the colonial and Revolutionary War periods but of the Civil War era in Yorktown. Frances Benjamin Johnston took these photographs that show the side [front visible] and rear of the custom house after the restoration was completed. *Library of Congress*

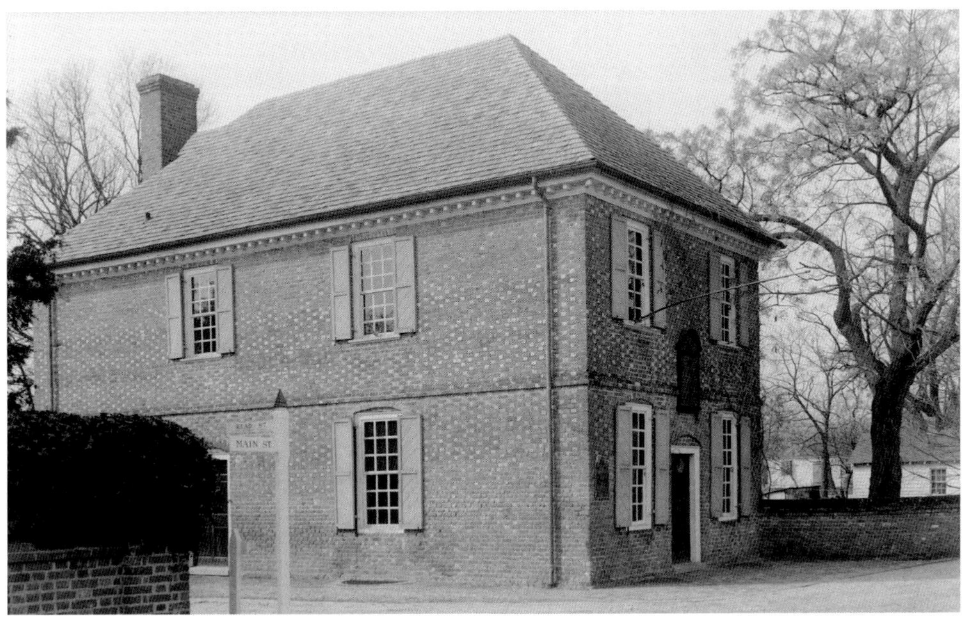

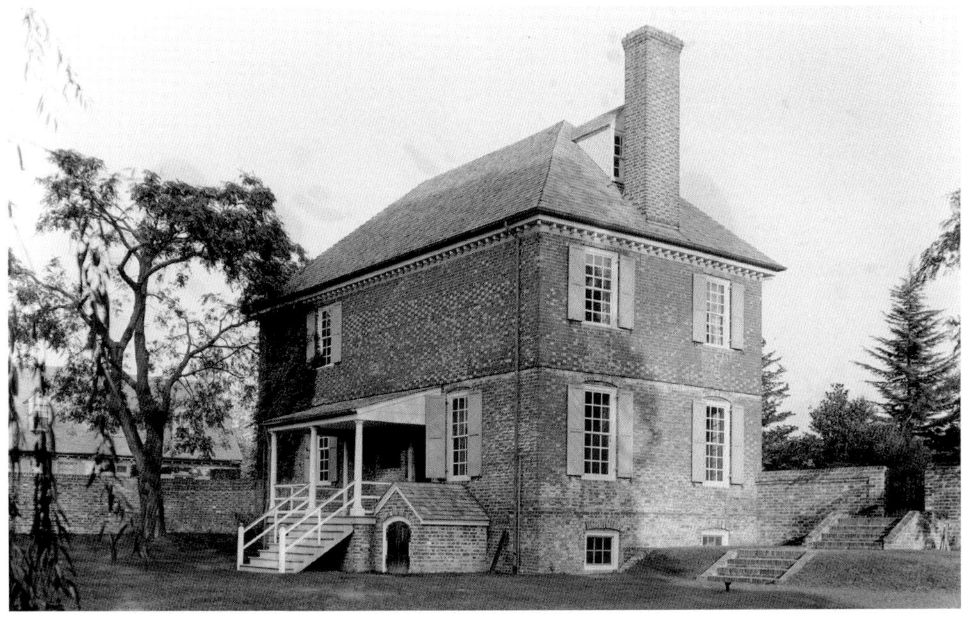

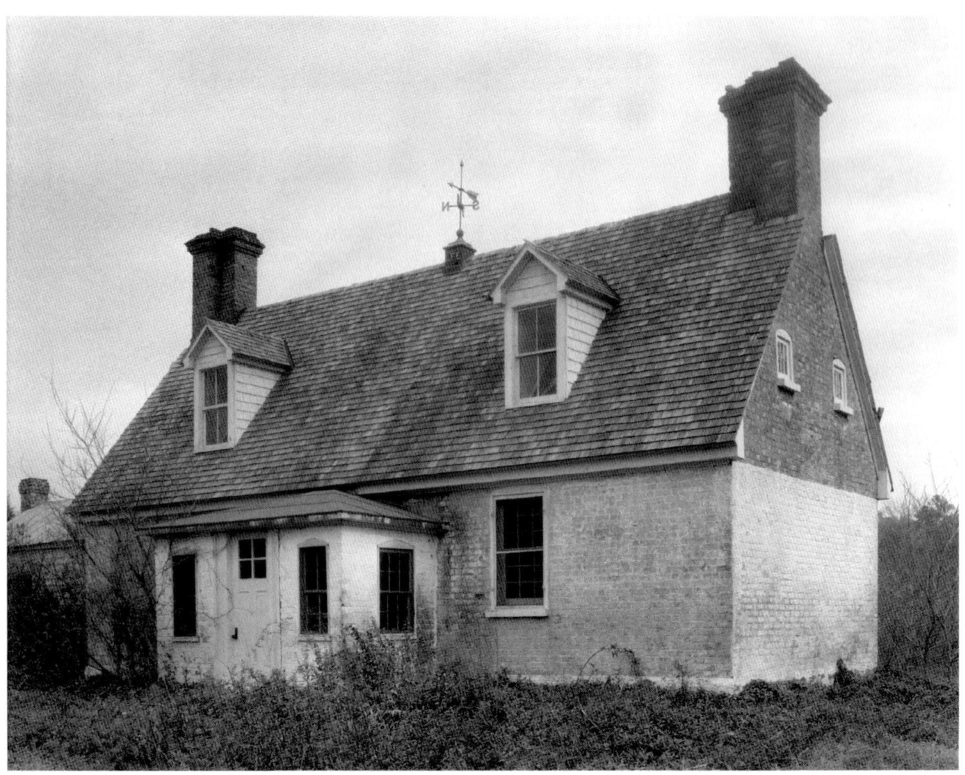

Kiskiack[3] [also called the Henry Lee House] exists as an eighteenth-century artifact characterized by extravagant brickwork popular in the mid-1720s. Kiskiack's most salient features are its T-shaped chimney stacks; implied by the detailing of these brick chimneys is a high level of craftsmanship, and thus the cost needed to construct them. The expense incurred by building in brick made such dwellings unusual in colonial Virginia, which was largely made up of communities filled with wood-frame houses. Kiskiack has been traditionally identified with Henry Lee who arrived from England in York County, Virginia, by 1640 and died there in 1657. Although county records do not substantiate this association, family birth and death records would appear to do so. The house's preservation is an effect of the belief that the property descended from Henry "Harry" Lee, the emigrant, to its last private owner, William Warren [Waring] Harrison Lee (1857–1936), who owned it until August 7, 1918, when it was taken by the federal government for the naval mine depot. When it passed out of Lee ownership, the Kiskiack farm was 265.33 acres, the original tract expanded with William Warren [Waring] Harrison Lee's purchases in 1911 and another in 1920 [he owned land within this tract until 1921 per the family history]. Lee family records indicate an alternate spelling of the name as "Kish Ki Oh Ke" [Kiskiack is also spelled Chiskiack, among others] for the Native American village and meaning "wide land" or "a broad place." The Indian village was located about three miles west of Yorktown on the "Charles York," now called the York River.[4] It was on this site, according to the family history, that Henry Lee was granted by colonial governor Sir William Berkeley (1605–1677) two hundred and forty-seven acres for the transportation of five persons to the Virginia colony from England in a land grant dated March 3, 1649. Family historical documentation would indicate that the residence was first constructed in 1650 to accommodate the arrival of Henry Lee's family but this has not been verified by archaeological studies of the structure or the surrounding property. Frances Benjamin Johnston took this picture of it in 1929 as part of the Carnegie Survey of Architecture of the South. *Library of Congress*

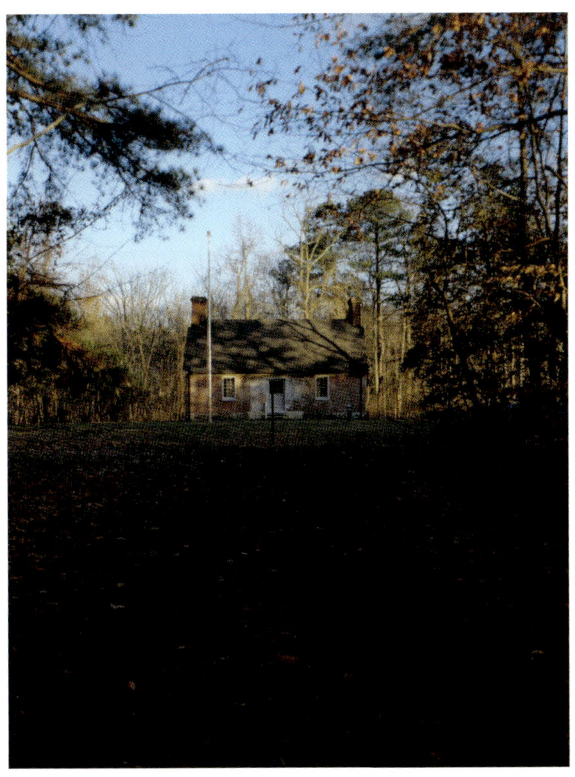

The last Lee family owner, William Warren [Waring] Harrison Lee, lived his entire life in Richmond, Virginia, and like most of the Lees from the eighteenth century forward, was an absentee owner of the property. The February 26, 1915 fire that destroyed the interior of the house was discovered by Lee's son William Henry Harwood Lee (1881–1935) in the early morning hours. All that remains of it is largely due to the efforts of the Henry Lee descendants to preserve the shell of this important piece of early Lower Tidewater architecture. By one account, offered by a naval officer assigned to the naval mine depot, Kiskiack was "rebuilt with the old walls on the original foundation [after this fire], the original type of architecture being carried through in detail."[5] Interpretations of this account implied that "old pink bricks" were used to rebuild the house on its foundations. Clearly some repairs were made, as evidenced in the archaeological test unit in the southeast corner and the mismatched, molded bricks marking the water table. After the federal government took over the property in the 1918 to 1919 period, the roof was further repaired, a back porch added and a bathroom installed on the second floor. These changes were completed in 1927 in preparation for occupancy. But the house remained vacant because it was sited in a restricted area of the depot. More changes were made in 1937, to include swapping the wood porch for a brick vestibule, lit by four windows and rebuilding a wood-frame wing on the north side. Years later, in 1953, the navy proposed demolishing this wing with the rear porch and bathroom. In the mid-1980s, due to recommendations made to the navy from Colonial Williamsburg, modern additions to Kiskiack were demolished, including the front and back porches and second floor bathroom. Despite all of these changes Kiskiack, located on the Naval Weapons Station Yorktown, is a rare survivor from the colonial period. Buffalo, New York native Jack Edward Boucher (1931–2012), a National Park Service photographer for forty-seven years, beginning in 1958, took this photograph of Kiskiack as part of a Historic American Buildings Survey (HABS) of the structure in February 1998. Boucher served as the chief photographer for the HABS and in the course of his career he created tens of thousands of photographs of an estimated seven to ten thousand buildings. As for Kiskiack, although the navy has stabilized the building, its chimneys persist in leaning. *Library of Congress*

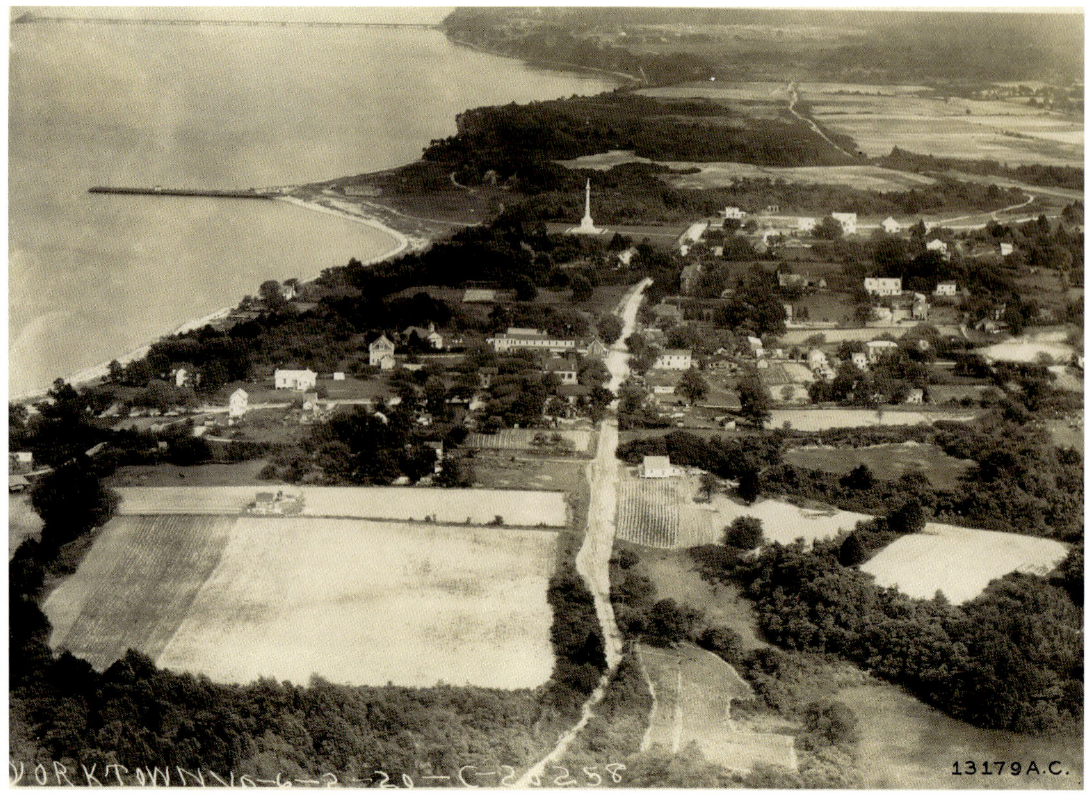

This aerial perspective of Yorktown was taken on December 6, 1923, by a Langley Field photographer. The road going up the center of the picture is Main Street. *National Archives*

Opposite page: The origin and construction date of the Cole Digges House [also called the Thomas Pate House], located at the corner of Main and Read Streets, has been under debate since the National Park Service elected to change the name to favor Digges, the son of Councilor Dudley Digges and the grandson of Edward Digges, who also served the Virginia colony as councilor as well as auditor-general, a Virginia agent in England, and governor for a two-year term, the latter during the period described as the Cromwellian Commonwealth. Called the Pate House until 2003, the house was originally thought to have been constructed by Thomas Pate, a ferryman and ordinary keeper at York Ferry, who owned the land from 1699 until his death in 1703. Yorktown law required that to retain ownership of property that a dwelling must be built within four months after purchase, thus pointing to a 1700 construction date. In Pate's will he gave "my House and Lott in York Town" to Joane Lawson, his caregiver in old age. The will specifies the property as Lot 42, where the Cole Digges House now stands. After extensive research and the use of dendrochronology to date the wood used in the house, the National Park Service has determined that Digges built the house in the early 1730s. The style of house was popular in the 1720s to 1750s. Tree-ring analysis performed on the wood used for the rafters of the house indicated that the wood was harvested in or around 1730. Surprised by the name change, descendants of Thomas Pate commissioned the Laboratory of Tree-Ring Science at the University of Tennessee and the Tree-Ring Laboratory at Columbia University to challenge the park service's findings. The 1730s tree ring date was confirmed, but the study points out that extensive renovations have been made since the Battle of Yorktown and that the wood used for the repairs may not be original. *Continued on next page*

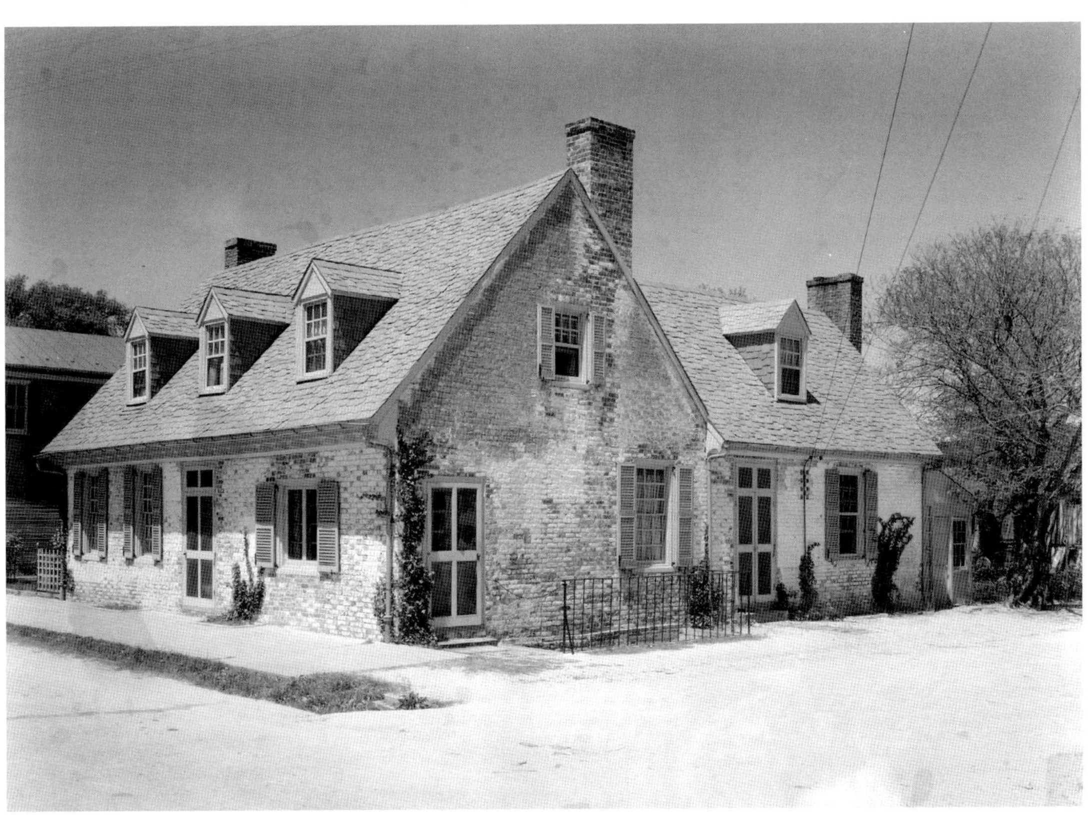

Continued from previous page: The house was damaged during the fighting at Yorktown and again during a fire in 1814 that burned much of the city. The existing nails and cutting techniques used to repair the rafters date from the early nineteenth century. Some theorized that the wood used for the repairs came from other old buildings that were damaged beyond repair during the 1814 fire, such as the second courthouse that was built in 1733. That would explain 1730s wood in a 1700 house. When the Yorktown Historic District was added to the National Register of Historic Places on October 15, 1966, it was noted that the house originally had exterior end chimneys, but the western stack was altered to allow a window in the gable, and the eastern chimney had been converted to an interior one. A modillion cornice was found at the roofline. The house was extensively remodeled after Helen McGraw Longyear Paul (1884–1960), a graduate of the Massachusetts Institute of Technology and the wife of a naval officer Carroll Paul[6] (1882–1937), bought the house in 1921. The National Park Service presently affirms the Cole Digges nomenclature. When Frances Benjamin Johnston photographed the house in 1933 for the Carnegie Survey of the Architecture of the South, it was logged as the "Thomas Pate House."
Library of Congress

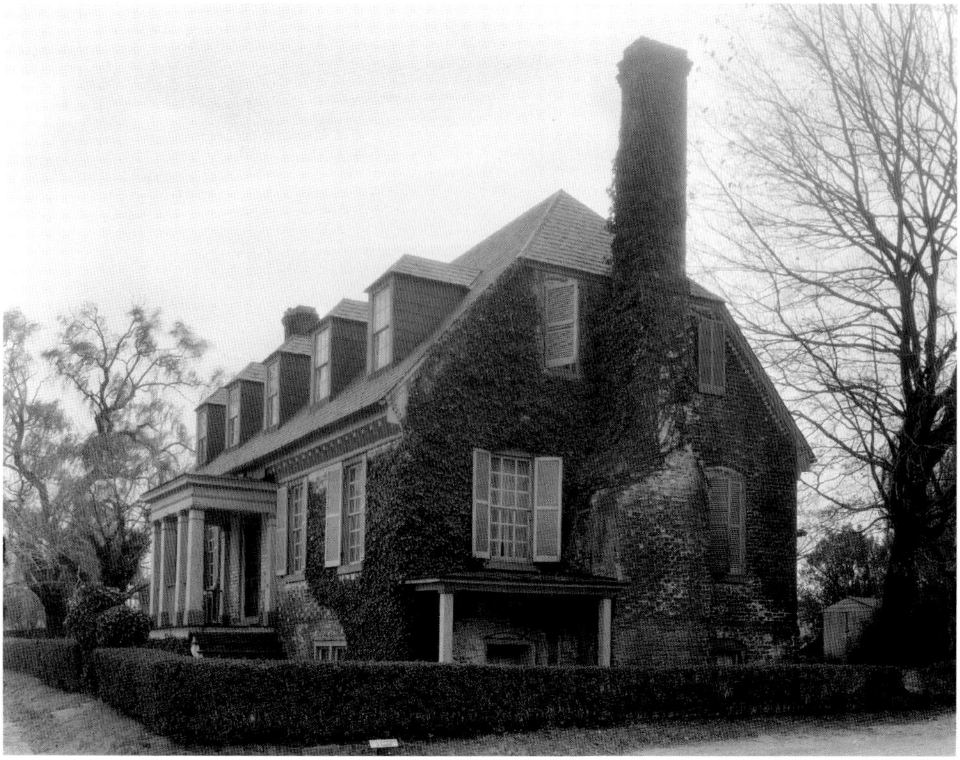

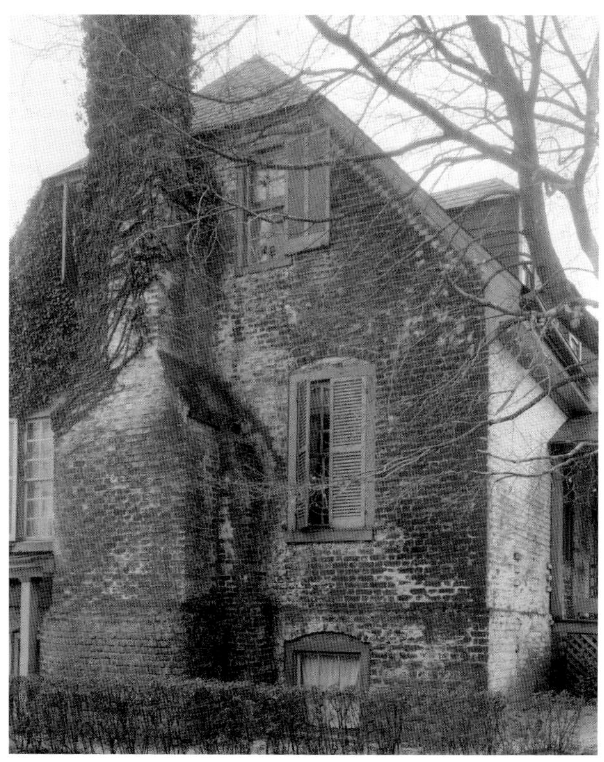

Opposite page: Standing on a half-acre lot at the corner of Main and Nelson Streets prominent as the head of the Great Valley that led directly down to the waterfront and to the York River, the one-and-a-half story, brick southern colonial-styled dwelling known as the Sessions-Pope-Sheild House [commonly known as the Sheild House] [Lot 56] is an excellent example of a mid-eighteenth-century masonry dwelling, with its Flemish bond brickwork and ornate north end chimney. The structure and its grounds have remained virtually untouched for nearly three hundred years. One architectural historian has identified the home as being among the earliest southern colonial dwellings with a jerkin-head roof. Also notable are the large exterior entrance door and a handsomely carved central hall entrance in the interior of the house. The Sheild House has been continuously occupied as a single-family dwelling since it was first built. Members of the current owner's family have occupied it for one hundred years. According to early colonial records Thomas Sessions (1640–1705), the first owner of the lot, was a carpenter or joiner and an active member of the community who frequently found himself a defendant in numerous court proceedings for nonpayment of his debts. Yet, despite this, he managed to build a dwelling on his property as required by law and he and his wife, Hester, disposed of the lots [56 and 57] and development by sale in January 1702.[7] But it is highly doubtful that the brick house shown here, photographed by Frances Benjamin Johnston in or about 1933 as part of the Carnegie Survey of the Architecture of the South, is that house. Of note, not only did Sessions retain ownership of Lot 56, but in 1699 he somehow managed to purchase the adjoining Lot 57, and now listed his occupation as "In[n]holder," to suggest that the Sessions House was not exclusively or even primarily a residence but served as an ordinary for the town. The property passed through various owners until Lot 56 was sold to Dr. Matthew Pope (1740–1791) in 1766, who most likely built the brick house that stands today. Based on available records, Pope appears to have been a successful Yorktown surgeon, serving in the Revolutionary War, where at one point he served as head of the Yorktown military hospital. After the war, Pope was active in local Yorktown affairs, being appointed as a trustee of the town in 1784, and later serving as mayor in 1788. After the doctor's death, the house again passed through a string of owners until Fanny Burwell Nelson Mercer (1848–1932), the daughter of William Nelson Jr. (1801–1849) and the former Martha Bryan Sheild (1818–1881) and the wife of Corbin Waller Mercer (1845–1910), sold it to her first cousin, Judge Conway Howard Sheild[8] (1870–1928), in 1901 for five hundred dollars. Since that time the property has remained in the Sheild family. Although not its principal significance, the Sheild House played a small role in the history of the area. During the Civil War, after troops under the command of Confederate major general John Bankhead "Prince John" Magruder at last abandoned Yorktown, the Sheild House served as the field headquarters for Union brigadier general Henry Morris Naglee (1815–1886), who, according to one historical account, used the front parlor as an office. During the Sheilds' ownership, a number of distinguished visitors have come to the house, including Presidents Woodrow Wilson, Warren Harding, Herbert Hoover, and Franklin Delano Roosevelt. While a number of local histories have previously tried to tie the house shown here to Sessions, physical and documentary evidence makes it clear that the date of construction occurred in the early period of Pope's ownership. The first illustration of Main Street Yorktown dated 1755 shows no evidence of a brick house like the Sheild House on Lot 56. An advertisement in the 1768 *Virginia Gazette*, published two years after Pope acquired the lot, provides a description of a brick house similar to the Sheild House. *Library of Congress*

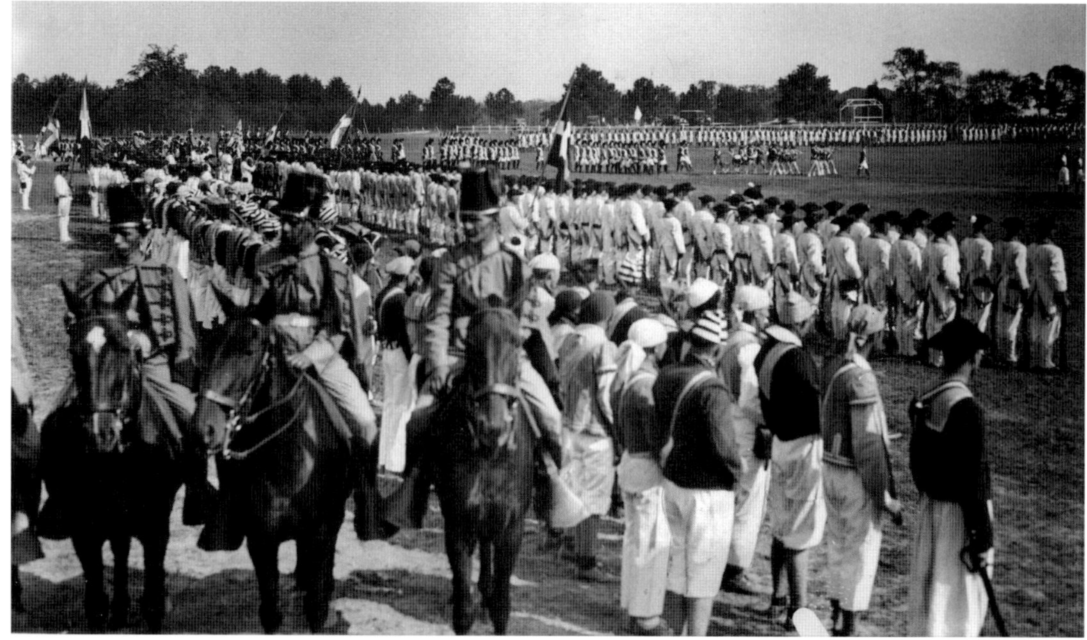

Infantry and cavalry troops were shown drawn up for battle at a rehearsal for the elaborate Yorktown sesquicentennial surrender pageant that was to begin the following day, October 16, 1931, and carry on for several days. The celebration of America's victory over the British included grand scenes such as the one shown here and the surrender of Lord Cornwallis to the American forces, and reenactments of significant events of the Revolutionary War and historic vignettes showcasing the original thirteen colonies. Fiennes Stanley Wykeham Cornwallis, First Baron Cornwallis [Lord Cornwallis] came from England to be an honored guest throughout the October 16–19, 1931 event. *Amy Waters Yarsinske*

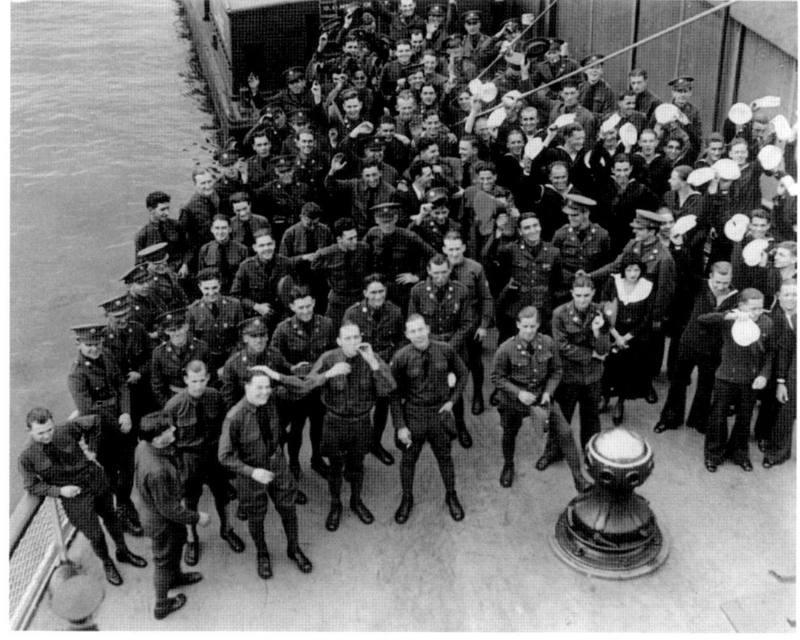

A contingent of New York State national guardsmen boarded the liner SS *Northland* (shown here) on October 15, 1931, bound for the Yorktown sesquicentennial in which they had been scheduled to participate. *Amy Waters Yarsinske*

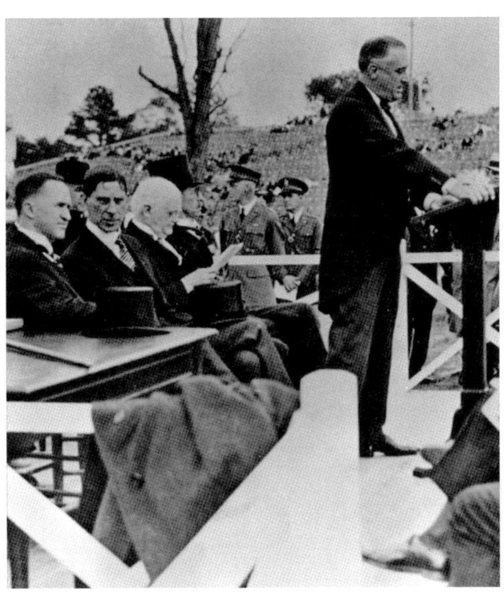

(Left to right) Director of the National Park Service Horace Marden Albright[9] (1890–1987), Secretary of Interior Ray Lyman Wilbur M.D.[10] (1875–1949), and Virginia governor John Garland Pollard (1871–1937) listened to New York governor Franklin Delano Roosevelt (1882–1945) deliver his address at the sesquicentennial anniversary of the celebration of the American victory at Yorktown. Roosevelt spoke on October 16, 1931, participating in the dedication of a bust of Lord Cornwallis that kicked off the celebration. *National Park Service*

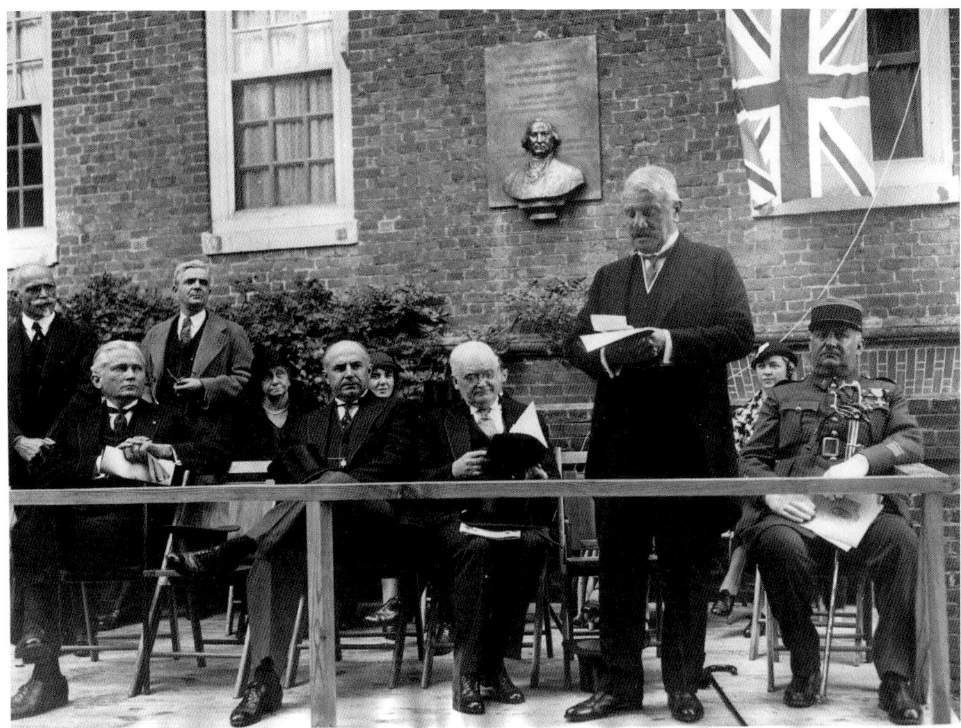

Fiennes Stanley Wykeham Cornwallis, First Baron Cornwallis [Lord Cornwallis][11] (1864–1935), of Great Britain, was photographed at Yorktown on October 16, 1931, speaking at the unveiling of a bust of his distinguished ancestor who was defeated by George Washington at Yorktown during the Revolutionary War. Dedication of the bust was at the Thomas Nelson House [also called York Hall], which also served as his ancestor Lord Cornwallis' Yorktown headquarters during the siege. The unveiling opened the sesquicentennial celebration. This scene was just one of many that played out at the sesquicentennial pageant at Yorktown held from October 16–19, 1931. *Amy Waters Yarsinske*

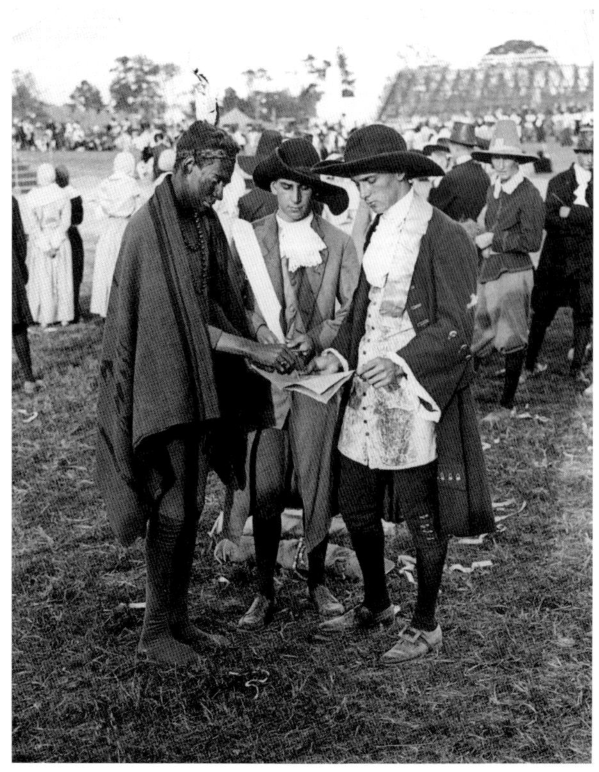

As part of the Yorktown sesquicentennial held at Yorktown, a pageant depicting scenes from the history of the original thirteen colonies of the United States took place on October 16, 1931. This photograph shows a reenactment of William Penn (1644–1718) signing the Treaty of Shackamaxon [also called the Great Treaty] in which he famously entered into a peace agreement with Tamanend (1625–1701), a chief of the Lenape Turtle Clan in 1683, during the Pennsylvania episode of the pageant. (Left to right) Ernest Davis Proudman Jr. (1915–2012), of Hampton, Virginia, depicts the Tamanend; Marvin Benton Page (1915–2002), of Messick, Virginia, played the aide to William Penn, and John Preston Hardy (1910–1984) took the role of William Penn. An Acme photographer took the picture. *Amy Waters Yarsinske*

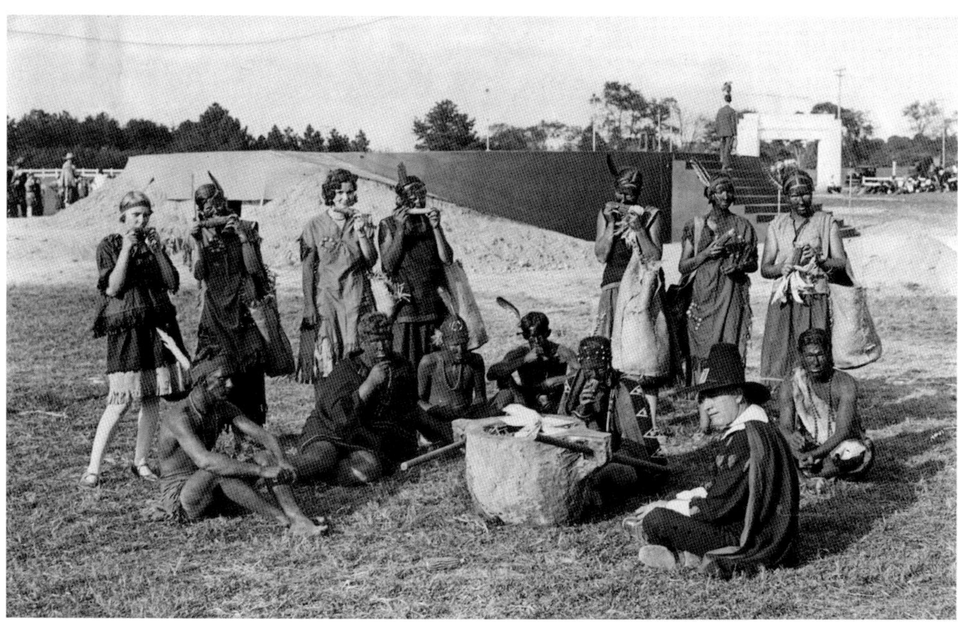

In this scene from the sesquicentennial pageant held on October 16, 1931, Roger Williams (1603–1683), played by James Walter Kenney (1880–1970), of Abingdon, Gloucester County, Virginia, and superintendent of the county's public schools, is shown reenacting a feast with Indians prior to landing at Narragansett, Rhode Island. *Amy Waters Yarsinske*

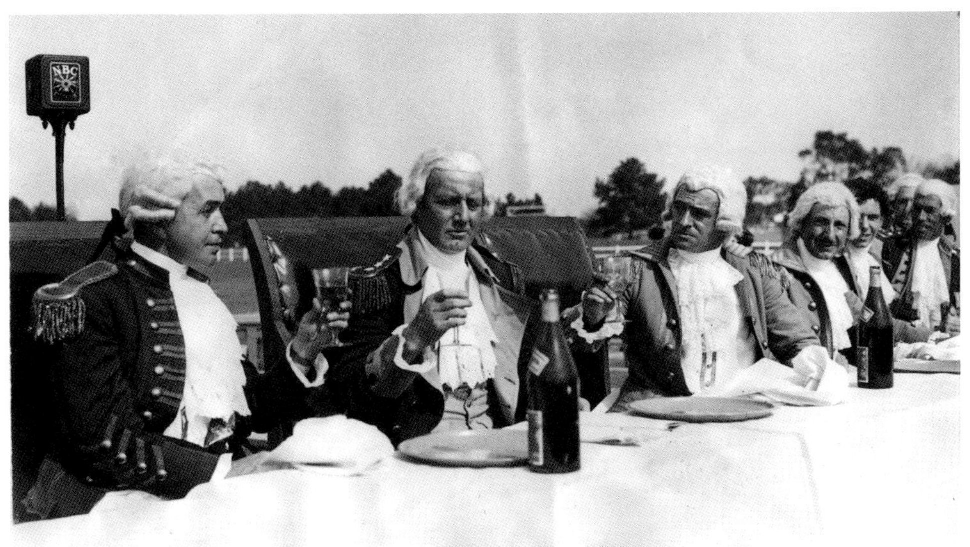

This reenactment of a historic scene when the leaders of three armies of the Revolutionary War celebrated the end of fighting with a huge open-air banquet at Yorktown following Lord Cornwallis' surrender on October 19, 1781, was held on that date one hundred and fifty years later. Reenactors portraying (left to right) British major general Charles Edward Cornwallis V, Lord Cornwallis, Continental Army general George Washington, and French army general Jean-Baptiste Donatien de Vimeur, Comte de Rochambeau, drink wine at the dinner. *Amy Waters Yarsinske*

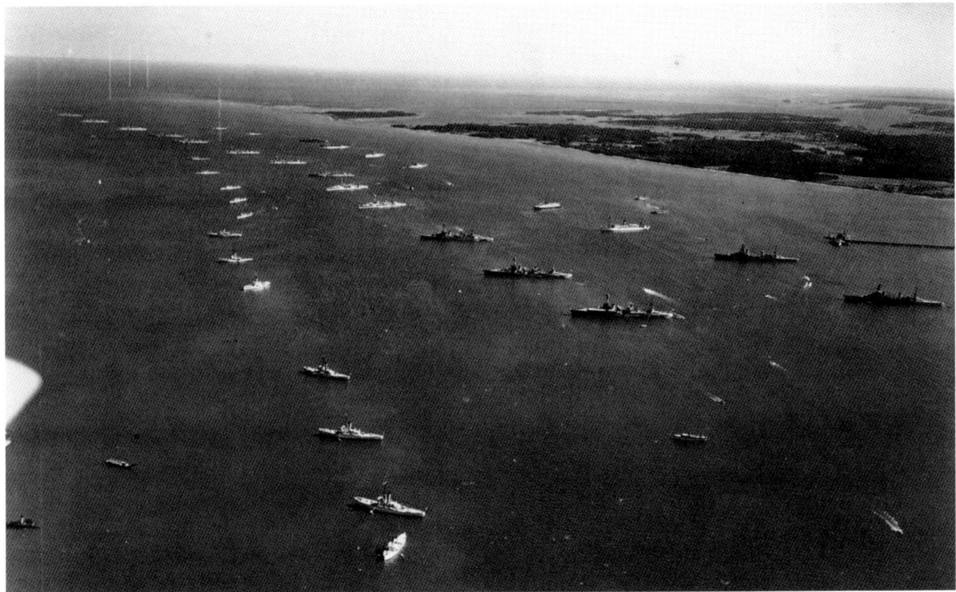

Warships were photographed anchored off Yorktown, Virginia, for the Battle of Yorktown sesquicentennial celebrations held between October 16–19, 1931. The picture shown here was taken from a United States Army Air Corps plane on October 17 and the ships include six United States Coast Guard cutters and thirteen United States Navy cruisers, seven destroyers, and the aircraft carrier USS *Langley* (CV-1), two French heavy cruisers, and other assorted ships. *Naval History and Heritage Command*

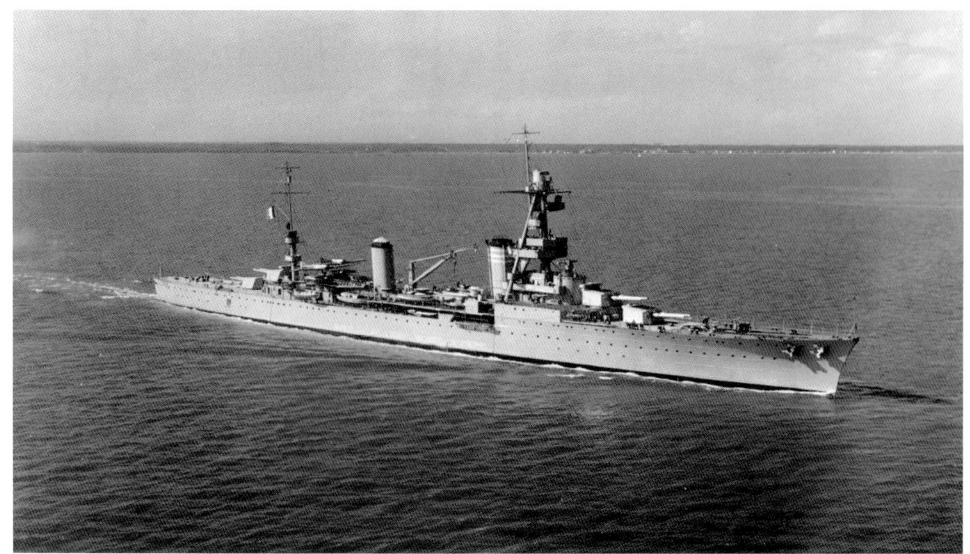

This is the French navy ship *Suffren*, a heavy cruiser and lead ship of the four-ship class, shown here on October 15, 1931, in Hampton Roads to attend the Yorktown sesquicentennial. The *Suffren*, the sixth ship named in honor of eighteenth-century French admiral comte Pierre André de Suffren de Saint Tropez, bailli de Suffren (1729–1788), was laid down at Arsenal de Brest on April 4, 1926, and decommissioned on October 1, 1947. *Naval History and Heritage Command*

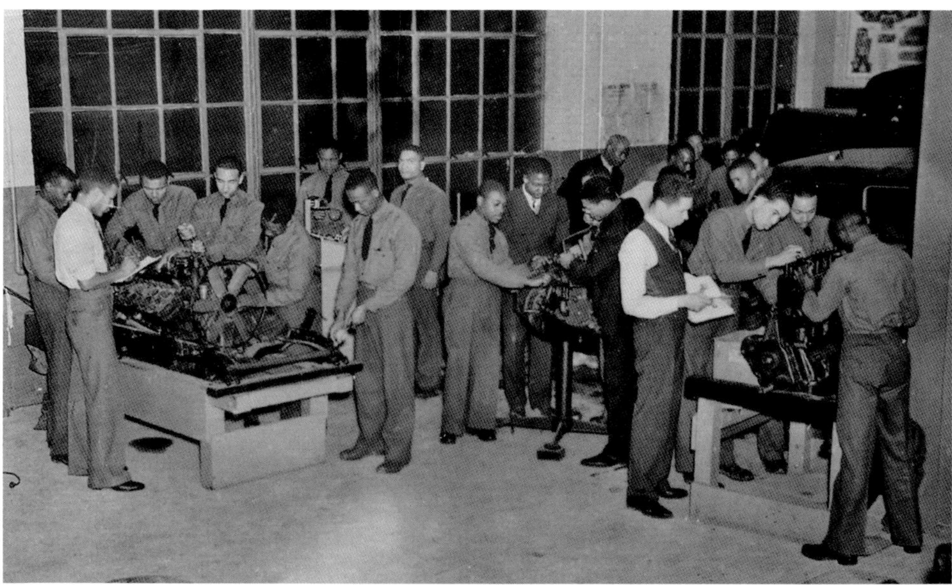

The Civilian Conservation Corps (CCC), Third Corps Area, sent African American company 1351 from Langley Field (shown here), where they began to learn vocational trades before deploying them to projects in Virginia's Historic Triangle [Jamestown–Williamsburg–Yorktown] to southside Hampton Roads. Here, men of the company are working with machinery. The picture was taken in the spring of 1933, before the company was sent to Vermont that July to work on a flood control project. This company was formed specifically to staff vocational projects for black veterans of World War I. *Franklin Delano Roosevelt Presidential Library and Museum*

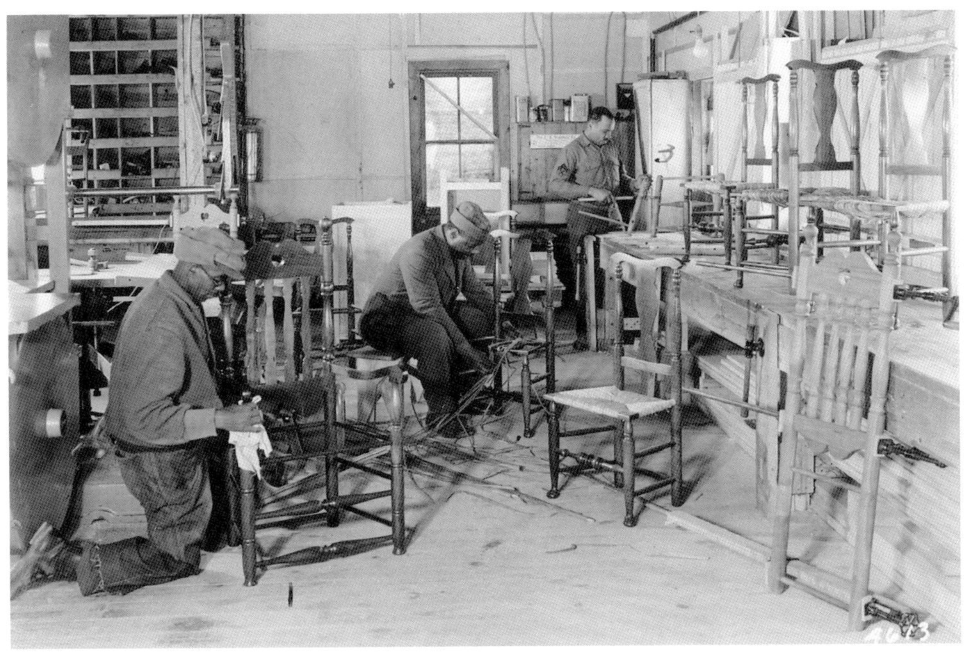

In this spring 1933 photograph, men of Civilian Conservation Corps (CCC) Company 1351 are shown furniture making in the Yorktown camp. *Franklin Delano Roosevelt Presidential Library and Museum*

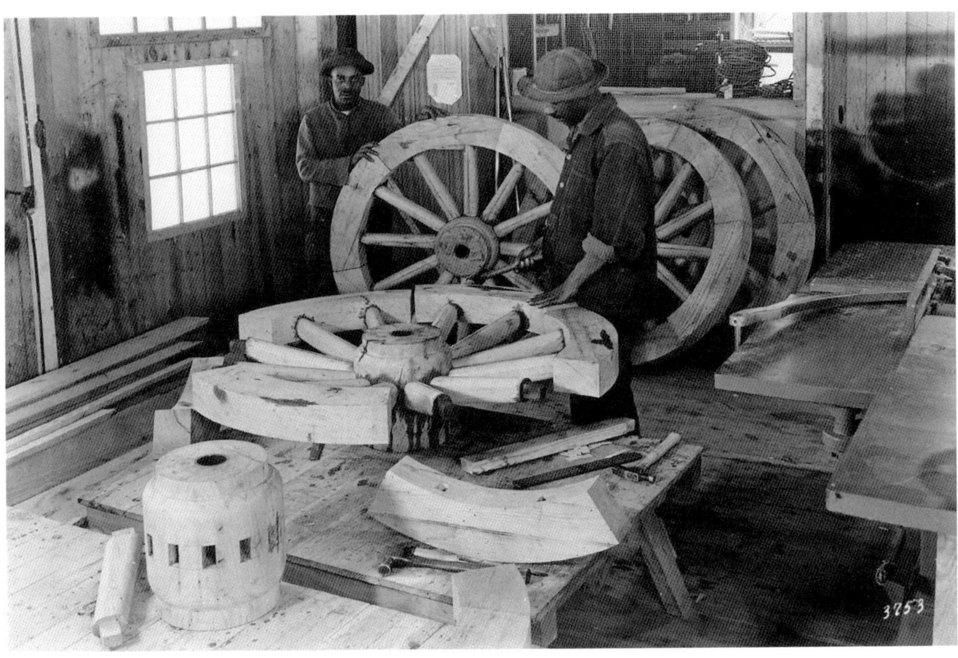

Men of CCC Company 1351, shown in this spring 1933 picture taken at Yorktown, were building wheels for cannon carriages. *Franklin Delano Roosevelt Presidential Library and Museum*

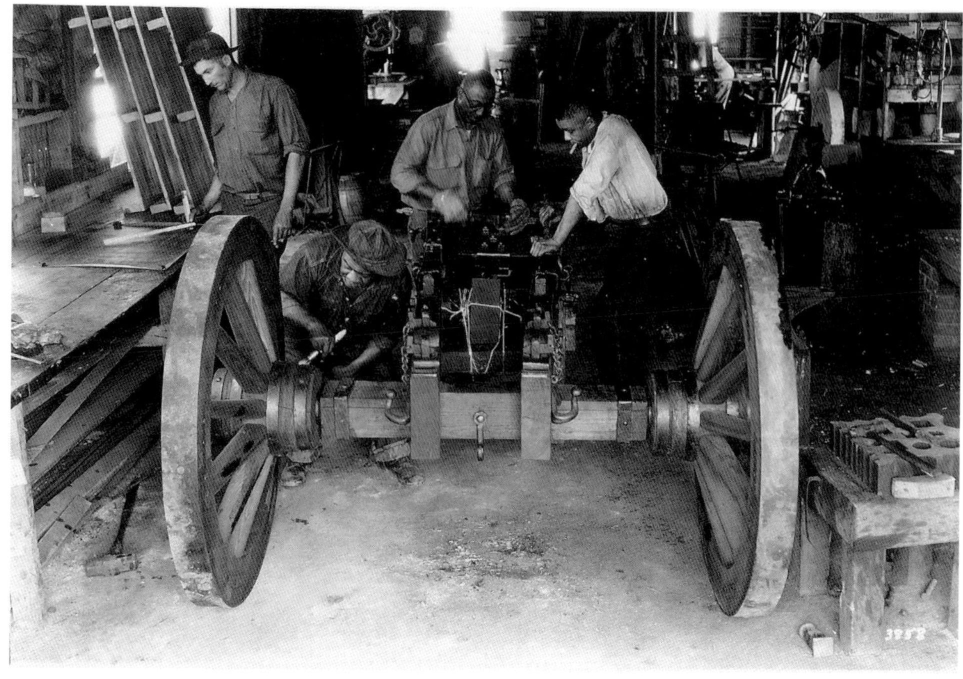

In this photograph, another CCC crew was building and assembling cannon carriages, photographed in or about the spring of 1933. The CCC operated a carpenter shop in Yorktown, where they built carriages like the one shown here to mount cannon on the battlefield. *National Park Service*

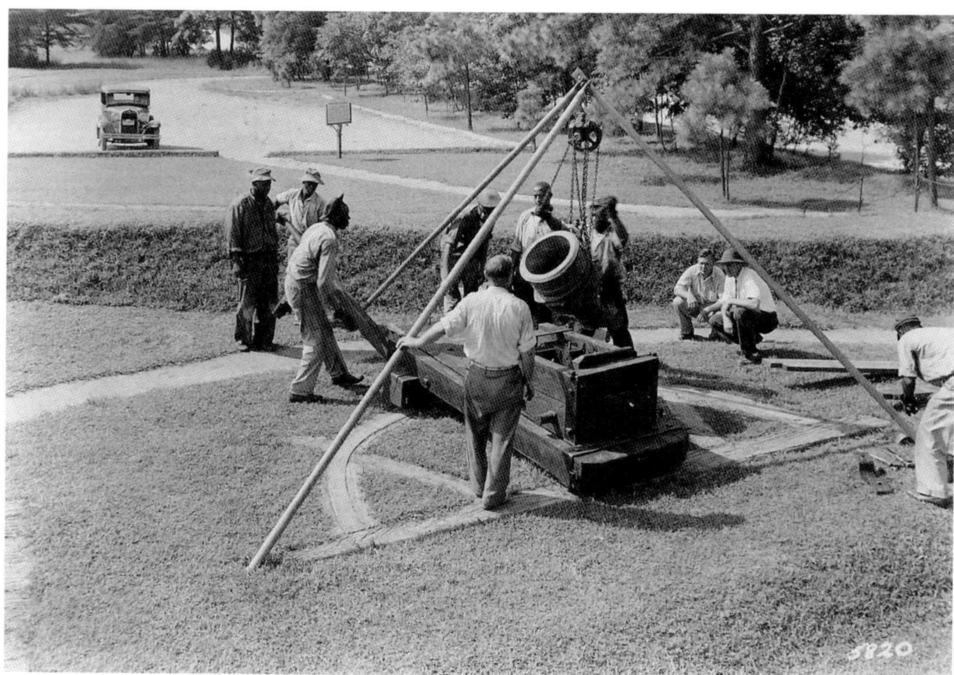

A CCC crew mounts a mortar in the Grand French Battery on the Yorktown Battlefield in or about 1933. Portions of the Riverview Golf Course can be seen in the background. *National Park Service*

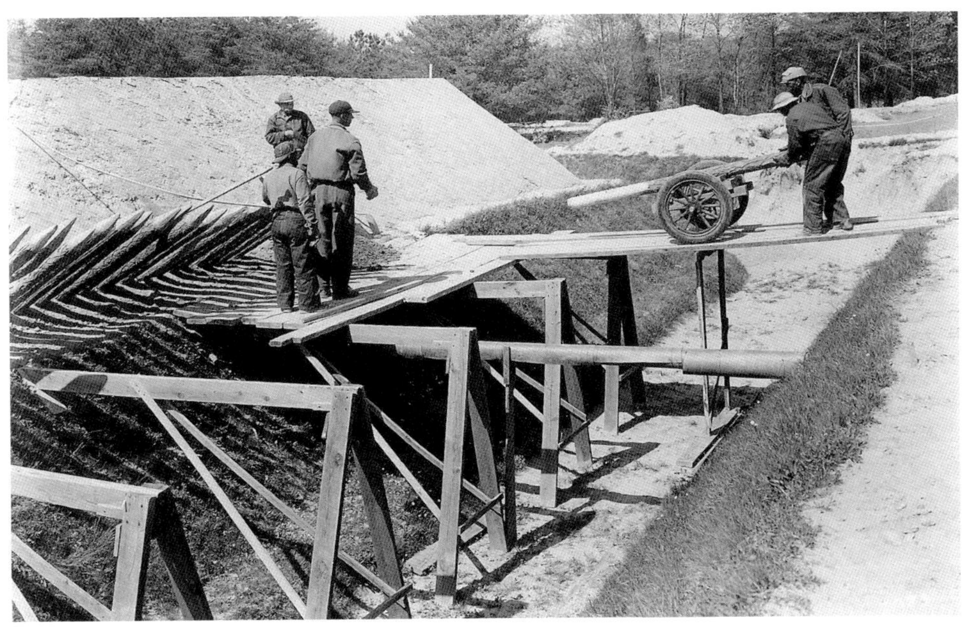

A Civilian Conservation Corps (CCC) crew installs fraises as part of the reconstruction of fortifications on the Yorktown Battlefield. Company 1351 and four additional African American CCC companies, developed the Colonial National Historical Park. The CCC enrollees worked under the direction of the National Park Service, which had just taken over the job of caring for military and historical parks from the United States Army. *National Park Service*

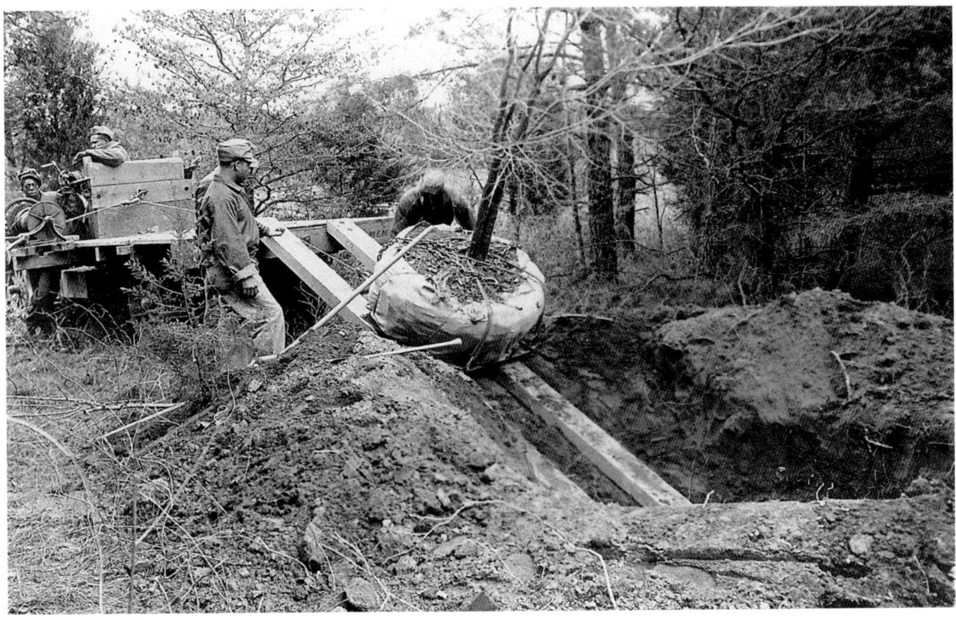

Meticulous landscaping is a hallmark of classically designed parkways. More than seventeen thousand trees and shrubs were planted between Yorktown and Williamsburg, including pines, cedars, dogwoods, redbuds, tulip and beech trees by CCC workers (shown here). *National Park Service*

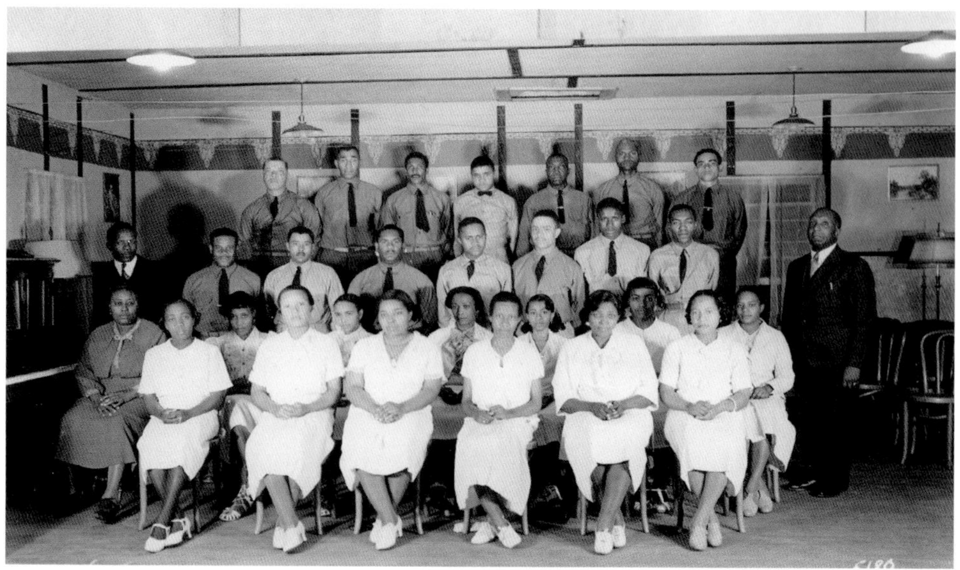

African Americans (shown here), among them World War I veterans, working in the Civilian Conservation Corps (CCC) camp NHP-2 at Yorktown formed a glee club. The young women who joined them and are also pictured lived nearby, meeting them at a church around the corner from camp, where there was a good piano. This glee club became very popular while the camp was in operation. Standing far right is Clarence Henry Brown (1900–1983), a Farmville, Virginia native with a four-year college degree and a carpenter by trade, who served as the educational adviser to the CCC camp for veterans; his assistant is in the dark suit to the left. The picture was taken in or about 1935. *National Archives*

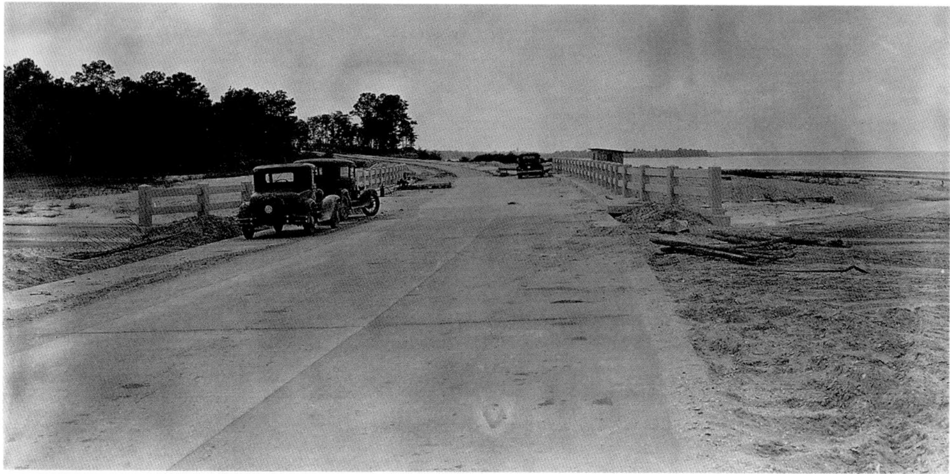

Indian Field Creek Bridge was built at the confluence of Indian Field Creek and the York River as part of Unit IV construction. At this section the roadway extends out over the York River on hydraulic fill. The low-level concrete slab bridge was designed to blend into the environment and provide maximum views of the river and tidal marshes. The bridge, built between 1932 and 1933 by the Sanford and Brooks Company, of Baltimore, Maryland, was one of three open deck bridges built along the first leg of the Colonial Parkway from Yorktown to Williamsburg. The bridge was rebuilt in 1980 by the J. Lawson Jones Construction Company, of Clarksville, Virginia. The bridge was just nearing completion when this picture was taken. *National Park Service*

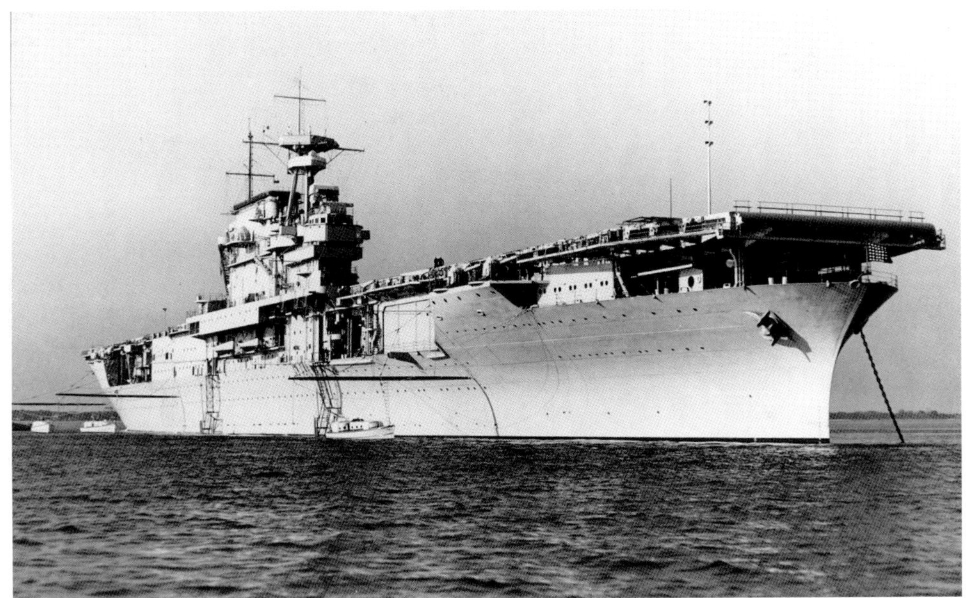

The third United States Navy ship to be named for Yorktown was the aircraft carrier USS *Yorktown* (CV-5), shown here at anchor in Hampton Roads on October 30, 1937. The ship was laid down on May 21, 1934, at Newport News Shipbuilding and Drydock Company and sponsored by first lady Eleanor Roosevelt. The *Yorktown* was commissioned at Naval Station Norfolk on September 30, 1937, with Captain Ernest Doyle McWhorter[12] (1884–1950) in command. After fitting out, the aircraft carrier trained in Hampton Roads and in the Southern Drill Grounds off the Virginia Capes into January of 1938, conducting carrier qualifications for her newly embarked air group. Just a few years later, during World War II combat action in the Pacific theater, this first aircraft carrier *Yorktown* sustained irreparable damage during the Battle of Midway, turned over on her port side and sank in three thousand fathoms of water on June 7, 1942, her battle flags still flying. *Yorktown* received three battle stars for her World War II service, two of them from the significant part she played in stopping Japanese expansion and turning the tide of the war at the Battles of the Coral Sea and Midway. *Naval History and Heritage Command*

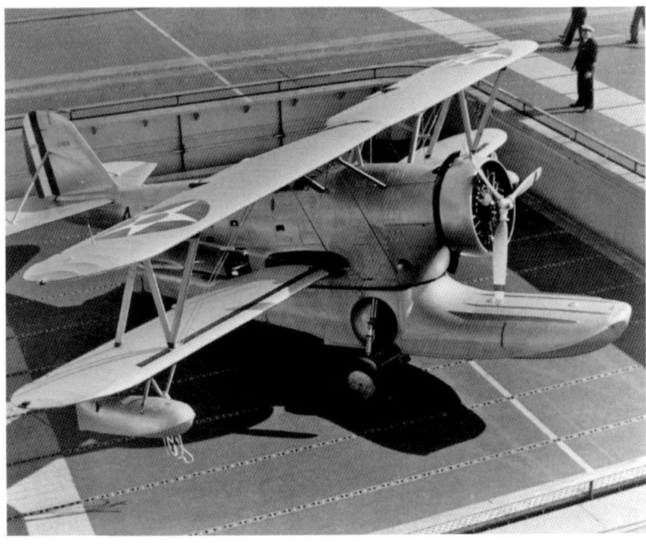

A Grumman J2F-1 utility plane [bureau number 0169] is shown on the midships elevator of the USS *Yorktown* (CV-5) on November 2, 1937. This J2F-1 was plane number four of the ship's utility squadron. *National Archives*

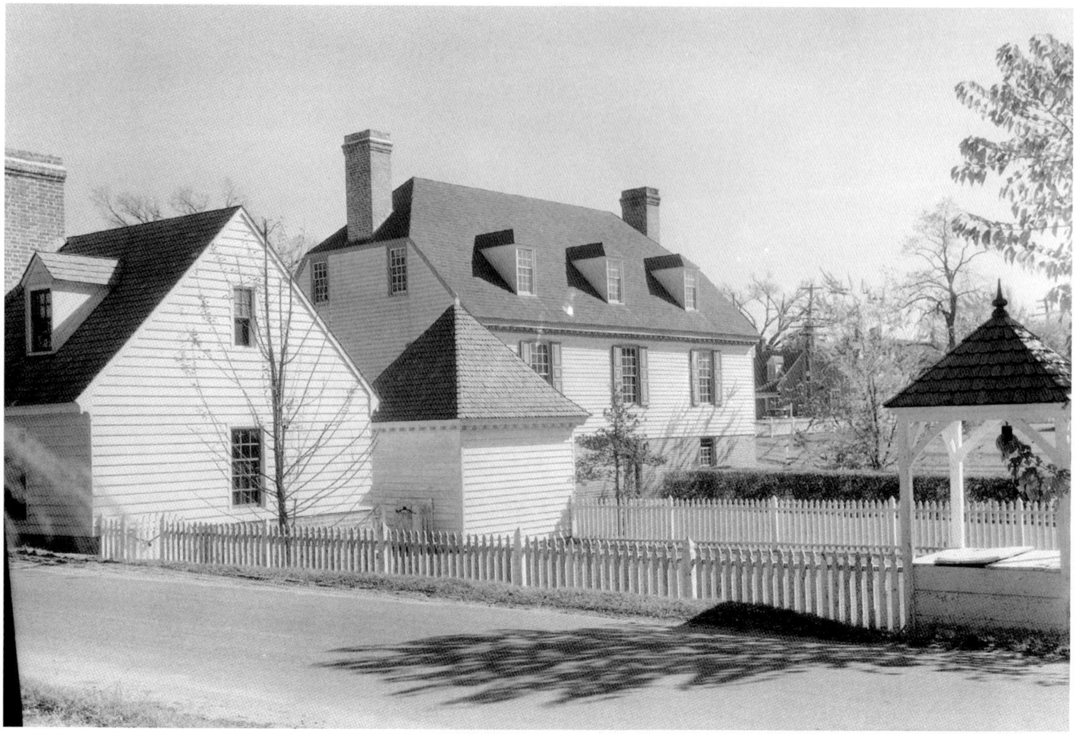

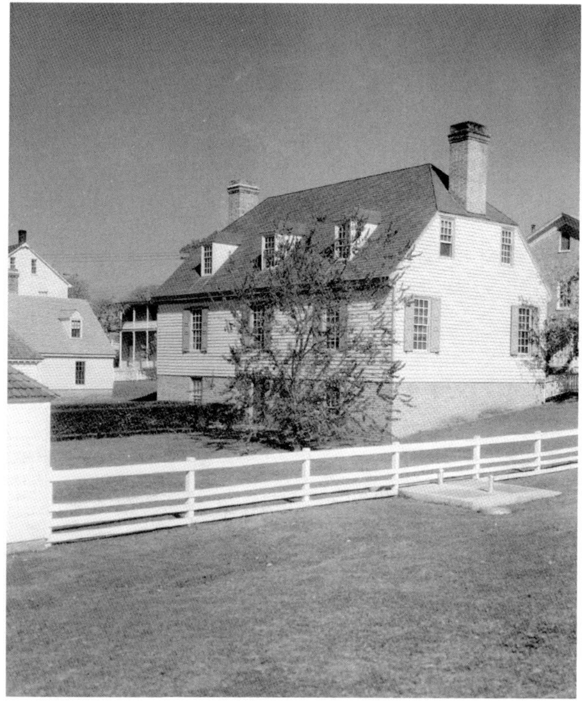

The original Swan Tavern [Lot 25] was built at the intersection of Main and Ballard Streets opposite the courthouse. The building is believed to have been erected by Thomas Nelson and Joseph Walker (1680–1723), who owned the property at that time, between 1719 and 1722. It was destroyed as the result of an explosion originating at the courthouse in 1863, and reconstructed by the National Park Service in 1934 from data accumulated through extensive research. Investigation of old ground lines showed that the basement [built of brick] must have been largely aboveground. This, coupled with the manner of the destruction of the superstructure, and the fact that another building had been built partly over the site in 1881, resulted in its almost complete demolition. The remains were excavated in 1932 and 1933. Insurance records dating to 1796 and 1806 revealed an original block fifty-two-feet, ten inches by thirty-one-feet, six inches, to which appendages had been constructed, apparently prior to the 1796 map. Within this main block was found a cross wall at about a third of the length. For the reconstruction, the insurance record of 1796 [which provided a sketch elevation], a Mathew Brady photograph taken in 1863, wills, inventories, deeds, and local precedent were relied upon to rebuild Swan Tavern. These views of Swan Tavern were taken by landscape architect Albert S. Burns (1905–1973) in or about 1935 as part of a Historic American Buildings Survey (HABS). *Library of Congress*

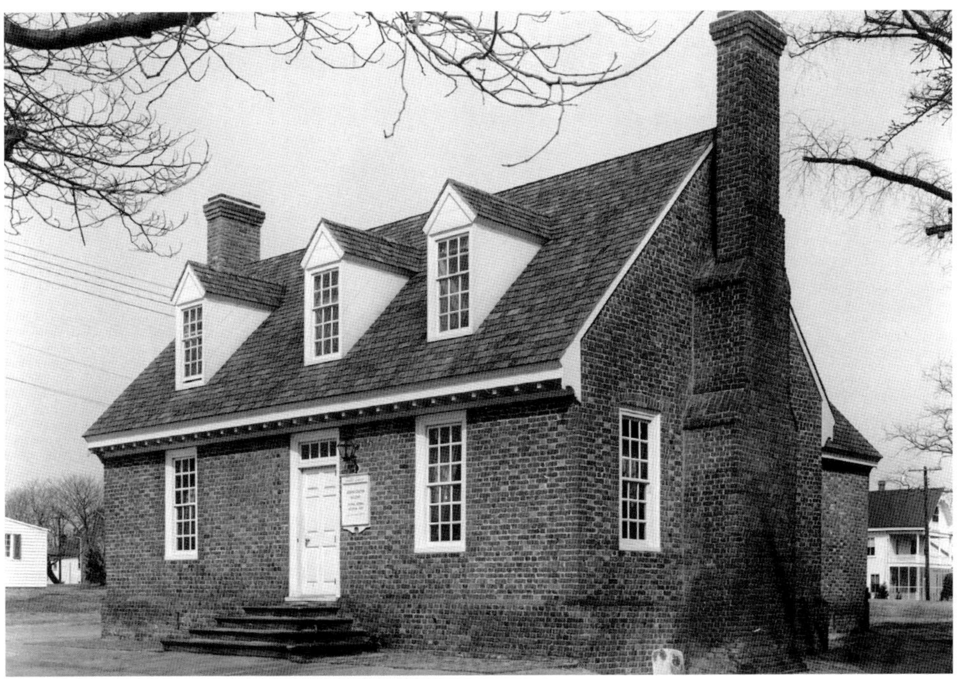

The Mungo Somerwell House [also called the Lightfoot House] [Lot 36], located at Main and Church Streets, is another structure with a date and origin in question. The home is named for Mungo Somerwell, who owned property in the first decade of the 1700s. York County Court records dated September 24, 1702, indicate: "On the Peticon [petition] of Mungo Somerwell to this court for his keeping the ferry in York Town of Same is accordingly granted." He was seeking a license just then to operate a ferry. Subsequent county records show that Somerwell, in addition to operating a ferry, simultaneously held several jobs, including that of merchant, keeper of an ordinary and town constable. When he died in February 1707, his widow, the former Elizabeth Leightonhouse, was ordered by the court to have his estate "appraised at his late dwelling house." This estate included the house as well as gardens, stables, warehouses and other appurtenances. Nearly a decade later, in 1716, the property was bought by Philip Lightfoot, and the house on the lot became known as the Lightfoot House. While it is possible that Lightfoot built it, there have been so many renovations over the years that today make it nearly impossible to unravel the correct construction date. The National Park Service has opted to go with the name of the original property owner and has thus, so it would appear, has also acknowledged a construction date between 1700 and 1707, making it the oldest house in Yorktown. Of note, the house is never mentioned in a list of the oldest houses and publicly it is largely believed to have been built in or around 1720, making it the Lightfoot House [which is what it was called when the home was photographed in 1935 as part of a field report turned into the Department of the Interior for a Historic American Buildings Survey (HABS)]. The National Park Service purchased the house in 1937, restoring it to its 1700s appearance. During the renovation, it was clear just how extensive the alterations to the house had been, particularly during the Civil War when it was used as a hospital. The park service first used the building as a visitor center and park headquarters. While it is still owned by the park service, the Mungo Somerwell House is used as a rental property. *Library of Congress*

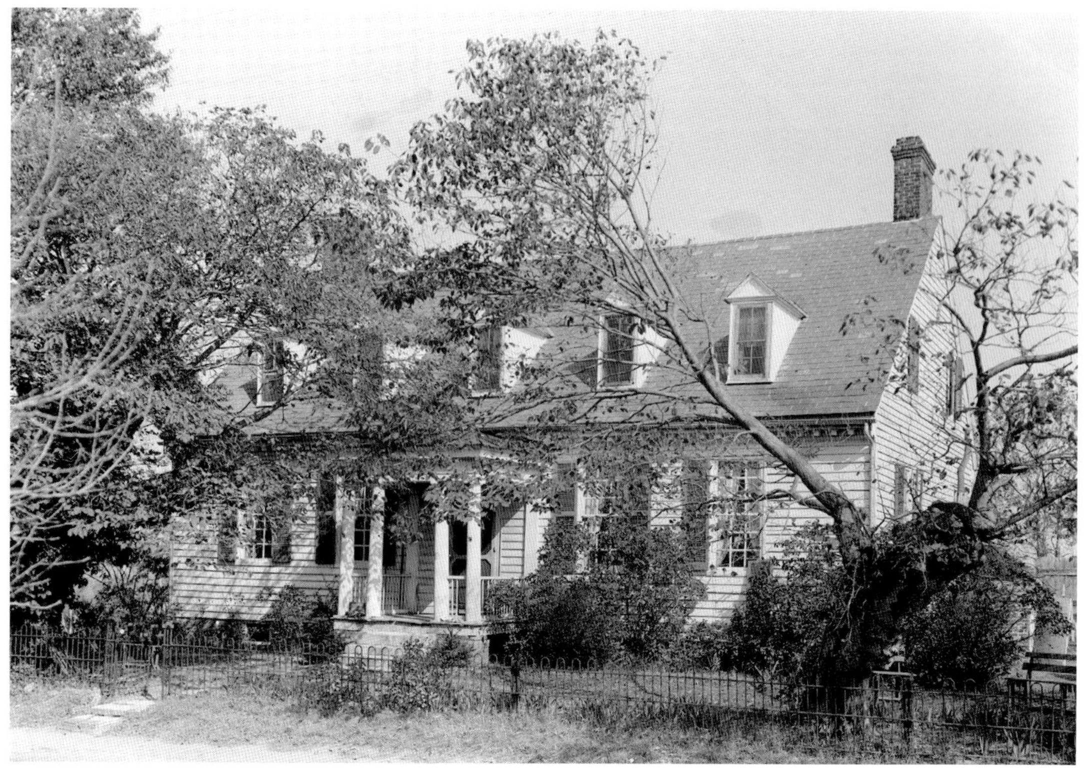

Above and top of next page: Dudley Digges (1723–1790) built this house on a half-acre parcel [Lot 77] between 1755 and 1760. When he took ownership of the property, it is believed that he dismantled an earlier thirty-six-by-eighteen-foot frame house with a cellar that had been built by Miles and Emanuel Wills soon after they were assigned the lot in 1706. Local legend has it that Digges' first wife, the former Martha Armistead (1721–1771), who died in childbirth while living in Yorktown, still haunts the house. Digges, a member of the Virginia General Assembly, was captured by the British during a raid at Charlottesville, Virginia, on June 4, 1781; he remained a prisoner until after the war. The house was damaged enough during the fighting at Yorktown that Digges moved to Williamsburg after the Revolutionary War and never returned to it. Major John Rowles West (1795–1852) bought the property from Elizabeth Digges Nicholson in 1821, which led to it being called the West House for a period of time. John West, a member of the Virginia governor's staff, married Elizabeth Page Nelson (1798–1839), the daughter of William Anderson Nelson (1763–1801) and the former Sarah Burwell (1767–1839) on February 11, 1818. According to documentation submitted by the wife of Judge Sydney Smith (1859–1938), the former Margaret Pond Crooks (1873–1950) and received by the National Park Service for the Historic American Buildings Survey (HABS) on February 28, 1938: "My father, Reverend Robert Nelson Crooks (1830–1916), bought the property in 1887, and after his death in 1916, Judge Smith (present owner) bought it from the heirs. During the war," she added, "three Revolutionary cannon balls went through the house, a twelve-inch sill in the basement being cut in half by one of them, two going through the first floor. There are marks now on the walls in each room where the ball penetrated. This is now the home of the writer of this." Smith went on to describe the old parlor with its wainscoted, original paint, five colors—pink, lavender, and white, with cornice of green and gold. The halls through the middle of the house she observed were wainscoted up to the chair rail; other rooms plaster. "Some architects believe that the front porch of this house was added later," she continued. "They do not believe there was any porch when the house was built. As to this I can't say, but I am positive the back porch is the original. The front porch has been repaired and I doubt its being the original." *Library of Congress*

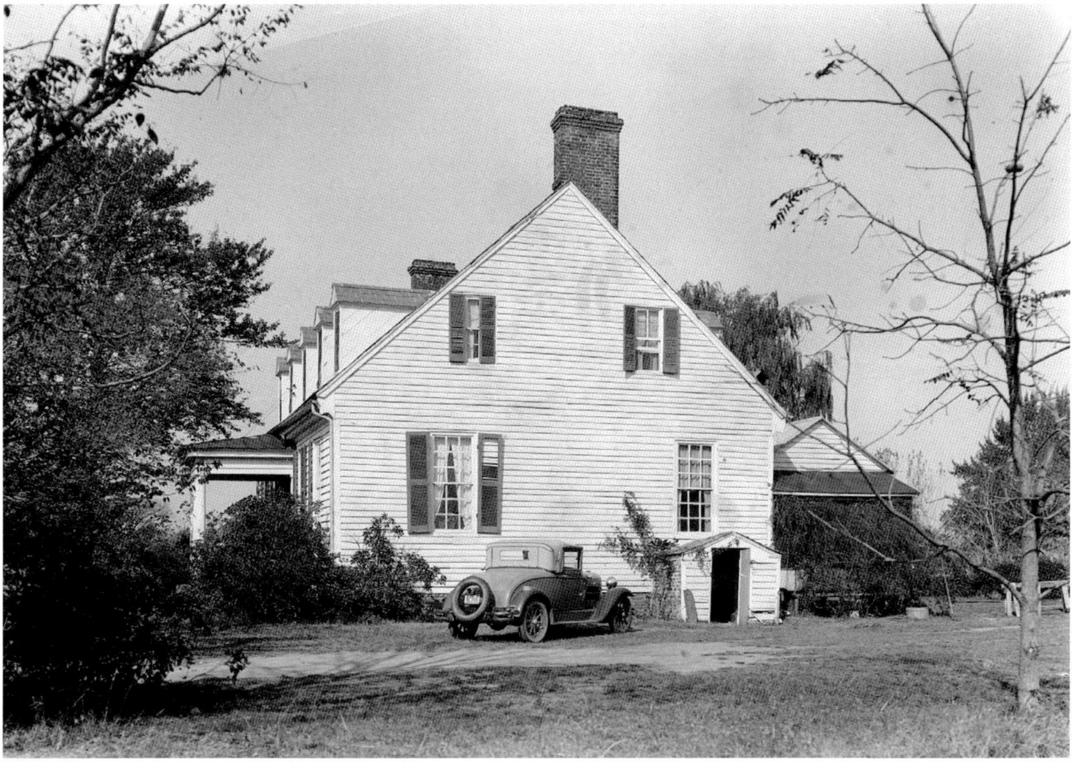

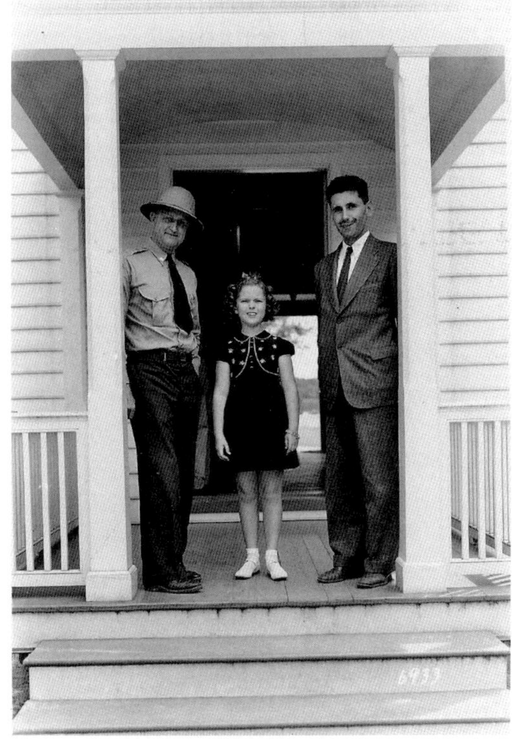

Shirley Jane Temple (1928–2014), Hollywood's number one box-office draw from 1935 to 1938, visited the Yorktown Battlefield on July 1, 1938, and was also shown the Augustine Moore House by acting chief ranger Harry Wray "Lighthorse" Doust (1890–1981) (left) and Colonial National Historical Park superintendent Benjamin Floyd Flickinger (1905–1992) (right). Accompanying her on the tour was her father, George Francis Temple (1888–1980). *National Park Service*

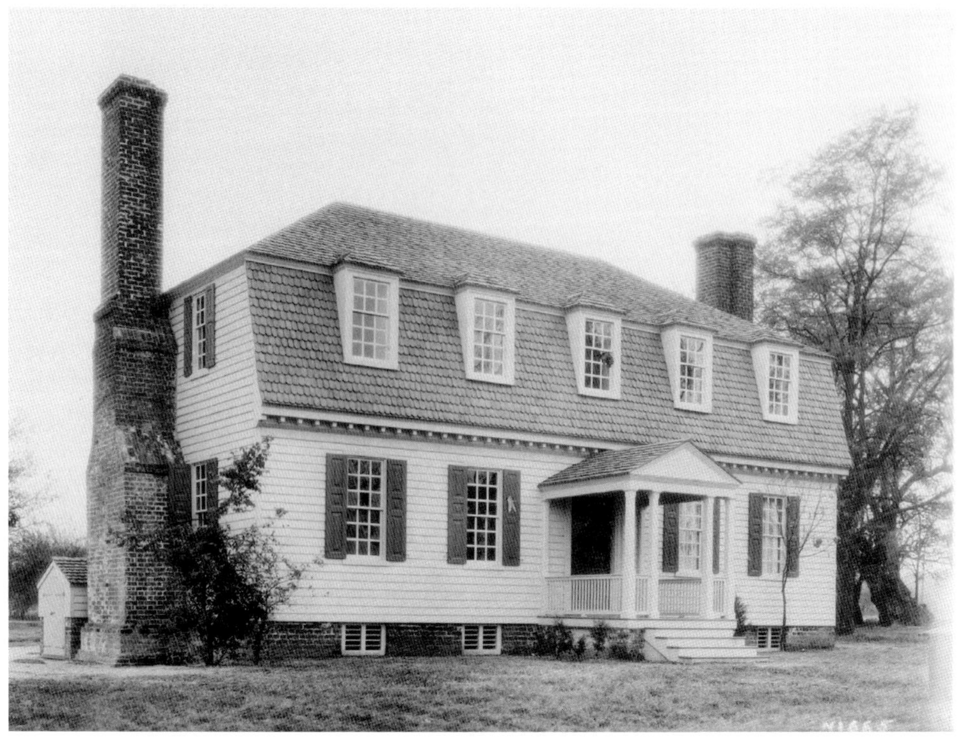

In the years between 1931 and 1934, the National Park Service, which had just established Colonial National Monument [later Colonial National Historical Park], restored the Augustine Moore House to its original colonial appearance. Archaeological assessments and historic images were used to assist in its restoration. The restoration was one of the first of its kind for the park service. The house was completed and formally dedicated on October 18–19, 1934, the one hundred and fifty-third anniversary of the surrender of Lord Cornwallis and the British army. The Augustine Moore House is shown as it looked before and after this early restoration. The photographs were included with Thomas Tileston Waterman's Historic American Buildings Survey dated November 2, 1940. *Library of Congress*

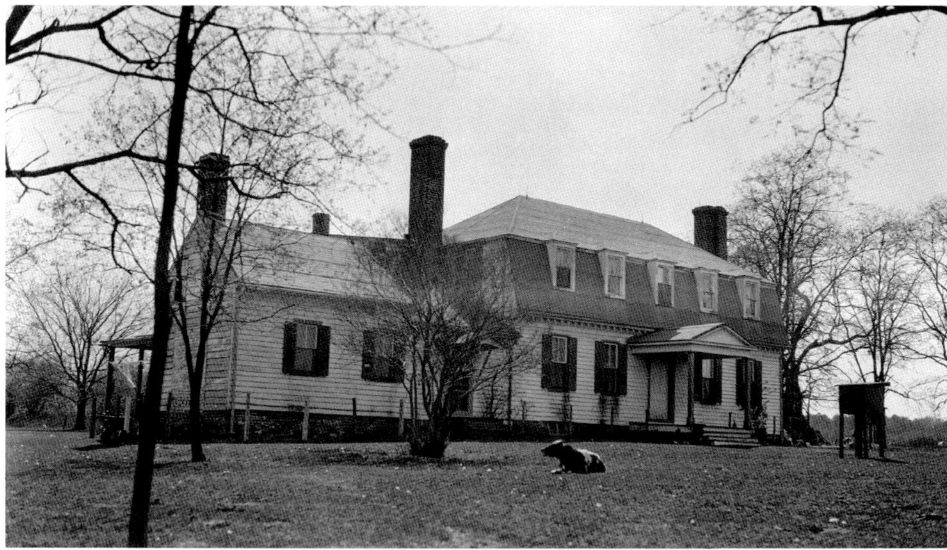

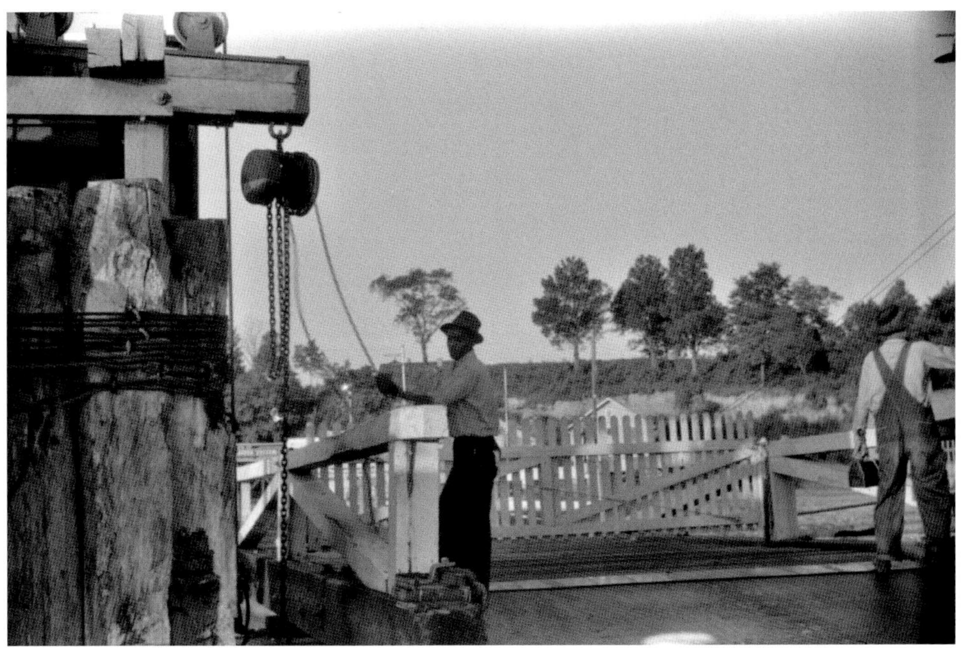

The Yorktown end of the Gloucester Point-Yorktown ferry was photographed by Jack Delano (1914–1997), a photographer for the Farm Security Administration (FSA), in July 1940 as part of the United States Farm Security Administration/Office of War Information documentation initiative that began prior to World War II. *Library of Congress*

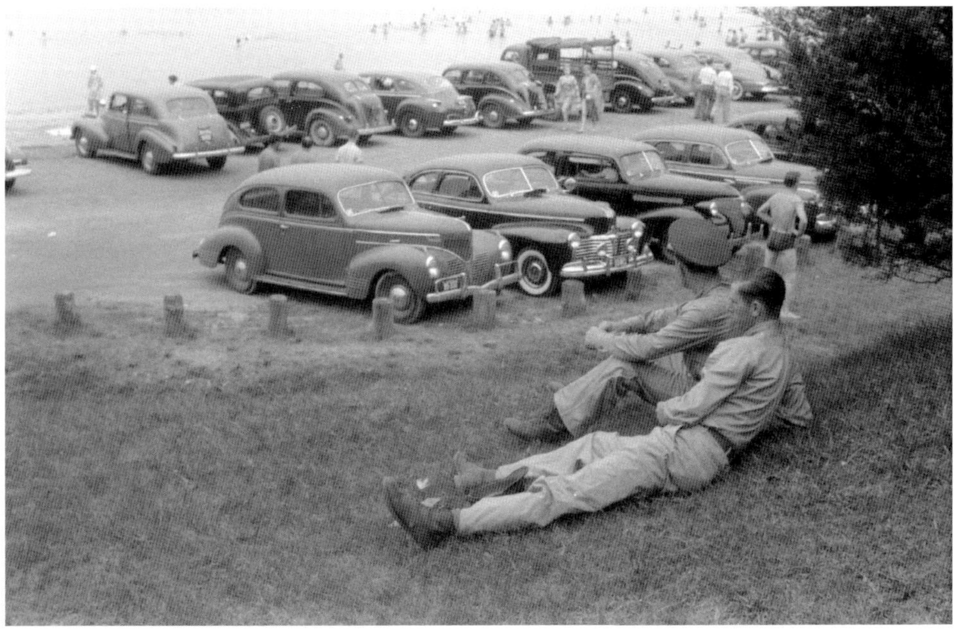

The soldiers in this Jack Delano photograph, dated June 1941, were watching the beachgoers at Yorktown. *Library of Congress*

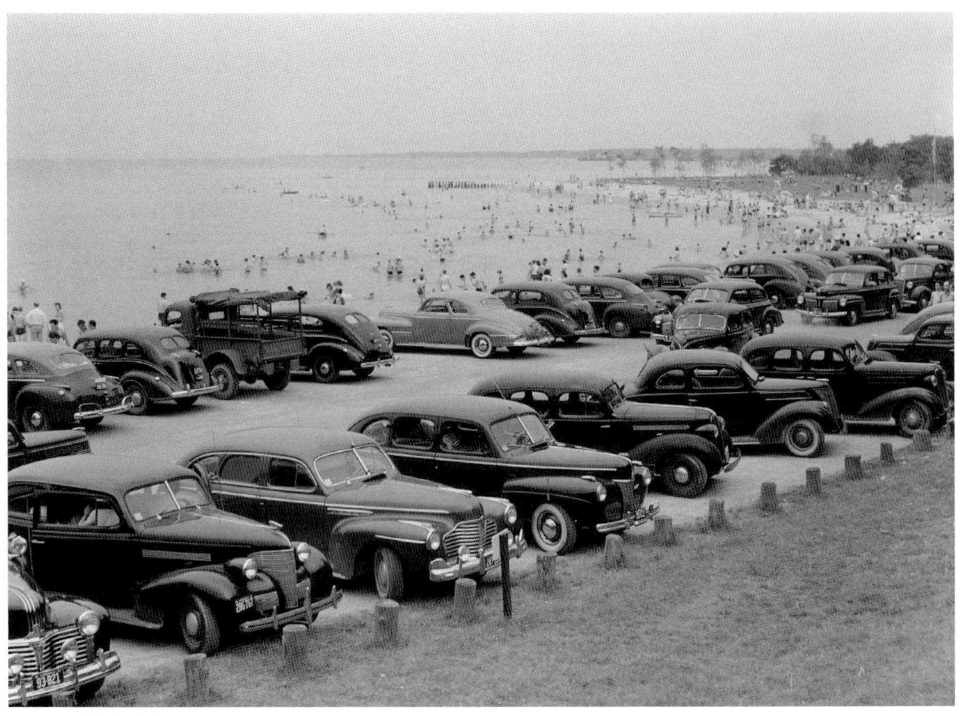

Farm Security Administration photographer Jack Delano took this picture, also in June 1941, of a crowded Yorktown beach. *Library of Congress*

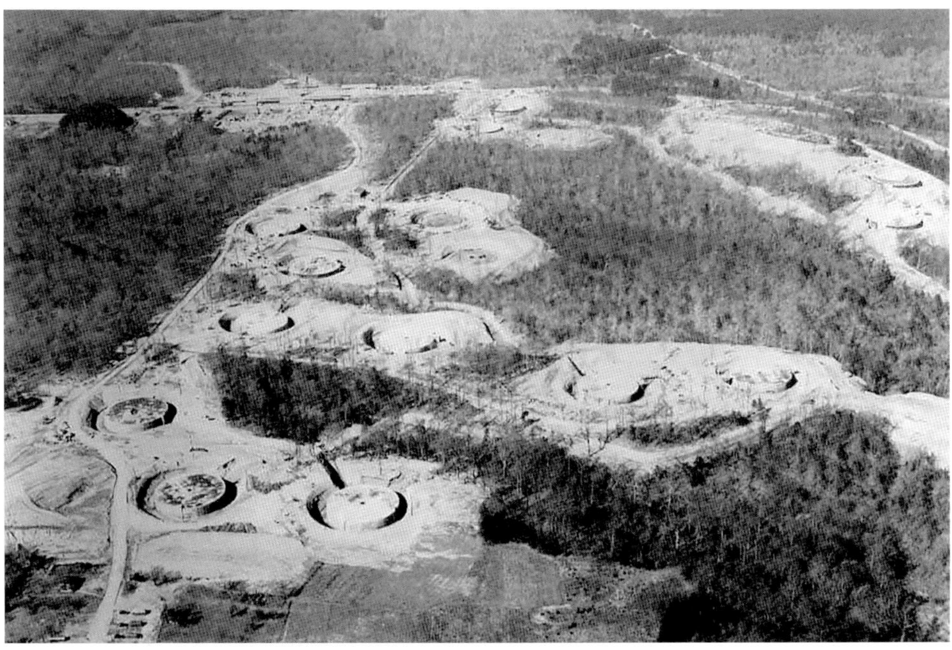

This aerial view shows the construction of fuel oil storage tanks on Naval Weapons Station Yorktown Cheatham Annex on February 19, 1943. When completed, there were twenty-three underground tanks installed, most with a fifty-thousand-barrel capacity. *National Archives*

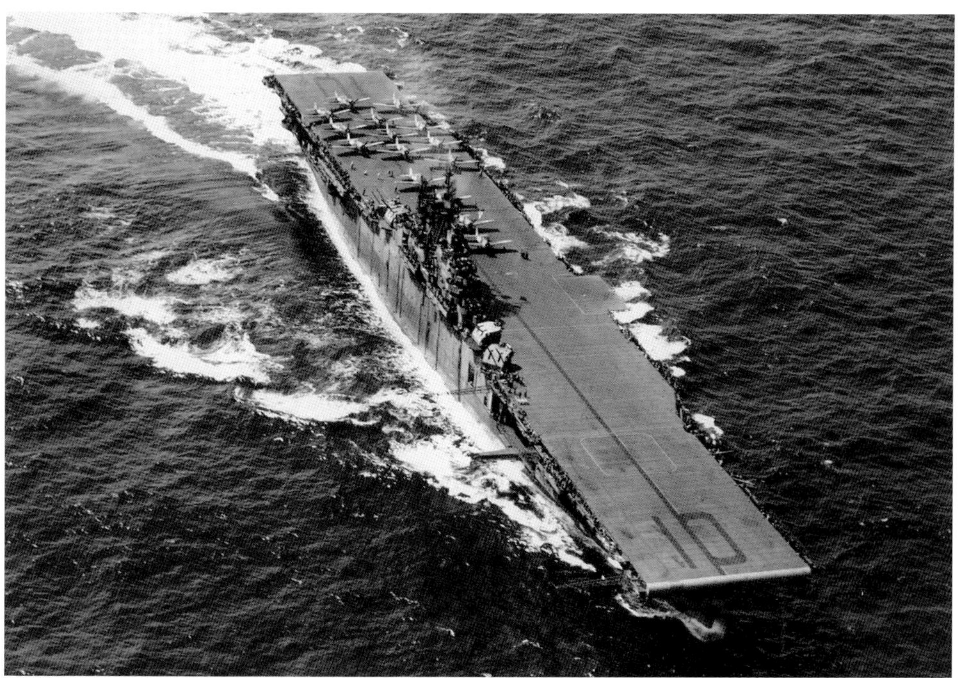

The fourth *Yorktown* (CV-10) was laid down on December 1, 1941, at Newport News Shipbuilding and Drydock Company as *Bon Homme Richard*; it was renamed *Yorktown* on September 26, 1942. The ship was sponsored by first lady Eleanor Roosevelt just like its predecessor. The ship was commissioned at Norfolk Navy Yard, Virginia, on April 15, 1943. *Yorktown* was freshly painted in Camouflage Measure 21 when this picture was taken. This photograph, taken just after it was commissioned, shows fifteen Fighter Squadron Five (VF-5) Grumman F6F-3 Hellcat aircraft on the deck. Note that the forward hull number on the flight deck is turned around, so that it was readable for aircraft approaching from the bow. Also note the extended hangar catapult on the starboard side forward of the gun turrets. *Yorktown* was decommissioned on June 27, 1970. During 1974, the Department of the Navy approved the donation of *Yorktown* to the Patriot's Point Development Authority, Charleston, South Carolina. She was formally dedicated as a memorial on the two hundredth anniversary of the United States Navy on October 13, 1975. *Yorktown* earned eleven battle stars and the Presidential Unit Citation during World War II and five battle stars for Vietnam service. *National Naval Aviation Museum*

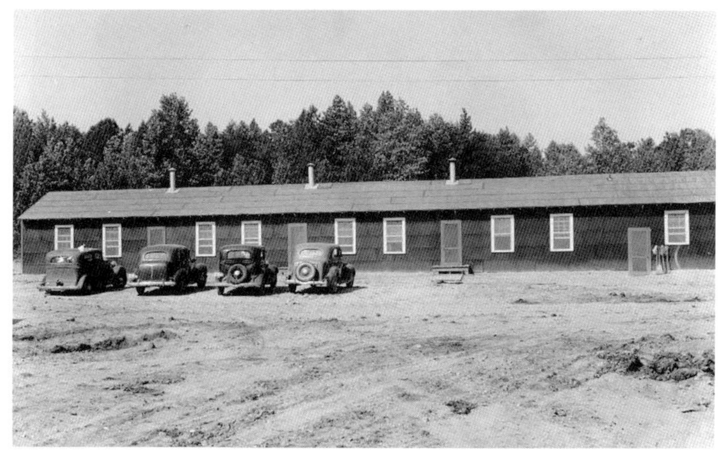

This is the rear elevation of the Marine Corps barracks on the Naval Weapons Station Yorktown Cheatham Annex. The photograph was taken on March 25, 1943. *National Archives*

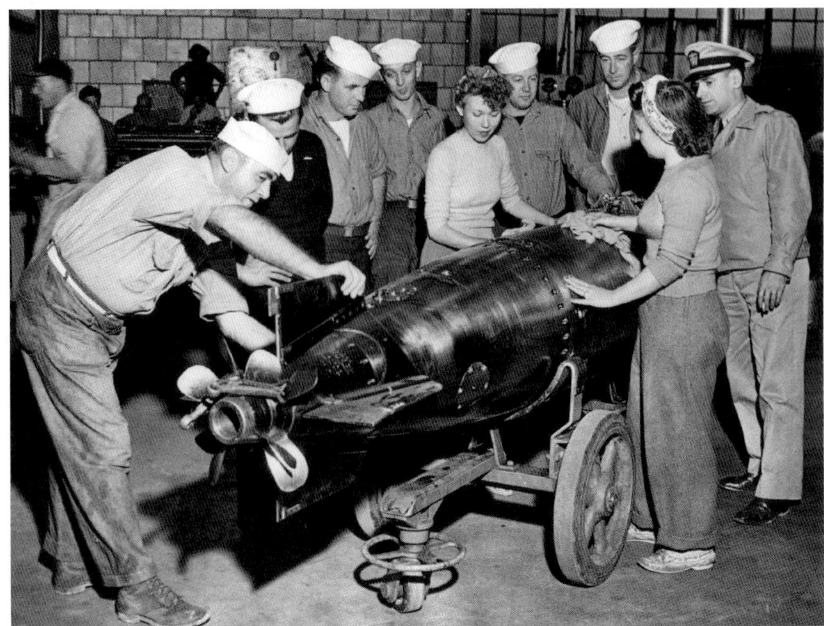

A group of navy sailors looked on as female defense workers at the Yorktown Naval Mine Depot polish a torpedo. The women, Bethany Janet Williams [later Smith] (1921–2012) (left), of Grafton [Hornsbyville], York County, Virginia, and Marie Gallagher, of Bayonne, New Jersey, worked in the depot's torpedo shop. The sailors, students at the Naval Mine Warfare School, watched closely as their instructor, (standing next to Gallagher) explained the process. The picture was taken by an Acme photographer on November 12, 1943. *Amy Waters Yarsinske*

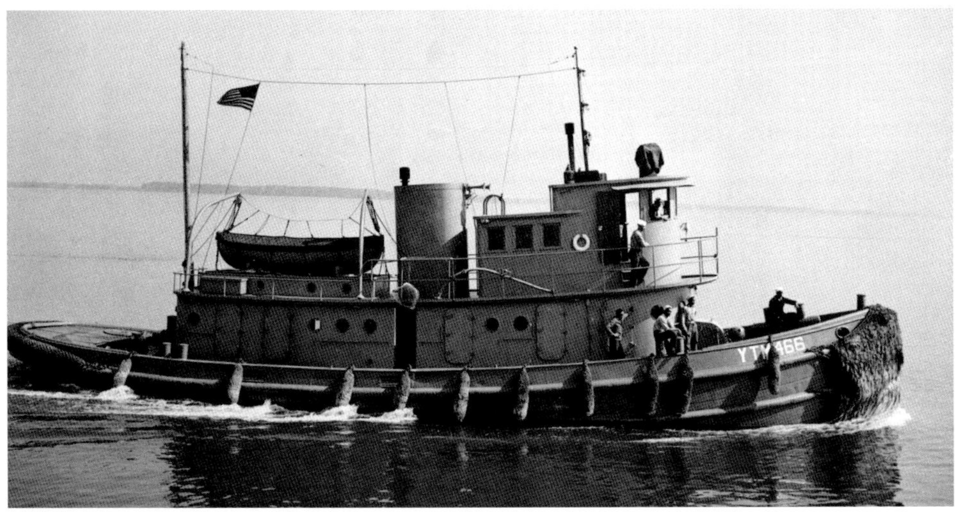

The navy tug YTM-466, operating out of the Mine Warfare School Yorktown, was photographed on May 17, 1945. The tug's captain Boatswain's Mate First Class Thomas Perdue and crew was all African American. The YTM-466 was built in 1940 as the commercial tug *Chipola* before being acquired by the navy in the same year; it was redesignated a harbor tug, medium (YTM) on May 15, 1944, and struck from the naval register on June 5, 1946. The boat was rebuilt into a yacht in the 1990s and was still operational as of May 2010. *National Archives*

ENDNOTES

1 Stoudt, John Baer. *Nicolas Martiau—The Adventurous Huguenot, The Military Engineer and The Earliest American Ancestor of George Washington*. Norristown, Pennsylvania: Norristown Press, 1932.

2 Thomas Garrett first came to market in 1618.

3 Historical consensus states that a group of Virginia Algonquians lived in the vicinity of the Kiskiack house, now located within the boundaries of the Naval Weapons Station Yorktown. No agreement, however, has been reached on the spelling of the Indian name that came to be associated with a people and a geographical area, be it an Indian settlement, Anglican parish, or a dwelling. Twentieth-century spellings include "Kisckiack" which refers to the Indian village. "Kis Kis Kiak" has been another spelling to identify the house. "Cheescake" meaning the house and "Chiskiack" the region has also been used. The last private owner probably preferred the "Kis Kis Kiak" spelling as that is what he chose for the memorial marker on the property for William Warren Lee. Newspaper articles generally adhered to the spelling adopted by HABS in 1935, "Kiskiack" after the map drawn by Captain John Smith and published in 1624 for his general history of the colony. Seventeenth-century source material merely adds to the array of spellings for Kiskiack. Captain John Smith used "Kiskiack" interchangeably with a "ch" format, "Chiskiack."

4 From 1612 Ottahotin was the werowance, or commander, of the Algonquian group affiliated with Powhatan that lived by the York River. He ruled over the Kiskiack Indians; because of its location on the Peninsula, Ottahotin's tribe was near the Jamestown settlement. Territory that had been theirs was opened for settlement rights by the British. The displaced Kiskiack Indians occupied the south bank of the Piankatank River by the summer of 1642. They stayed there until 1677. The Kiskiack Indians also lived on the northeast shore of the York River for a period of time. The Kiskiack Indian population dwindled along with that of the other Virginia Algonquians, essentially extinct by 1700.

5 Department of the Interior/National Park Service. Historic American Building Survey [HABS]. Kiskiack (Naval Mine Depot) [HABS No. VA-183] Yorkville vicinity, York County, Virginia [1997].

6 The Pauls were brought to Yorktown, Virginia, by his naval career. Carroll Paul was a naval officer assigned to the naval mine depot there. He would leave the navy to become president of the Longyear Corporation. Helen Longyear Paul was a member of the Daughters of the American Revolution (DAR).

7 Sessions sold to Robert Snead, gentleman, and there was reference to Snead's House (formerly that of Sessions) three months later. Snead added on a store and storehouse under the hill on the waterfront at the mouth of the Great Valley adjacent to the landing here which was already "Comonley Called Sessions Landing." Snead did not remain in ownership long, selling to John Penton, merchant, in October 1703. He in turn sold to John Martin, another merchant, just a month later. Then in June 1705, Martin sold it back to Penton. In each instance the conveyance was for Lots 56 and 57 and "the Store and Store house and Still house" under the hill. In September 1708, it was Penton's turn to sell again. Through his power of attorney vested in Michael Archer, the sale went to Nicholas Phillips. It involved Lot 56 where Thomas Sessions had built his home either in 1692 or no later than 1693. This also included the storehouses "under the hill" but not Lot 57. The property remained in the Phillips family for nearly forty years. When Nicholas died in 1715 it passed to his son, William, in these words: "I give & bequeath to my son Wm. Phillips & ye male heirs of his body lawfully begotten for Even that my Lott on half acre of Land & warehouse under ye bank situate in York Town lately in ye tenure & occupation of Jno. Penton & his under tenants." It was not William Phillips, however, but Thomas, his brother, who in March 1746 sold Lot 56 for one hundred and forty pounds sterling to John Norton of King William County, a merchant. And so, another merchant was based here. After almost twenty years he disposed of half of his lot to still another merchant, George Wilson, for one hundred and twenty-five pounds sterling current money of Virginia. It was the inland half of the lot and had no face on Main Street. It would appear that John Norton went on to regain the ownership of all of Lot 56 and that George Wilson came in some way into possession of Lot 57 just behind it. John Norton then sold his lot [Lot 56—noted in 1763 as his "Store Lott"] and its improvements to Matthew Pope in 1766 and he, in turn, bequeathed it to Mary, the wife of Robert Carter, by will probated in 1792. It was in 1796 that Robert Canter and his wife sold it to Thomas Nelson for five hundred pounds sterling. Lot 56 remained in Nelson hands until May 1821, at which time the property was sold along with adjacent Lot 60 to Dr. Frederick Bryan Power (1793–1843). It was then described as "A house and lot in the Town of York situate as follows, the house on the northwest corner of the square next to Thomas Nelson's house…" It was Power who took out the first insurance coverage now of record on the property. This was in 1838 and the plot plan and description showed the "Dwelling of Brick" to be one and one-half stories covered with wood. Its measurements were forty-six feet by twenty-six feet.

8   The judge was the husband of Catherine Stryker Sheild (1869–1946), the founder and director of the Association for the Preservation of Virginia Antiquities (APVA) Yorktown Chapter. She was the director from 1921 to 1946.

9   Albright, a native of Bishop, California, was the son of a miner. He graduated from the University of California Berkeley in 1912 and then earned a law degree from Georgetown University before going to work for Stephen Mather, who had become the assistant secretary in charge of national parks. Albright worked side by side with Mather to stand up the National Park Service four years later, in 1916, and helped acquire land in the east to form new national parks. On January 12, 1929, Albright succeeded Mather as the second director of the National Park Service, a post he held until August 9, 1933.

10   Wilbur was a medical doctor who also served as the third president of Stanford University before becoming the thirty-first United States secretary of Interior on March 5, 1929, a post he held until March 4, 1933. Wilbur subsequently became a sharp critic of Franklin Roosevelt's New Deal.

11   The Baron Cornwallis was a title that has been created twice, once in the peerage of England and again in the peerage of the United Kingdom. The holders of the first creation were later made Earl Cornwallis and Marquess Cornwallis. The second creation came in 1927 when the Fiennes Cornwallis was created Baron Cornwallis, of Linton in the County of Kent. Cornwallis was the grandson of Charles Wykeham Martin; the great-grandson of James Mann, Fifth Earl Cornwallis; the second great-grandson of James Cornwallis, Fourth Earl Cornwallis; the third great-grandson of Charles Cornwallis, First Earl Cornwallis; the fourth great-grandson of Charles Cornwallis, Fourth Baron Cornwallis; the fifth great-grandson of Charles Cornwallis, Third Baron Cornwallis; the sixth great-grandson of Charles Cornwallis, Second Baron Cornwallis; the seventh great-grandson of Frederick Cornwallis, First Baron Cornwallis; and the eighth great-grandson of Jane Cornwallis, and Elizabeth Richardson, First Lady Cramond.

12   McWhorter retired from the navy as a rear admiral.

V

Where the Past is Always Prologue

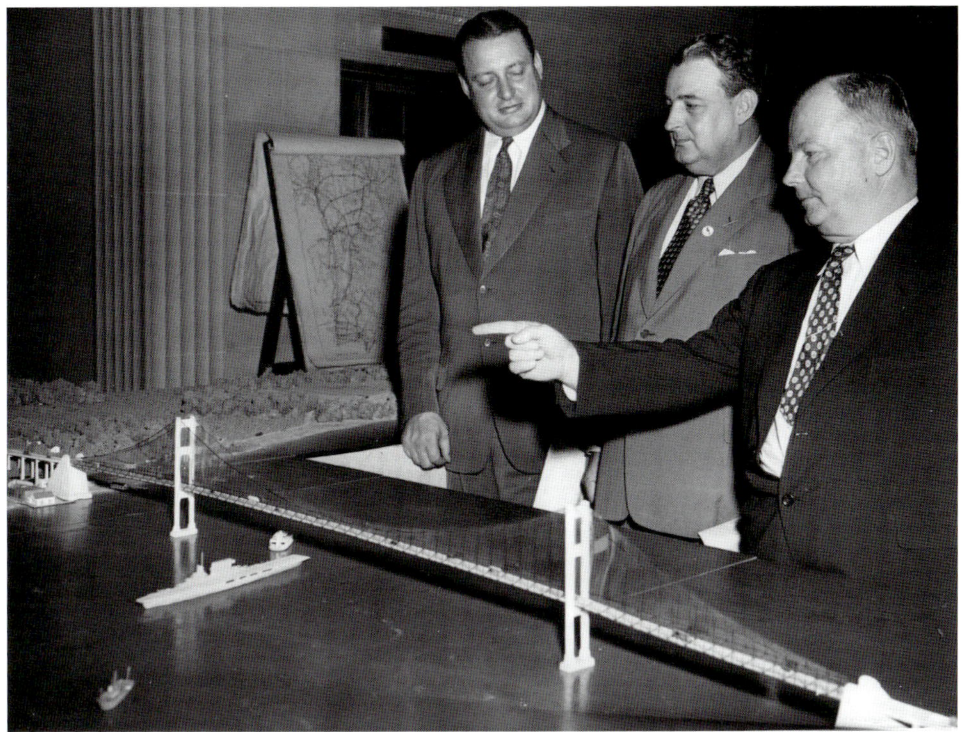

Secretary of the Interior Julius Albert Krug (1907–1970), Virginia governor William Munford Tuck (1896–1983), and Virginia state highway commissioner James Aylor Anderson (1892–1964), a Virginia state highway commissioner, inspect a model of the proposed bridge over the York River at the Interior Department in Washington, D.C., on July 23, 1946. *Amy Waters Yarsinske*

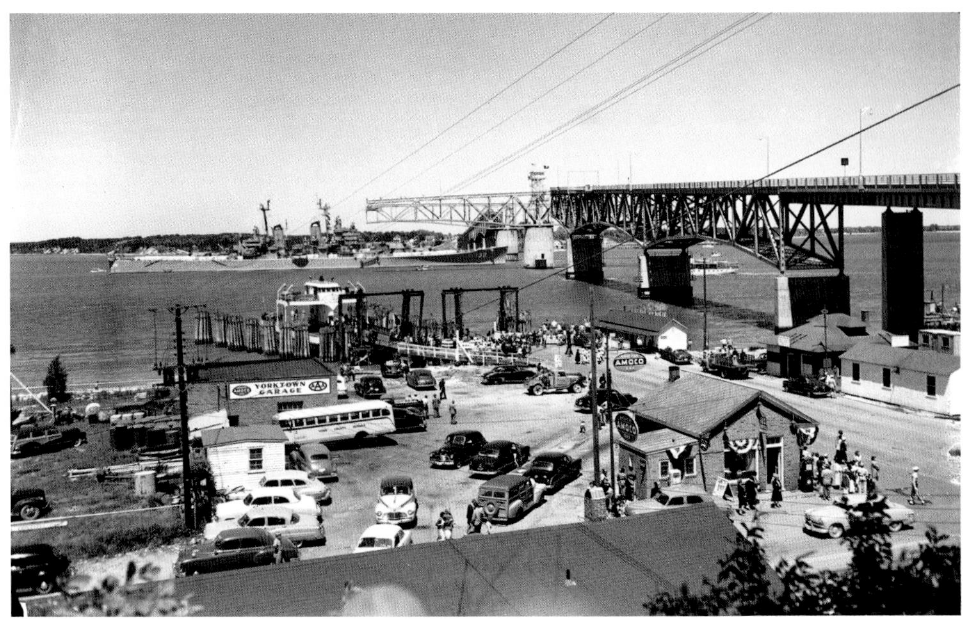

Dedication ceremonies were held on May 7, 1952, in Yorktown for the George Preston Coleman Memorial Bridge. With the backdrop of the York River, businesses and landmarks identified in this photograph include the United States Navy *Baltimore*-class heavy cruiser USS *Macon* (CA-132), the Yorktown garage, and the Gloucester-Yorktown Ferry Terminal. *Sargeant Memorial Collection, Norfolk Public Library*

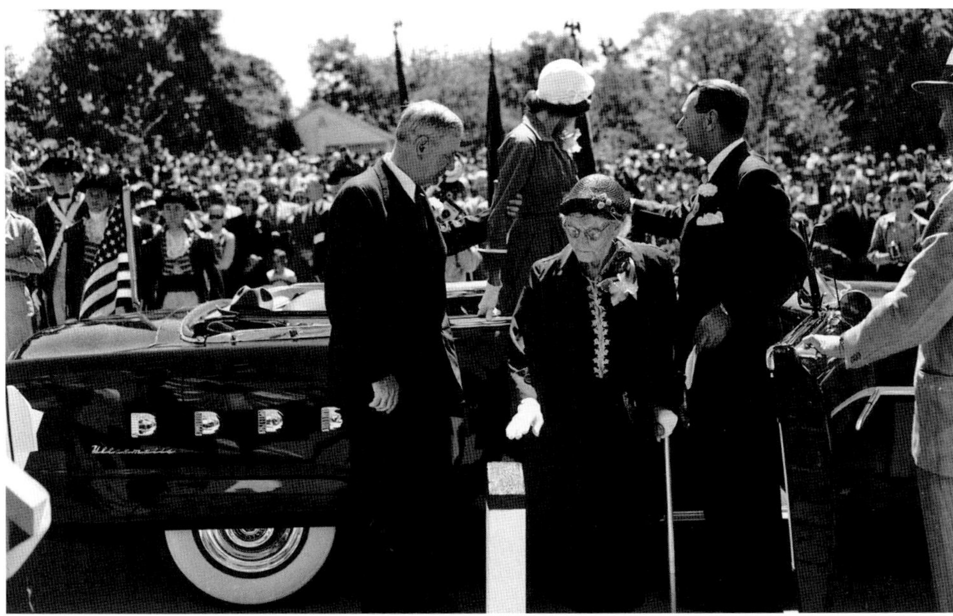

In this photograph, taken on May 7, 1952, Virginia governor John Stewart Battle (1890–1972) (left) assists members of the Coleman family on their arrival at the dedication and opening ceremony for the George Preston Coleman Memorial Bridge. Mary Haldane Begg Coleman (1875–1967), the widow of former head of the Virginia Highway Commission and mayor of Williamsburg George Preston Coleman[1] (1870–1948) is shown right foreground with the cane. *Sargeant Memorial Collection, Norfolk Public Library*

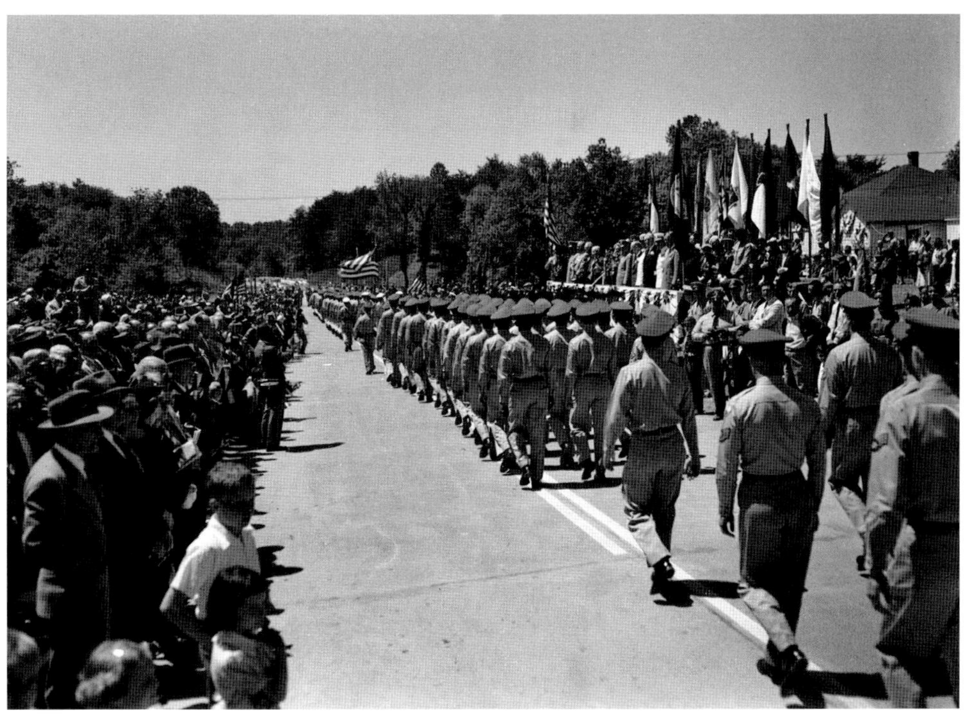

A military parade in honor of the opening of the George Preston Coleman Memorial Bridge opening on May 7, 1952, featured all branches of the military and several special reenactor groups. Here, the troops are shown moving past the reviewing stand. *Sargeant Memorial Collection, Norfolk Public Library*

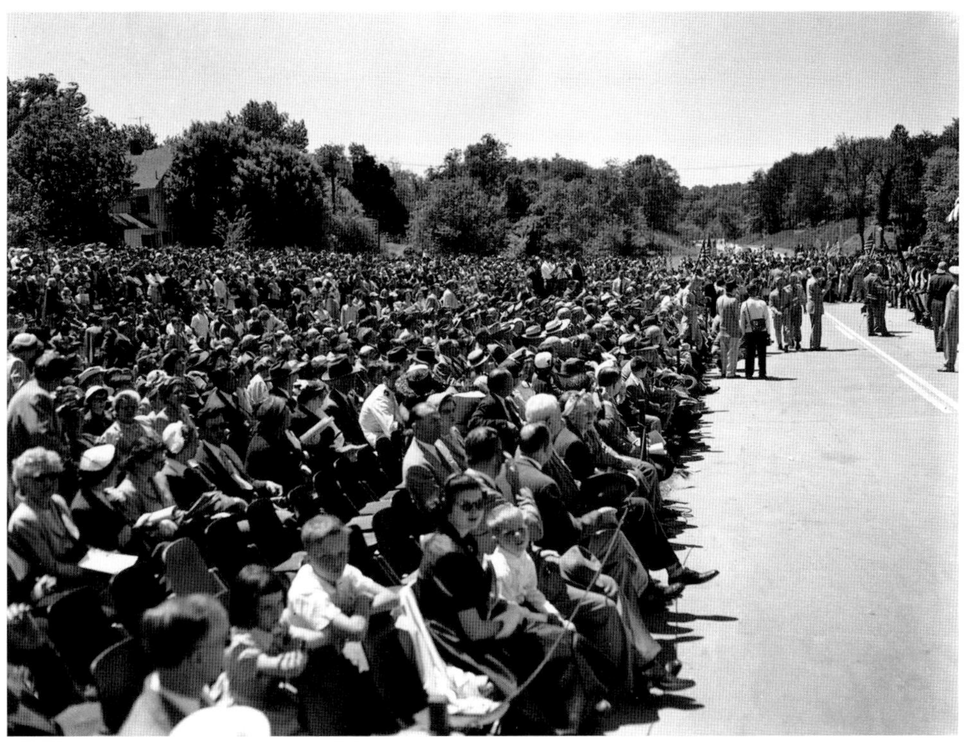

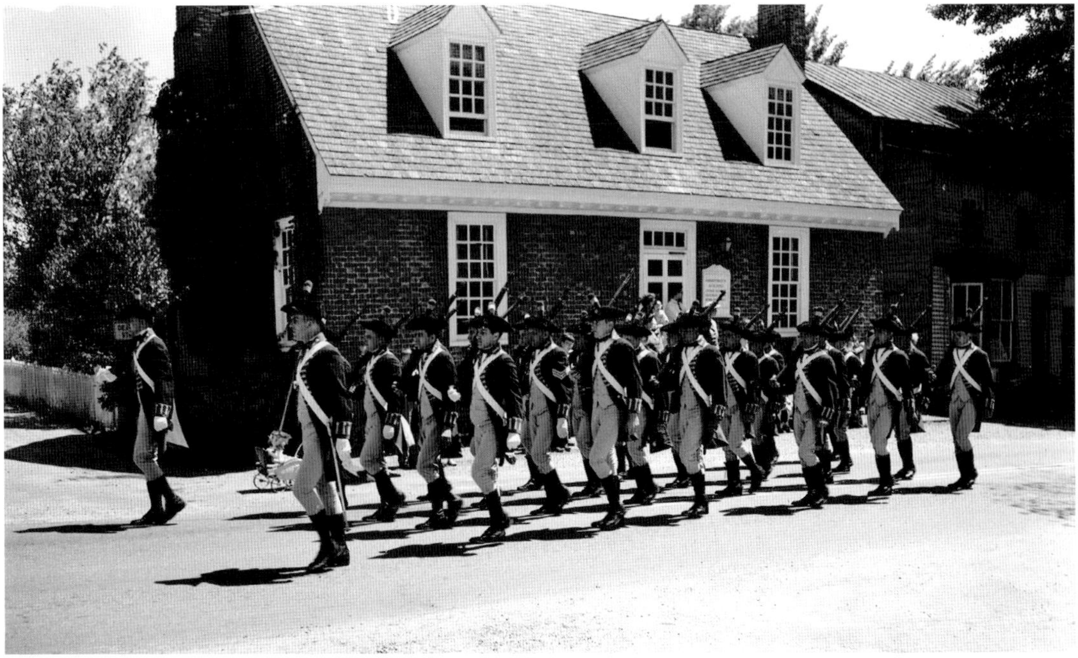

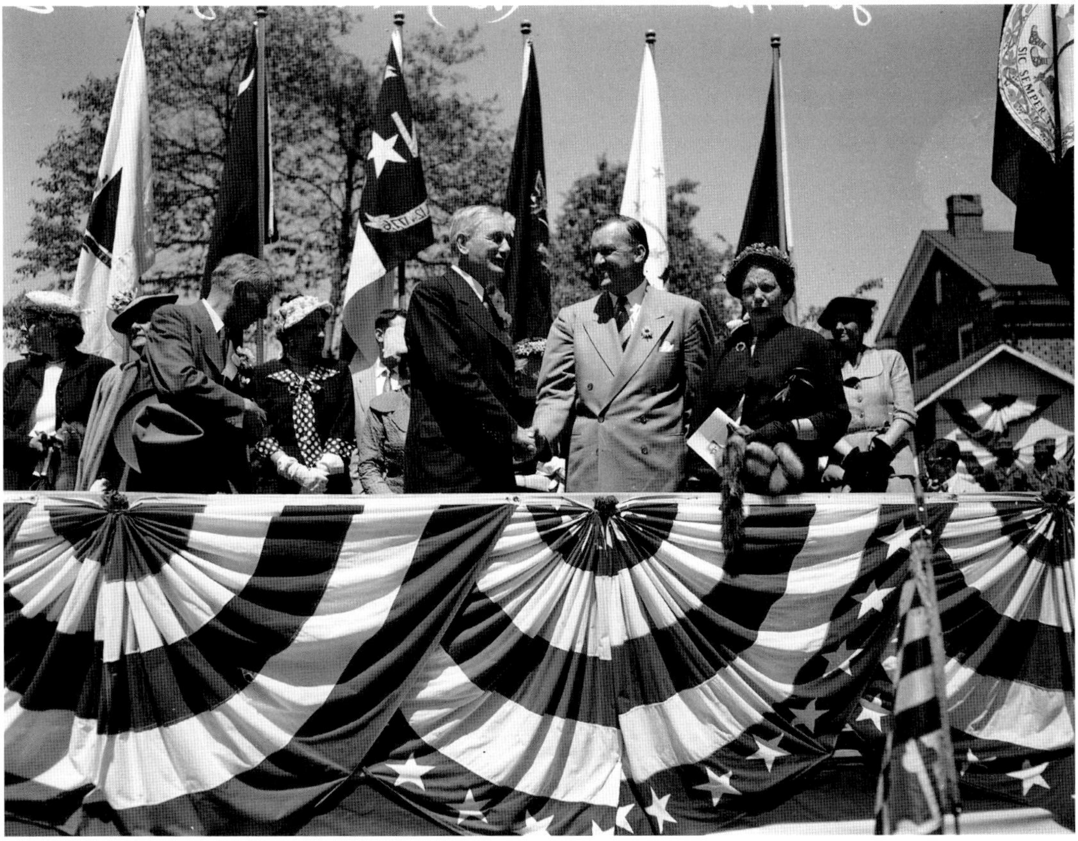

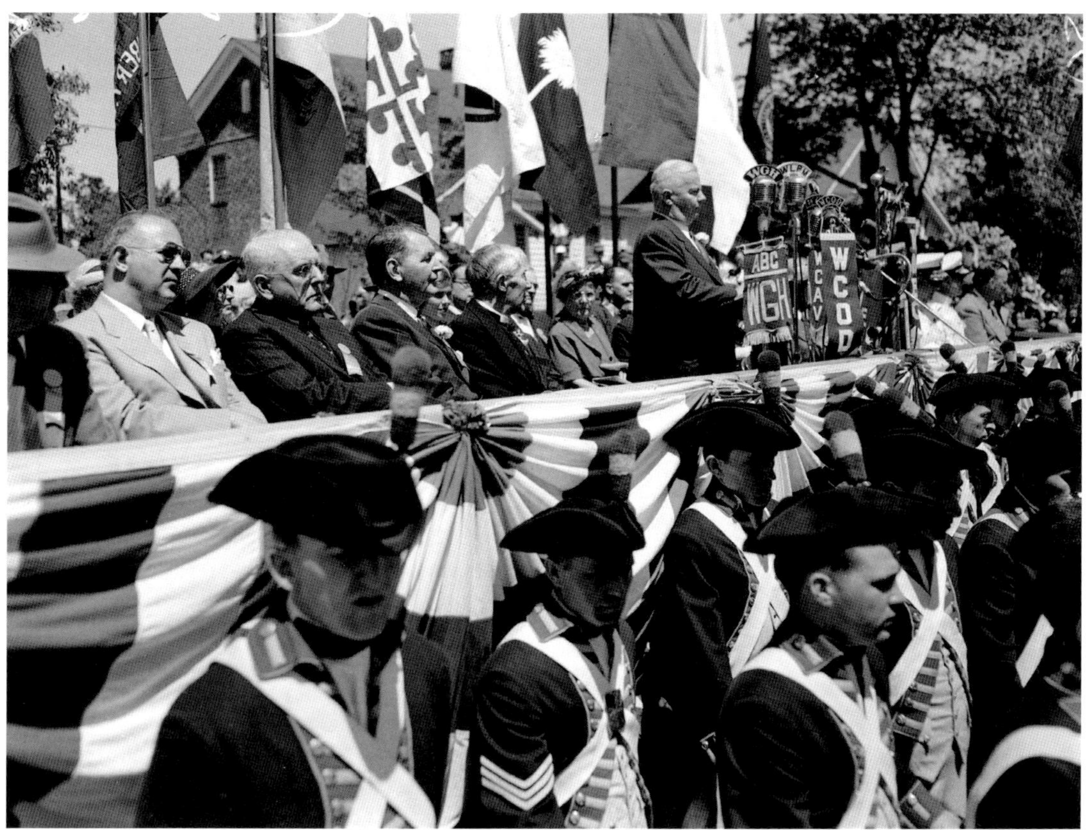

Virginia highway commissioner James Aylor Anderson was photographed delivering his speech at the George Preston Coleman Memorial Bridge dedication on May 7, 1952. *Sargeant Memorial Collection, Norfolk Public Library*

Opposite page:

Above: The Monticello Guard Fife and Drum Corps, shown here on the walk from Yorktown's Main Street to the reviewing stand, participated in the dedication ceremonies for the George Preston Coleman Memorial Bridge on May 7, 1952. *Sargeant Memorial Collection, Norfolk Public Library*

Below: Virginia governor John Stewart Battle and Maryland governor Theodore Roosevelt McKeldin[2] (1900–1974) shake hands on the platform during dedication ceremonies held for the George Preston Coleman Memorial Bridge on May 7, 1952. *Sargeant Memorial Collection, Norfolk Public Library*

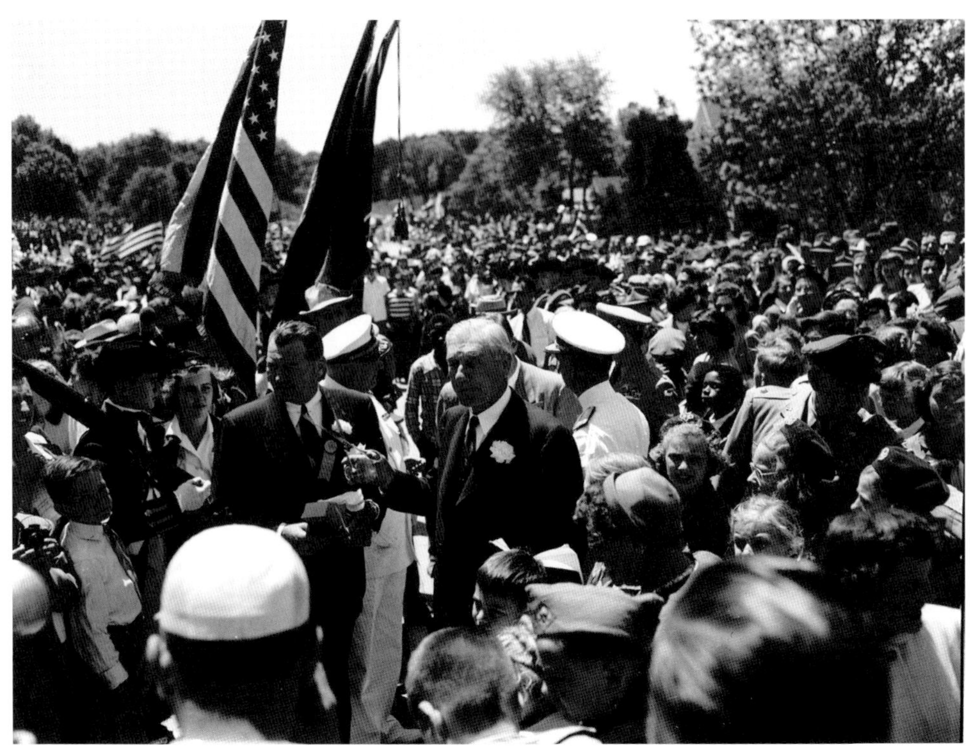

Virginia governor John Stewart Battle cut the ribbon opening the George Preston Coleman Memorial Bridge on May 7, 1952 (shown here). *Sargeant Memorial Collection, Norfolk Public Library*

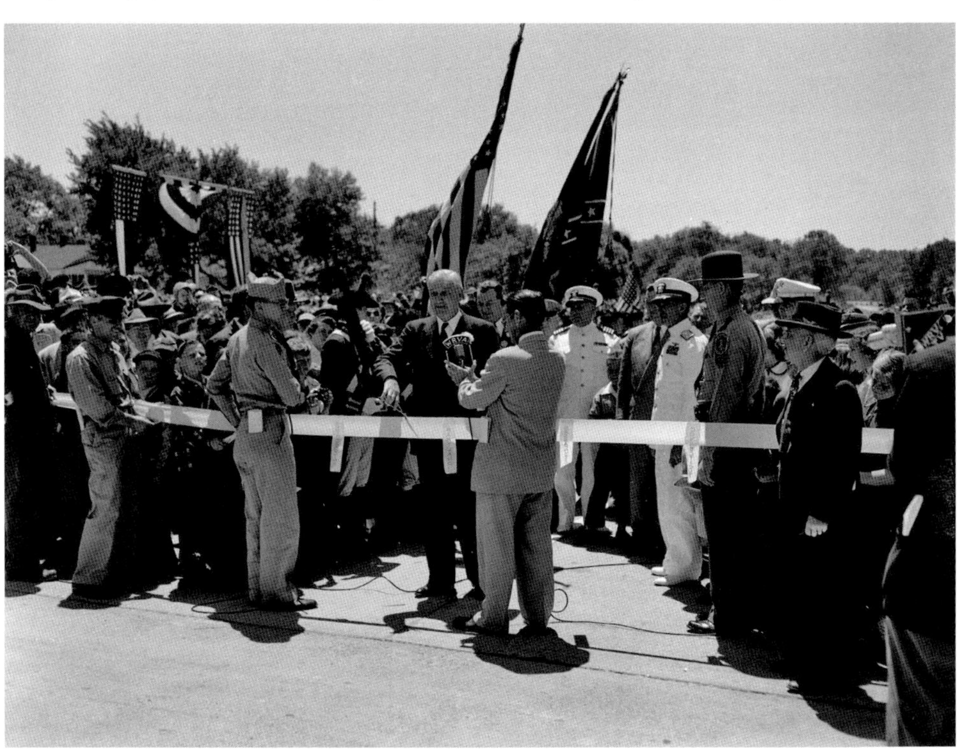

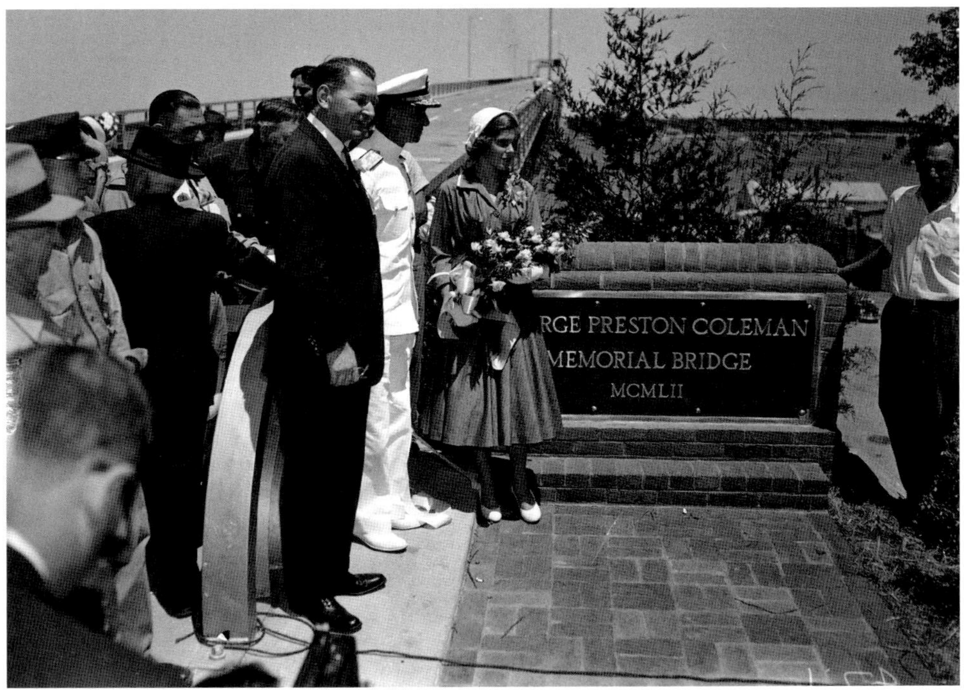

The George Preston Coleman Memorial Bridge signage was unveiled as part of the dedication ceremonies. *Sargeant Memorial Collection, Norfolk Public Library*

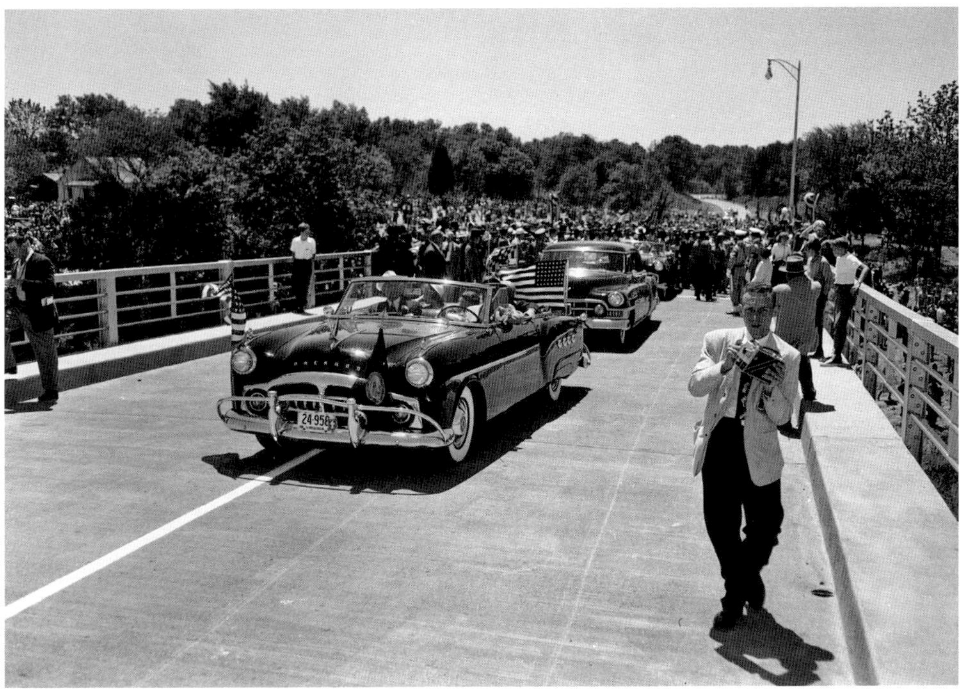

Virginia governor John Stewart Battle rode in the first automobile (shown here) to cross the George Preston Coleman Memorial Bridge on May 7, 1952. *Sargeant Memorial Collection, Norfolk Public Library*

This is the George Preston Coleman Memorial Bridge spanning the York River at U.S. Route 17 [U.S. 17]. In this view, also taken looking northeast from the Yorktown side of the George Preston Coleman Memorial Bridge, Piers 2S, 1S, and 1N (right to left) are shown along with the barrier gate and bridge house above. The bridge is a 3,750-foot, steel deck-truss structure comprised of plate girder approach spans, a series of cantilevered fixed spans, and two center-pivot swing spans which operate in tandem. Built between 1950 and 1952, the bridge was a key element in a larger program of post-World War II transportation improvements throughout the lower Tidewater region and connects Yorktown to Gloucester Point. Designed by the prominent New York City engineering firm of Parson, Brinkerhoff, Hall and Macdonald, the George Preston Coleman Memorial Bridge is a significant example of hollow-pier construction utilizing the open-dredge caisson method, and among the few bridges with double swing spans still in operation today. The picture was taken by Rob Tucher in February 1993 for the Historic American Engineering Record (HAER) documentation of the bridge. *Library of Congress*

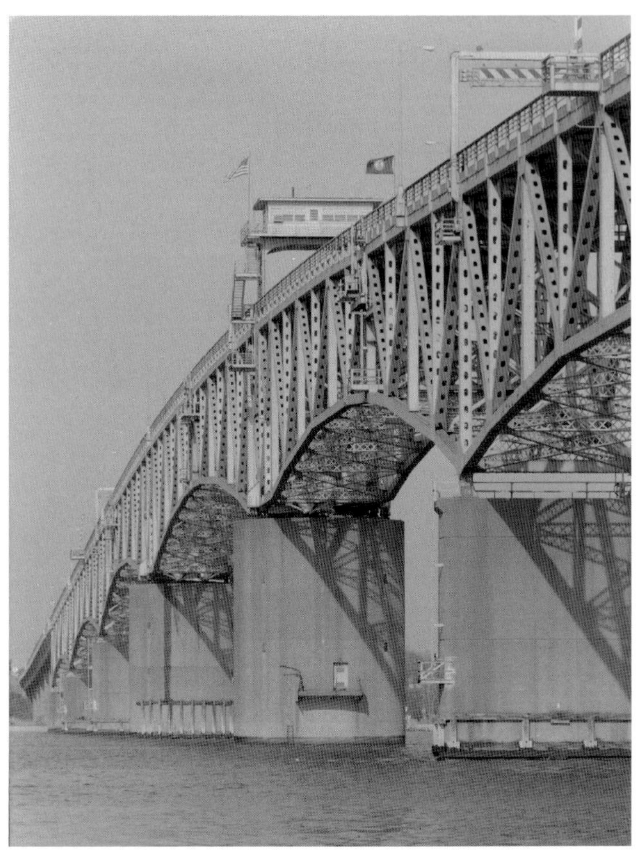

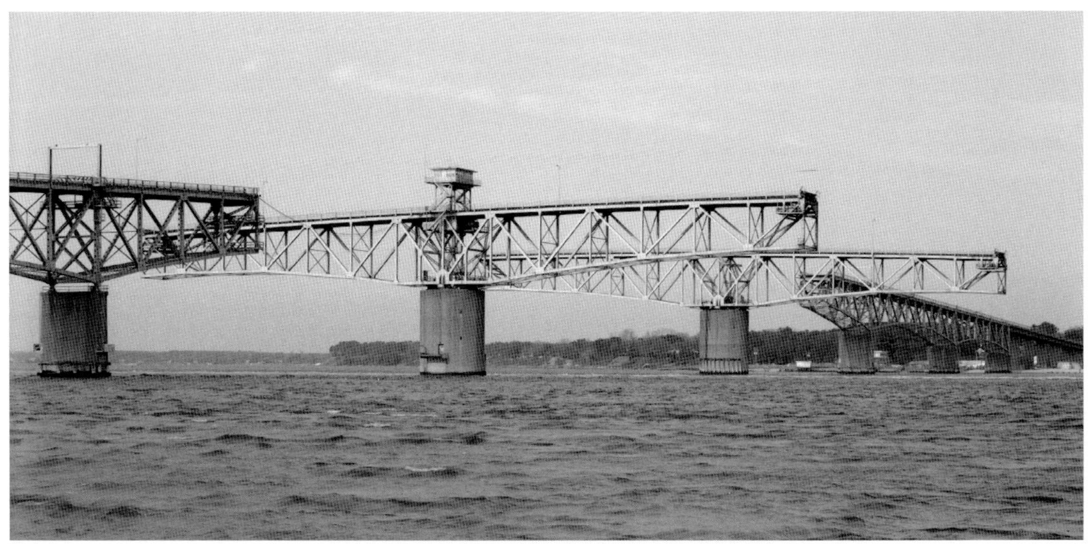

This view looking northwest from the Yorktown side shows the swing spans of the George Preston Coleman Memorial Bridge in full open position. The picture was taken by Rob Tucher in February 1993 for the Library of Congress Prints and Photographs Division HAER. Tucher has years of experience working as an architectural historian. *Library of Congress*

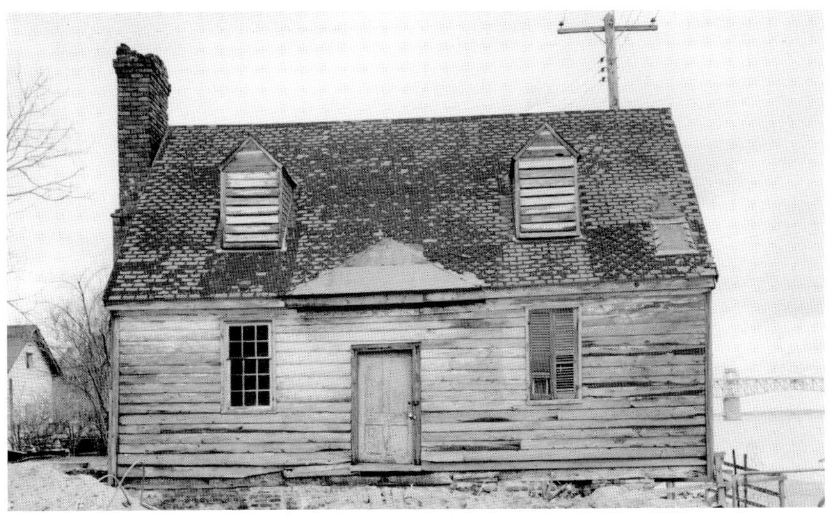

The Thomas Archer House, located on Water Street [Lot 123] below the bluffs, is currently the only visible structure on the Yorktown waterfront with colonial associations. The fire of 1814 has been assumed to have destroyed the house but shortly afterwards, about 1820, it was rebuilt on its original stone foundations above its basement which was likely filled at that point. The rebuilder of the house could have been Nathanial Taylor, whose family remained in it until 1840. The National Park Service rebuilt the structure in 1960. From an archaeological study performed in 1958 by John Wallace Griffin (1919–1993), the National Park Service's regional archaeologist from that year to 1971, the following was recorded: "Physically, it [the house] was slightly larger than most of the waterfront buildings, and judging from the surviving details, may have been somewhat more pretentious than the present building. It has been generally assumed that the house burned in the great fire of 1814 leaving only the foundation walls and .... chimney." The evidence uncovered showed the foundations suffered from a major fire. The foundations are eighteenth century and unique to Yorktown, possibly deposited here by English ships in colonial days. The stone walls consist of granite, limestone, coral and marl but major portions of river rock, with some brick and slate used for filing holes. The chimney below the five-foot-seven-inch level is from the eighteenth century and the upper portion that which was rebuilt. The one and one-half story, wood frame house has a central passage floor plan with a room to either side of the passage on the main floor and two rooms in the attic or garret level. The enclosed stair rises east of the passage. The room to the west of the passage is heated, and the west room in the attic is also heated. Dormer windows punctuate the slope of the gable roof and provide light to the attic rooms. In the photograph shown here, taken on March 27, 1959, by photographer Thomas Leslie Williams[3] (1912–1998), Colonial Williamsburg Foundation's first official photographer, for the Historic American Buildings Survey (HABS), we see the south elevation. *Library of Congress*

Right: This perspective of the Thomas Archer House shows the south [front] and east side of the building. The picture was also taken by Thomas Leslie Williams on March 27, 1959. *Library of Congress*

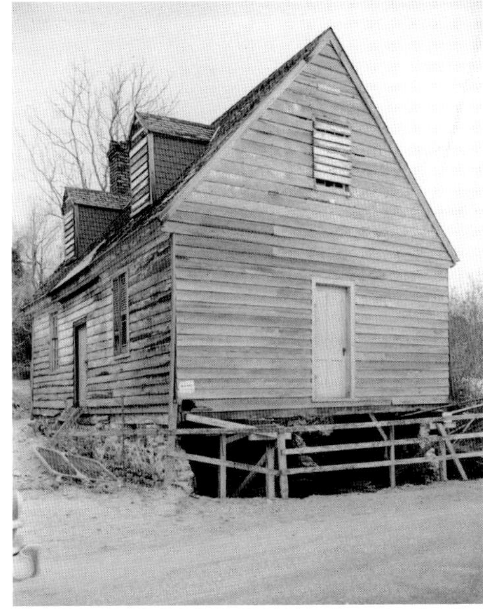

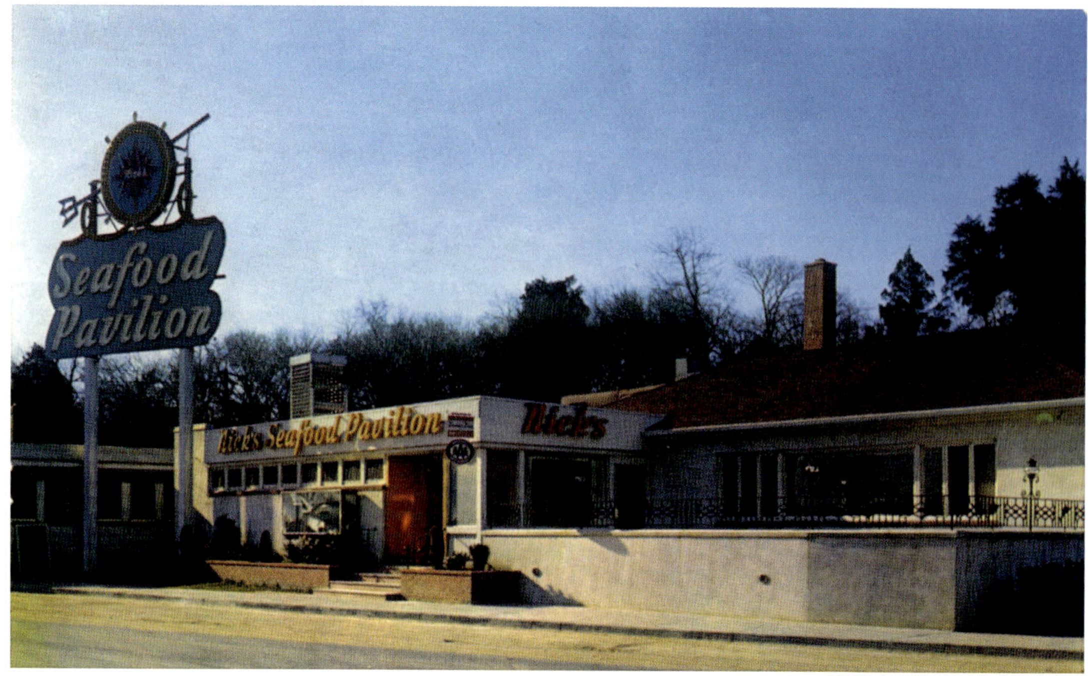

Nick's Seafood Pavilion, the legendary Water Street seafood house facing the historic York River owned by restauranteurs and philanthropists Nicholas Minas "Mister Nick" and Mary Pappas "Miss Mary" Mathews, immigrants from Greece who opened the restaurant in 1944, was visited yearly by thousands of patrons from all over the world from celebrities like John Wayne, Tony Bennett and Elizabeth Taylor to kings and queens and leading American political figures. The first postcard (*above*), dating to the 1960s, shows the restaurant as it was for decades before further additions were made such as those seen in the second picture taken a decade later (*opposite above*). The restaurant is no longer there [it closed for good in late 2003] and the building was demolished shortly thereafter.[4] When the new American Revolution Museum at Yorktown was dedicated on April 1, 2017, it was dedicated to the late Nick and Mary Mathews, benefactors of the Jamestown-Yorktown Foundation who donated the land on which the museum is built and supported museum programs [via the museum's predecessor Yorktown Victory Center] during their lifetimes and through their estate. *Amy Waters Yarsinske*

Opposite below: This interior picture of Nick's Seafood Pavilion does not do justice to the eclectic décor throughout the restaurant, from the entry to what children called "the tree room"—the real trees growing through the floor and ceiling that were tempting enough to climb. There was the old dining room, the Triton Room and the Nile Room, which had a gurgling fountain to imitate the Nile River. The artwork throughout the restaurant included bronze and marble statues, memorable paintings and all of the walls were purple. The three large and themed dining rooms, the result of four expansions, seated 450 people and were nearly always packed on weekends, when the wait to be seated could be up to one-and-a-half hours and patrons stood in long lines that wrapped around the parking lot. The Mathewses left their estate to the Jamestown Educational Trust, which sold the property to York County in March 2002. *Amy Waters Yarsinske*

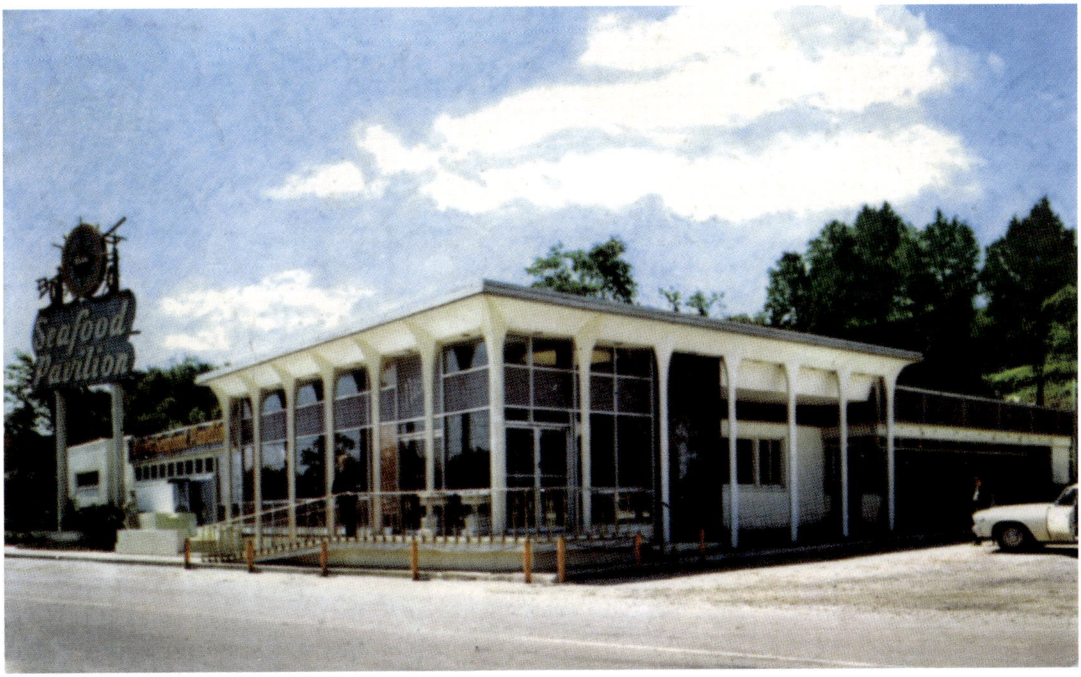

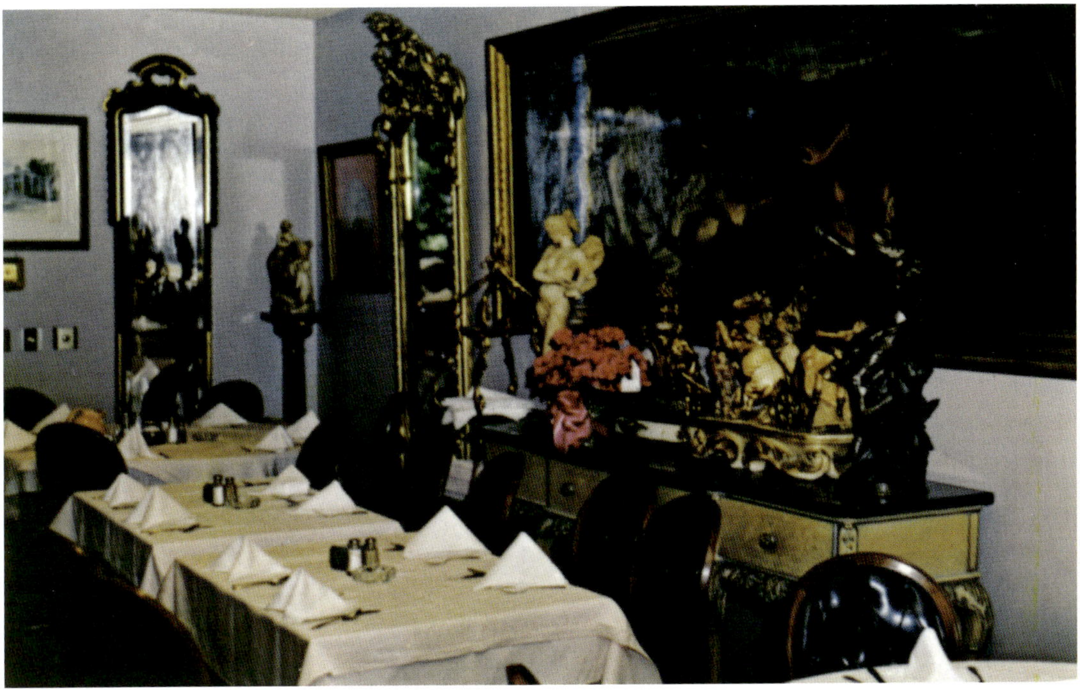

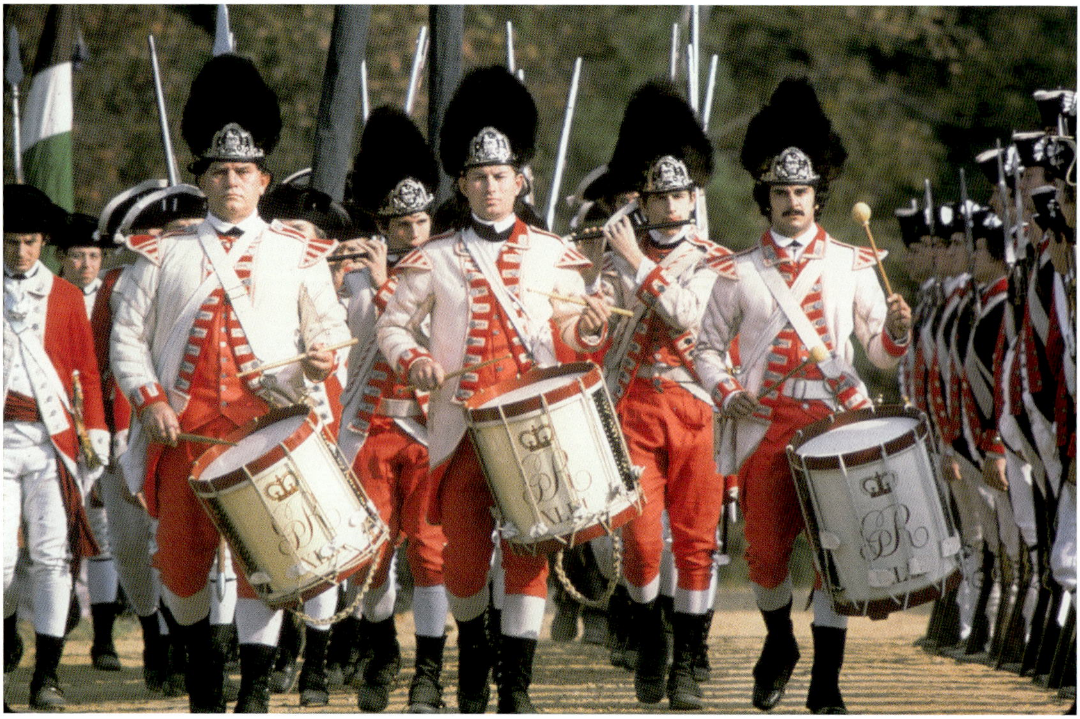

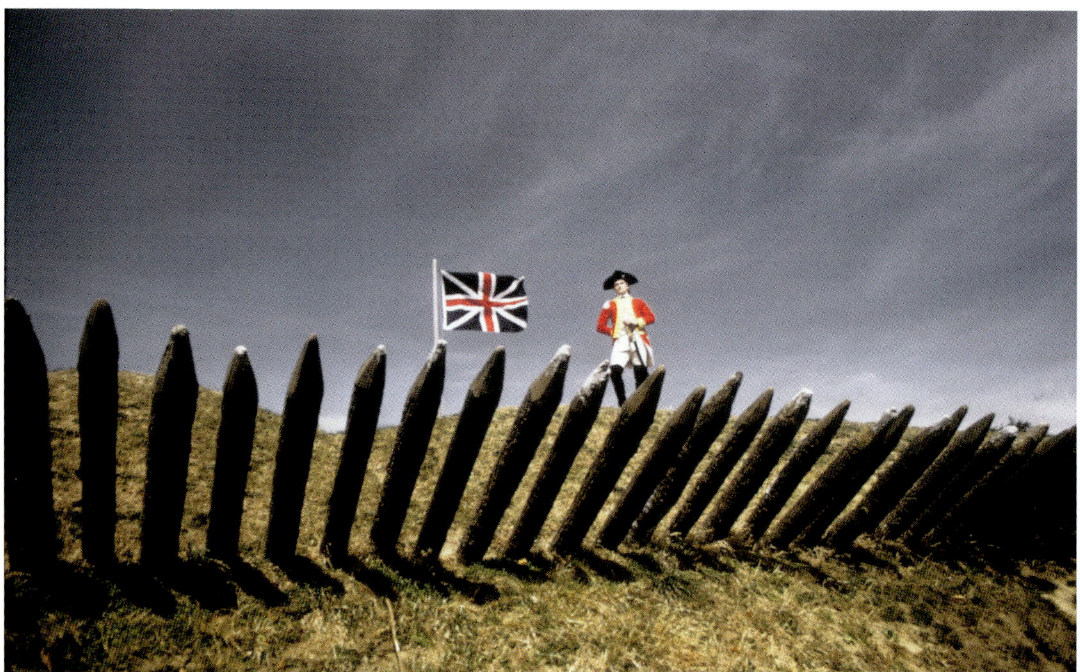

The National Park Service published a series of photographs (*on this page and opposite above*) of reenactments on the Yorktown Battlefield in the 1970s that provide visual evidence of the scope of the events held there during key anniversary commemorations. *National Park Service*

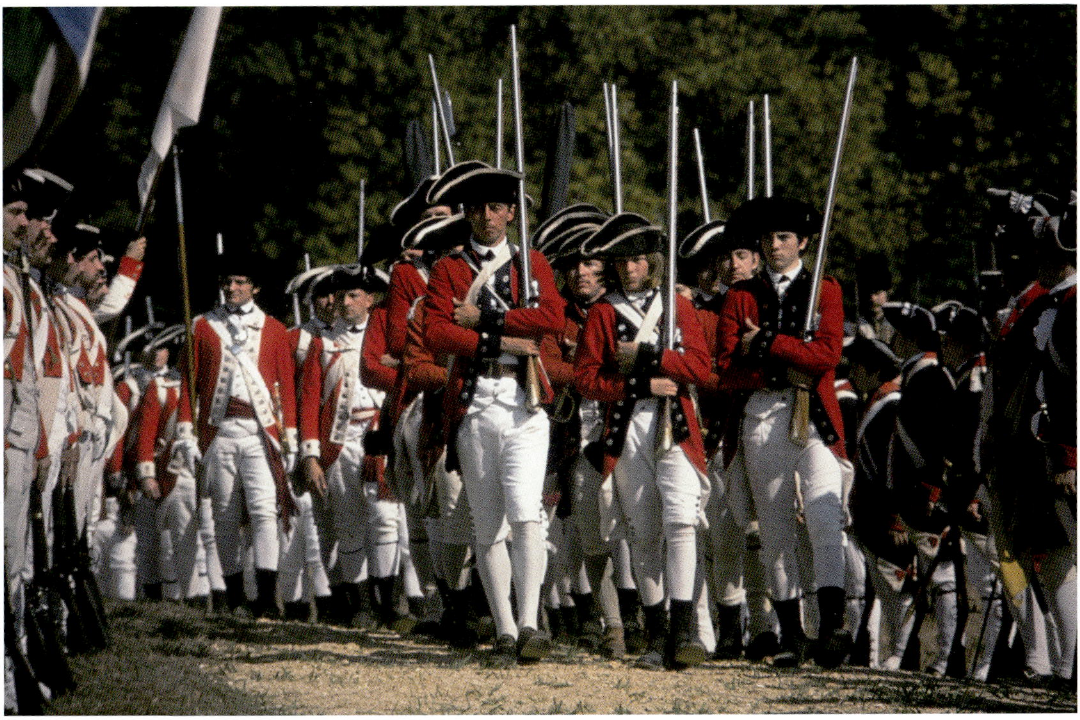

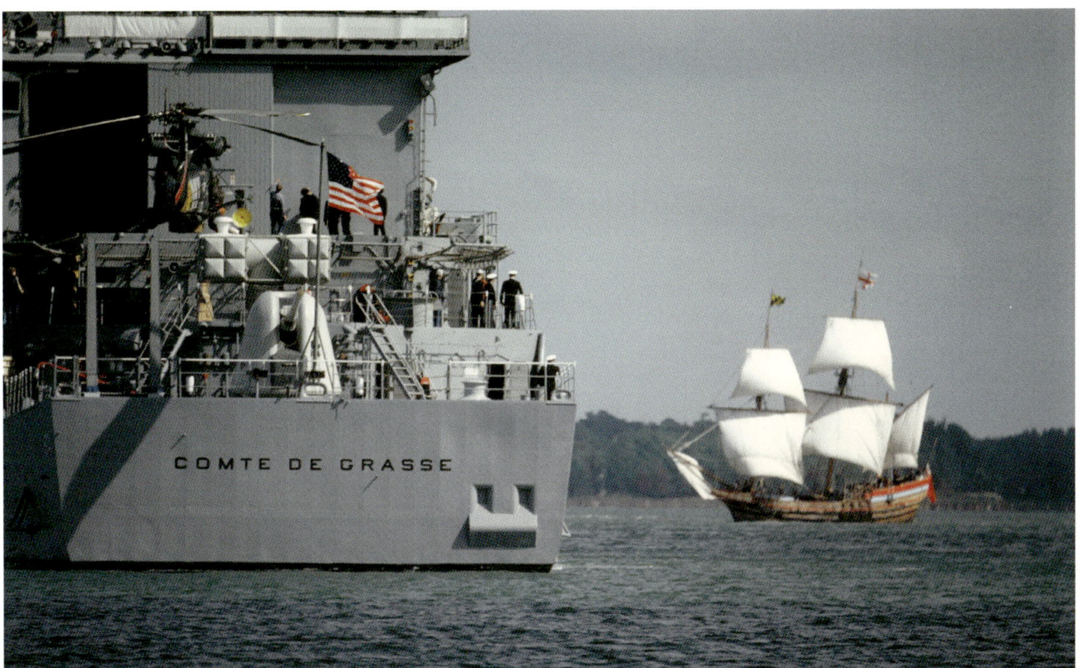

This is a stern view of the destroyer USS *Comte de Grasse* (DD-974) with an SH-2F Seasprite helicopter on board during a reenactment of the Battle of Yorktown. A replica sailing ship is in the background. The picture was taken on October 15, 1981, by Journalist First Class Peter Dwaine Sundberg (1947–2005). *National Archives*

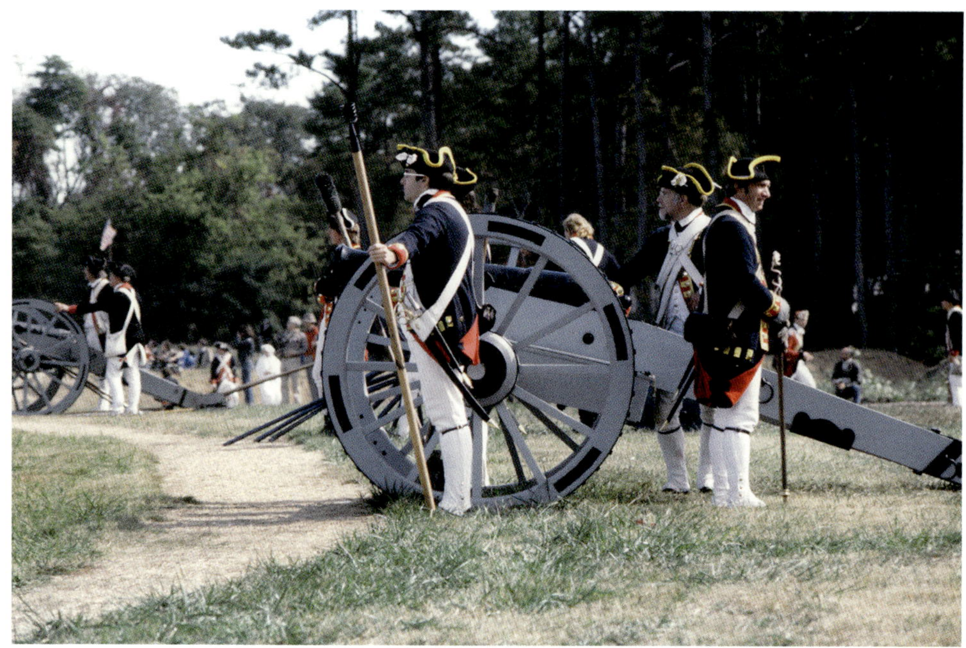

Members of Great Britain's Fourth Royal Artillery Unit, dressed in Revolutionary War uniforms, demonstrate cannon firing at the Yorktown Bicentennial Celebration. The picture was taken on October 16, 1981, by air force sergeant Marvin Dwayne Lynchard. *National Archives*

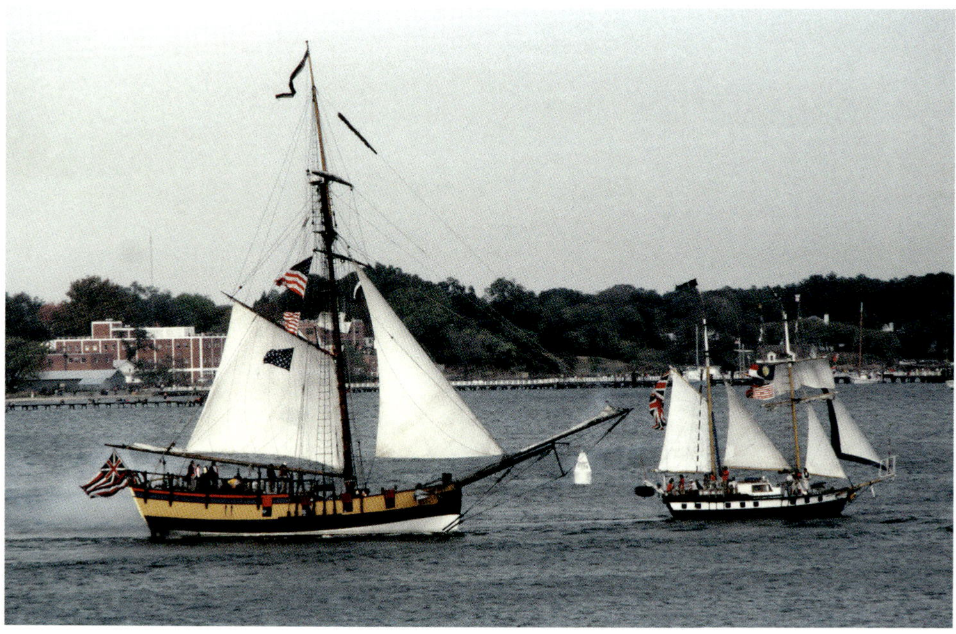

A mock sea battle between American and British ships took place on the York River during the Yorktown Bicentennial Celebration. The photograph was taken on April 16, 1981. *National Archives*

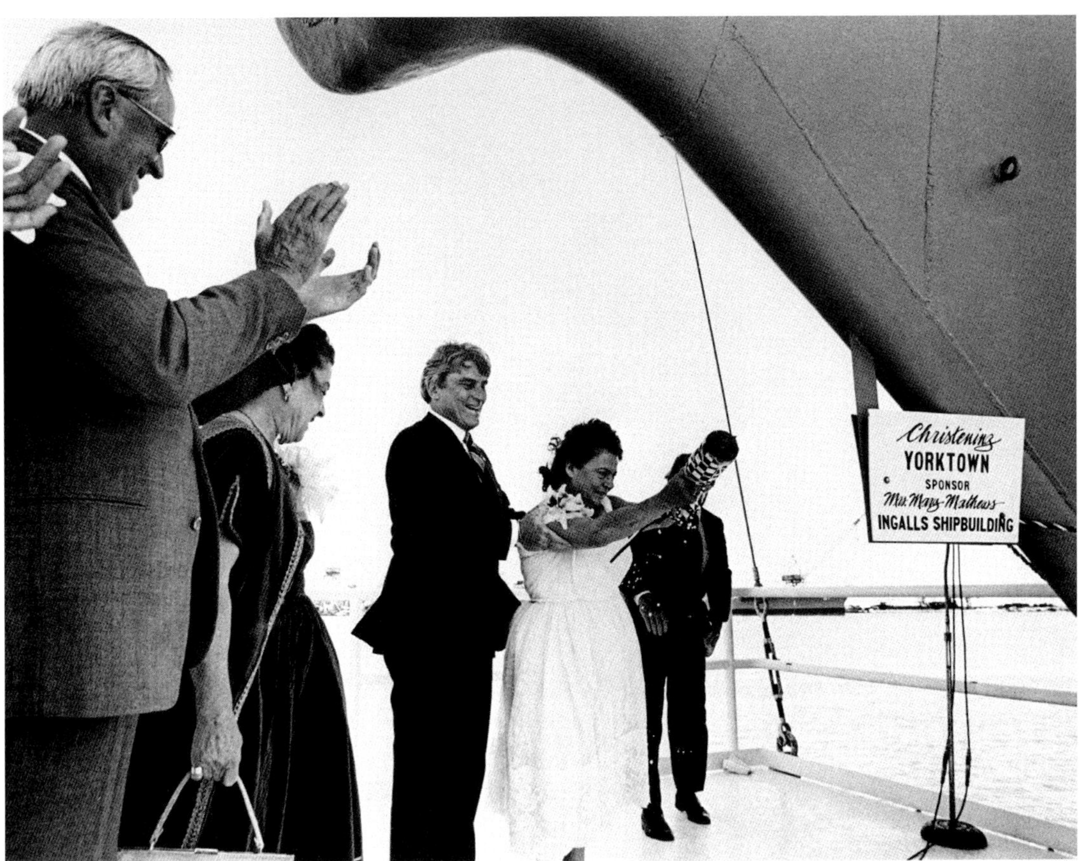

USS *Yorktown* (CG-48), an Aegis guided missile cruiser, was launched January 17, 1983, and sponsored by Mary Pappas Mathews, widow of Nicholas Minas "Mister Nick" Mathews, owner of Nick's Seafood Pavilion and a prominent citizen of Yorktown, Virginia.[5] *Yorktown* was commissioned on July 4, 1984, at Yorktown, Virginia, and was designed to take advantage of the American Aegis technology. Among its various weapon systems were surface to air missiles (SAMs), anti-ship/anti-submarine missiles, torpedo launchers, and a mounted cannon. *Yorktown*'s first deployment was from August 1985 to April 1986 and it was during this at-sea period that the ship was involved in the *Achille Lauro* hijacker intercept, two Black Sea excursions (in 1986 and 1988), and a trio of operations off the Libyan coast including Operation El Dorado Canyon and Operation Attain Document and Prairie Fire. *Yorktown* was decommissioned and struck from the navy record on December 10, 2004. Mary Mathews, sponsor, christened the Aegis guided missile cruiser *Yorktown* (CG-48) on May 15, 1983, at Ingalls Shipbuilding. She was joined on the platform by (from left to right): Leonard Erb, president of Ingalls Shipbuilding; Helen Pappas Fiore (1908–1998), matron of honor and Mary Mathews' sister; Virginia Republican senator John William Warner (1927–2021), and Albert Colmer Weeks (1927–2011), Ingalls Shipbuilding's director of public relations. *National Archives*

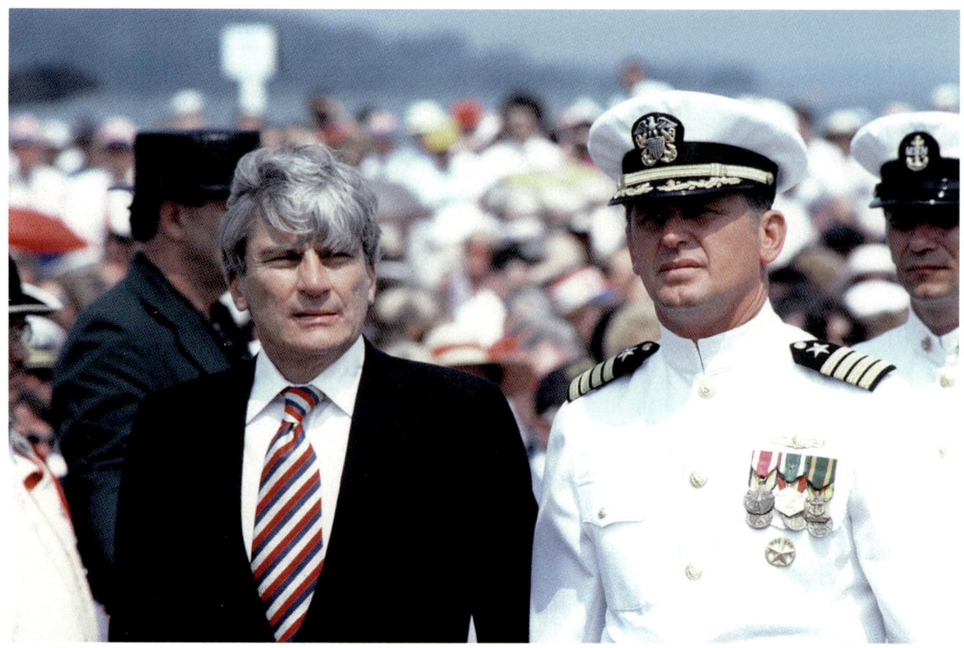

United States Senator John William Warner (left) stood with Captain Carl Allan Anderson, the first commanding officer of the USS *Yorktown* (CG-48) during the July 4, 1984 commissioning ceremony. The picture was taken by Photographer's Mate Joan Zopf. *National Archives*

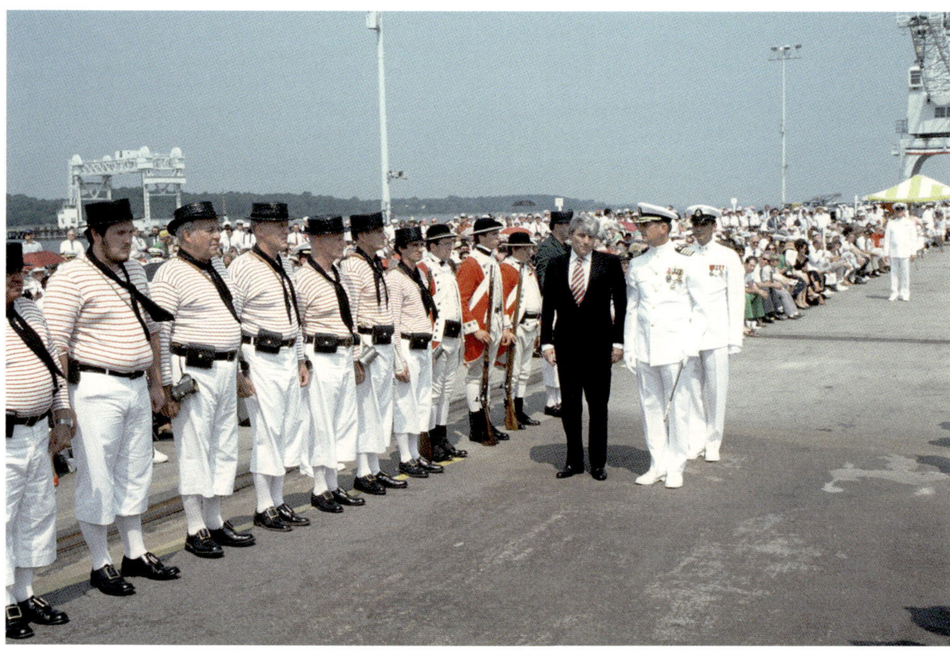

As part of the day's July 4, 1984 commissioning festivities, Senator John Warner, accompanied by Captain Carl Allan Anderson, the *Yorktown*'s commanding officer, inspected a group of men wearing the uniform of the Colonial Navy of Massachusetts. Photographer's Mate Third Class Joan Zopf took the picture. *National Archives*

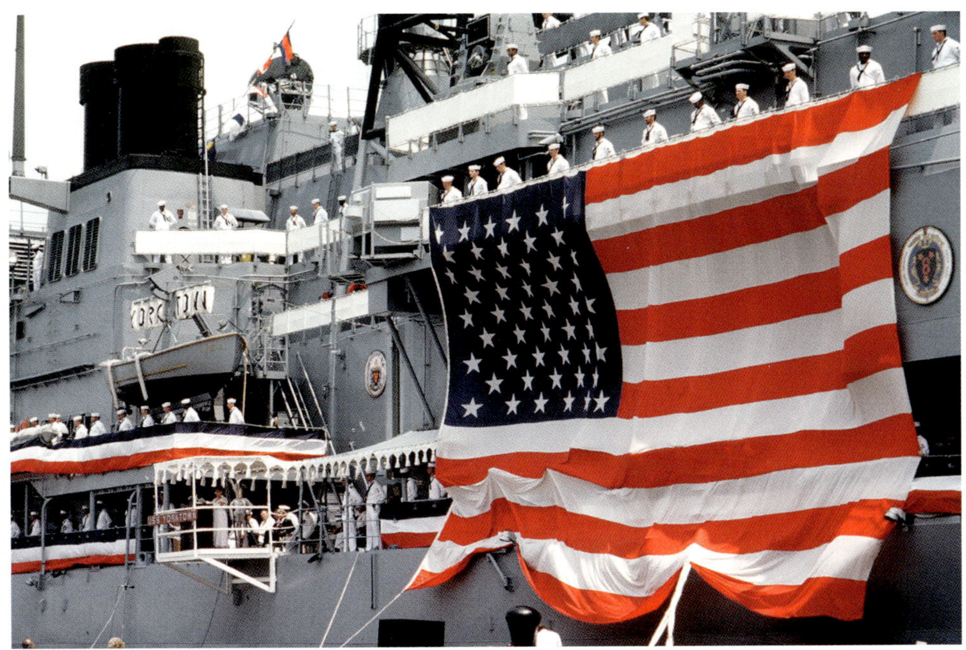

The crew of the USS *Yorktown* (CG-48) manned the rail during the ship's commissioning ceremony at Naval Weapons Station Yorktown on July 4, 1984. The picture was taken by Photographer's Mate Third Class Joan Zopf. *National Archives*

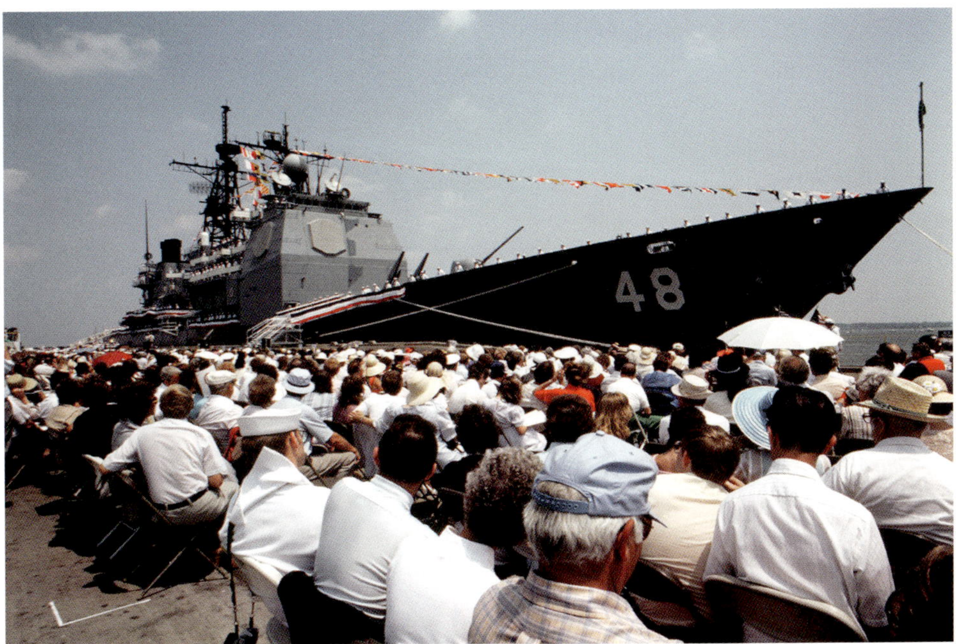

Hundreds of onlookers watched the July 4, 1984 commissioning of the USS *Yorktown* (CG-84). The picture was taken by Photographer's Mate Third Class Joan Zopf. *National Archives*

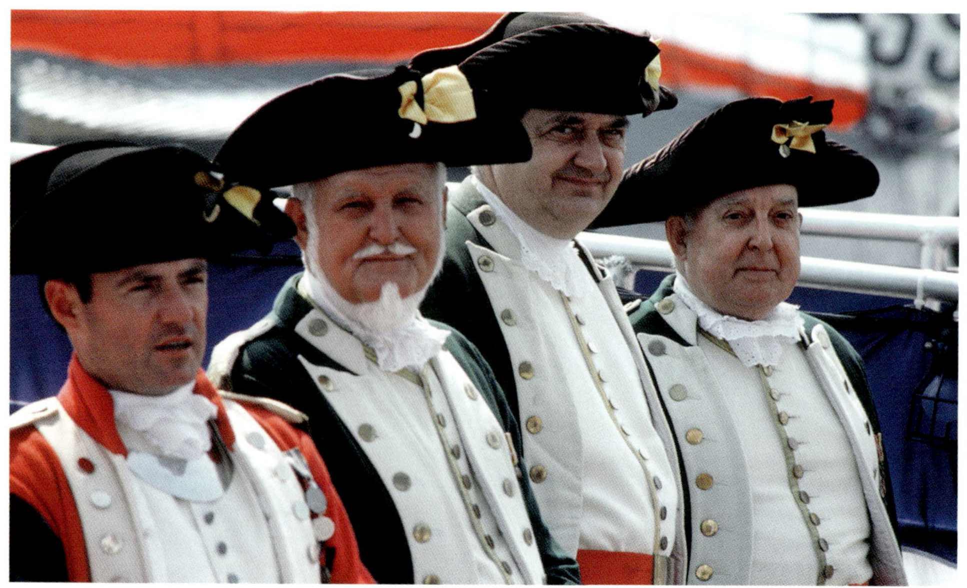

(Left to right) Frank Noble, Ralph Lesley Malloch (1918–1989), William L. "Bill" Brayton and John M. Babcock (1914–1987), wearing the uniform of the Colonial Navy of Massachusetts, attended and participated in the July 4, 1984 commissioning ceremony of the USS *Yorktown* (CG-48). The reenactor group was founded in 1967. This moment was preserved by Photographer's Mate Third Class Joan Zopf. *National Archives*

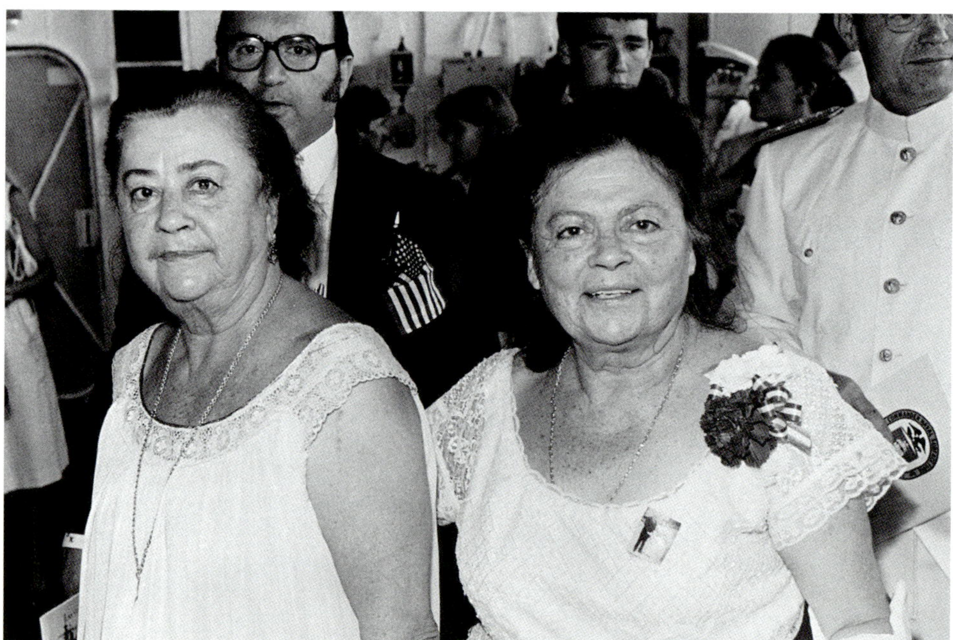

Helen Pappas Fiore (left), matron of honor, and Mary Pappas Mathews, ship's sponsor, pause for a picture at the conclusion of the commissioning ceremony for the Aegis guided missile cruiser USS *Yorktown* (CG-48) on July 4, 1984, at the Naval Weapons Station Yorktown. Mathews is wearing a picture taken with her husband—Nicholas Minas Mathews—on her dress—her way of sharing the honor of day with him. *National Archives*

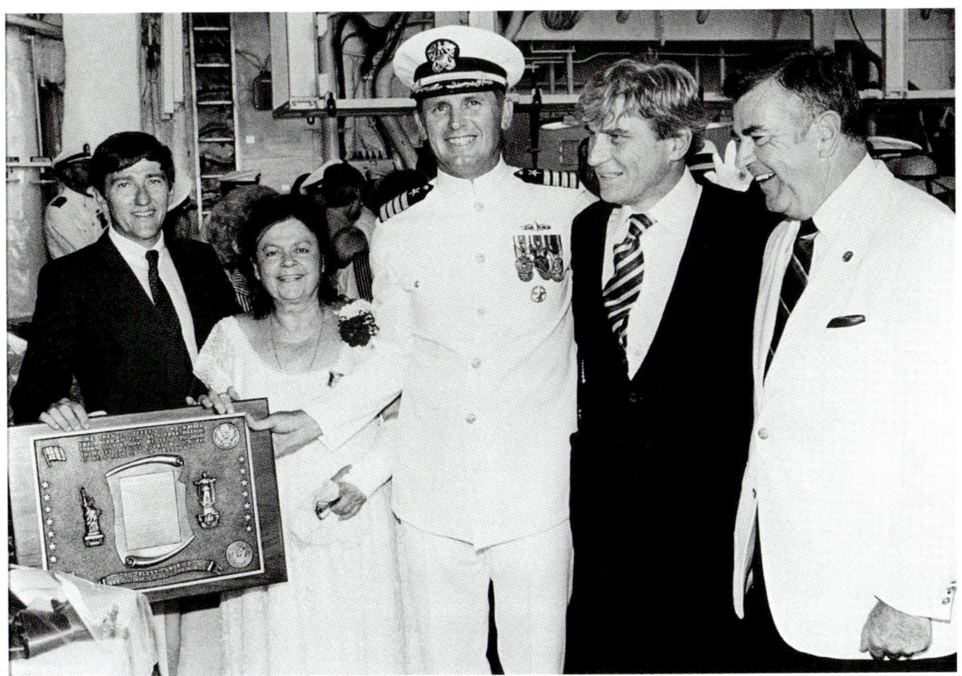

Participants in the commission ceremony of the USS *Yorktown* (CG-48) stand with the plaque presented to the ship. Shown here (left to right) are John Francis Lehman Jr., secretary of the navy; Mary Pappas Mathews, sponsor; navy captain Carl Allan Anderson, commanding officer; Virginia Republican senator John William Warner, and Virginia Republican congressman Herbert Harvell Batemen (1928–2000), representing the first district. *National Archives*

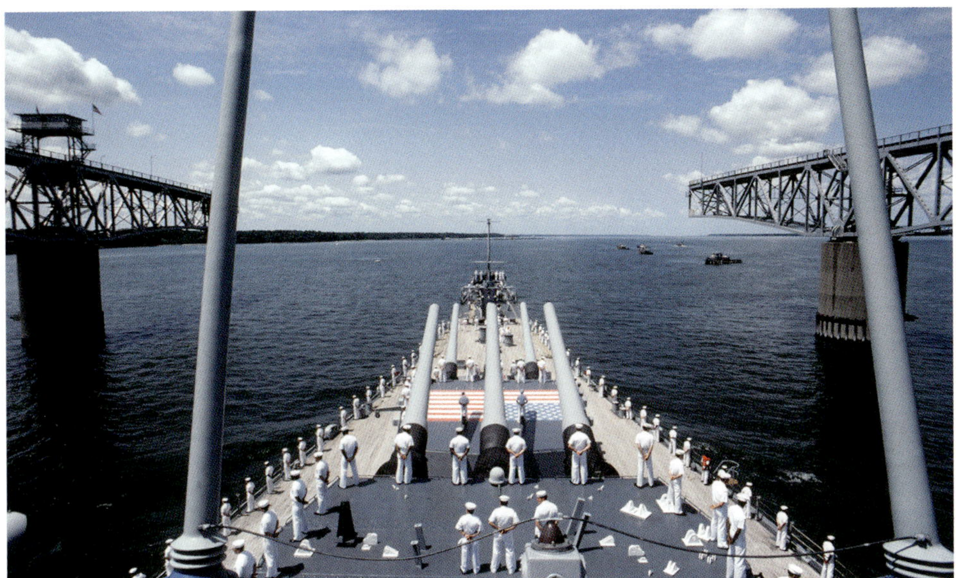

The crew of the battleship USS *Iowa* (BB-61) mans the rails as the ship passes through the George Preston Coleman Memorial Bridge en route to Naval Weapons Station Yorktown on August 1, 1984. The picture was taken by Photographer's Mate First Class Jeffery Hilton. *National Archives*

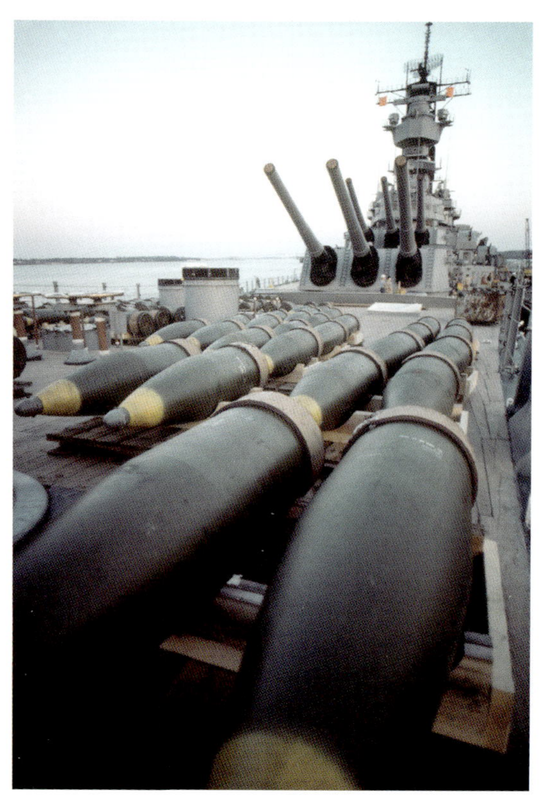

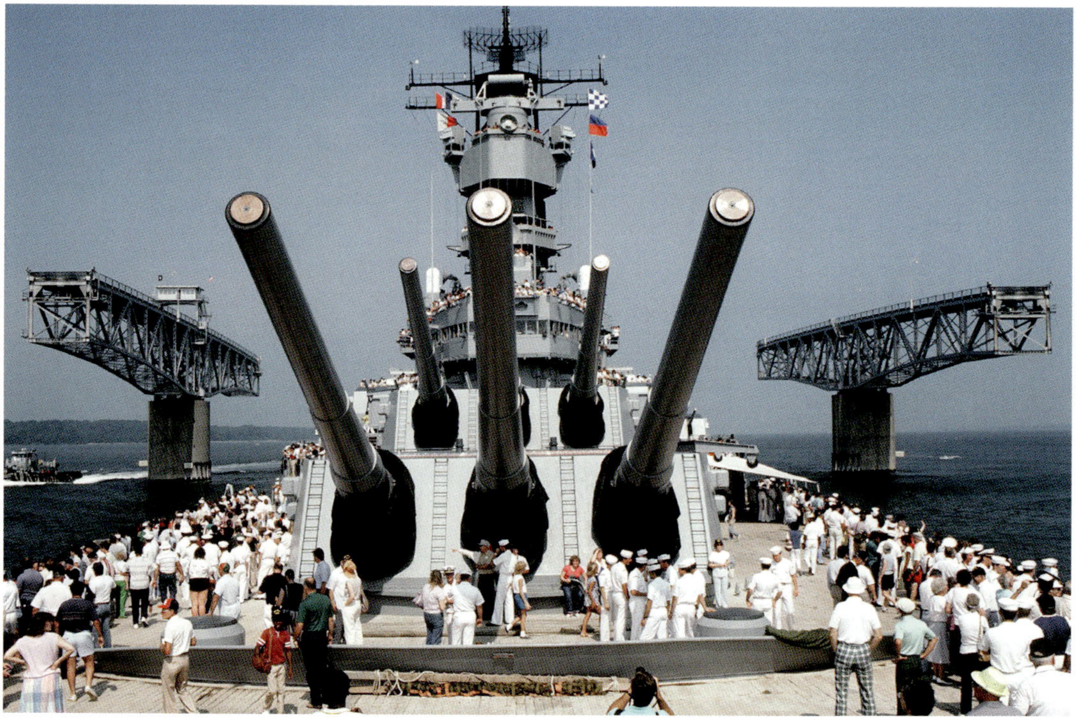

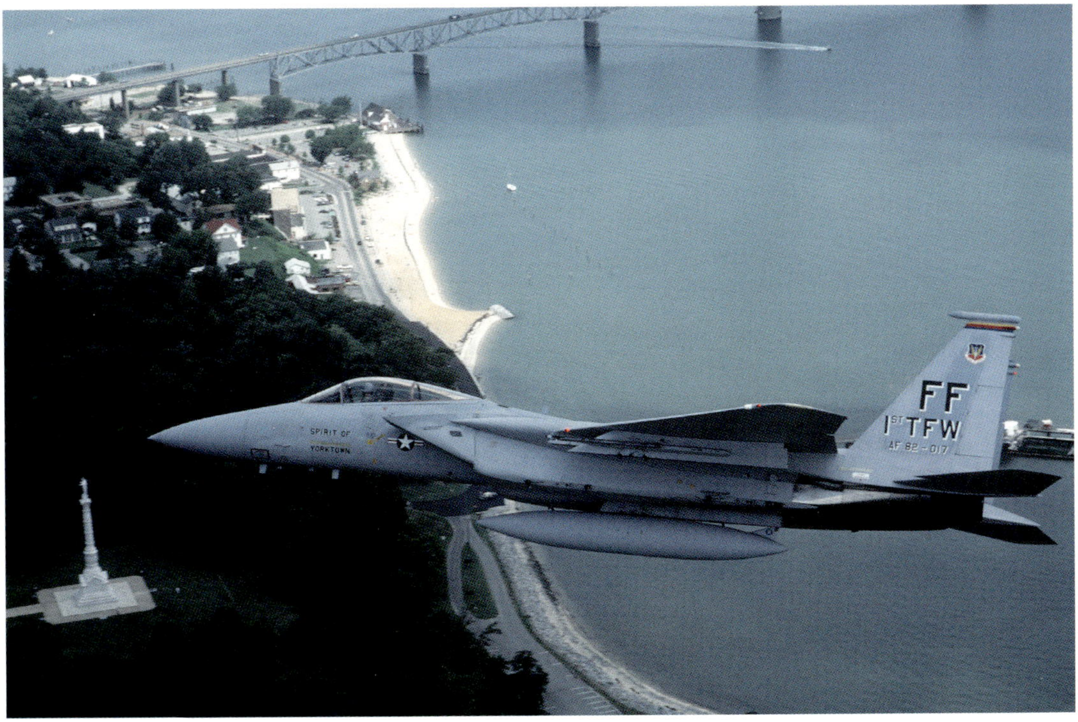

This air-to-air port side view of a First Tactical Fighter Wing F-15 Eagle painted below the cockpit with the name "Spirit of Yorktown" flies over Yorktown on August 5, 1986. *National Archives*

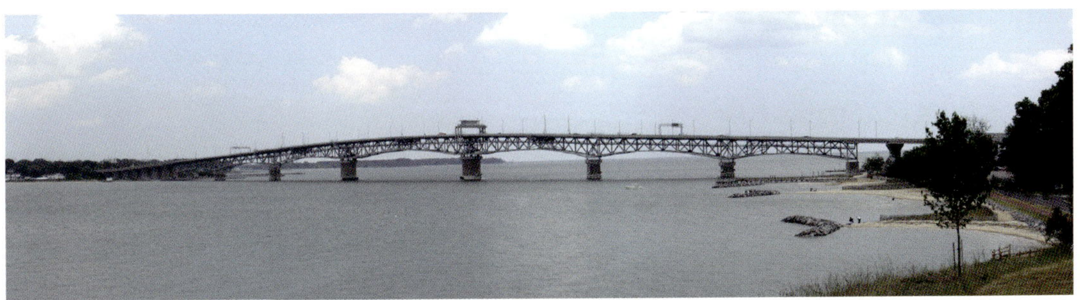

This panoramic photograph of the George Preston Coleman Memorial Bridge was taken on May 18, 2006. *Mike Durkin*[6]

Opposite page:

Above: Projectiles used in the sixteen-inch fifty caliber Mark 7 guns of the battleship USS *Iowa* (BB-61) were being offloaded at Naval Weapons Station Yorktown when Photographer's Mate First Class Jeffery Hilton took these pictures on March 1, 1985. The *Iowa* had to offload its ordnance before entering Naval Station Norfolk. *National Archives*

Below: Photographer's Mate First Class Jeffery Hilton took this picture of the battleship USS *Iowa* (BB-61) as it passed through the George Preston Coleman Memorial Bridge after it left the Naval Weapons Station Yorktown en route to Naval Station Norfolk during a six-hour dependents' day cruise on August 16, 1985. *National Archives*

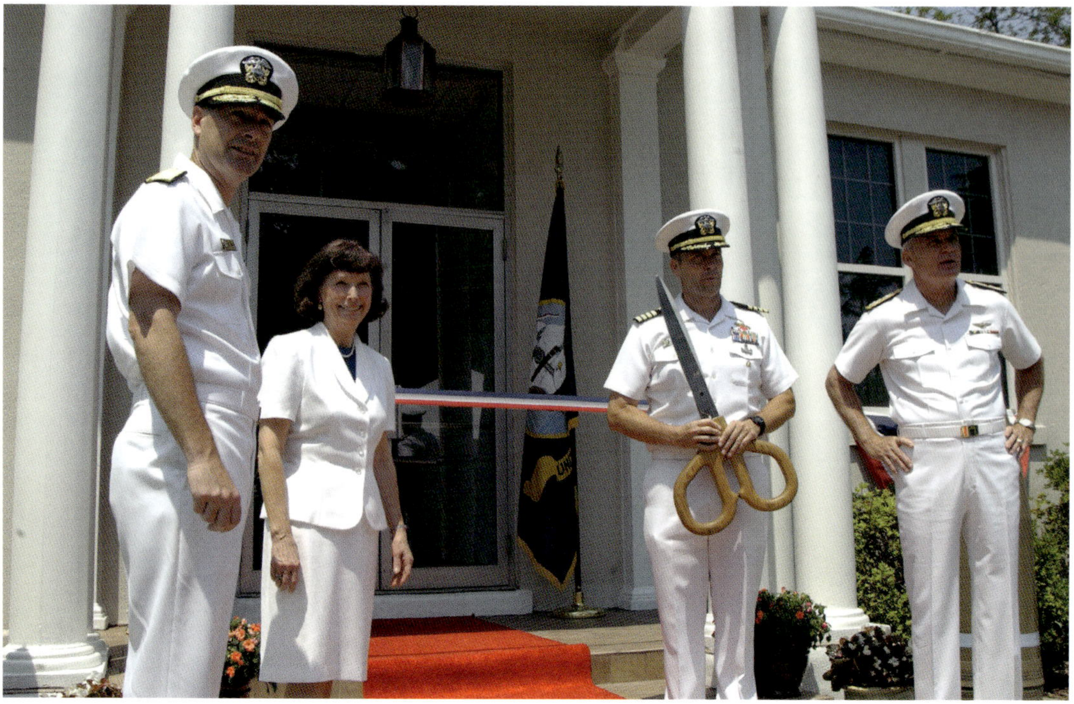

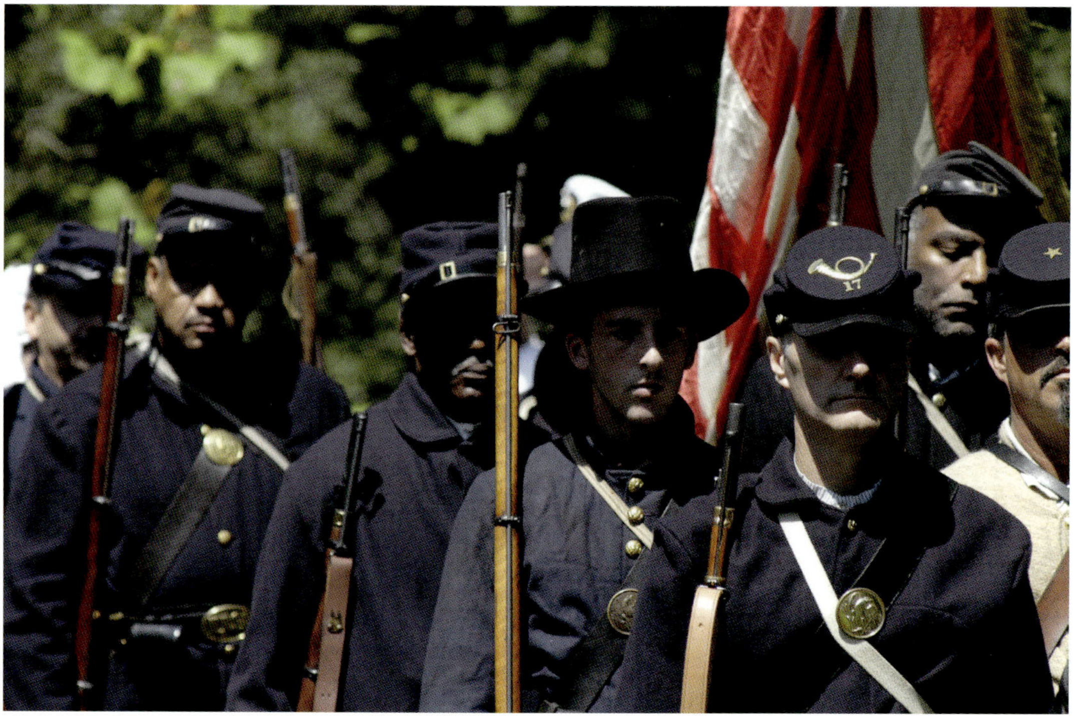

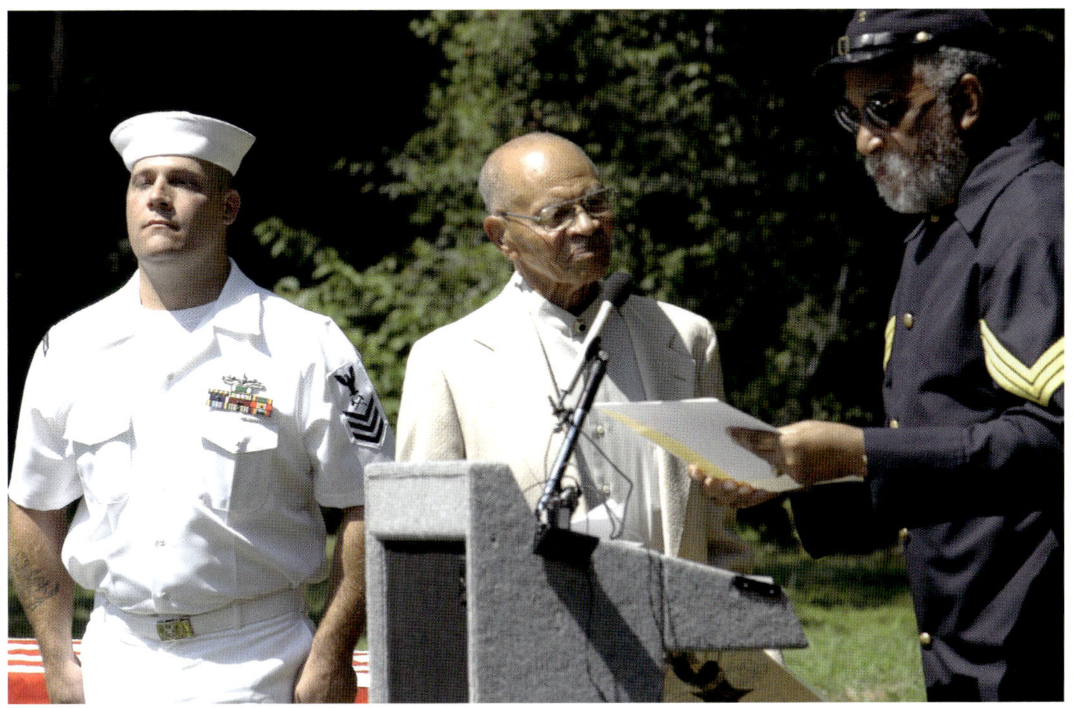

Reverend Dr. Edward Curtis Alexander (right), on behalf of the Thirty-Eighth United States Colored Troops Company C [Edward Ratcliff's unit], read an award to Edward Radcliffe (center), a descendant of Civil War Medal of Honor recipient United States Army sergeant major Edward Ratcliff, during the dedication of a memorial marker for the Civil War hero. Standing at attention (left) is navy hull technician first class John Frush, of Naval Weapons Station Yorktown. The photograph was taken by Mass Communication Specialist Third Class Chad A. Hallford during the end of summer ceremony. *United States Navy*

Opposite page:

Above: The commanding officer of Naval Weapons Station Yorktown, Captain Gerard O'Regan, was photographed on June 8, 2006, as he prepared to cut the ribbon for the official opening of the Naval Munitions Command as navy supply corps rear admiral Raymond E. Berube, executive director of the Navy Munitions Command Atlantic Frances Goodwin Holt Ph.D., and Admiral John B. Nathman looked on. The Navy Munitions Command was stood up just then to align all current ashore ordnance support operations in the United States and Asia into one worldwide unit to consolidate resource requirements, standardize policies and streamline procedures for a more responsive, flexible and efficient fleet ordnance support structure. The picture was taken by Photographer's Mate Airman Christopher Hall. *United States Navy*

Below: These Civil War reenactors paraded the Colors on August 5, 2006, during the dedication of a memorial marker for Sergeant Major Edward Ratcliff (1835–1915), of the United States Army, a Civil War Medal of Honor recipient for his actions at the Battle of Chaffin's Farm. Born a slave, he was freed when the Union army took Yorktown. Ratcliff was serving as a first sergeant in Company C of the Thirty-Eighth Regiment United States Colored Troops by September 29, 1864. On that day, his unit was at the Battle of Chaffin's Farm for which he was awarded the Medal of Honor six months later, on April 6, 1865. After he died at the age of eighty, Ratcliff was buried at Cheesecake Cemetery, Charles Corner, York County, now part of Naval Weapons Station Yorktown. The picture was taken by Mass Communication Specialist Third Class Chad A. Hallford. *United States Navy*

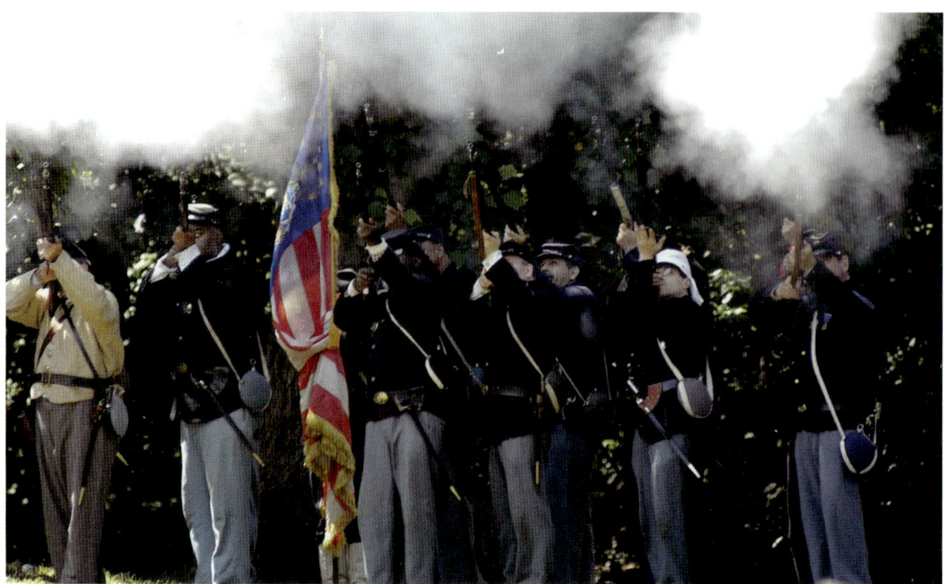

Civil War reenactors performed a twenty-one-gun salute at the dedication of a memorial marker at Cheesecake Cemetery, Yorktown, Virginia, for Sergeant Major Edward Ratcliff, of the United States Army, a Civil War Medal of Honor recipient. The cemetery is on the United States Naval Weapons Station. The navy hosted the event. The photograph was taken on August 5, 2006, by Mass Communication Specialist Third Class Chad A. Hallford. *United States Navy*

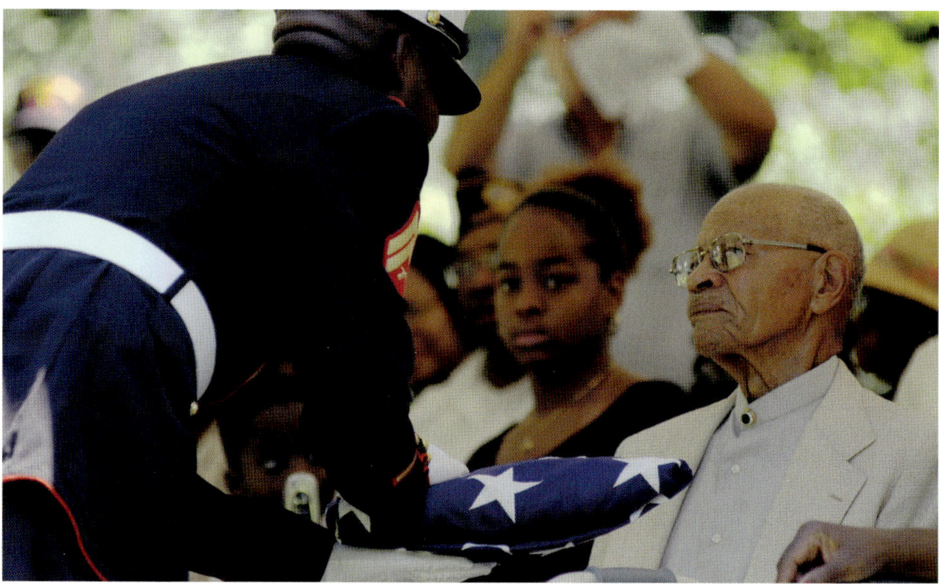

United States Marine Corps corporal Edward Radcliffe (left) presented his grandfather, Edward Radcliffe, with a flag that was flown over Naval Weapons Station Yorktown during the unveiling of a memorial marker at Cheesecake Cemetery for Civil War hero and Medal of Honor recipient sergeant major Edward Ratcliff, of the United States Army. The Radcliffes are both descendants of the honoree. The picture was taken, along with others shown here, by Mass Communication Specialist Third Class Chad A. Hallford during the August 5, 2006 events. *United States Navy*

The youngest Edward Ratcliff descendant, Jaylen, stood over the grave of his ancestor, army sergeant major Edward Ratcliff, the first African American to be awarded the Medal of Honor, during a wreath-laying ceremony at Naval Weapons Station Yorktown on December 10, 2011. More than eighteen Ratcliff descendants attended the ceremony, which was part of the annual Wreaths Across America campaign to lay holiday wreaths at the graves of veterans across the United States. Mark O. Piggott took the picture. *United States Navy*

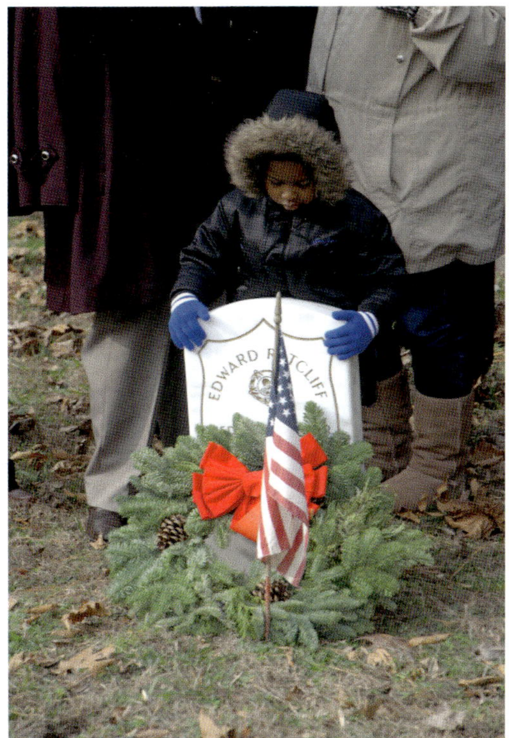

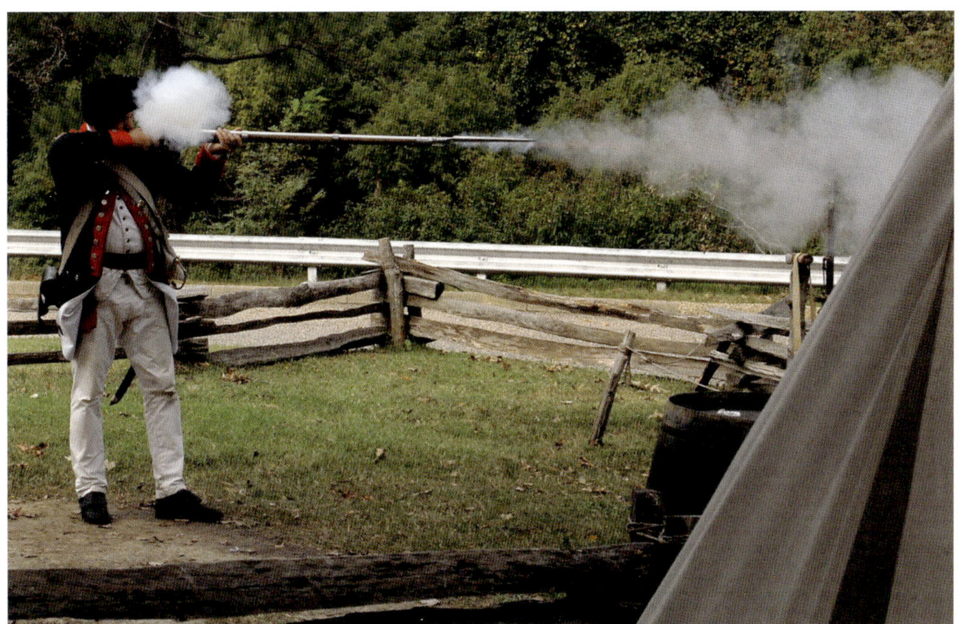

Retired navy chief aviation structural mechanic Don Kevin Reimert, a historical interpreter, fires a flintlock musket during a demonstration held for the two hundred and twenty-fifth anniversary of the end of the Revolutionary War, part of the Yorktown celebratory events. The picture was taken by Mass Communication Specialist Second Class Christopher Delano on October 19, 2006. *United States Navy*

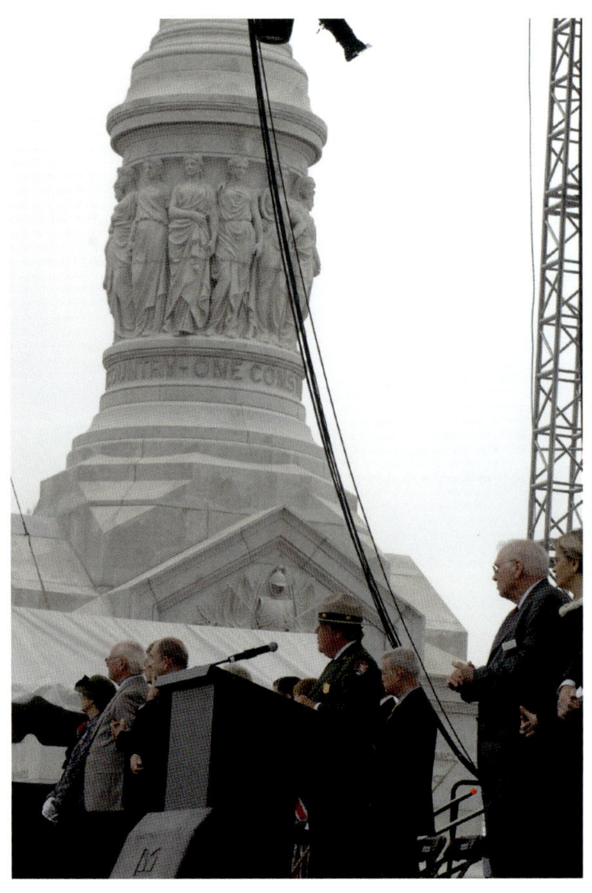

Secretary of the Interior Dirk Arthur Kempthorne joined a platform of dignitaries that also included Virginia senators John William Warner and George Allen, fourteenth secretary of the army John Otho Marsh Jr., then French ambassador to the United States Jean-David Levitte, and former French defense minister Michèle Jeanne Honorine Alliot-Marie to kick off the two hundred and twenty-fifth anniversary celebration of the Battle of Yorktown. Kempthorne delivered the keynote address in shadow of the Yorktown Victory Monument on October 19, 2006. The pictures were taken by Department of Interior staffer Tami Hellemann. *Department of the Interior*

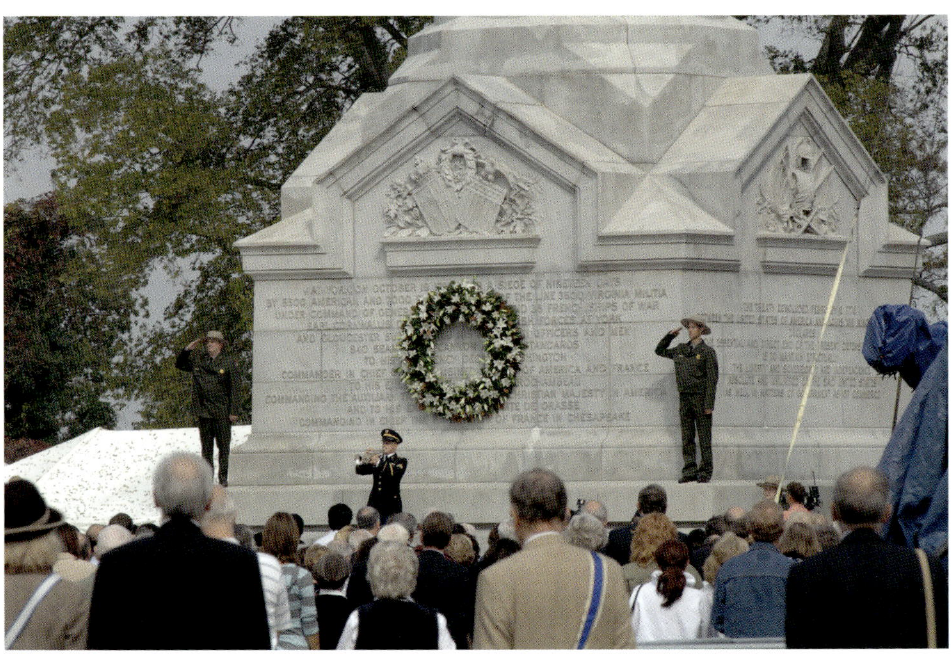

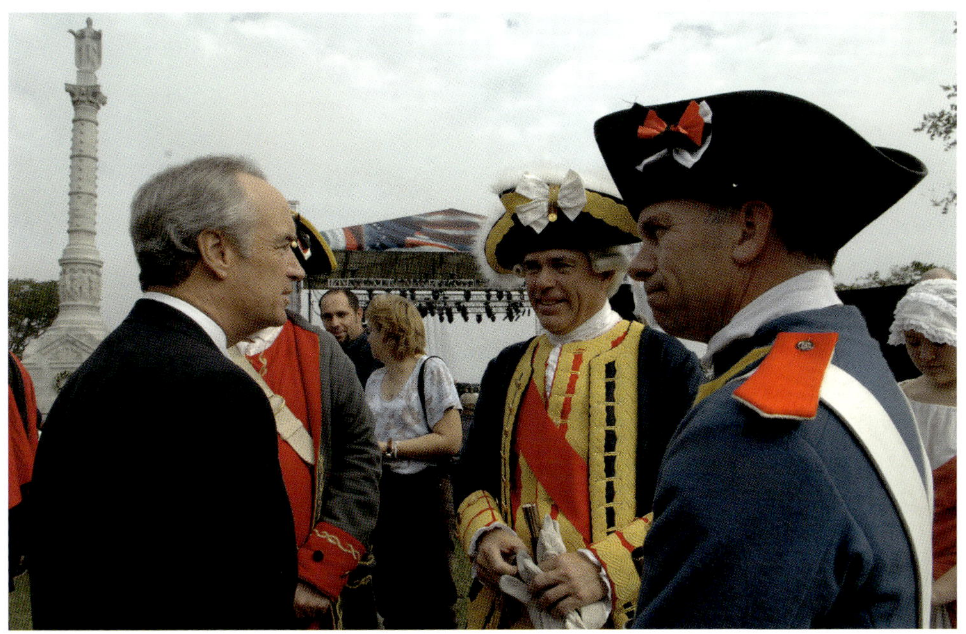

Secretary of the Interior Dirk Kempthorne was photographed by Tami Hellemann, an Interior staffer, speaking to reenactors during his visit to Yorktown on October 19, 2006. *Department of the Interior*

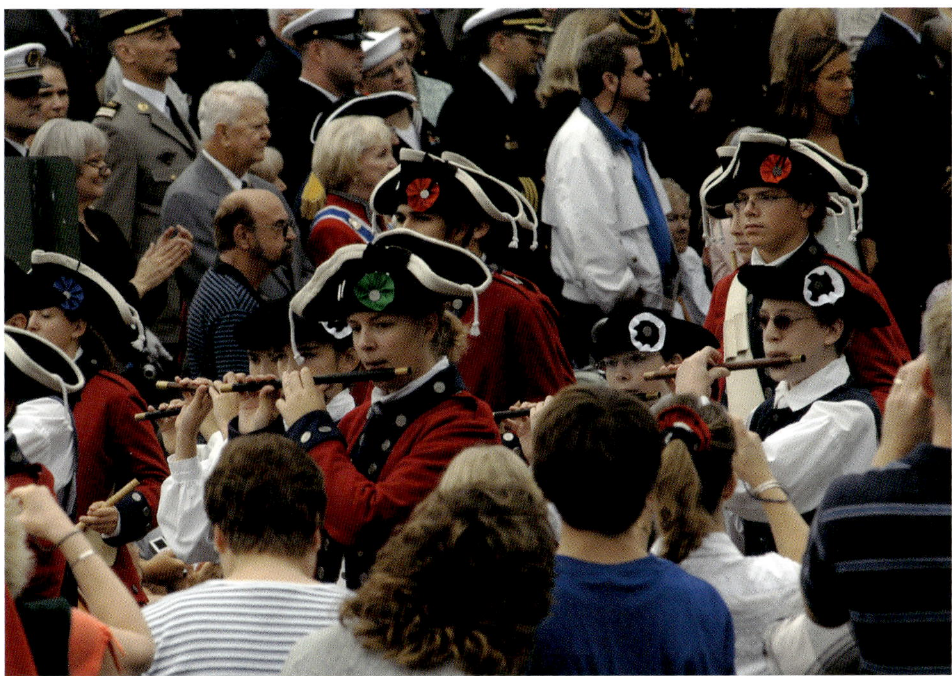

The Fife and Drums of York Town performed for a crowd of onlookers during the Revolutionary War Yorktown Victory Celebration on October 19, 2006. The team was photographed by Mass Communication Specialist Second Class Christopher Delano. *United States Navy*

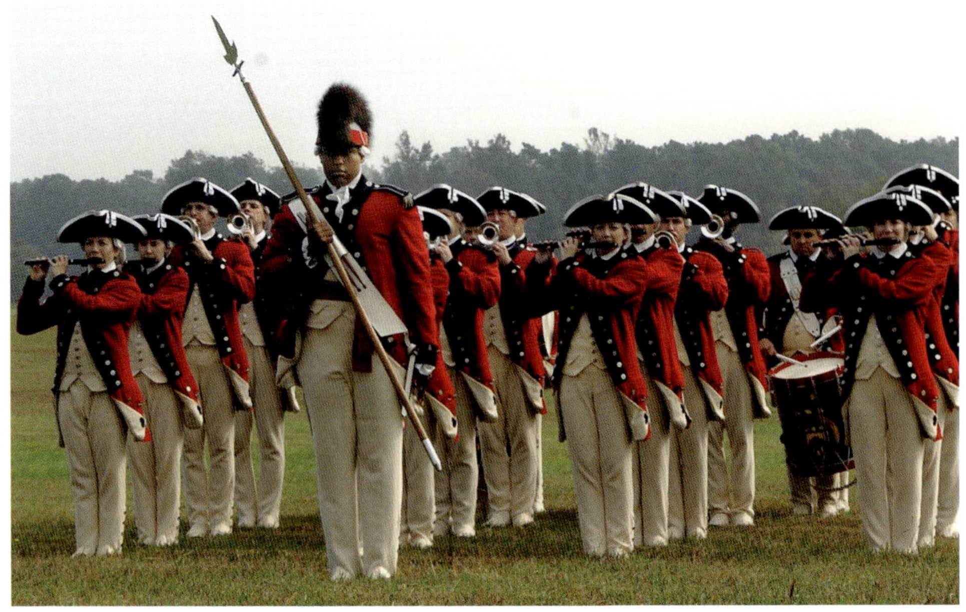

The Old Guard Fife and Drum Corps performed at a celebration commemorating the two hundred and twenty-fifth anniversary of the American victory at Yorktown, Virginia, during the Revolutionary War on October 19, 2006. The picture was taken by army specialist Van Der Weide. *United States Army*

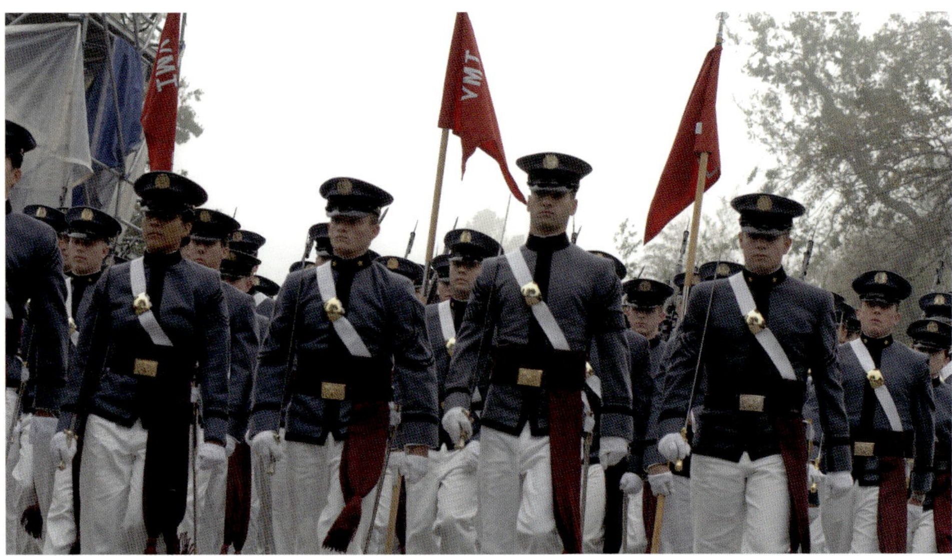

The Virginia Military Institute Corps of Cadets marched in the Revolutionary War Yorktown Victory Celebration on October 19, 2006 (shown here). The picture was taken by Interior Department staffer Tami Hellemann. *Department of the Interior*

Opposite above: The Bagad Lann Bihoué (shown here) is a Bagad, Breton pipe band [Music of Brittany]; it is the Bagad of the French navy and the only remaining French and professional military Bagad. The band represents the French navy and France in multiple national and international events like the two hundred and twenty-fifth anniversary of the American victory at Yorktown on October 19, 2006. *Continued on next page*

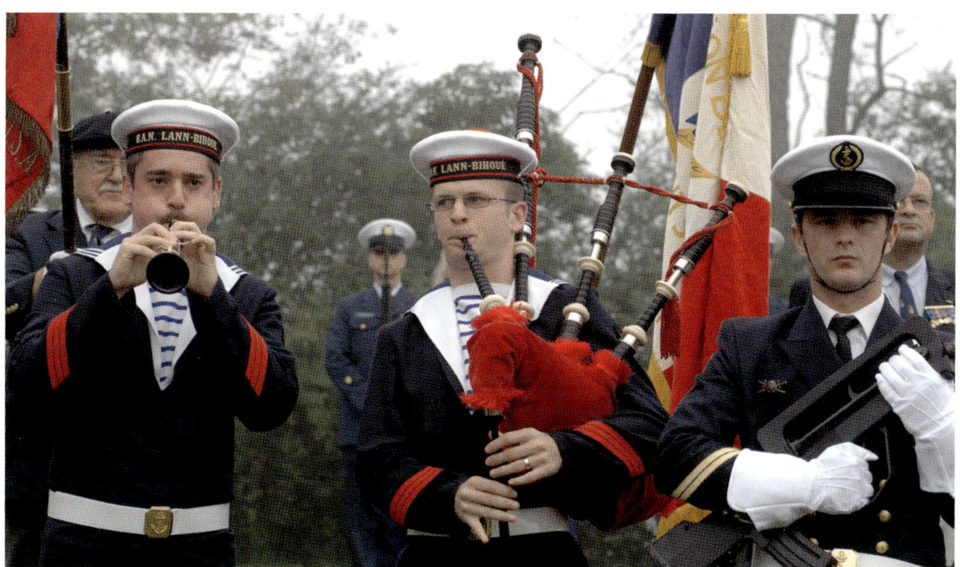

Continued from previous page: The band has performed regularly in front of heads of state and remains a source of cultural influence in Brittany as in the rest of France. The Bagad Lann Bihoué was created in 1952 on the naval air base Lann-Bihoué near Lorient [Morbihan, a department of Brittany]. Having almost been disbanded twice in 1969 and in 2000, it secured its existence in 2001 by becoming a professional band. It has recorded about fifteen albums during its sixty years of existence and has participated in several songs or albums from other artists. The picture was taken by Interior Department staffer Tami Hellemann. *Department of the Interior*

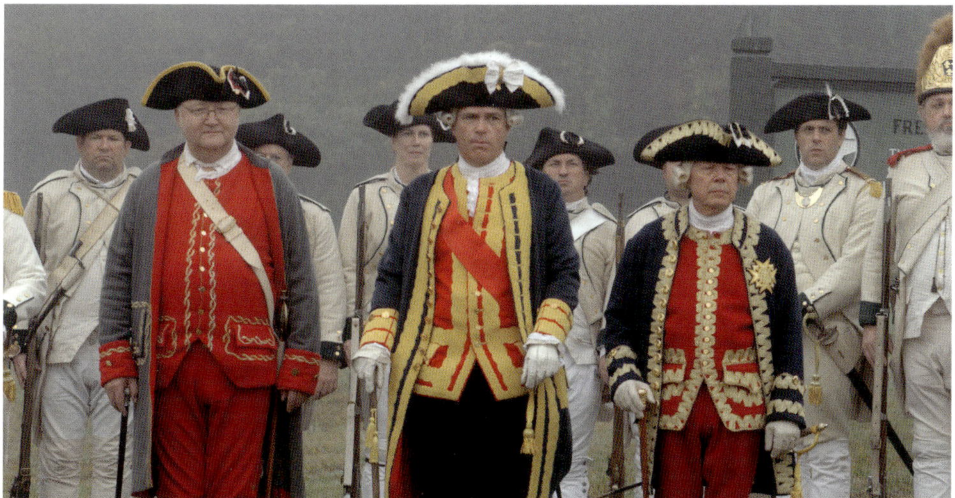

Featured here are reenactors filling the roles of officers of the French Armée Auxilaire participating in the American Revolutionary War, including from left to right: Commissaire des Guerres Claude Blanchard [depicted by Robert A. Selig Ph.D.]; Francois-Joseph Paul, Comte de Grasse, Lieutenant-général d'Armée Navale, l'amiral de la flotte francaise à Yorktown [depicted by Bill Rose], and Lieutenant-général Jean-Baptiste Donatien de Vimeur, Comte de Rochambeau, commander of the royal corps d'armée [played by John Welsh, an attorney]. The scene was photographed on October 19 2006, by Interior Department staffer Tami Hellemann. *Department of the Interior*

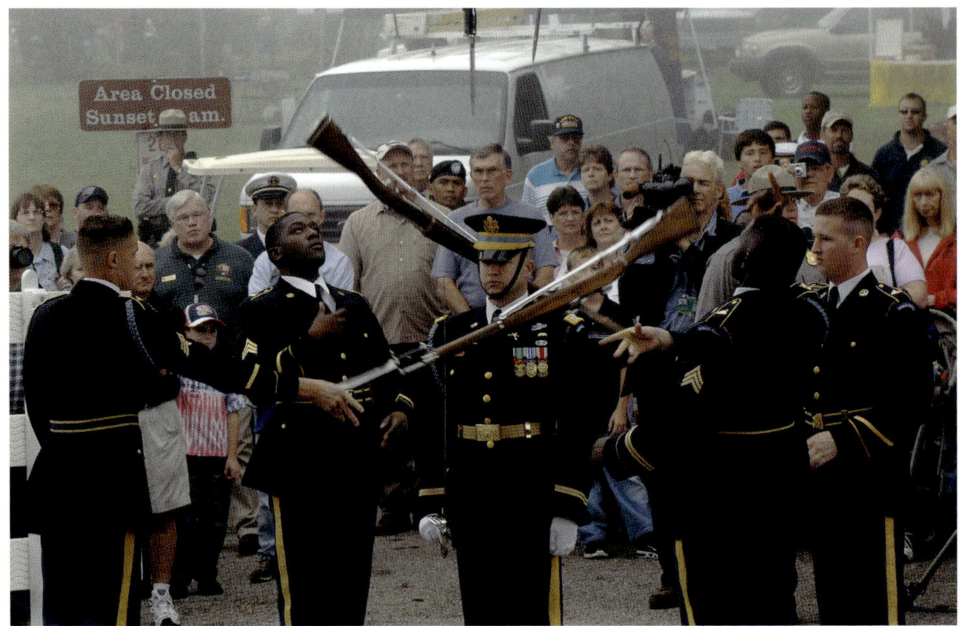

Mass Communication Specialist Second Class Christopher Delano took this picture of the United States Army Drill Team executing a precision rifle presentation during the two hundred and twenty-fifth anniversary of the Revolutionary War Yorktown Victory Celebration held on October 19, 2006. *United States Navy*

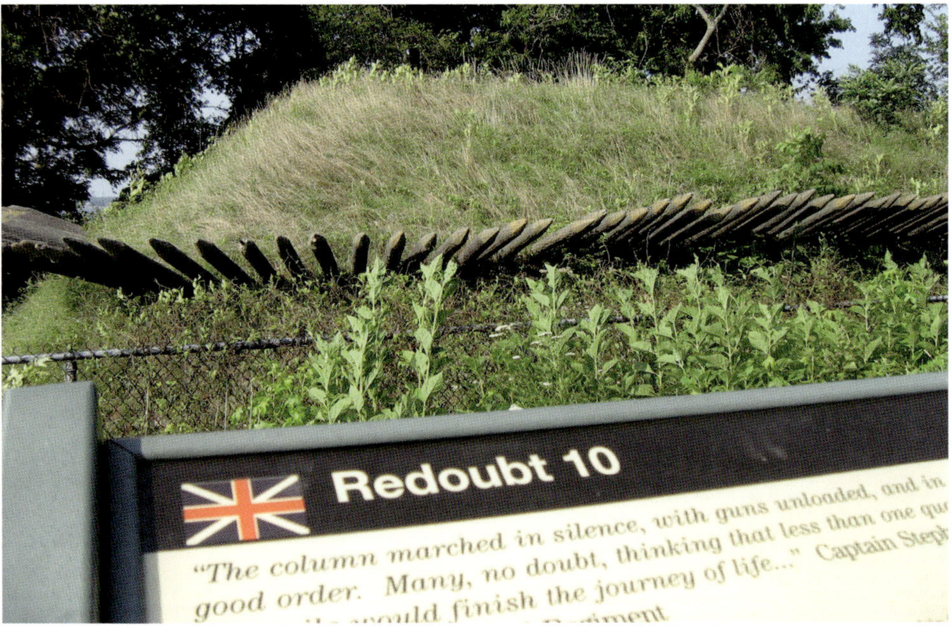

Redoubt No. 10 on the Yorktown Battlefield was photographed on June 16, 2007. *Yellowute*[7]

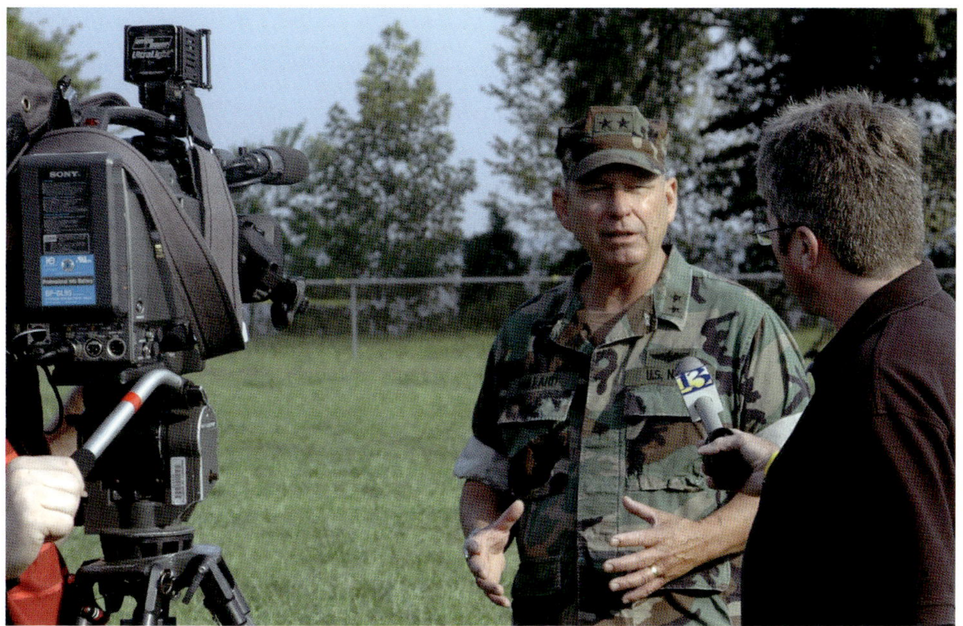

Rear Admiral Donald K. Bullard, commander of Navy Expeditionary Combat Command (NECC) just then, spoke to WVEC-13 military reporter Mike Gooding during a media day at Naval Weapons Station Yorktown Cheatham Annex on September 11, 2007. The event was part of NECC's integrated maritime security exercise COMET 2007. Senior Chief Mass Communications Specialist Dave Nagle took the photograph. *United States Navy*

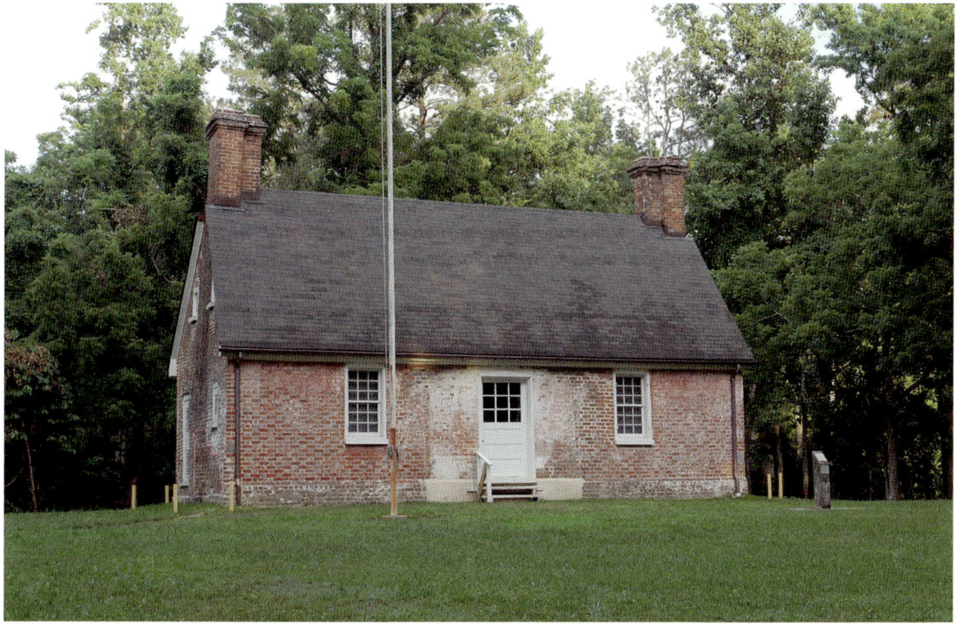

The only original plantation house still standing on Naval Weapons Station Yorktown, Kiskiack was named after the American Indian tribe in the area. Today, the house is listed on the Virginia Historic Landmark registry. Mark Piggott took the photograph on August 1, 2008. *United States Navy*

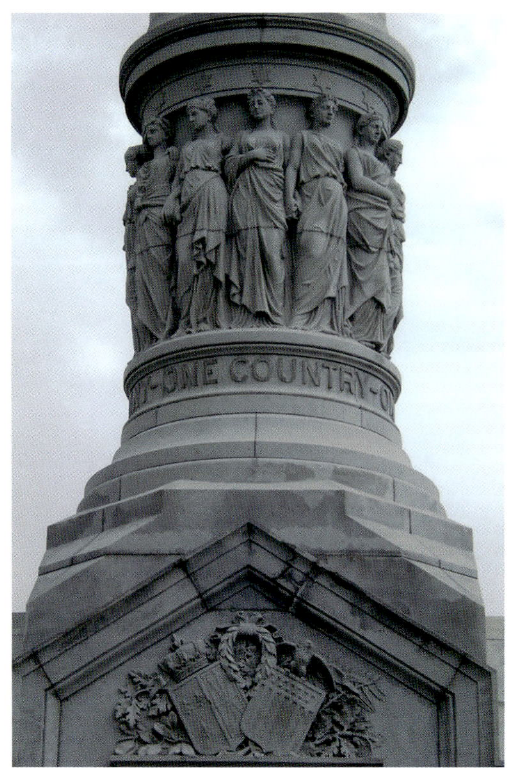

Sarah Stierch took this picture of the Yorktown Victory Monument [detail] on May 4, 2009. *Sarah Stierch*[8]

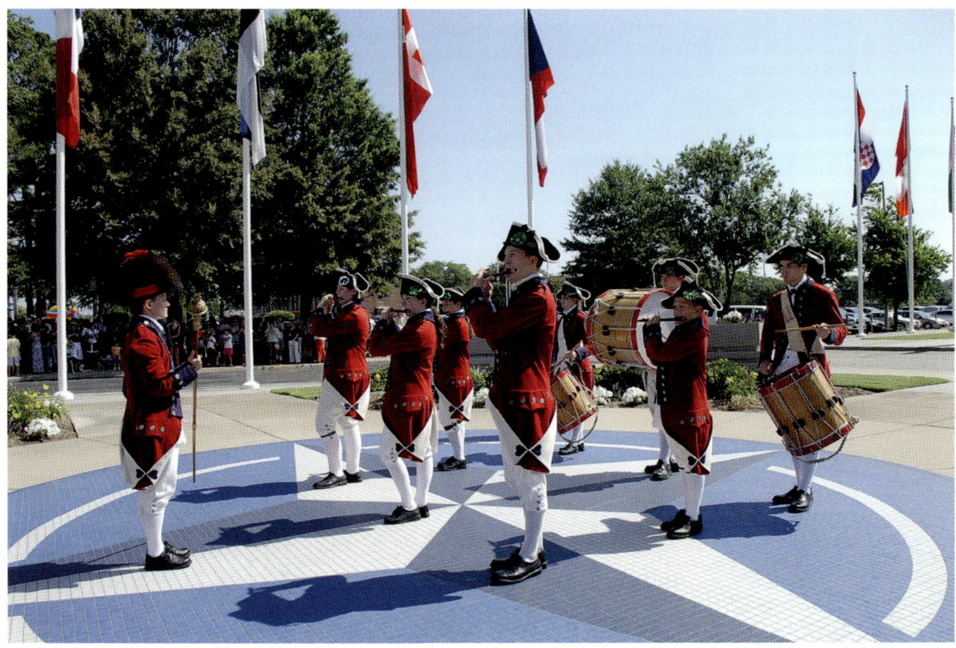

Members of the Fife and Drums of York Town played patriotic music during the NATO Allied Command Transformation (ACT) National Day celebrations at the ACT headquarters in Norfolk, Virginia, on July 2, 2009. The photograph was taken by army captain Robin Ochoa. *United States Army*

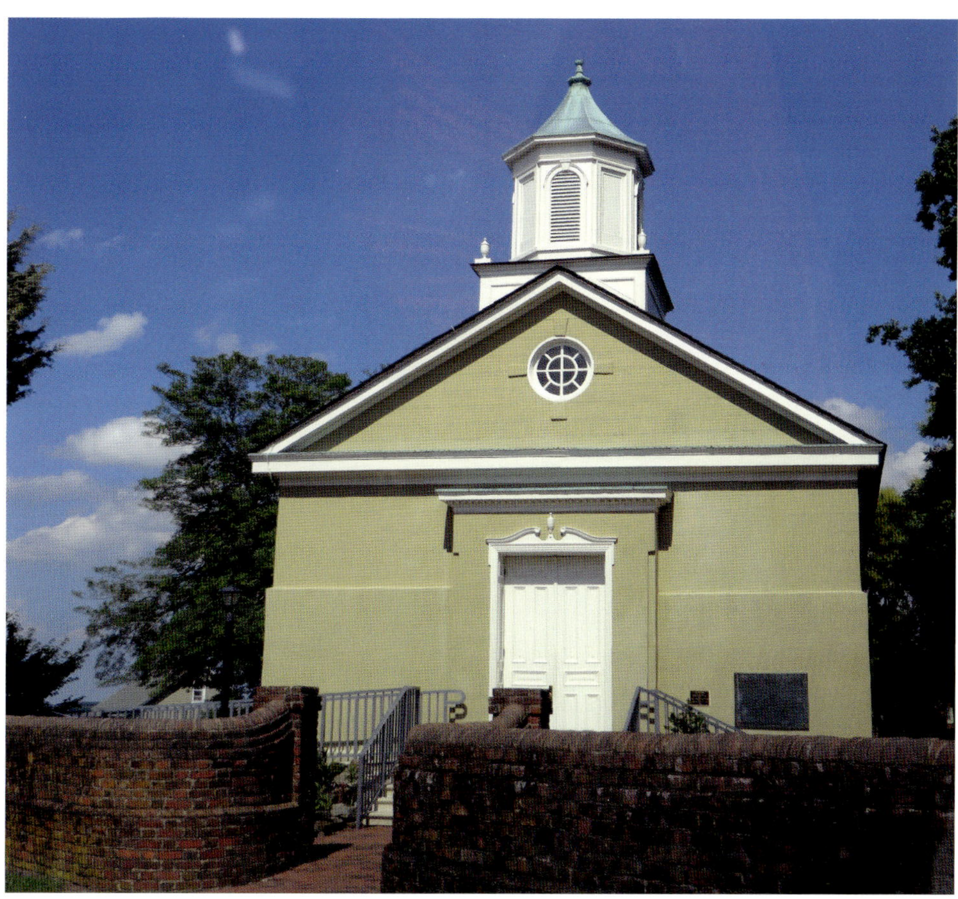

Grace Episcopal Church [also historically known as York-Hampton Parish Church], located at Yorktown's Church and Main streets, was built by the Episcopalians in 1697 and later updated with a Greek Revival style. Thomas Nelson Jr., a signer of the Declaration of Independence and several other Founding Fathers attended the church. The building was added to the National Register of Historic Places in 1970. The picture of the church (shown here) was taken on June 14, 2014. *Ken Lund*[9]

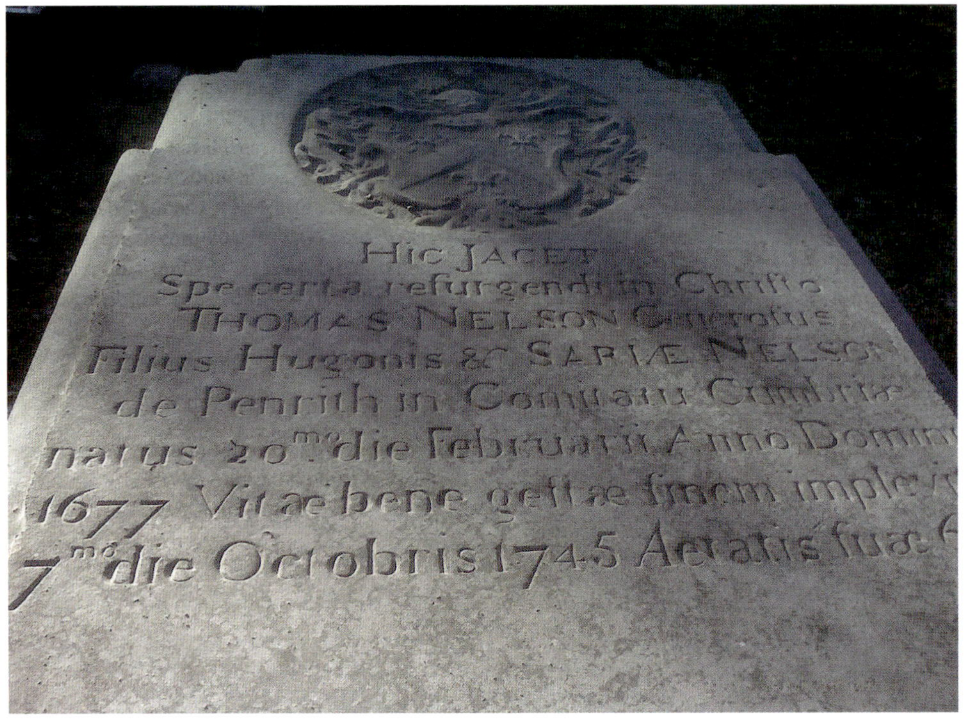

This is the tomb and flat stone top of Thomas "Scotch Tom" Nelson in Grace Episcopal Church Cemetery, photographed on January 21, 2011. *Michael Kotrady*[10]

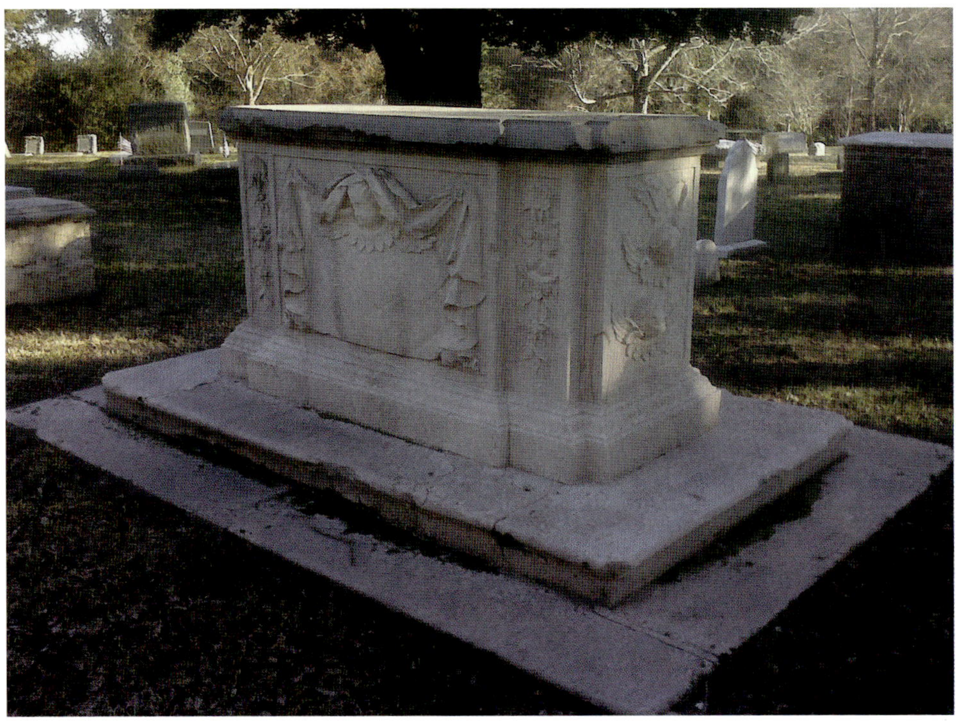

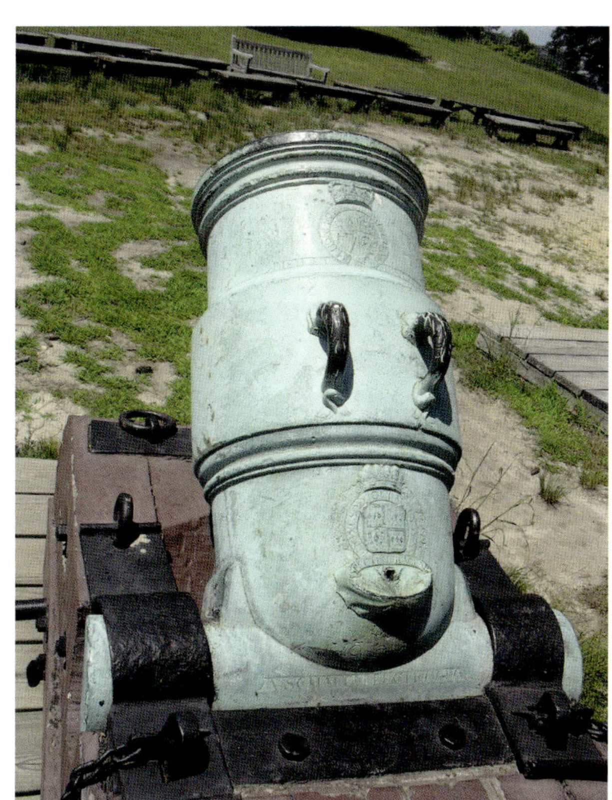

These full—and close-up views of a Revolutionary War mortar on display at the Yorktown Battlefield were photographed on May 27, 2012. The close-up shows the mortar markings. *DrStew82*[11]

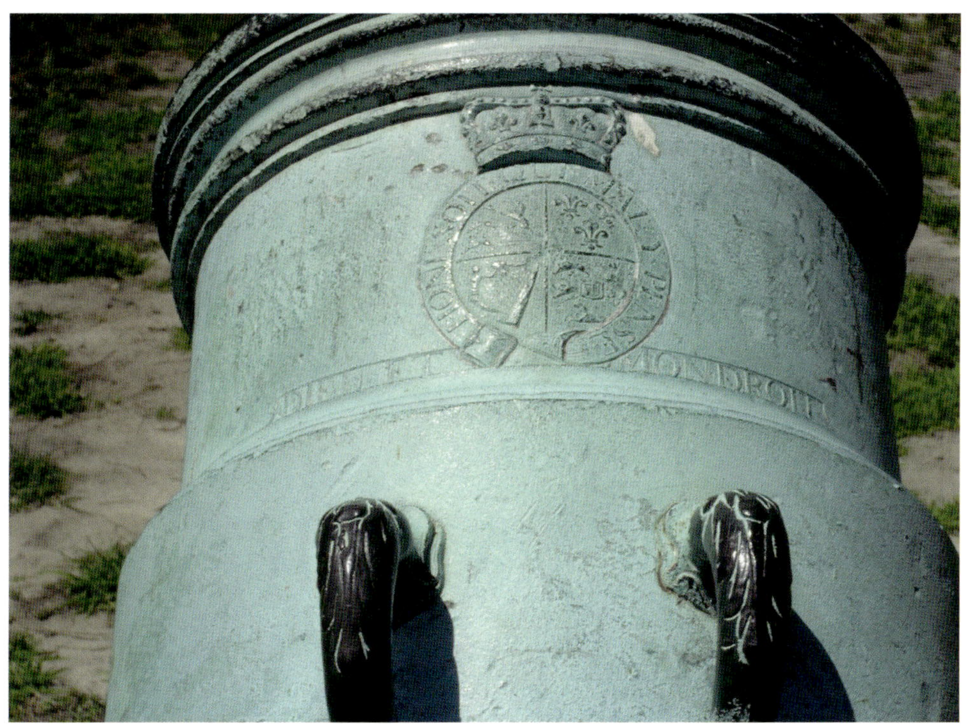

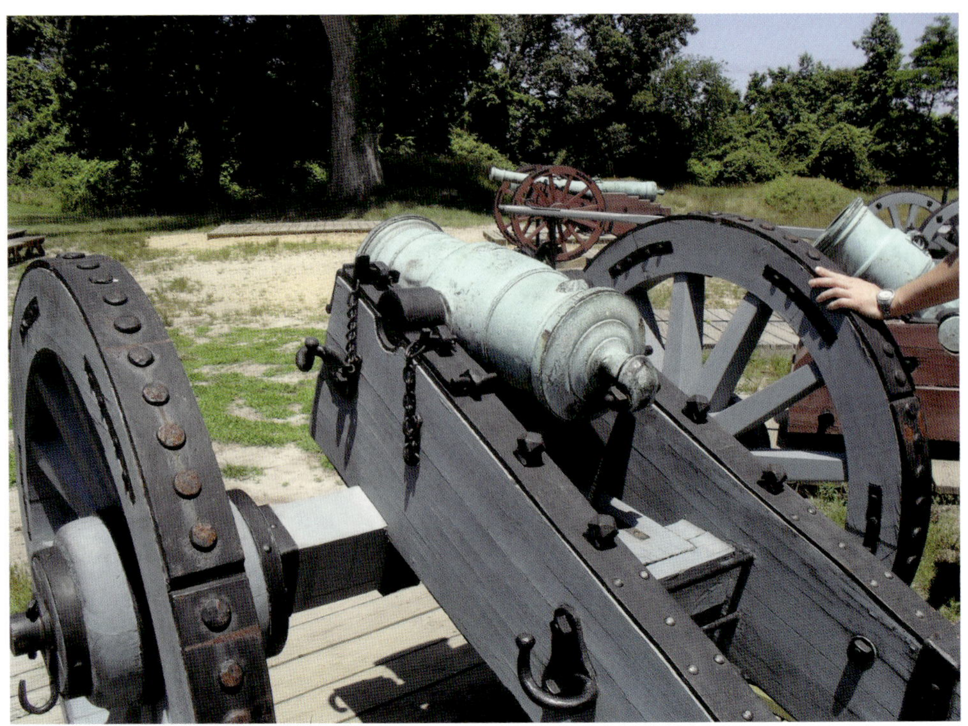

A Revolutionary War field gun on display at the Yorktown Battlefield is shown in this May 27, 2012. *DrStew82*[12]

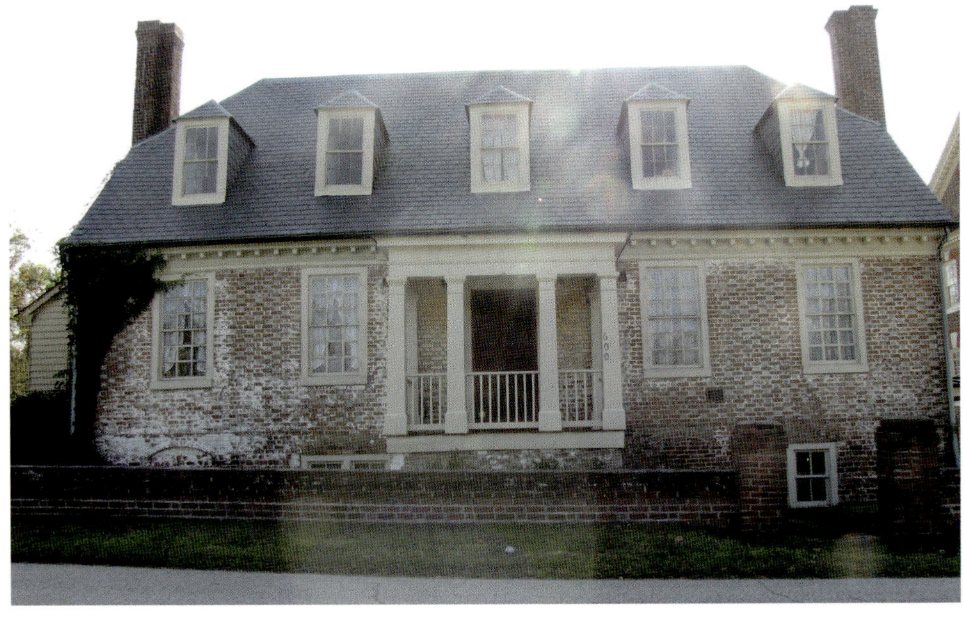

The Sessions-Pope-Sheild House is pictured here as it looked on September 22, 2012. *SKM2000*[13]

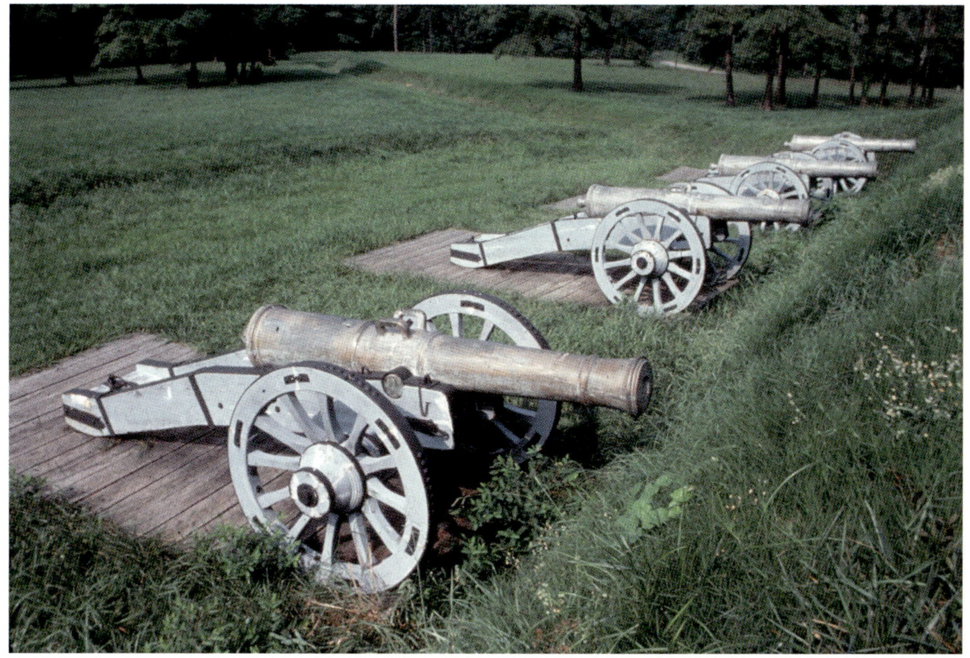

The Grand French Battery was the largest gun emplacement on the Allies first siege line during the siege of Yorktown. The battery is shown as it looked on July 16, 2010. *National Park Service*

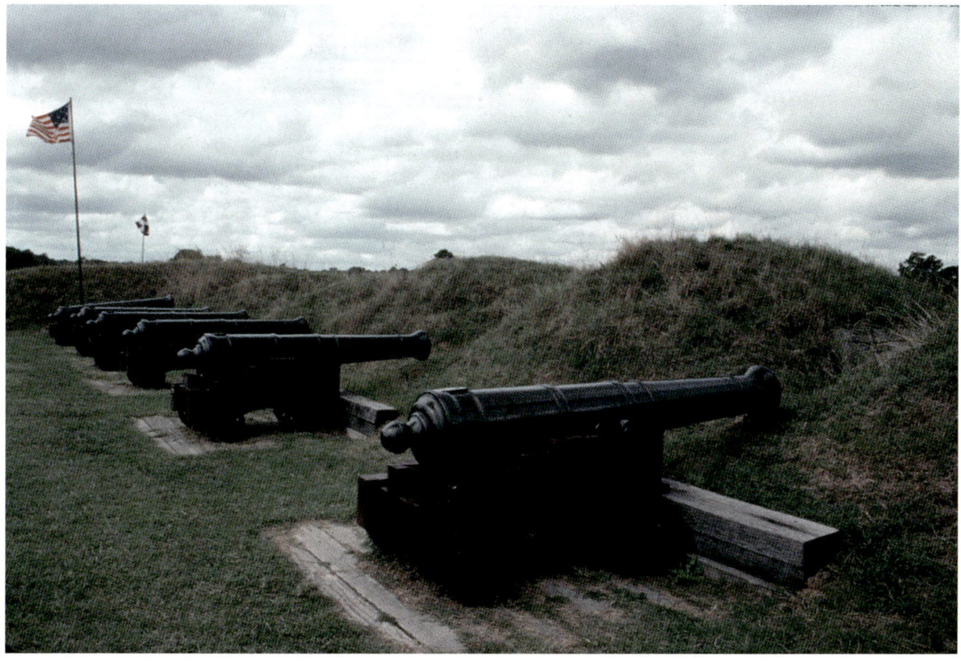

The American Battery, shown in this contemporary photograph, was the largest American artillery position at the siege of Yorktown. *National Park Service*

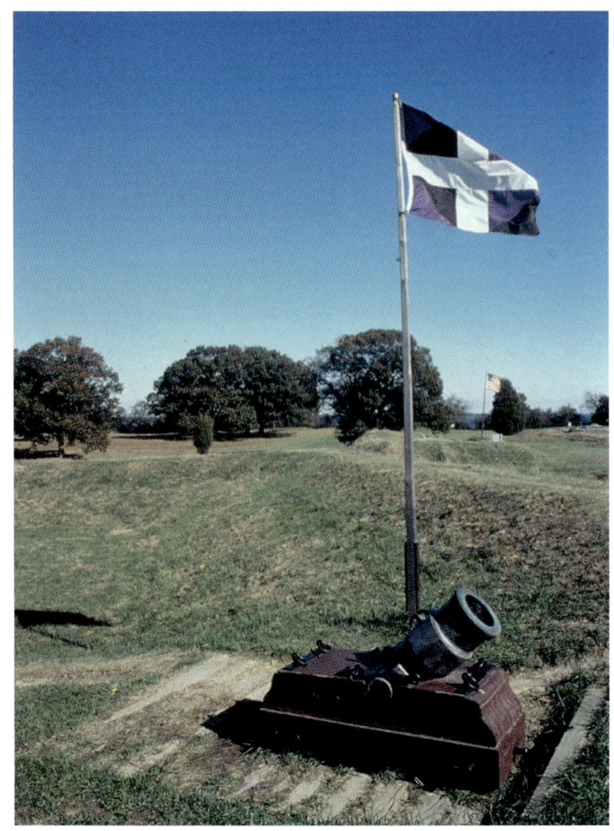

Left: Redoubt No. 9, site of a French attack on the night of October 14, 1781, during the siege of Yorktown, is shown in this July 16, 2010 photograph. *Cliff from Arlington*[14]

Below: The re-created *Betsy*, a British supply ship scuttled during the siege, is shown on display inside the now defunct Yorktown Victory Center, located at the Yorktown Battlefield, Colonial National Historic Site. This picture was taken on June 14, 2014. The center has been replaced by the American Revolution Museum at Yorktown. *Ken Lund*[15]

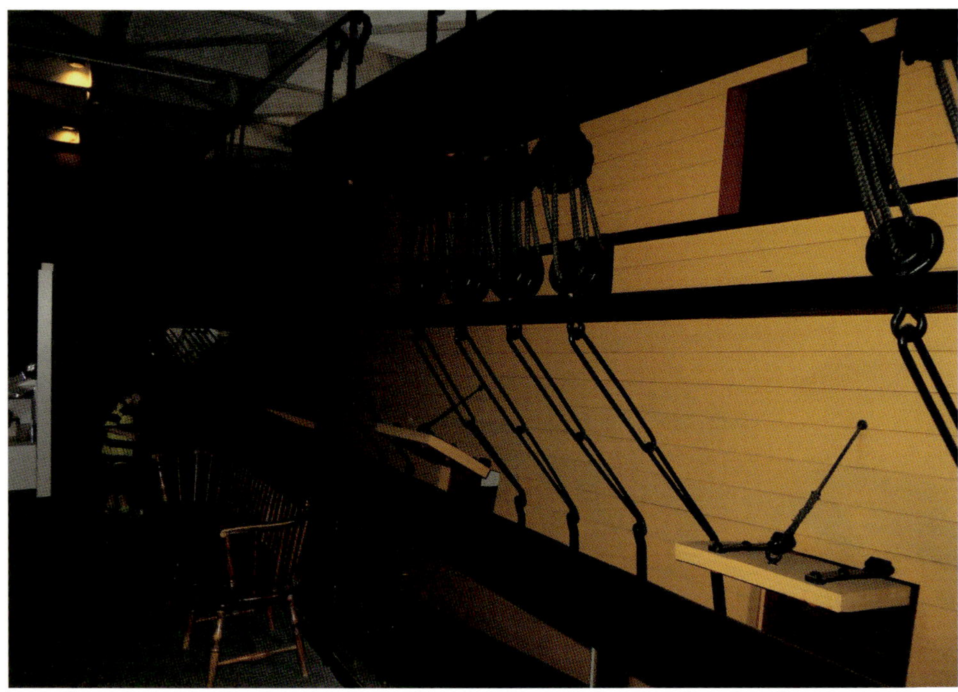

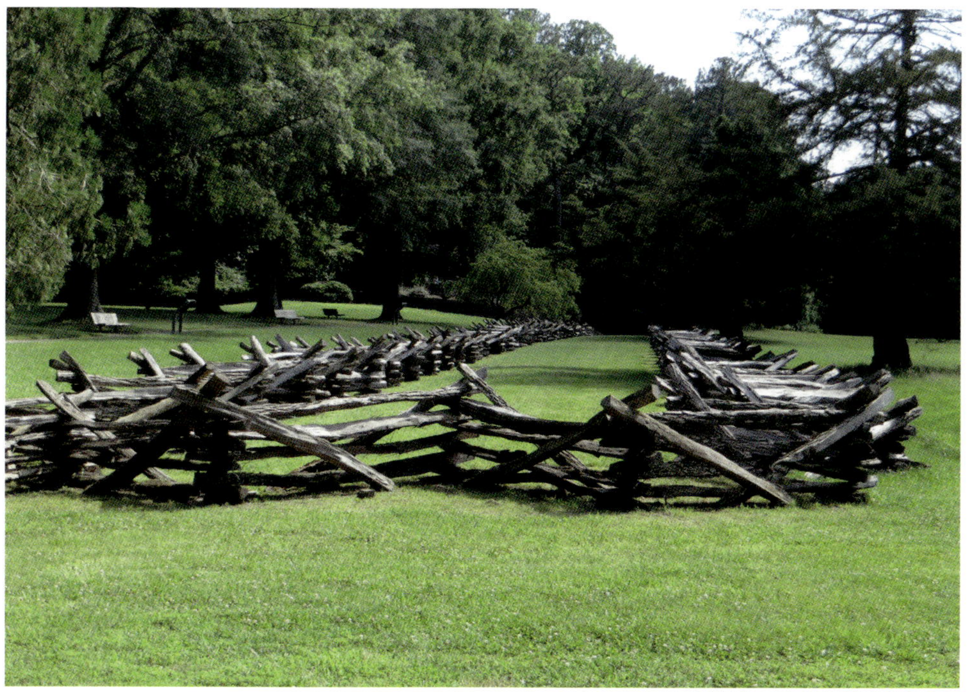

On this stretch of the Yorktown Battlefield [also called Surrender Road] on October 19, 1781, the British army laid down their weapons to end the siege and effectively grant independence to the American colonies. The picture was taken on June 14, 2014. *Ken Lund*[16]

Endnotes

1 Coleman was head of the Virginia Highway Commission from 1913 to 1922 and the mayor of Williamsburg, Virginia, from 1929 to 1934.

2 McKeldin was mayor of Baltimore twice from 1943–1947 and 1963–1967, and was the fifty-third governor of Maryland from 1951 to 1959.

3 Williams served in the navy during the Second World War, where he was stationed at Camp Peary to establish the photography laboratory. The May 13, 1998 *Daily Press* noted that he was loaned during the war to the Colonial Williamsburg Foundation to record the ongoing restoration of historic landmarks because it did not have an official photographer just then. He also worked out of Naval Station Norfolk during the war. He went back to the Colonial Williamsburg Foundation after being released by the navy and also became the official photographer for the College of William and Mary, working there for thirty-five years.

4 Nicholas Minas Mathews (1906–1983) and Mary Pappas Mathews (1918–1998) were major contributors to the Yorktown Victory Center [they are now buried behind the former center] and equally enthusiastic Yorktown, Virginia boosters.

5 Nicholas Minas Mathews died on April 13, 1983, on the trip down to Mississippi in which Mary Pappas Mathews, sponsor of the USS *Yorktown* (CG-48), was set to christen the ship.

6 By Mike Durkin from Forest Hills, NY (yorktown_pano_view.jpg) [CC BY-SA 2.0 (http://creativecommons.org/licenses/by-sa/2.0)], via Wikimedia Commons

7 By Yellowute at English Wikipedia (Transferred from en.wikipedia to Commons.) [Public domain], via Wikimedia Commons

8 By Sarah Stierch (Own work) [CC BY 4.0 (http://creativecommons.org/licenses/by/4.0)], via Wikimedia Commons

9 By Ken Lund from Reno, Nevada, USA (Grace Church, Yorktown, Virginia) [CC BY-SA 2.0 (http://creativecommons.org/licenses/by-sa/2.0)], via Wikimedia Commons

10 By Michael Kotrady (Own work) [CC BY-SA 3.0 (http://creativecommons.org/licenses/by-sa/3.0)], via Wikimedia Commons

11 By DrStew82 (Own work) [CC BY-SA 4.0 (http://creativecommons.org/licenses/by-sa/4.0)], via Wikimedia Commons

13 By DrStew82 (Own work) [CC BY-SA 4.0 (http://creativecommons.org/licenses/by-sa/4.0)], via Wikimedia Commons

14 By SKM2000 (Own work) [CC BY-SA 3.0 (http://creativecommons.org/licenses/by-sa/3.0)], via Wikimedia Commons

15 By Cliff from Arlington, Virginia, USA (British Field Cannon Uploaded by Morgan Riley) [CC BY 2.0 (http://creativecommons.org/licenses/by/2.0)], via Wikimedia Commons

16 By Ken Lund from Rcno, Nevada, USA [CC BY-SA 2.0 (http://creativecommons.org/licenses/by-sa/2.0)], via Wikimedia Commons

143 By Ken Lund from Reno, Nevada, USA [CC BY-SA 2.0 (http://creativecommons.org/licenses/by-sa/2.0)], via Wikimedia Commons

VI

HISTORY COMES ALIVE

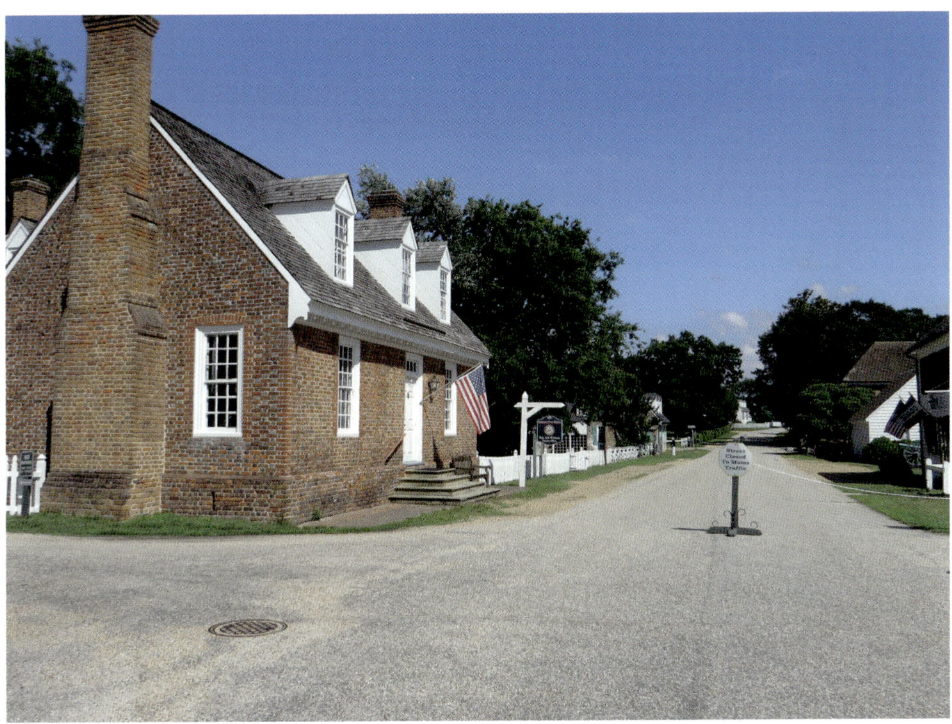

While Yorktown itself is not officially part of Colonial National Historical Park, many of the homes in the historic district are owned by the National Park Service. The Thomas Nelson House and the Poor Potter site are open during the summer, but only as staffing permits. All other buildings are either private residences or continue to be operated as businesses, including a few museums and art galleries. This view of Main Street in Historic Yorktown, set on the York River, remains the area in which the architecture is almost exclusively original. The old courthouse, several small shops, the Thomas Nelson House, and the Yorktown Victory Monument all sit along the trajectory of this road. The picture shown here was taken on June 14, 2014. The house in the foreground (left) is the Mungo Somerwell House, which dates to the early eighteenth century. Beyond it, on the left, is the Cole Digges House. *Ken Lund*[1]

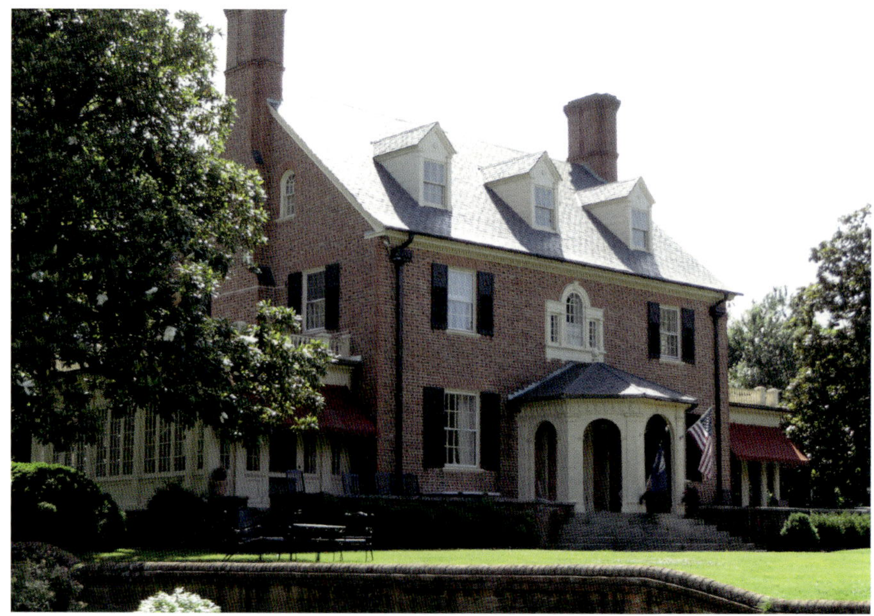

Located on Main Street in the heart of the historic area, the Hornsby House Inn was originally built in 1933 by John William "J. W." Hornsby, a waterman and Amoco Oil and Gas distributor for the Virginia Peninsula born in 1888 in Seaford, York County, who constructed this grand style colonial-style home overlooking the York River for his wife and six children. The house was designed by William Graves Perry, the lead architect for John Davison Rockefeller Jr.'s Colonial Williamsburg. The Hornsby home became a well-known center of southern hospitality for friends, neighbors, extended family and business associates, according to the inn's historical narrative. John William Hornsby died in 1951 but his only daughter Marian Hornsby Bowditch (1921–2006) and her husband[2] and four sons moved into the house to help care for her mother. Today, two of Marian's sons, David and Phillip, operate the inn. The Hornsby House Inn is shown in this June 14, 2014. *Ken Lund*[3]

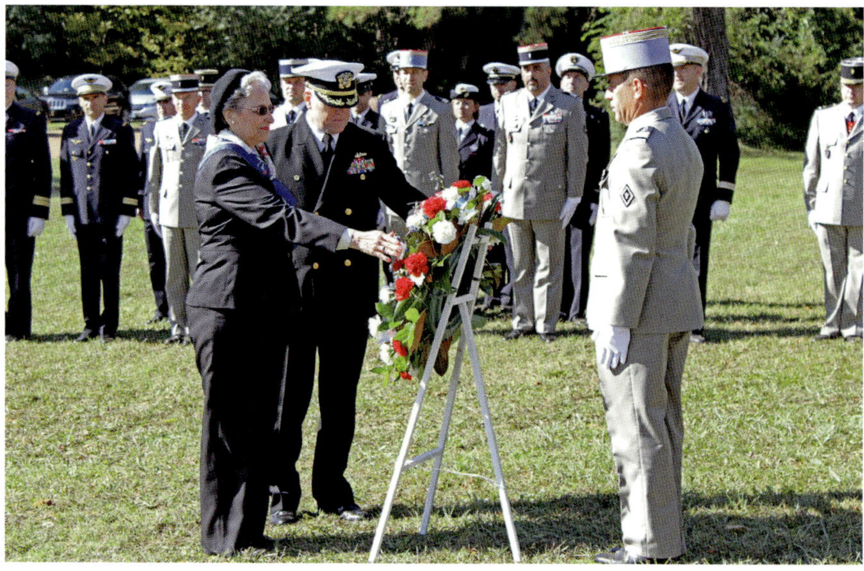

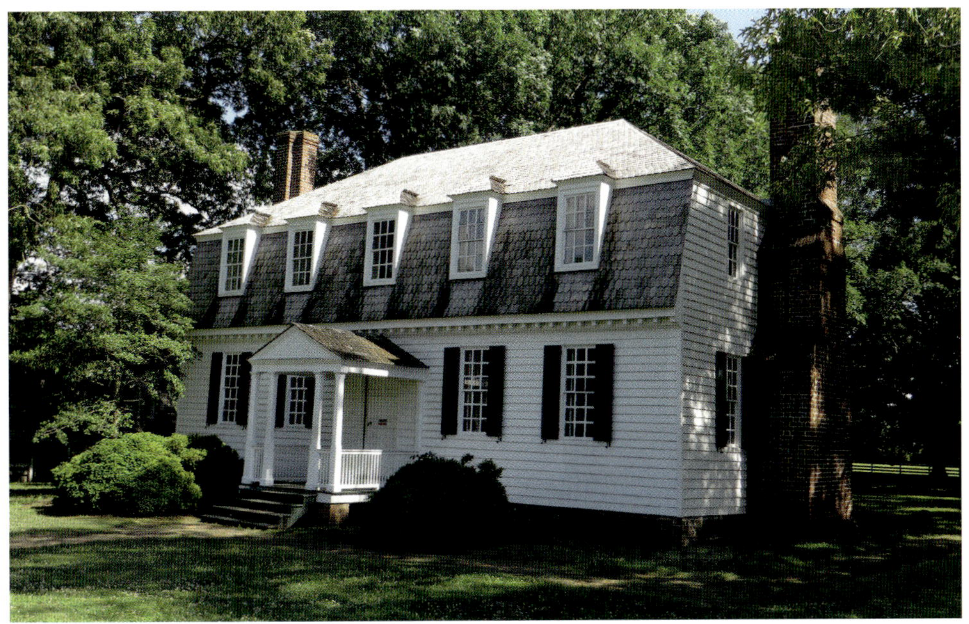

The Augustine Moore House is shown here, June 14, 2014. *Ken Lund*[4]

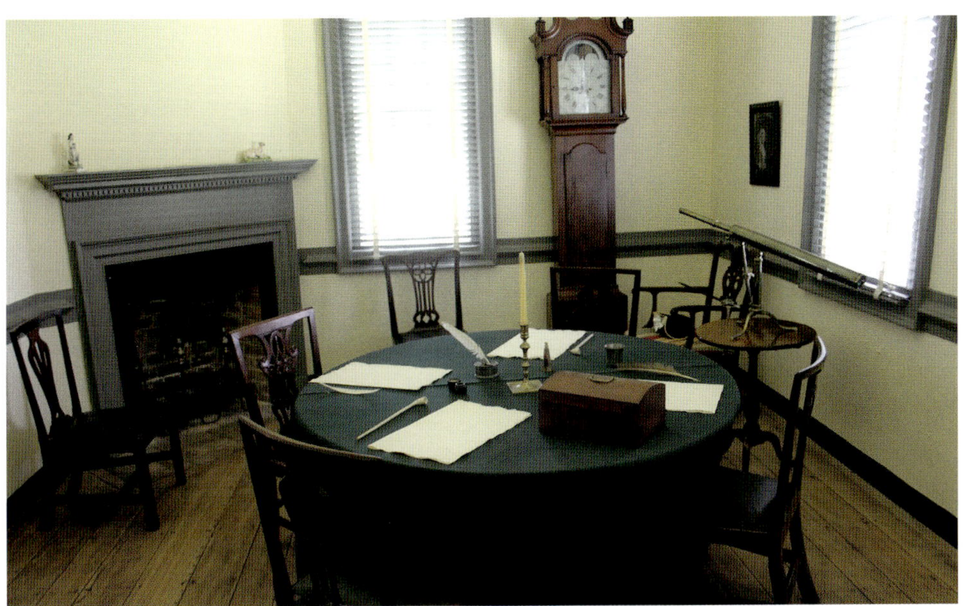

The interior of the Augustine Moore House, where the Articles of Capitulation were drawn, is shown in this July 24, 2012 photograph. *Navin75*[5]

Opposite below: Mark O. Piggott took this picture of Captain Paul C. Haebler, commanding officer of Naval Weapons Station Yorktown, joined by Brenda Duda, vice president of the Alliance Française Chapitre de Grasse, to lay one of six wreaths at the French memorial on the Yorktown Battlefield as part of the Yorktown Day celebration on October 19, 2014. Yorktown Day annually marks the anniversary of the American-French victory in 1781 over the British, effectively securing American independence. *United States Navy*

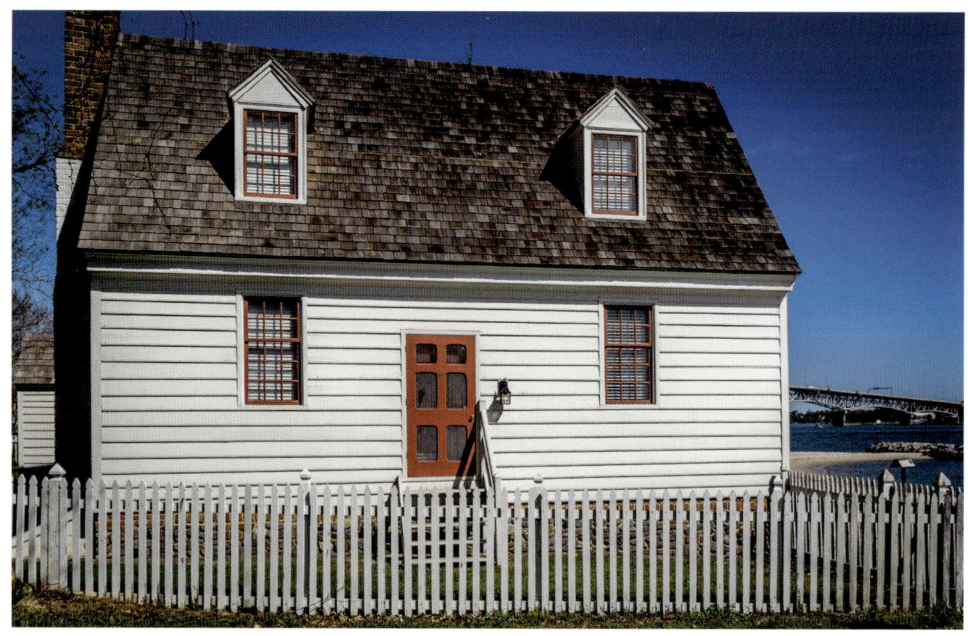

The Thomas Archer House, the York River in the background, is shown in this April 23, 2015 photograph. *Mobilus In Mobili*[6]

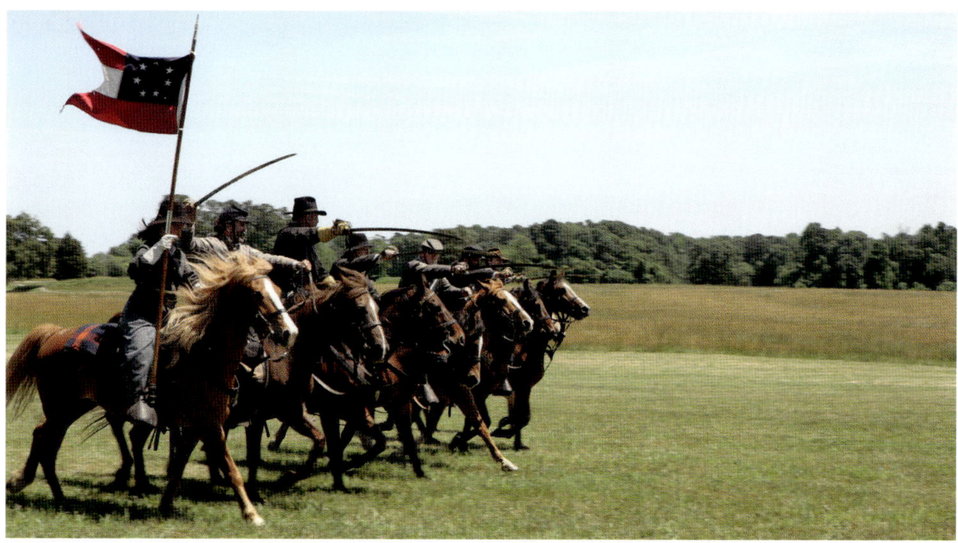

This May 23, 2015 photograph shows a Confederate cavalry reenactment that took place on the Yorktown Battlefield. *Reneftorres*[7]

The Arleigh Burke-class guided missile destroyer USS *Mitscher* (DDG-57) (right) provided a warm welcome to the French tall ship replica *Hermione* in the vicinity of the Battle of the Virginia Capes off the Virginia coast on June 2, 2015. The original *Hermione* brought French general Marquis de Lafayette to America in 1780 to inform Continental Army general George Washington that a French army was headed for the United States to assist in the war effort. The symbolic return of the *Hermione* that June paid homage to Lafayette and to the Franco-American alliance that brought victory at the Battle of Yorktown in 1781. *Continued on next page*

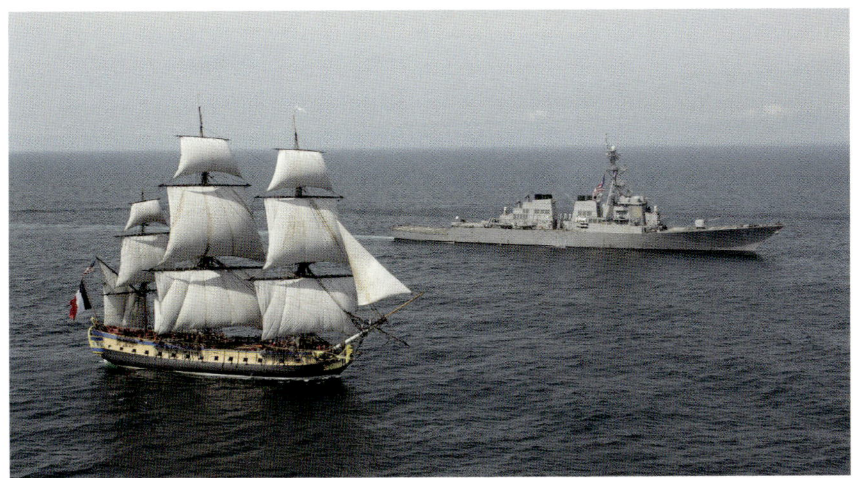

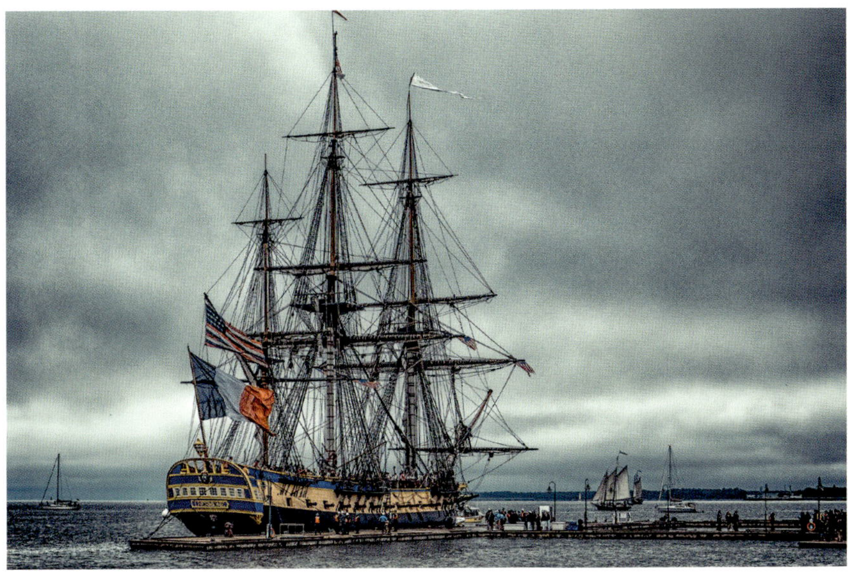

The *Hermione* is a thirty-two-gun [all non-functional] *Concorde*-class frigate consisting of twenty-six twelve-pounder long guns in the main battery and six six-pounder guns on the galliards, completed in Rochefort, France, by the Asselin organization, a replica of the 1779 *Hermione*, which achieved fame by ferrying French general Marquis de Lafayette to the United States in 1780 to allow him to rejoin the American side in the Revolutionary War. Unlike the original *Hermione*, which took only a year to build, this replica, begun in July 1997, was not launched for seaworthiness trials until September 7, 2014, and cost $22 million to complete. The new *Hermione* arrived at Yorktown on June 5, 2015, after sailing from France. After leaving Yorktown, the *Hermione* visited a string of richly historic sites, to include Mount Vernon, Alexandria, Annapolis, Baltimore, Philadelphia, New York City, Greenport, Newport, Boston and Castine, as well as Lunenberg, Nova Scotia. The ship was captained just then by Yann Cariou, a thirty-year veteran of the French navy. *Mobilus In Mobili*[8]

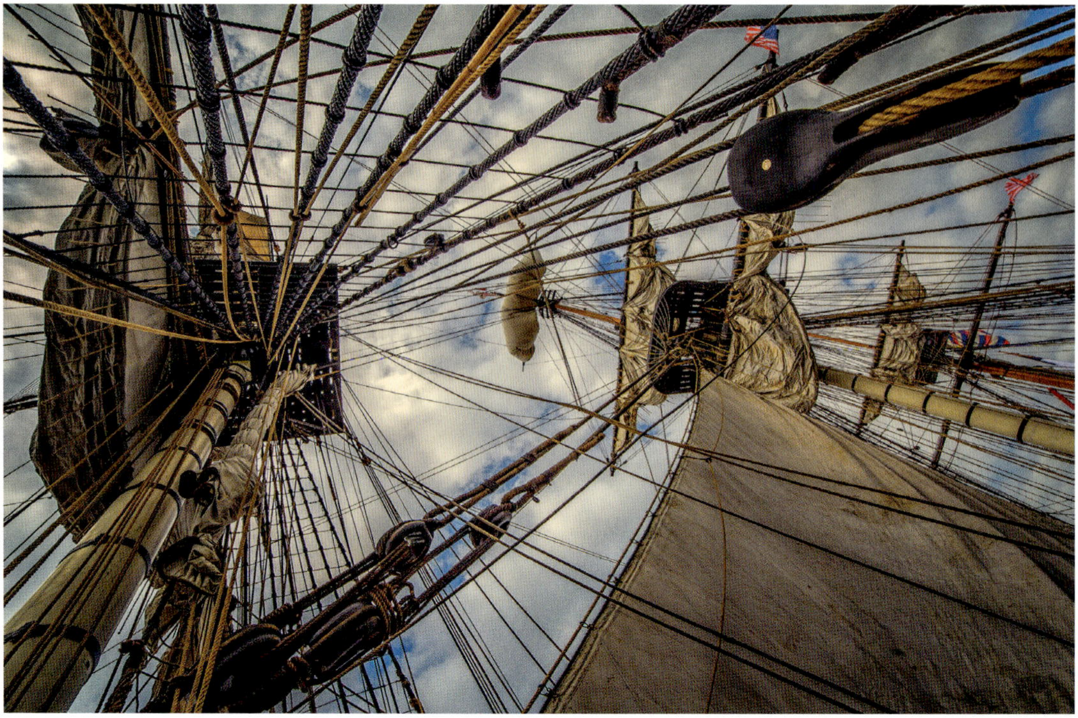

This is the rigging of the *Hermione*, called the "frigate of freedom," photographed on June 6, 2015. The *Hermione* is a ship forever linked to the legend of the Marquis de Lafayette, who once stated: "From the first moment I heard the name of America, I loved it; from the instant I knew it struggled for freedom, I was consumed with the desire to shed my blood for her. I will count the days I got the chance to serve it, everywhere and anytime, among the happiest days of my life."[9] *Mobilus In Mobili*[10]

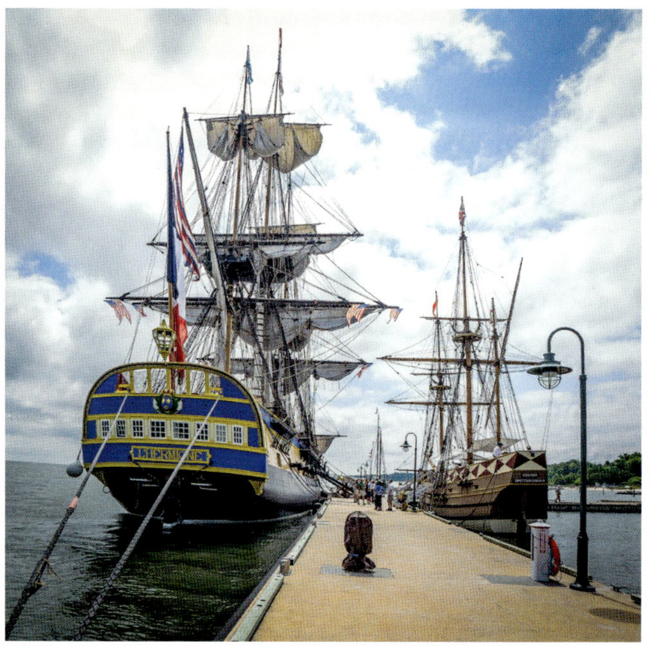

The *Hermione* (left) was docked at Yorktown across the pier from the smaller replica of the *Godspeed* from Jamestown. *Godspeed*, under Captain Bartholomew Gosnold, was one of the three ships to make the 1606/7 voyage to the New World with Virginia Company of London settlers. The journey resulted in the establishment of the first permanent English settlement in the new Virginia Colony. The picture was taken on June 6, 2015. *Mobilus In Mobili*[11]

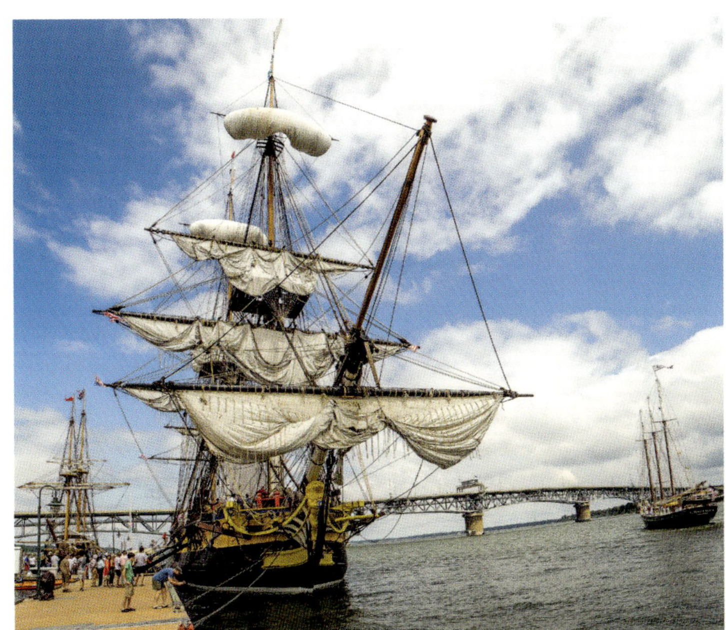

The *Hermione* was set to leave Yorktown after the ship's historic visit when this picture was taken on June 6, 2015. *Mobilus In Mobili*[12]

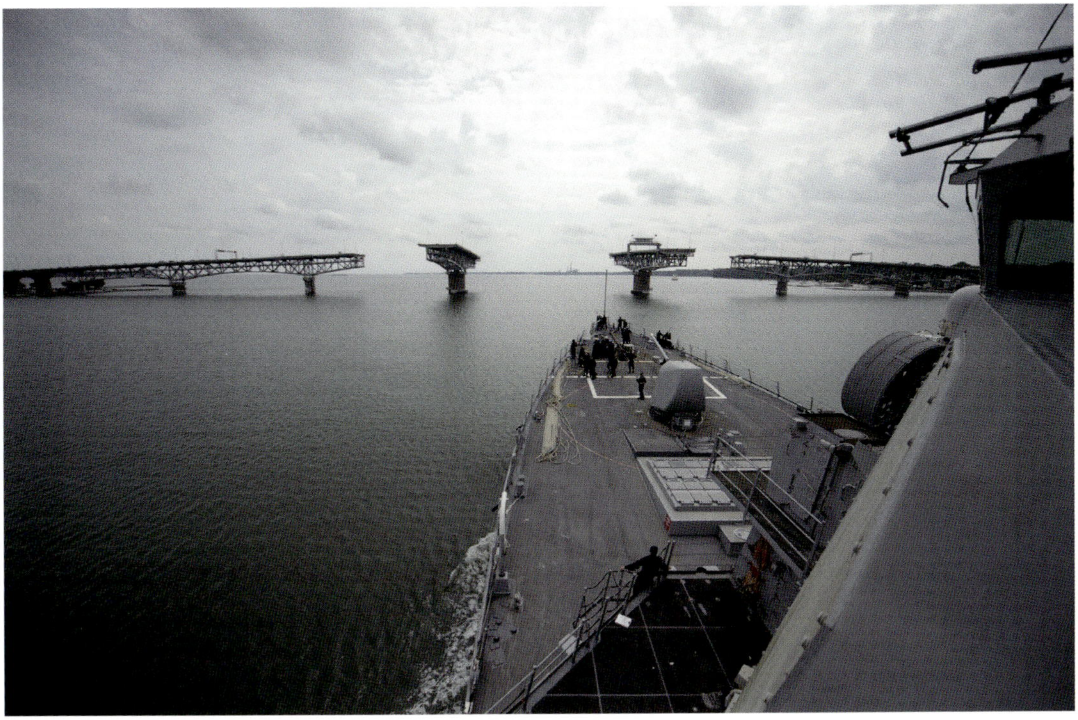

The guided-missile destroyer USS *Carney* (DDG-64) was photographed on September 11, 2015, as it prepared to transit through the George Preston Coleman Memorial Bridge. *Carney* was the fourth *Arleigh Burke*-class destroyer to be forward deployed to Rota, Spain, to serve as part of the Obama administration's European phased adaptive approach to ballistic missile defense in Europe at the time this picture was taken by Mass Communication Specialist Third Class Jonathan B. Trejo. *United States Navy*

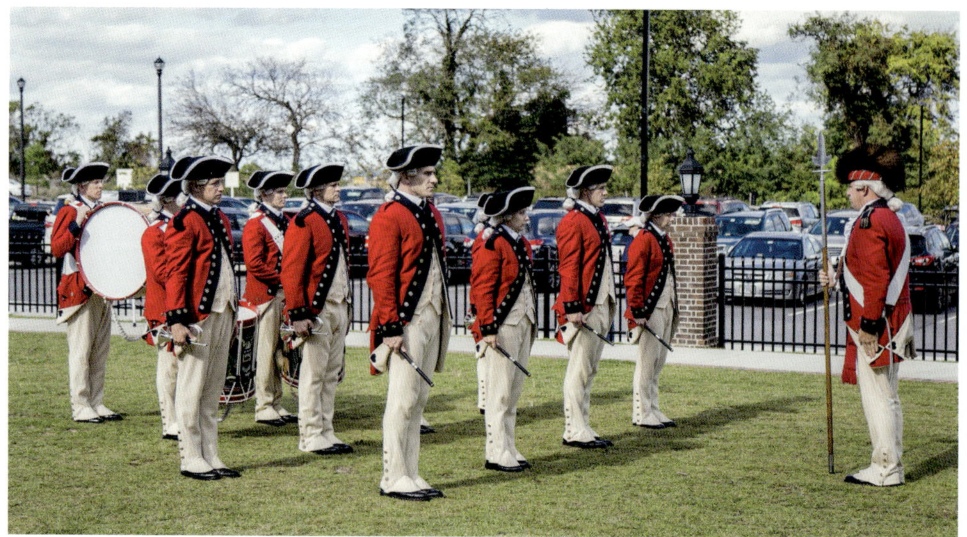

The Old Guard Fife and Drum Corps is the only unit of its kind in the armed forces, and is part of the Third United States Infantry Regiment [The Old Guard]. The Fife and Drum Corps is headquartered at Fort Myer, Virginia, and is shown in this October 18, 2015 photograph participating in the reenactment of the October 1781 battle at Yorktown. *Mobilus in Mobili*[13]

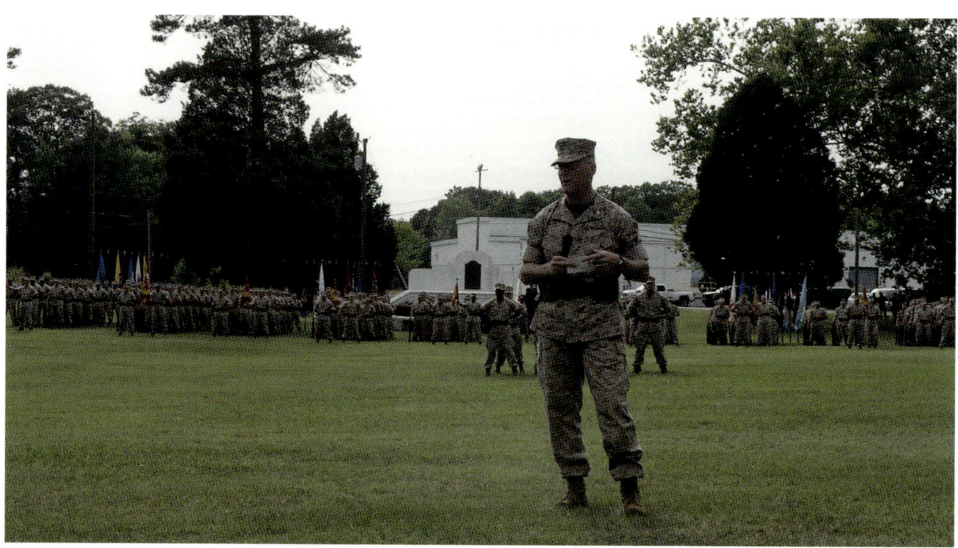

United States Marine Corps colonel James M. Bright, outgoing regimental commanding officer of the Marine Corps Security Force, addressed the guests at a change-of-command ceremony June 19, 2015, at Naval Weapons Station Yorktown. Bright passed command to Colonel John W. Evans Jr. The Marine Corps Security Force Regiment is the Marine Corps' largest regiment with over four thousand marines and sailors spread across the globe. The photograph was taken by Marine Corps corporal Taylor Schrick. *United States Marine Corps*

Opposite below: In front of the American Revolution Museum at Yorktown which replaced the Yorktown Victory Center, is this flag court, photographed on September 12, 2016, which flies the flags of the first thirteen states. The museum was officially dedicated on April 1, 2017. *Elizabeth Rowe*[14]

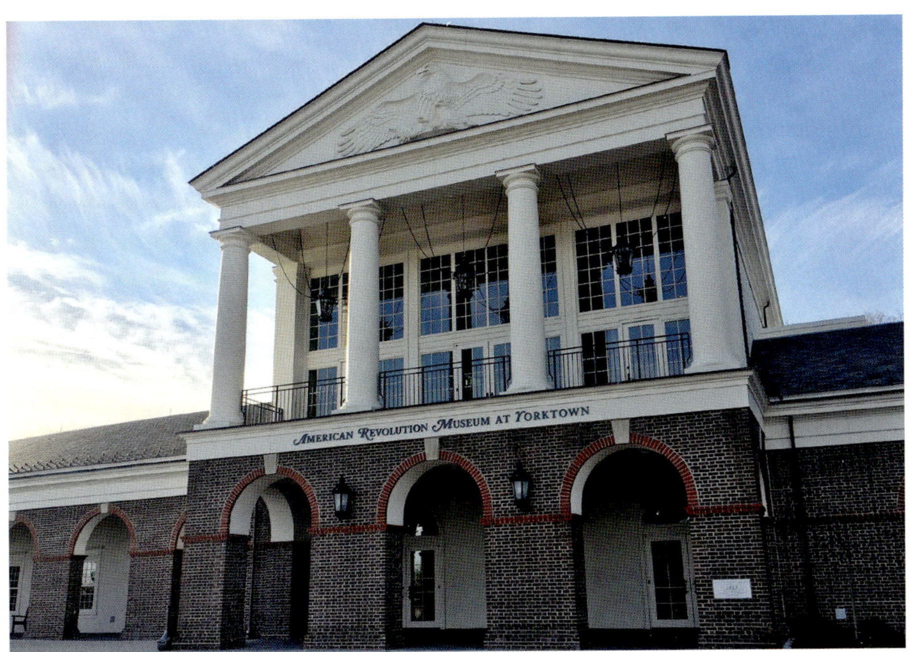

Work began in mid-2012 on transforming the Yorktown Victory Center into the American Revolution Museum at Yorktown. The project included reorganization of the twenty-two-acre site, an eighty-thousand-square-foot structure encompassing expanded exhibition galleries, classrooms and support functions, and enlarged and enhanced outdoor living-history areas. Museum operations transitioned to the new museum in late winter 2015, as work continued on development of permanent exhibition galleries, an introductory film, and the outdoor encampment and farm. The film and galleries debuted on October 15, 2016, along with the new museum name, and a grand opening celebration took place from March 23–April 4, 2017, officially launching the American Revolution Museum at Yorktown. This is the main entrance to the new museum, photographed on December 14, 2016. *Jamestown-Yorktown Foundation*

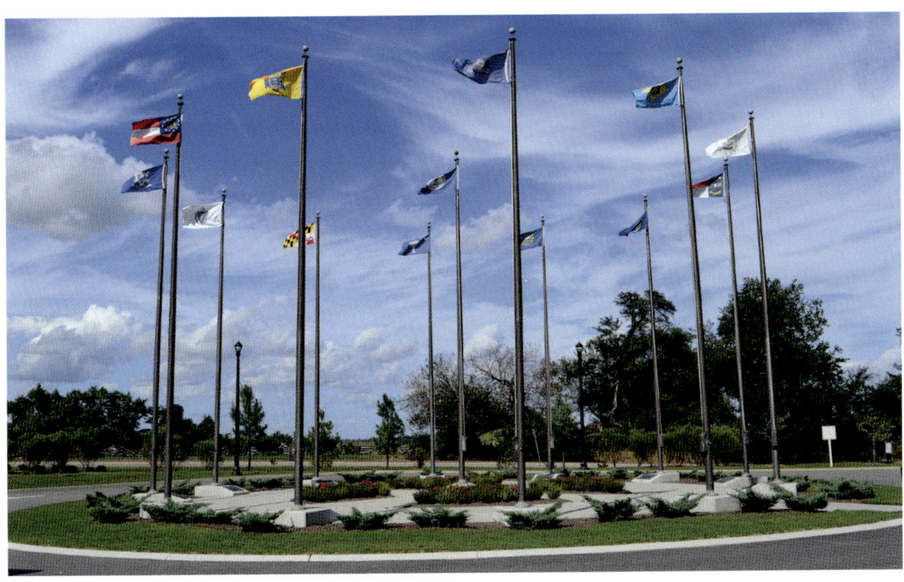

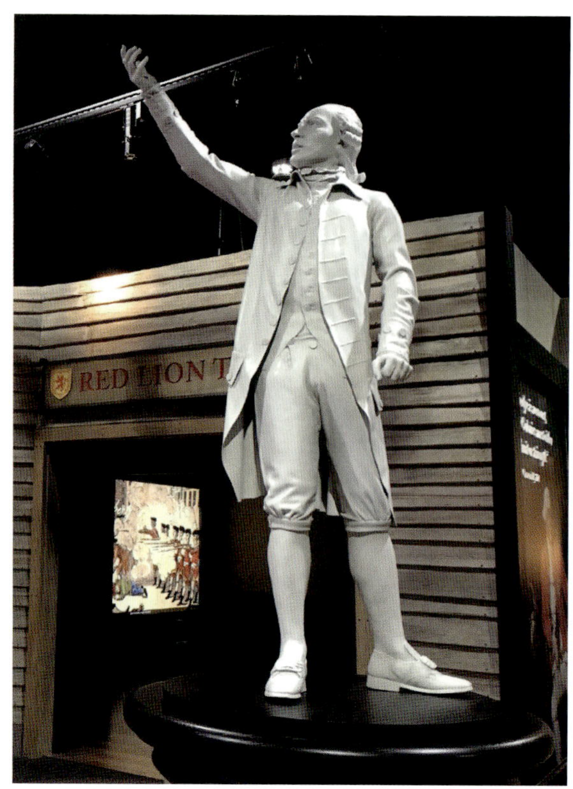

A statue depicting Patrick Henry standing outside the Red Lion Tavern is among the exhibits of the American Revolution Museum at Yorktown. *Jamestown-Yorktown Foundation*

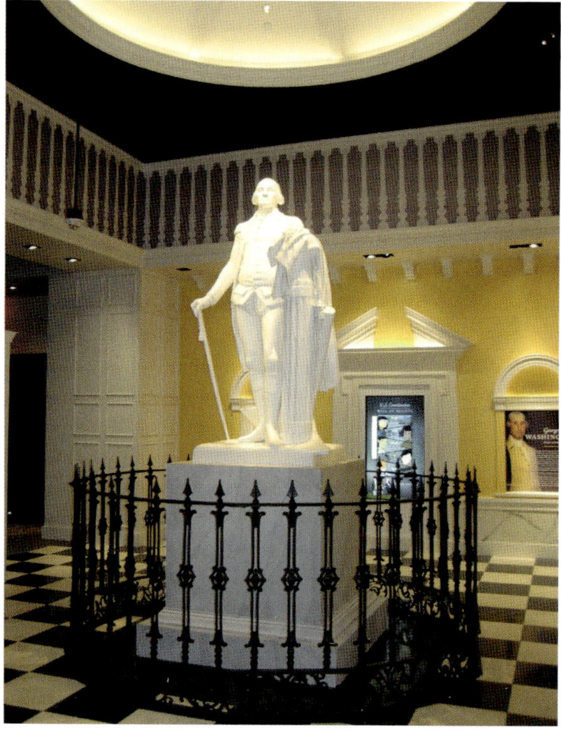

A life-size statue of George Washington that was formerly exhibited at the United States Capitol stands in the section of exhibition galleries of the American Revolution Museum at Yorktown that chronicle the development of the United States government. The picture was taken on October 1, 2016. *Jamestown-Yorktown Foundation*

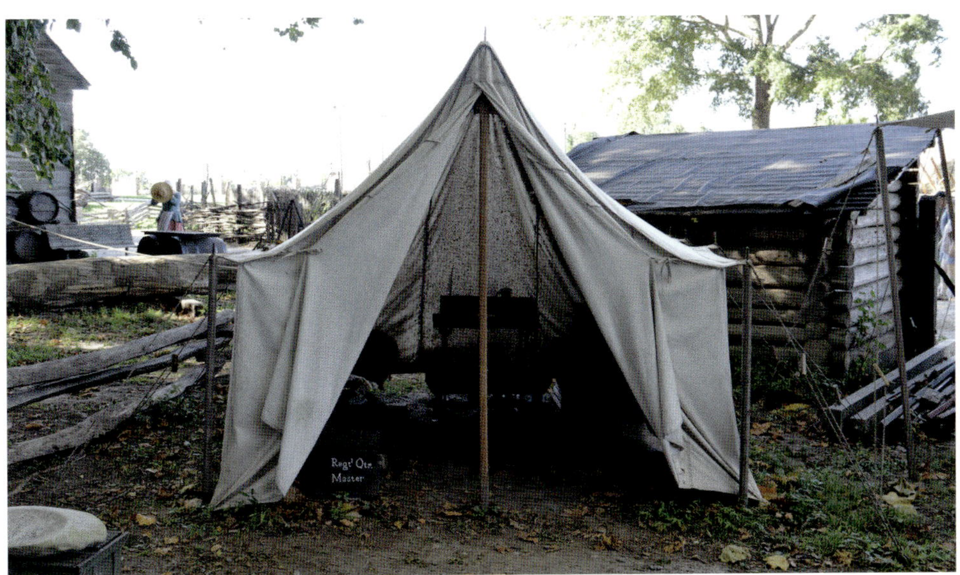

The living-history Continental Army encampment and Revolutionary period farm continue as an integral part of the museum experience at the American Revolution Museum at Yorktown site. An informational pavilion aids visitors with the transition from indoor galleries to the outdoor exhibit areas, where they engage in a number of hands-on activities, from military drills to watering and weeding crops. The encampment and farm support gallery storylines and expand the museum's capacity for visitor-participatory demonstrations. According to the museum, the encampment (shown here), represents a portion of an American regiment with tents for officers and soldiers as well as surgeon's and quartermaster's quarters, and also includes a drill field and an artillery demonstration area with tiered seating that from the outside looks like a redoubt. Beyond the encampment, the farm has a larger house, kitchen and tobacco barn and a new building representing quarters for enslaved people, along with spaces for crop fields, kitchen garden and orchard. The use of a specific eighteenth-century York County family provides a frame of reference for historical interpretation. The photographs were taken September 12, 2016. *Elizabeth Rowe*[15]

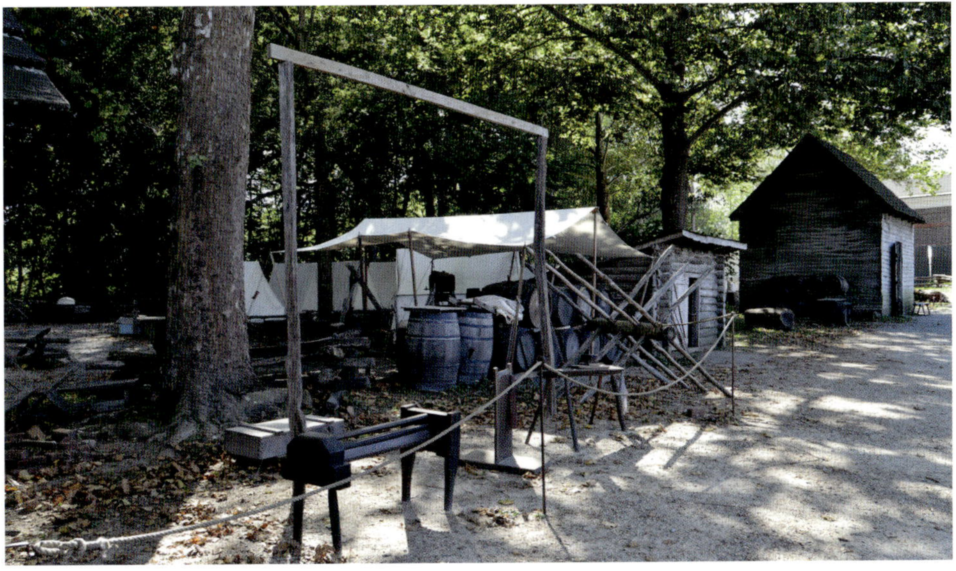

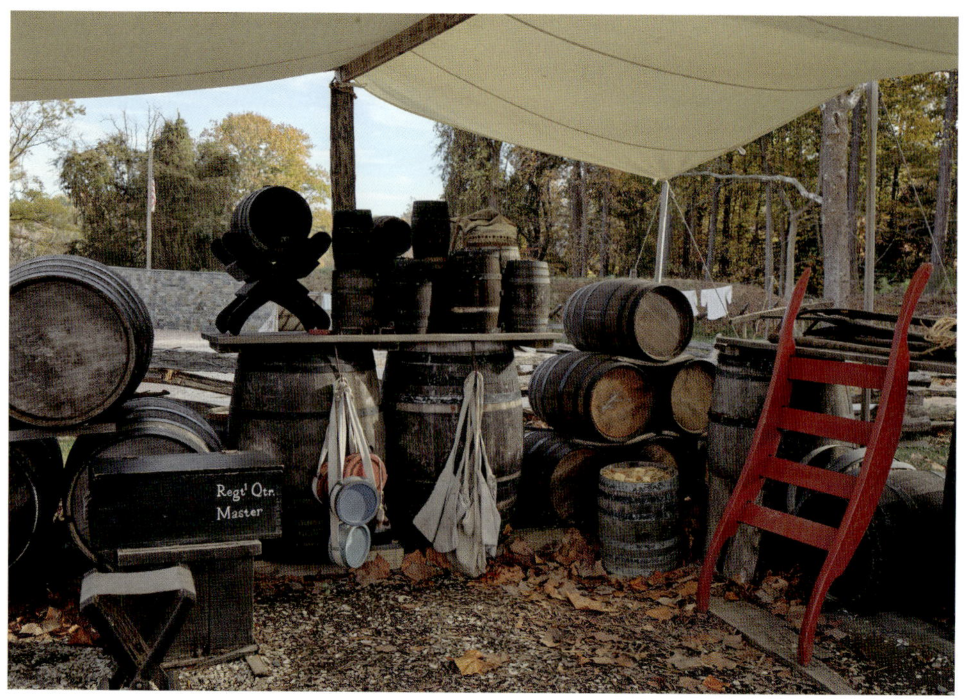

The American Revolution Museum's recreated quartermasters' quarters is shown in this November 21, 2019 Carol M. Highsmith photograph. *Library of Congress*

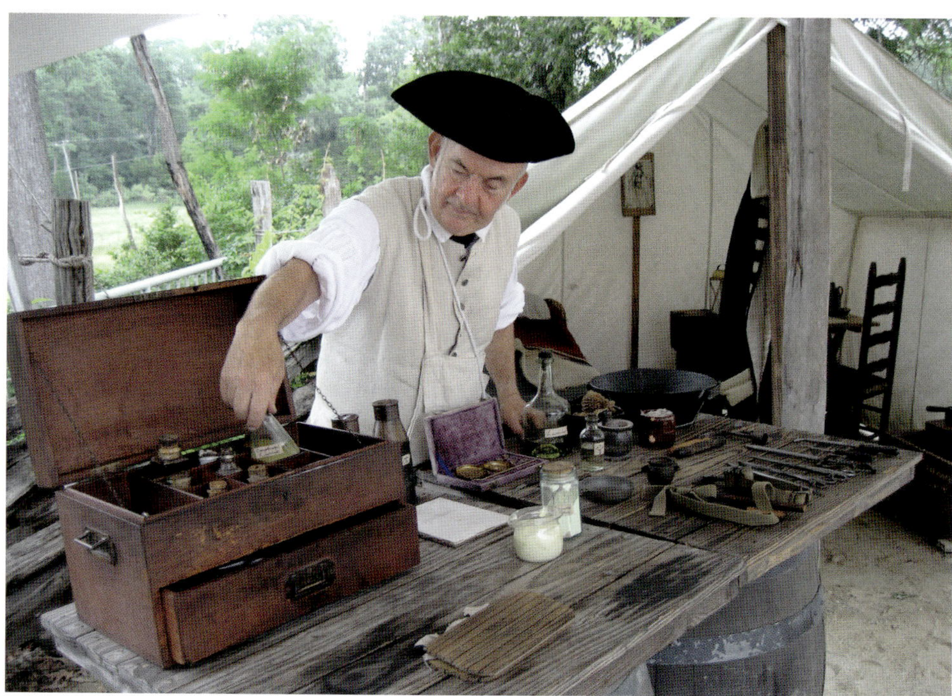

The surgeon's tent at the American Revolution Museum at Yorktown Continental Army encampment is shown in this contemporary view. *Jamestown-Yorktown Foundation*

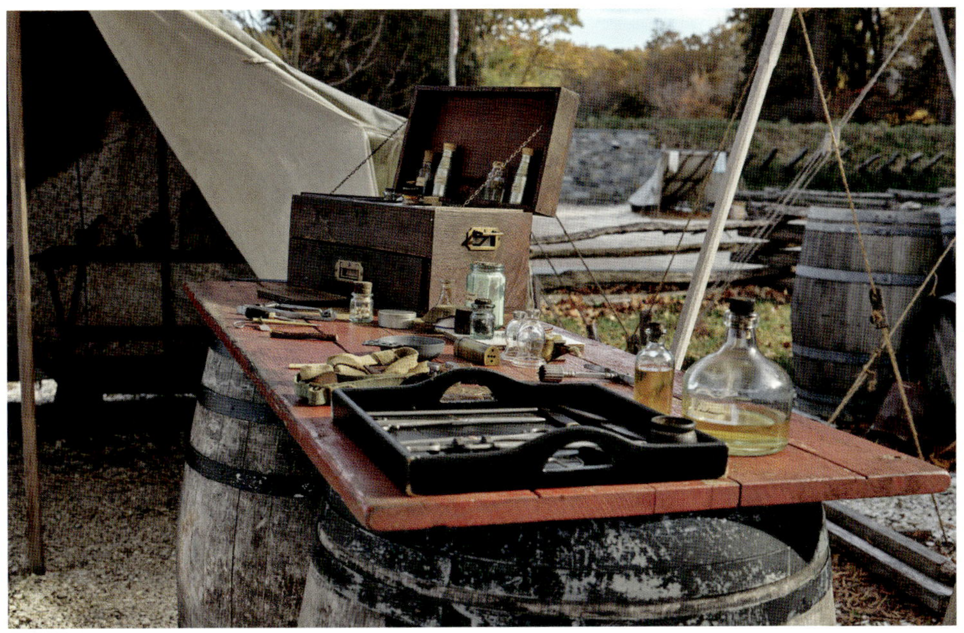

In addition to the surgeon's tent, the American Revolution Museum painstakingly recreated the medical supplies that would be found therein. Carol Highsmith took her photograph of a surgeon's wares on November 21, 2019, providing greater detail of instruments and implements that would have been employed by a colonial period field surgeon. *Library of Congress*

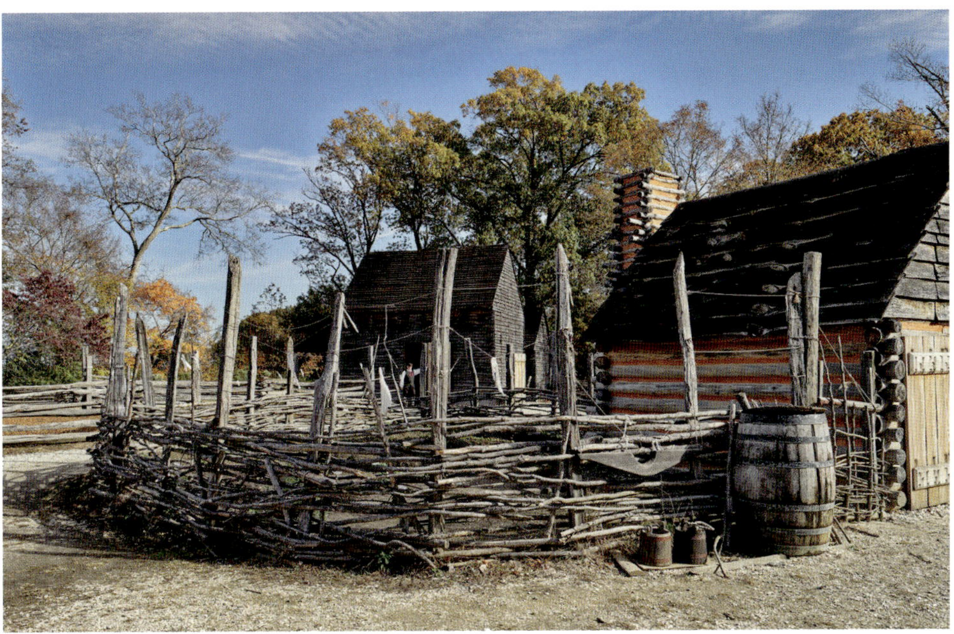

At the American Revolution Museum at Yorktown, the re-created Revolutionary-era farm features a tobacco barn (left) and quarters for enslaved people. Tobacco and corn were the main crops an eighteenth-century farmer in lower Tidewater would have sold for cash. The picture was taken on November 21, 2019, by Carol M. Highsmith. *Library of Congress*

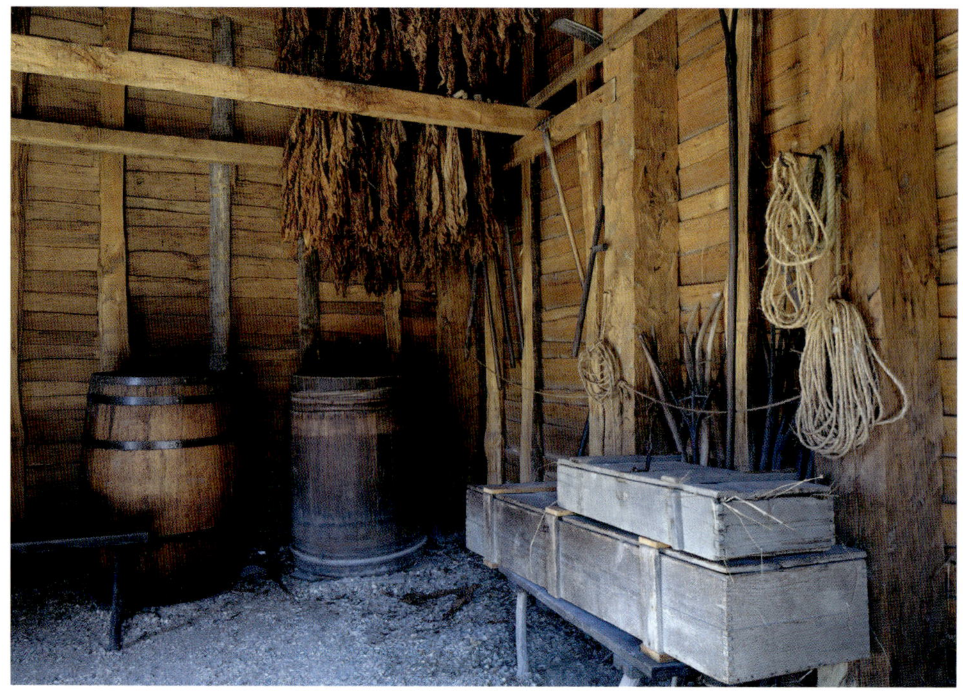

Carol Highsmith took this picture of the scene inside the recreated tobacco barn at the American Revolution Museum on November 21, 2019. *Library of Congress*

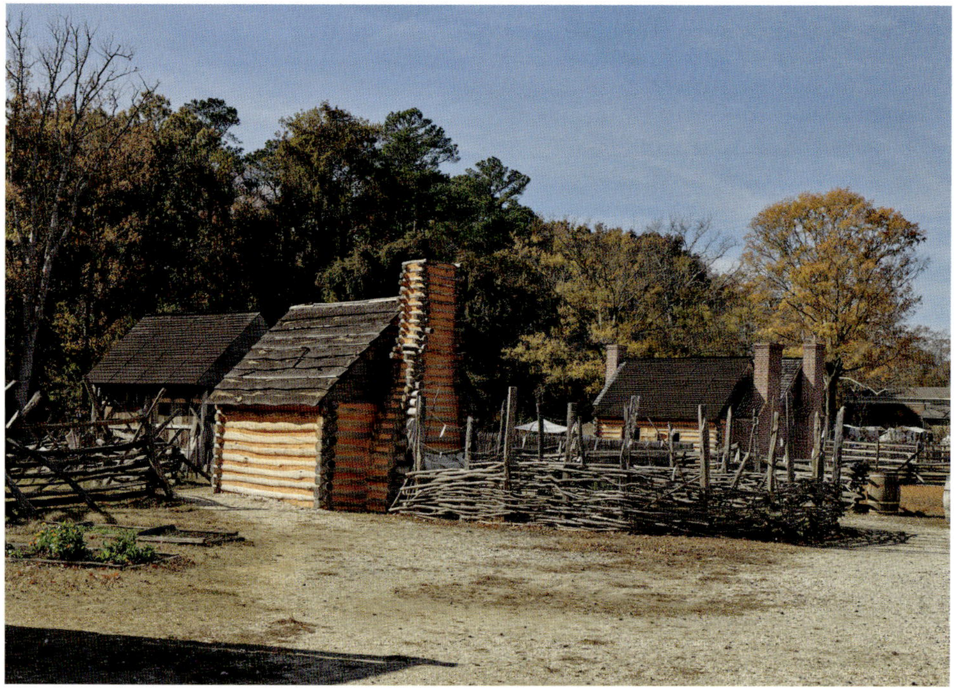

The American Revolution Museum's living-history exhibits include this slave cabin (foreground), photographed by Carol Highsmith on November 21, 2019. *Library of Congress*

The American Revolution Museum at Yorktown farm exhibit offers a unique opportunity to witness a typical rural lifestyle at the time of the Revolution. The setting includes a dwelling, separate kitchen and the tobacco barn [also shown here]. With guidance from eighteenth-century reference materials, it is known that dozens of varieties of vegetables and herbs were planted and harvested year-round, providing a source of food, medicine, fabric dye and insect repellant. Much of this has been replicated at the museum's farm. Breeds of fowl commonly found at that time included chickens, Muscovy ducks and American wild turkey, which also roam the exhibit site. Here, a visitor picks beans in the farm garden. *Jamestown-Yorktown Foundation*

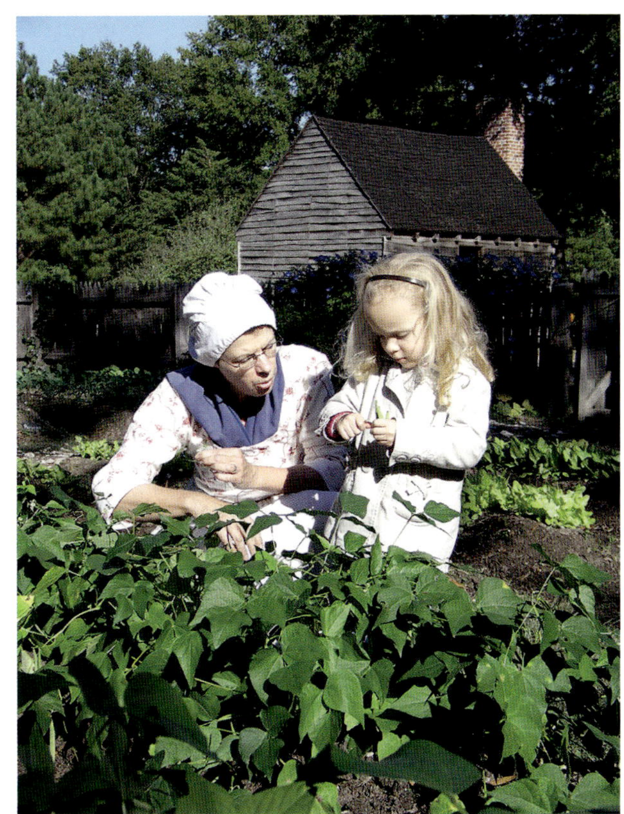

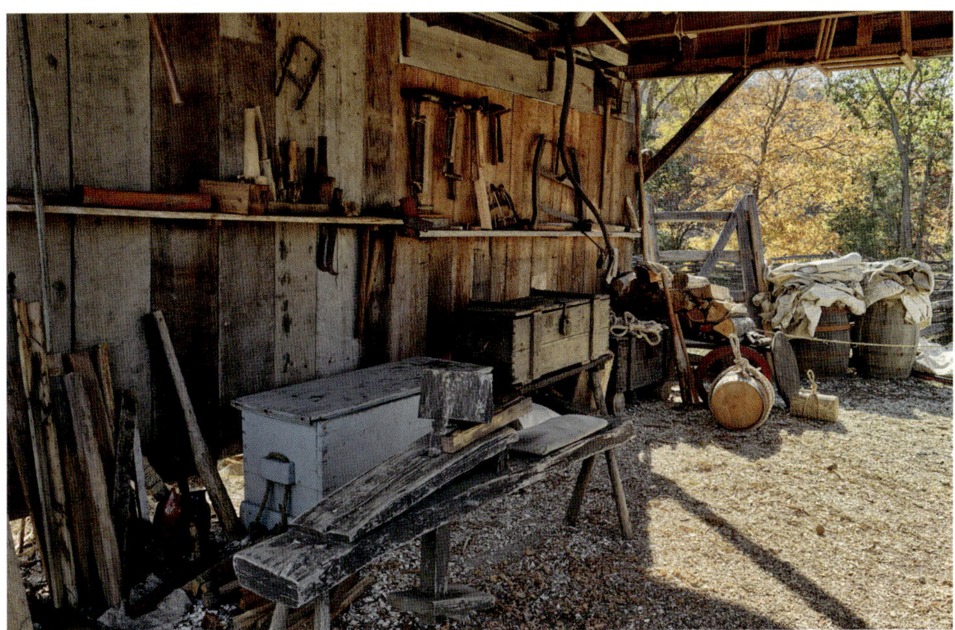

The American Revolution Museum recreated this colonial period tool shed as part of its outdoor exhibit. Carol Highsmith took the picture on November 21, 2019. *Library of Congress*

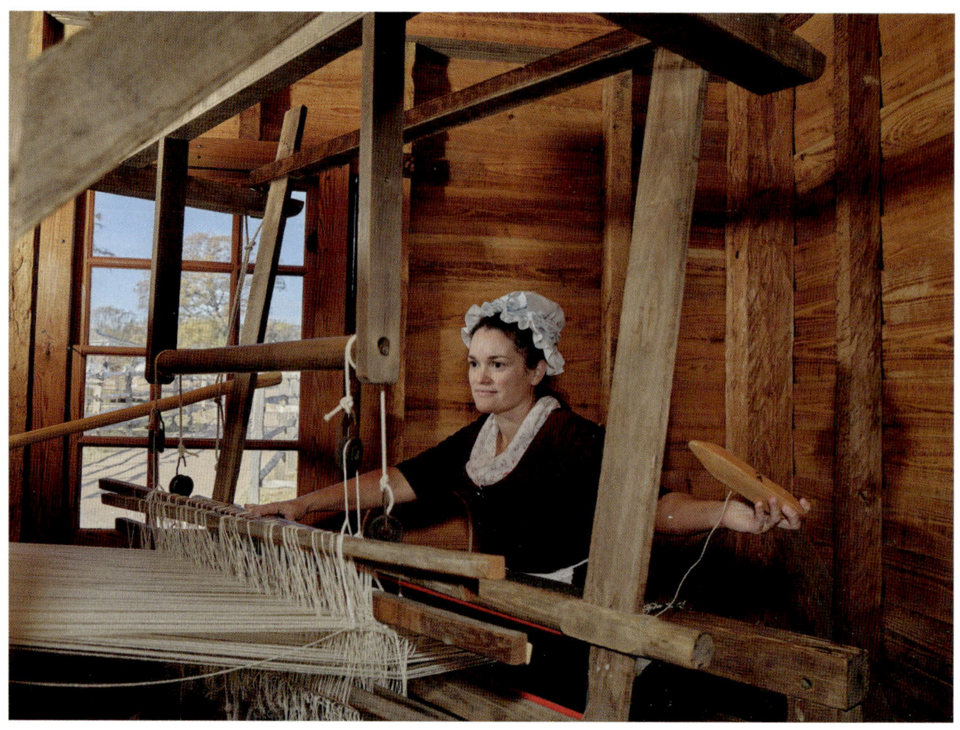

Sara Rivera works a loom at the American Revolution Museum. Carol Highsmith took the photograph on November 21, 2019. *Library of Congress*

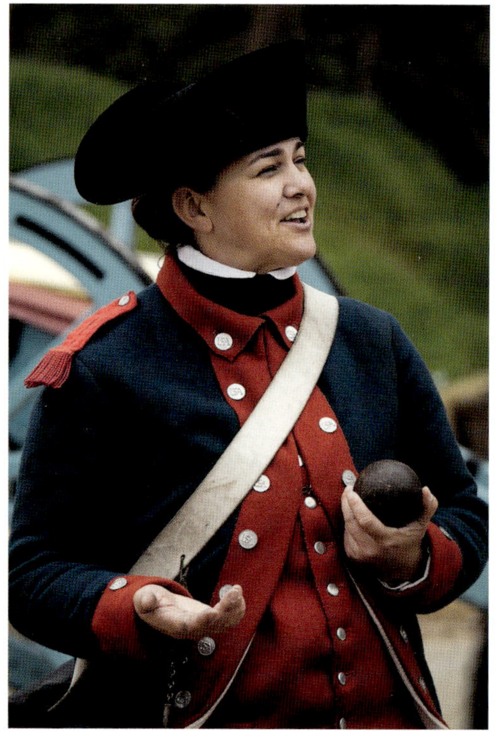

A Continental Army encampment historical interpreter led visitors in a demonstration of military tactics and weaponry as part of the grand opening celebration for the American Revolution Museum at Yorktown events honoring the role of New Hampshire in the Revolutionary War. The picture was taken on March 31, 2017. *Jamestown–Yorktown Foundation*

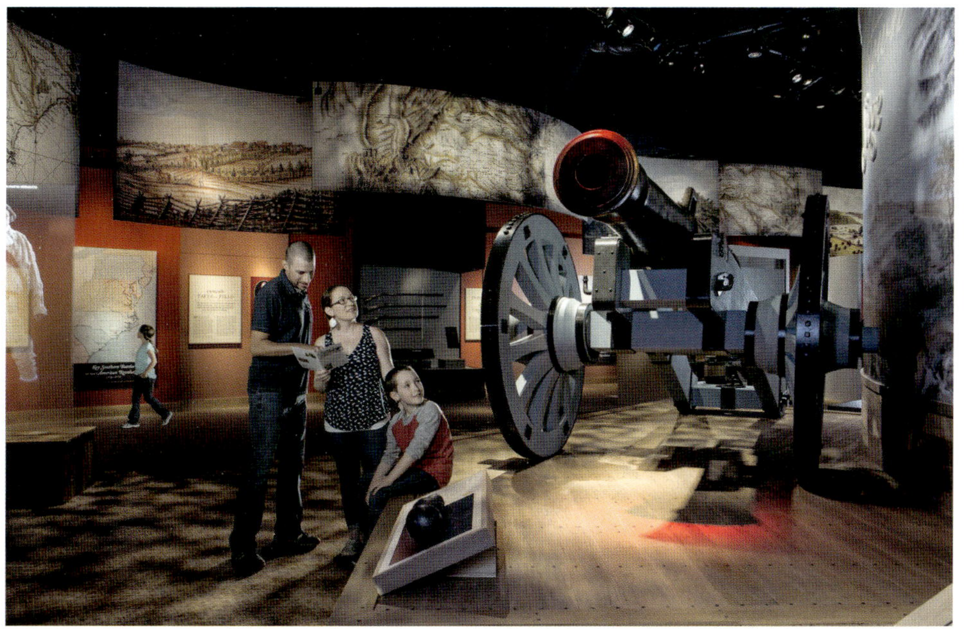

A family observes a reproduction of a twenty-four-pounder French siege gun, representative of the largest guns used during the 1781 Yorktown siege. The cannon (shown here) sits outside "The Siege of Yorktown" experiential theater. *Jamestown–Yorktown Foundation*

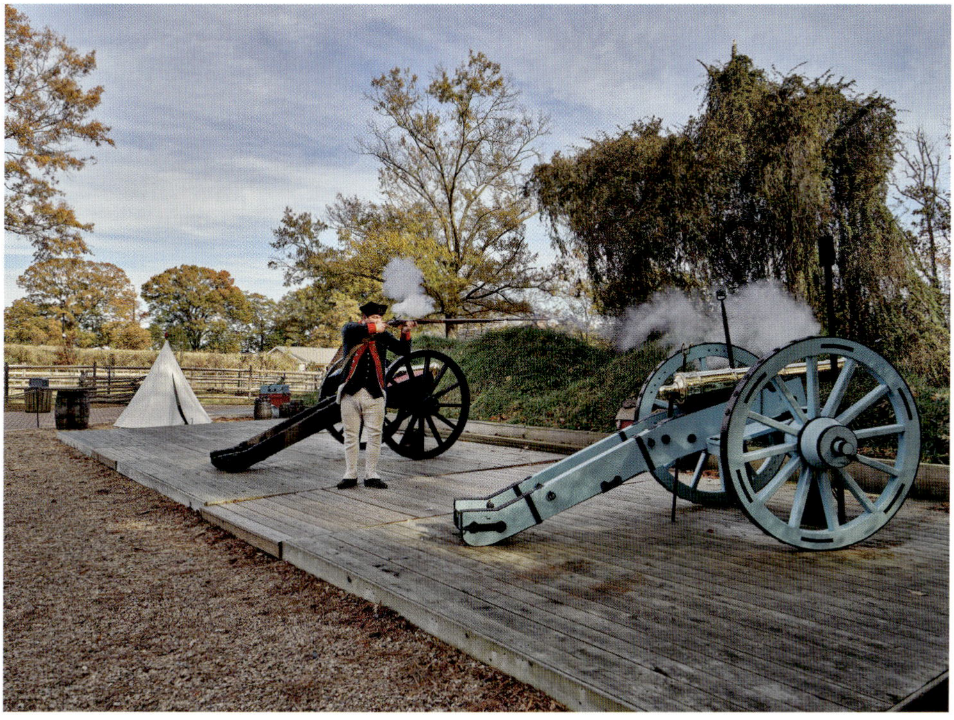

Costumed interpreter Andrew Raha fires a musket at the American Revolution Museum. The picture was taken on November 21, 2019, by Carol Highsmith. *Library of Congress*

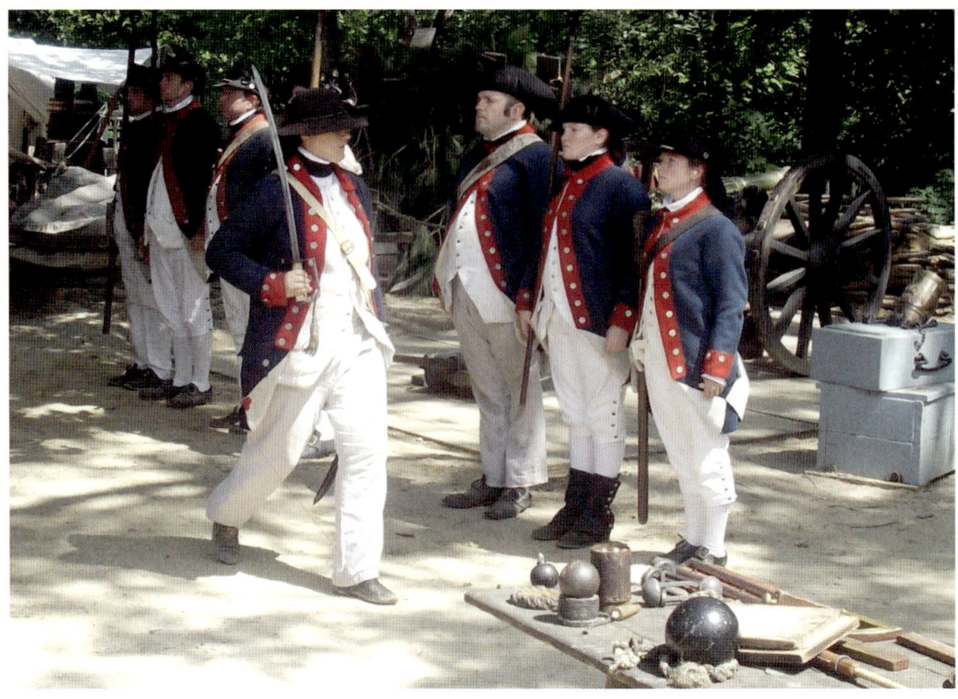

An artillery inspection in the American Revolution Museum at Yorktown re-created Continental Army encampment (shown here) took place over the October 17–18, 2015 Yorktown Victory Weekend. *Jamestown–Yorktown Foundation*

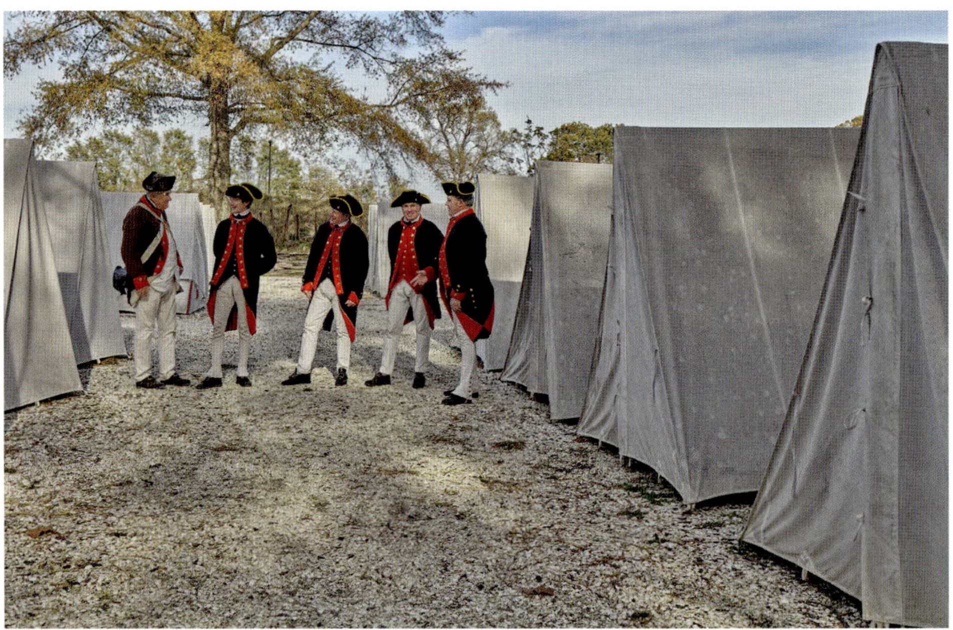

Costumed interpreters Glenn Bittner, James Thomas Richardson, Louis Crispin Simmons, and James Woodard (right to left) converse with an unidentified interpreter (far left) at the American Revolution Museum on November 21, 2019. Carol M. Highsmith took the photograph. *Library of Congress*

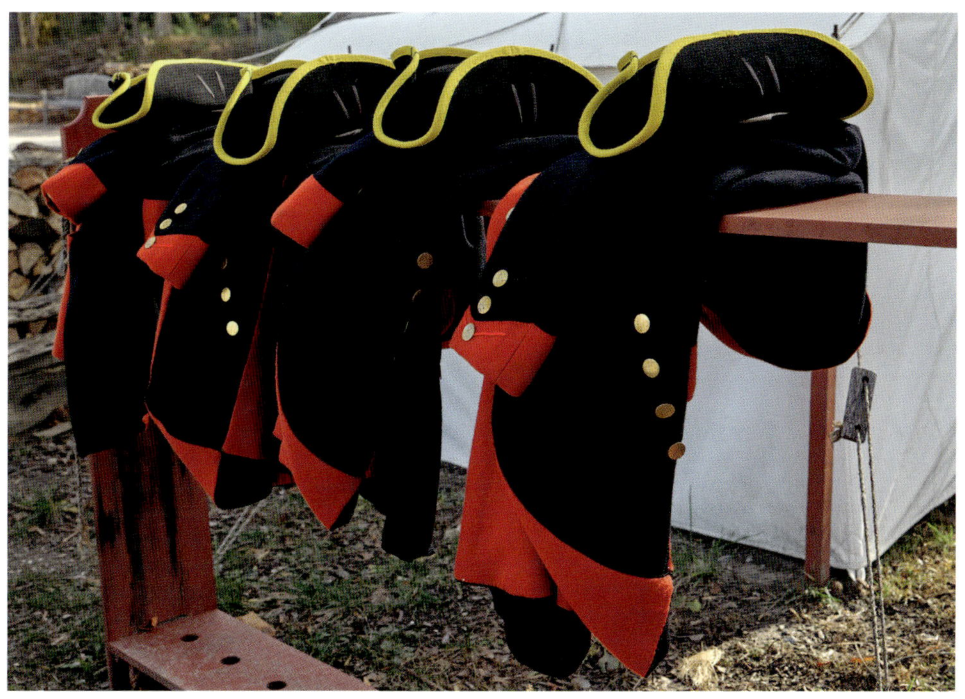

Artillerymen's hats and jackets get an airing in the reenactors' encampment at the American Revolution Museum. Carol Highsmith took the photograph on November 21, 2019. *Library of Congress*

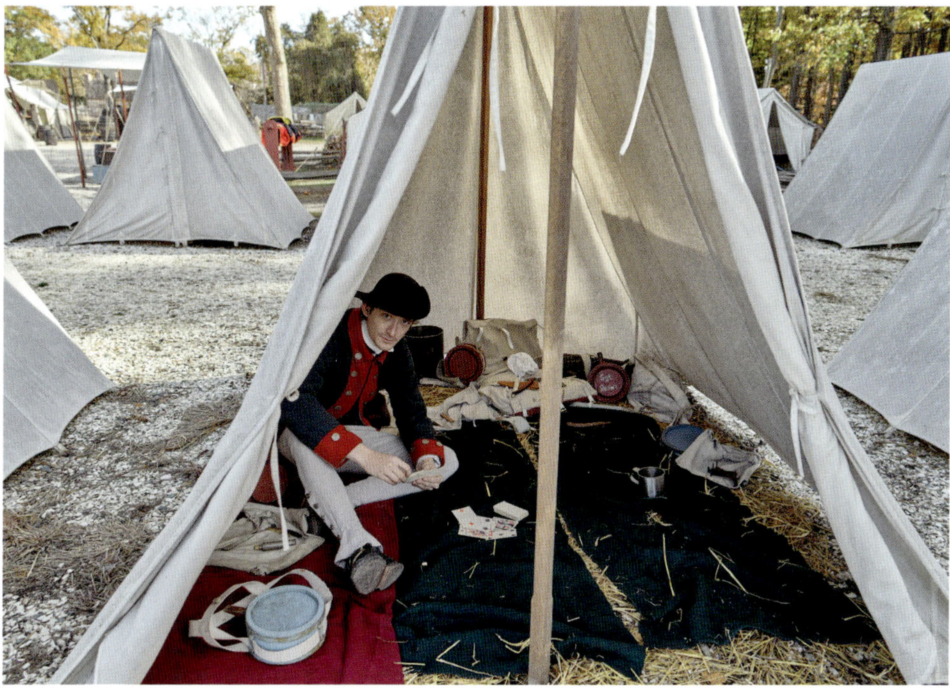

Carol Highsmith took this picture on November 21, 2019, as costumed interpreter James Thomas Richardson plays cards inside a soldier's tent at the American Revolution Museum. *Library of Congress*

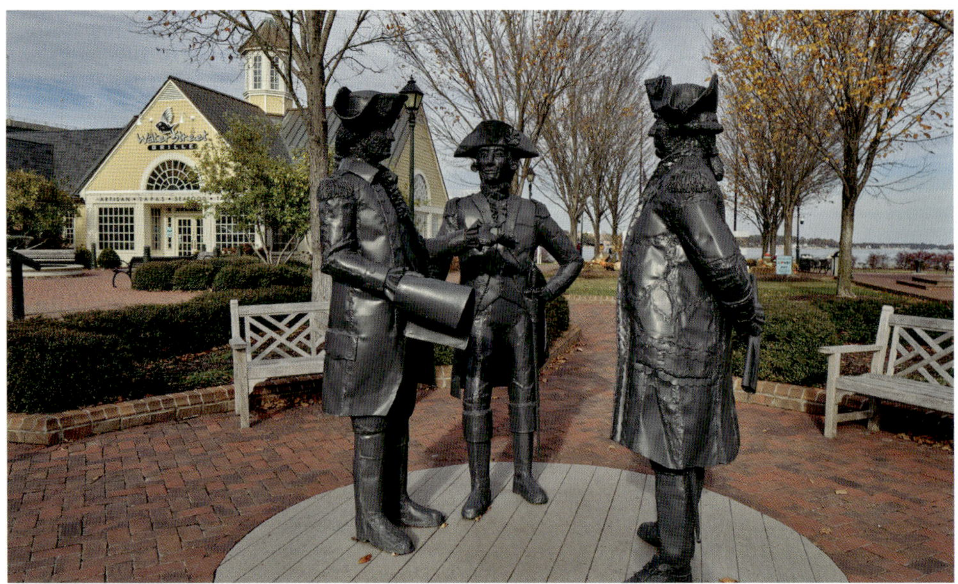

Prominently displayed along the waterfront in Yorktown, Virginia, are life-sized statues of General George Washington (left) and Admiral François Joseph Paul de Grasse, also known as Comte de Grasse (right). Installed in 2005 and enjoyed by tens of thousands of visitors annually, the statues commemorate two important meetings that took place on board de Grasse's flagship the *Ville de Paris* during the 1781 Yorktown campaign. The statues, shown in this March 25, 2017 photograph, are the work of Williamsburg sculptor Cyd Player. The artist added a statue of Marquis de Lafayette (center) to this display on October 18, 2017. Carol M. Highsmith took this photograph on November 21, 2019. *Library of Congress*

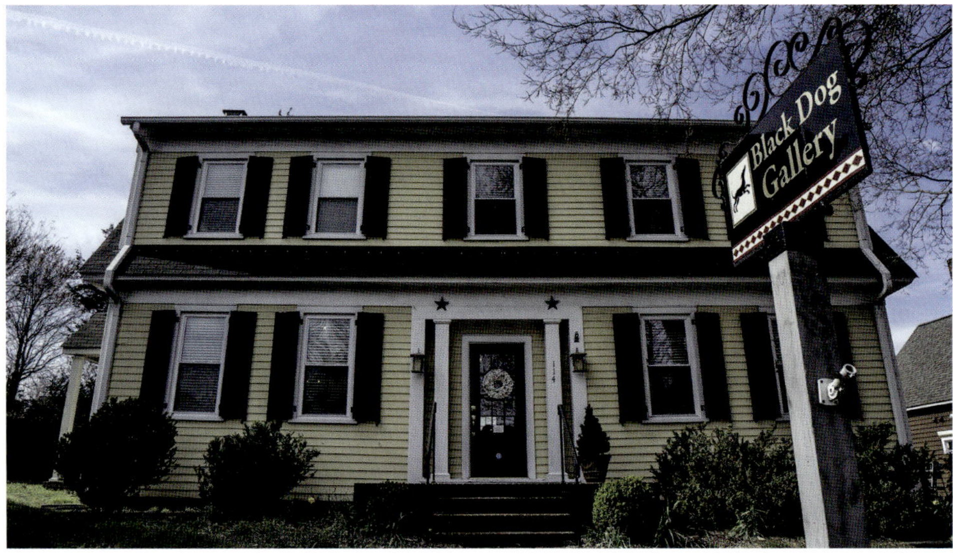

The Black Dog Gallery, shown in this March 25, 2017 picture, is located on Yorktown's Ballard Street. Established in 1992 by sister and brother Virginia and Joe Lascara, the gallery specializes in hand-painted eighteenth-century floor cloths, period frames, antique and contemporary prints. Designers, historians and curators of some of America's finest museums and homes utilize the skill and expertise of the gallery in their renovations, restorations and projects.[16]

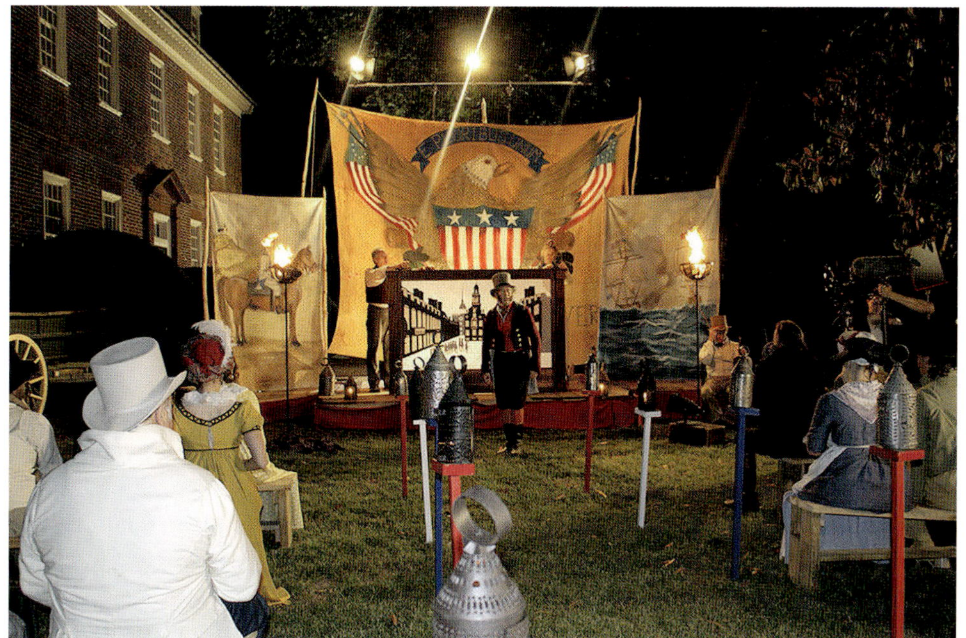

The "Liberty Fever" narrative, a new feature at the American Revolution Museum at Yorktown, is delivered by an early nineteenth-century storyteller reenactor who has traveled the country, gathering stories about the American Revolution. He shares these accounts with his audience using a moving panorama presentation of the time period. Through silhouettes and shadow puppets interwoven with live-action film segments, the viewer is afforded the opportunity to witness "liberty fever" in the stories of people who lived during the Revolution. *American Revolution Museum at Yorktown* [formerly the Yorktown Victory Center][17]

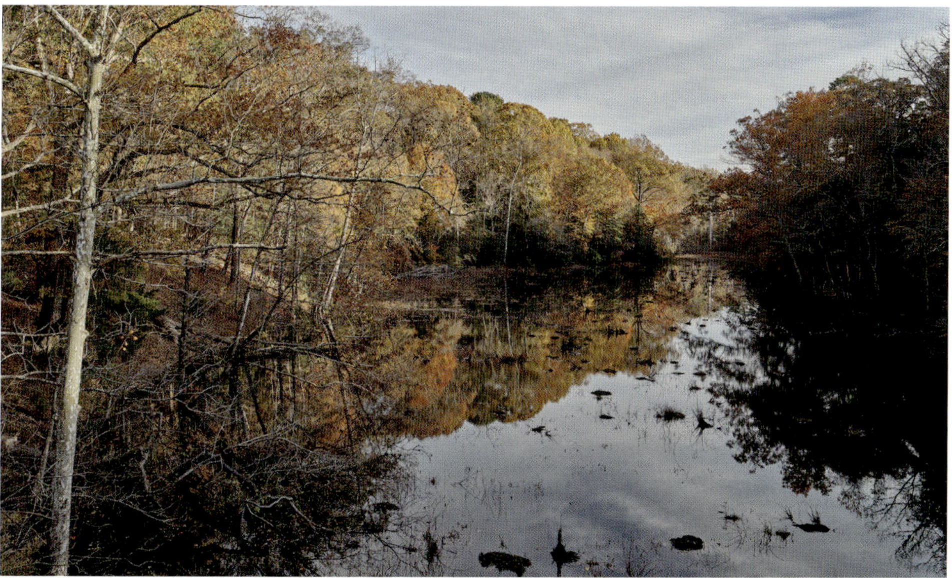

This fall scene in the Yorktown Battlefield portion of the Colonial National Historical Park is shown in this November 21, 2019 Carol M. Highsmith photograph. *Library of Congress*

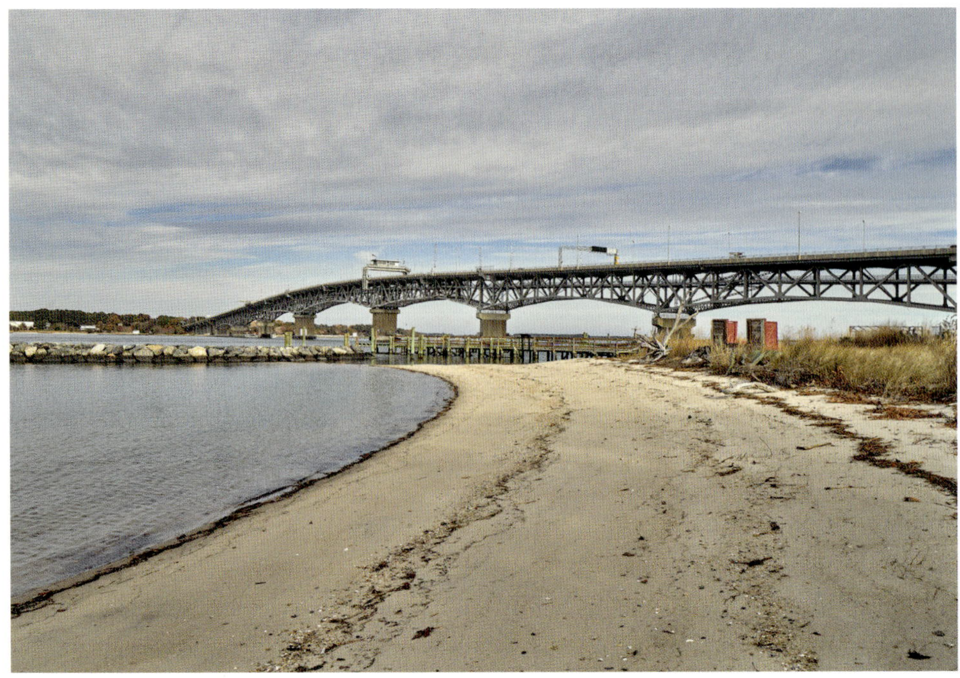

Carol Highsmith took these November 21, 2019 photographs of the George Preston Coleman Memorial Bridge that spans the York River between Yorktown and Gloucester Point. Highsmith stood on the Yorktown beach to take the second photograph. The toll bridge was named for Coleman, who from 1913 to 1922 was the chief of the Virginia Department of Highways and Transportation. The bridge has become one of the sites of a special program to establish and encourage nesting locations for the Virginia peregrine falcon population. *Library of Congress*

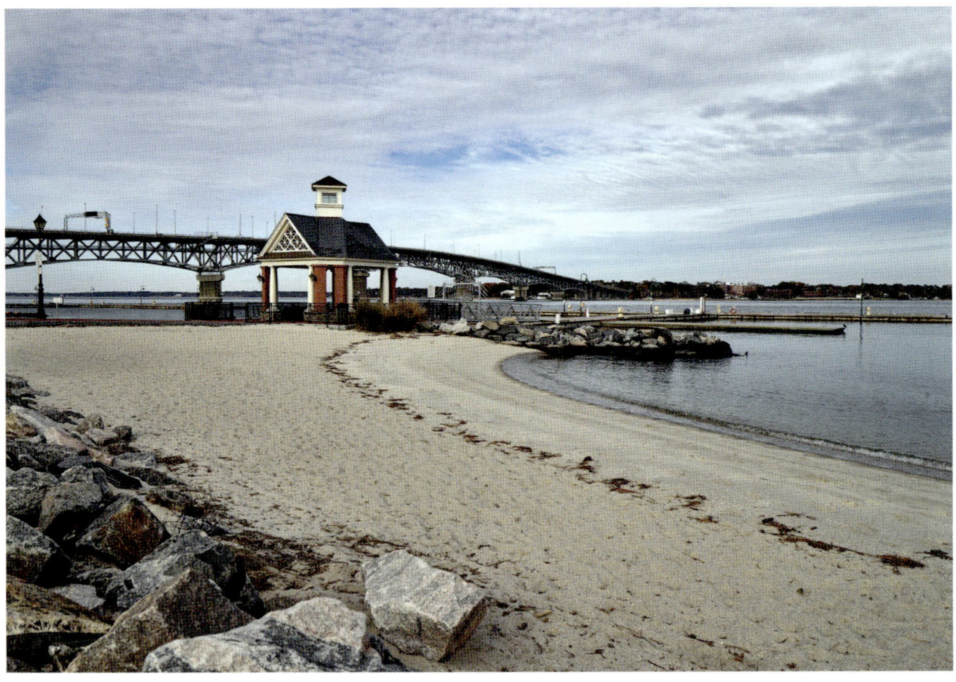

1 By Ken Lund from Reno, Nevada, USA [CC BY-SA 2.0 (http://creativecommons.org/licenses/by-sa/2.0)], via Wikimedia Commons

2 John William and Georgiana White (1888–1956) Hornsby's only daughter Marian Jeanette (1921–2006) met Willits Henry "Bill" Bowditch (1912–1994) at the beginning of World War II when he was a student at the Naval Mine Warfare School [in 1942] and the couple married on January 23, 1943. The Bowditchs had four sons: Willets Henry Bowditch Jr., John Watts "Bill" Bowditch (1944–2012), David Hornsby Bowditch and Phillip Marian Bowditch. Bill Bowditch was the founder of Bowditch Ford and a Peninsula business and civic leader for decades. He was a past president of the Peninsula (1958–1960) and Virginia State (1966–1968) Chambers of Commerce; served on boards of the College of William and Mary and Mary Baldwin College; led the state's first trade mission to Europe (1967), and aided civic charities and arts organizations for many years, to include his tenure as president of the Peninsula Art Association and his involvement with the United Way. Of note, Bill Bowditch served in the Pacific theater during World War II as the naval aide and flag lieutenant to Rear Admiral George Hudson Fort (1891–1956) and later to Rear Admiral Jerauld Wright (1898–1995). He resigned from the United States Navy as a lieutenant commander in 1946.

3 By Ken Lund from Reno, Nevada, USA [CC BY-SA 2.0 (http://creativecommons.org/licenses/by-sa/2.0)], via Wikimedia Commons

4 By Ken Lund from Reno, Nevada, USA [CC BY-SA 2.0 (http://creativecommons.org/licenses/by-sa/2.0)], via Wikimedia Commons

5 By Navin75 (Interior, Moore House Uploaded by Morgan Riley) [CC BY-SA 2.0 (http://creativecommons.org/licenses/by-sa/2.0)], via Wikimedia Commons

6 By Mobilus In Mobili (https://www.flickr.com/photos/mobili/17079263009/) [CC BY 2.0 (http://creativecommons.org/licenses/by/2.0)], via Wikimedia Commons

7 By Reneftorres (Own work) [CC BY-SA 4.0 (http://creativecommons.org/licenses/by-sa/4.0)], via Wikimedia Commons

8 By Mobilus In Mobili (https://www.flickr.com/photos/mobili/18683194672/) [CC BY 2.0 (http://creativecommons.org/licenses/by/2.0)], via Wikimedia Commons

9 L'Hermione, la Frégate de la liberté: https://www.hermione.com/en/the-hermione-project/the-history/

10 By Mobilus In Mobili (https://www.flickr.com/photos/mobili/17920470163/) [CC BY 2.0 (http://creativecommons.org/licenses/by/2.0)], via Wikimedia Commons

11 By Mobilus In Mobili (https://www.flickr.com/photos/mobili/18357155029/) [CC BY 2.0 (http://creativecommons.org/licenses/by/2.0)], via Wikimedia Commons

12 By Mobilus In Mobili (https://www.flickr.com/photos/mobili/20075690491/) [CC BY 2.0 (http://creativecommons.org/licenses/by/2.0)], via Wikimedia Commons

13 By Mobilus In Mobili (https://www.flickr.com/photos/mobili/21665302393/) [CC BY-SA 2.0 (http://creativecommons.org/licenses/by-sa/2.0)], via Wikimedia Commons

14 By Elizabeth Rowe (Own work) [CC BY-SA 4.0 (http://creativecommons.org/licenses/by-sa/4.0)], via Wikimedia Commons

15 By Elizabeth Rowe (Own work) [CC BY-SA 4.0 (http://creativecommons.org/licenses/by-sa/4.0)], via Wikimedia Commons

16 Stock photo [CC0] [public domain]

17 http://www.historyisfun.org/blog/creating-a-new-museum/

Bibliography

Primary Sources

Department of the Interior/National Park Service. Division of History. Office of Archaeology and Historic Preservation. Yorktown's Main Street. From Secretary Nelson's to the Windmill and Military Entrenchments Close In and Around the Town of York. [Charles E. Hatch Jr. resource study] [March 1974]. Colonial National Historical Park, Virginia.

— Grace Church: General Study [Charles E. Hatch Jr. paper] [May 1970]. Colonial National Historical Park, Yorktown, Virginia.

— The Edmund Smith House: A History [Charles E. Hatch Jr. paper] [August 1969]. Colonial National Historical Park, Yorktown, Virginia.

— Yorktown and the Siege of 1781 [Charles E. Hatch Jr. historical handbook series number fourteen] [first published 1954 and revised 1957].

Department of the Interior/National Park Service. Cultural Landscapes Inventory [2012]. Nelson House. Colonial National Historical Park. Yorktown, Virginia.

Department of the Interior/National Park Service. Historic American Building Survey [HABS]. Kiskiack (Naval Mine Depot) [HABS No. VA-183] Yorkville vicinity, York County, Virginia [1997].

— Ballentine House [originally Dewsville] [HABS No. VA-596] Yorktown, York County, Virginia [May 1960].

— Moore House [HABS No. VA-80] Yorktown, York County, Virginia [November 2, 1940].

— Ringfield [HABS No. VA-318] Indian Fields, Near Yorktown, York County, Virginia [1940].

— West House [HABS No. VA-82] Yorktown, York County, Virginia [February 23, 1938].

— Sheild House [HABS No. VA-81] Yorktown, York County, Virginia [December 29, 1937].

— Swan Tavern [HABS No. VA-83] Yorktown, York County, Virginia [1937].

— Nelson House [HABS No. VA-58, VA-58-A, VA-58-B] Yorktown, York County, Virginia [December 29, 1937].

Department of the Interior/National Park Service. Historic American Engineering Record [HAER]. Yorktown Battlefield Tour Road [HAER No. VA-117] Yorktown vicinity, York County, Virginia [1995].

— George Preston Coleman Memorial Bridge [HAER No. VA-57] Spanning the York River at U.S. Route 17, Yorktown, York County, Virginia [1993].

— Colonial National Monument Parkway [HAER No. VA-48] Running from Jamestown Island to Yorktown via Williamsburg, James City County, Williamsburg City, and York County, Virginia [1988].

Department of the Interior/National Park Service. National Register of Historic Places [NRHP] Inventory Form. Sessions-Pope-Sheild House [NRHP], Yorktown, Virginia [June 23, 2003].

—Old Custom House [NRHP], Yorktown, Virginia [March 31, 1999].

—William Gooch Tomb and York Village Archaeological Site [NRHP], Yorktown, Virginia [January 18, 1974].

—Yorktown Shipwrecks [NRHP], Yorktown, Virginia [October 9, 1973].

—Grace Church [NRHP], Yorktown, Virginia [September 15, 1970].

—Lee House [Kiskiack] [NRHP], Naval Weapons Station, Yorktown, Virginia [November 12, 1969].

—Yorktown Historic District [NRHP], Yorktown, Virginia [October 15, 1966].

Department of the Interior/National Park Service. Office of History and Historic Structures/Eastern Service Center [September 1970]. Ringfield Plantation [Charles E. Hatch Jr. paper]. Colonial National Historical Park, Yorktown, Virginia.

National Oceanic and Atmospheric Administration (NOAA). War Record of J. W. Donn, including reminiscences of Frederic W. Dorr [July 1861 to June 1865] by John W. Donn, assistant, United States Coast Survey. http://www.history.noaa.gov/stories_tales/donn.html

Books

Crozier, William Armstrong, ed. *The Buckners of Virginia and the allied families of Strother and Ashby*. New York, New York: The Genealogical Association, 1907.

Eberlein, Harold Donaldson. *The Architecture of Colonial America*. Boston, Massachusetts: Little, Brown and Company, 1924.

McIlwaine, H. R. ed. *Legislative Journals of the Council of Colonial Virginia* [in three volumes]. Volume I. Richmond, Virginia: Virginia State Library Board, 1918.

Miller, Francis Trevelyan ed. *The Photographic History of the Civil War* [in ten volumes]. New York, New York: The Review of Reviews Company, 1911.

Smith, Margaret Ponds Crooks. *Old Yorktown and Its History*. Yorktown, Virginia: [by the author], 1920.

Stevens, John Austin. *Yorktown Centennial Handbook*. New York: C. A. Coffin and Rogers, 1881.

Stoudt, John Baer. *Nicolas Martiau—The Adventurous Huguenot, The Military Engineer and The Earliest American Ancestor of George Washington*. Norristown, Pennsylvania: Norristown Press, 1932.

Periodicals, Pamphlets and Papers

Burnett, Jim, "Did the Great Depression save the Yorktown Battlefield?" *National Parks Traveler*, December 8, 2008. https://www.nationalparkstraveler.org/2008/12/did-great-depression-save-yorktown-battlefield

Cawley, Jon, "NPS: business sought to occupy colonial home in Yorktown," *Daily Press*, January 5, 2012. http://articles.dailypress.com/2012-01-05/news/dp-nws-yorktown-house-20120105_1_yorktown-battlefield-park-service-colonial-era-home

Erickson, Mark St. John, "Lost black township in York County lives on in memory," Daily Press, February 22, 2016. http://www.dailypress.com/news/hampton/dp-nws-black-history-slabtown-20160220-story.html

—"The Great Fire of 1814 left once-flourishing Yorktown in blackened ruins," *Daily Press*, March 1, 2014. http://www.dailypress.com/features/history/our-story/dp-the-great-fire-of-1814-left-yorktown-in-blackened-ruins-20140228-post.html

Knemeyer, Nelda N., "Willits H. Bowditch, Ford dealer, leader in business, dead at 82," *Daily Press*, April 13, 1994. http://articles.dailypress.com/1994-04-13/news/9404130113_1_bill-bowditch-gentleman-friendly-rivalry

Patterson, Henry Kirk White (1855–1935) *War Memories of Fort Monroe and Vicinity*. Fort Monroe, Virginia: Pool and Deuschle, 1885. Patterson was a soldier in the artillery who became a minister.

Piggot, Mark O., "Naval Weapons Station Yorktown celebrates 90 years of ordnance support," *Navy News Service*, August 7, 2008. http://www.navy.mil/submit/display.asp?story_id=38849

Robertson Jr., James I., "Notes on (Civil War) camp," *New York Times*, April 14, 2012. https://opinionator.blogs.nytimes.com/2012/04/14/notes-on-civil-war-camp/

Schnaars, Christopher, "Yorktown's oldest home isn't," *Chicago Tribune*, October 20, 2002. http://articles.chicagotribune.com/2002-10-20/business/0210200353_1_oldest-house-yorktown-custom-house

Websites

American Revolution Museum at Yorktown—https://www.historyisfun.org/

National Park Service—https://www.nps.gov/

The Watermen's Museum—https://watermens.org/

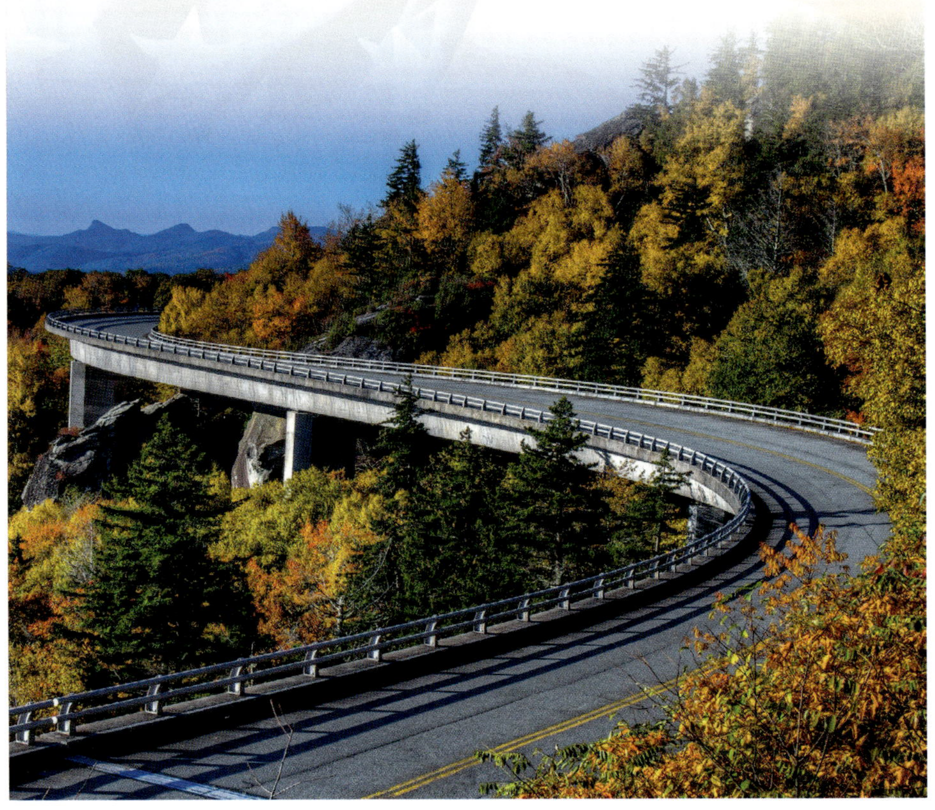

BLUE RIDGE PARKWAY
Through Time
978-1-63500-067-2
$28.99

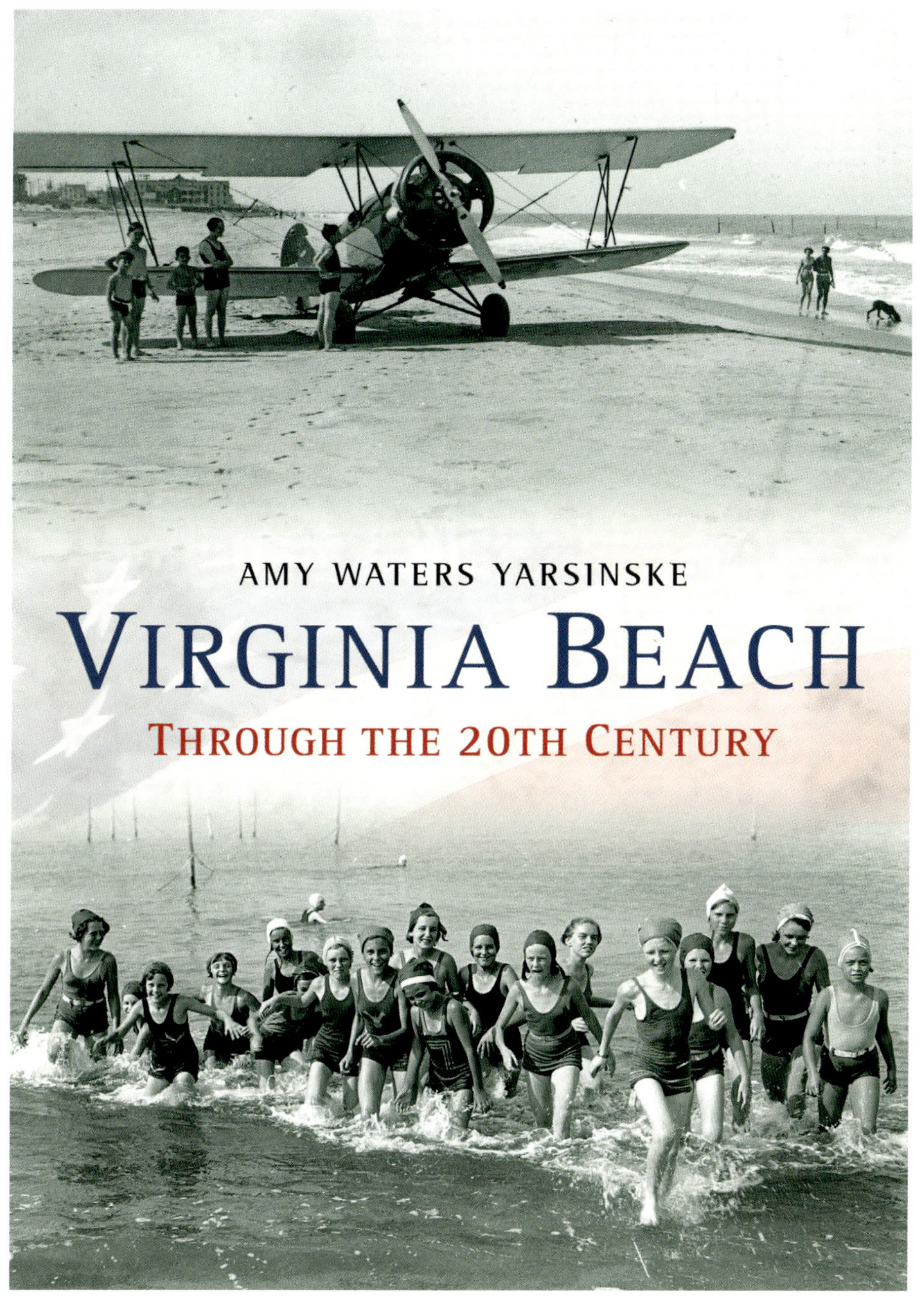

AMY WATERS YARSINSKE
VIRGINIA BEACH
THROUGH THE 20TH CENTURY